# A
# Treasury of
# Classic
# Poetry

# A
# Treasury of
# Classic
# Poetry

**BARNES & NOBLE**

NEW YORK

Cover design by Patrice Kaplan
Marbled endpapers © Andy Magee/shutterstock

Barnes & Noble, Inc.
122 Fifth Avenue
New York, NY 10011

ISBN 978-1-4351-4541-2

Printed and bound in China

2 4 6 8 10 9 7 5 3

# Contents

## JOHN DRYDEN

## ALEXANDER POPE

## SAMUEL JOHNSON

## THOMAS GRAY

## ROBERT BURNS

## WILLIAM BLAKE

### SONGS OF INNOCENCE

## EMILY DICKINSON

## ALFRED, LORD TENNYSON

## EDWARD FITZGERALD

# INTRODUCTION

The poems selected for this volume span more than 500 years, from the poetry of courtly love that Thomas Wyatt wrote while serving in the court of Henry VIII to T. S. Eliot's modernist masterpiece, "The Waste Land," published in the third decade of the twentieth century. Although the contents are limited to poems in the English language, all of the poets represented were critically acclaimed in their respective eras. In many cases, their poems rank among the best works of literature in their time. A number of these poems were immensely popular and found a wide readership, and some of their writers enjoyed the kind of renown in their time that we confer on celebrities today. Many of the selections—especially the sonnets of Shakespeare, and the poems of John Donne, Ben Jonson, and Robert Burns—feature lines that are among the most quoted in literature, and familiar to readers who have never read the poem in which they appear.

A variety of poetic forms—ode, sonnet, dramatic monologue—are represented, as is nearly every genre popular in the centuries covered: lyric, narrative, elegy, satirical, even epic if John Dryden's "Mac-Flecknoe" and Alexander Pope's "The Rape of the Lock"—both mock heroic epics—can lay claim to that designation. When selecting the more than 300 poems collected in *A Treasury of Classic Poetry* we decided to include only those poems that could be printed in their entirety. A number of the greatest poems written during the five-century interval covered run to full book length and thus are not excerpted here, among them Geoffrey Chaucer's *The Canterbury Tales*, Edmund Spenser's *The Faerie Queene*, John Milton's *Paradise Lost*, Alexander Pope's *The Dunciad*, William Wordsworth's *The Prelude*, Lord Byron's *Childe Harold's Pilgrimage* and *Don Juan*, Alfred, Lord Tennyson's *The Idylls of the King* and *In Memoriam*, and Robert Browning's *The Ring and the Book*, not to mention the dramatic verse of William Shakespeare, Christopher Marlowe, Ben Jonson, and other poet playwrights.

The contents are organized in rough chronological order by the birth date of each poet, though some liberties were taken to group the work of certain poets, notably the so-called metaphysical poets—John Donne, Robert Herrick, Andrew Marvell, George Herbert, Richard Crashaw, and Henry Vaughan—and the English Romantic poets: William Blake, William Wordsworth, Samuel Taylor Coleridge, Lord Byron, Percy Bysshe Shelley, and John Keats. While the poets in these groupings shared certain sensibilities, and often were aware of each others' work, it should be remembered that they were not members of formal schools, and that the categories their works are corralled into today were imposed retroactively by scholars and critics.

Readers who choose to read the poems as they are ordered in this volume have the opportunity to explore poetry in the English language as it has evolved over 500 years, an evolutionary path that was by no means straight or predictable but that ineluctably was influenced by the events and the temper of the times. In less than a century after Sir Thomas Wyatt wrote the first sonnets in English, the English literary renaissance was in its full glory, and Elizabethan poets Edmund Spenser, William Shakespeare, Christopher Marlowe, and Ben Jonson were writing poems rich with colorful description and symbolism that would influence generations of poets to come. In the early seventeenth century, the metaphysical poets flourished, writing lyric poems on love and devotional themes remembered for their clever allusions and carefully crafted metaphors. The century is dominated by John Milton, in whom one sees the culmination of the poetic traditions that flowered during the Elizabethan era, and John Dryden, whose work anticipates that of the Restoration era poets. Poetry reaches it apogee in the eighteenth century in the poems of Alexander Pope, whose verse is the model of neoclassical precision and orderliness. Thomas Gray and the graveyard poets who emerged at the end of the eighteenth century bridge the popular gothic tradition in literature and the emerging Romantic era. The English Romantic poets, strongly influenced by Shakespeare and Milton, set the tone for most poetry written for the next two centuries, with poems that take a more liberal approach to the language and structure of verse and that are notably self-conscious about the poetic imagination and how it shapes perceptions of the world. At the same time that Alfred, Lord Tennyson, Robert Browning, and other Victorian era poets sustained this new Romantic tradition through the end of the nineteenth century, a Romantic tradition emerged in American poetry, distinguished by the philosophically insightful poems of Emily Dickinson, the profoundly personal lyrics of What Whitman, and the portraiture of ordinary people and small-town life of Edward Arlington Robinson, Edgar Lee Masters, and inevitably Robert Frost. In the early twentieth century, Wilfrid Owen and Rupert Brooke wrote poems based on their experiences in World War I, a cataclysmic historical event that also radically influenced artistic sensibilities in the war's aftermath. Experiments in verse seen previously in the poems of Gerard

Manly Hopkins became a regular feature of the imagist poems of William Carlos Williams and Wallace Stevens, and the modernist approach to poetry seen in Eliot's "The Waste Land."

The foregoing brief historical survey cannot do justice to the wide variety of poems collected in this volume or the poetic traditions they represent. Each poem can—and should—be read and enjoyed on its own terms. A fuller appreciation comes with the understanding that each represents a significant contribution to a literary legacy that continues to this day.

# SIR THOMAS WYATT
## (1503–1542)

## They Flee from Me

They flee from me that sometime did me seek,
With naked foot stalking within my chamber:
Once have I seen them gentle, tame, and meek,
That now are wild, and do not once remember,
That sometime they have put themselves in danger
To take bread at my hand; and now they range
    Busily seeking in continual change.

    Thanked be Fortune, it hath been otherwise
Twenty times better; but once especial,
In thin array, after a pleasant guise,
When her loose gown did from her shoulders fall,
And she me caught in her arms long and small,
And therewithal so sweetly did me kiss,
And softly said, "Dear heart, how like you this?"

    It was no dream; for I lay broad awaking:
But all is turn'd now, through my gentleness,
Into a bitter fashion of forsaking;
And I have leave to go of her goodness;
And she also to use new fangleness.
But since that I unkindly so am served;
How like you this, what hath she now deserved?

## Whoso List to Hunt

Whoso list to hunt? I know where is an hind!
But as for me, alas! I may no more,
The vain travail hath wearied me so sore;
I am of them that furthest come behind.
Yet may I by no means my wearied mind
Draw from the deer; but as she fleeth afore
Fainting I follow; I leave off therefore,
Since in a net I seek to hold the wind.
Who list her hunt, I put him out of doubt
As well as I, may spend his time in vain!
And graven with diamonds in letters plain,
There is written her fair neck round about;
   "Noli me tangere; for Cæsar's I am,
    And wild for to hold, though I seem tame."

## Varium et Mutabile

   Is it possible?
That so high debate,
So sharp, so sore, and of such rate,
Should end so soon, that was begun so late.
Is it possible?
   Is it possible?
So cruel intent,
So hasty heat, and so soon spent,
From love to hate, and thence for to relent,
Is it possible?
   Is it possible?
That any may find,
Within one heart so diverse mind,
To change or turn as weather and wind,
Is it possible?
   Is it possible?
To spy it in an eye,
That turns as oft as chance or die,

The truth whereof can any try;
Is it possible?
     It is possible,
For to turn so oft;
To bring that low'st that was most aloft;
And to fall highest, yet to light soft;
It is possible!
     All is possible!
Who so list believe,
Trust therefore first and after preve;
As men wed ladies by license and leave;
All is possible!

## Forget Not Yet the Tried Intent

Forget not yet the tried intent
Of such a truth as I have meant;
My great travail so gladly spent,
          Forget not yet!
Forget not yet when first began
The weary life ye know, since whan
The suit, the service, none tell can;
          Forget not yet!
Forget not yet the great assays,
The cruel wrong, the scornful ways,
The painful patience in delays,
          Forget not yet!
Forget not! oh! forget not this,
How long ago hath been, and is
The mind that never meant amiss,
          Forget not yet!
Forget not then thine own approv'd,
The which so long hath thee so lov'd,
Whose steadfast faith yet never mov'd:
          Forget not this!

## My Lute, Awake

My lute, awake, perform the last
Labour, that thou and I shall waste;
And end that I have now begun:
And when this song is sung and past,
My lute, be still, for I have done.

As to be heard where ear is none;
As lead to grave in marble stone;
My song may pierce her heart as soon.
Should we then sigh, or sing, or moan?
No, no, my lute, for I have done.

The rocks do not so cruelly
Repulse the waves continually,
As she my suit and affection:
So that I am past remedy;
Whereby my lute and I have done.

Proud of the spoil that thou hast got
Of simple hearts through Love's shot,
By whom unkind thou hast them won:
Think not he hath his bow forgot,
Although my lute and I have done.

Vengeance shall fall on thy disdain,
That makest but game on earnest pain;
Think not alone under the sun
Unquit to cause thy lovers plain;
Although my lute and I have done.

May chance thee lie withered and old
In winter nights, that are so cold,
Plaining in vain unto the moon;
Thy wishes then dare not be told:
Care then who list, for I have done.

And then may chance thee to repent
The time that thou hast lost and spent,
To cause thy lovers sigh and swoon:
Then shalt thou know beauty but lent,
And wish and want as I have done.

Now cease, my lute, this is the last
Labour, that thou and I shall waste;
And ended is that we begun:
Now is this song both sung and past;
My lute, be still, for I have done.

# SIR PHILIP SYDNEY
## (1554–1586)

## The Bargain

My true love hath my heart, and I have his,
   By just exchange one for another given:
I hold his dear, and mine he cannot miss,
   There never was a better bargain driven:
      My true love hath my heart, and I have his.

His heart in me keeps him and me in one,
   My heart in him his thoughts and senses guides:
He loves my heart, for once it was his own,
   I cherish his because in me it bides:
      My true love hath my heart, and I have his.

## Philomela

The Nightingale, as soon as April bringeth
   Unto her rested sense a perfect waking,
While late-bare Earth, proud of new clothing, springeth,
   Sings out her woes, a thorn her song-book making;
      And mournfully bewailing,
      Her throat in tunes expresseth
      What grief her breast oppresseth,
For Tereus' force on her chaste will prevailing.

*O Philomela fair, O take some gladness*
*That here is juster cause of plaintful sadness!*
*Thine earth now springs, mine fadeth;*
*Thy thorn without, my thorn my heart invadeth.*

Alas! she hath no other cause of anguish
  But Tereus' love, on her by strong hand wroken;
Wherein she suffering, all her spirits languish,
  Full womanlike complains her will was broken.
    But I, who, daily craving,
    Cannot have to content me,
    Have more cause to lament me,
Since wanting is more woe than too much having.

*O Philomela fair, O take some gladness*
*That here is juster cause of plaintful sadness!*
*Thine earth now springs, mine fadeth;*
*Thy thorn without, my thorn my heart invadeth.*

## His Lady's Cruelty

With how sad steps, O moon, thou climb'st the skies!
  How silently, and with how wan a face!
What! may it be that even in heavenly place
That busy archer his sharp arrows tries?
Sure, if that long-with-love-acquainted eyes
Can judge of love, thou feel'st a lover's case:
I read it in thy looks; thy languish'd grace
To me, that feel the like, thy state descries.
Then, even of fellowship, O Moon, tell me,
Is constant love deem'd there but want of wit?
Are beauties there as proud as here they be?
Do they above love to be loved, and yet
  Those lovers scorn whom that love doth possess?
  Do they call "virtue" there—ungratefulness?

# EDMUND SPENSER

## (1552–1599)

## Epithalamion

Ye learnèd sisters, which have oftentimes
Beene to me ayding, others to adorne,
Whom ye thought worthy of your gracefull rymes,
That even the greatest did not greatly scorn
To heare theyr names sung in your simple layes,
But joyèd in theyr praise;
And when ye list your owne mishaps to mourne,
Which death, or love, or fortunes wreck did rayse,
Your string could soone to sadder tenor turne,
And teach the woods and waters to lament
Your dolefull dreriment:
Now lay those sorrowfull complaints aside;
And, having all your heads with girlands crownd,
Helpe me mine owne loves prayses to resound;
Ne let the same of any be envide:
So Orpheus did for his owne bride!
So I unto my selfe alone will sing;
The woods shall to me answer, and my Eccho ring.

Early, before the worlds light-giving lampe
His golden beame upon the hils doth spred,
Having disperst the nights unchearefull dampe,
Doe ye awake; and, with fresh lusty-hed,
Go to the bowre of my beloved love,
My truest turtle dove;
Bid her awake; for Hymen is awake,
And long since ready forth his maske to move,

With his bright Tead that flames with many a flake,
And many a bachelor to waite on him,
In theyr fresh garments trim.
Bid her awake therefore, and soone her dight,
For lo! the wishèd day is come at last,
That shall, for all the paynes and sorrowes past,
Pay to her usury of long delight:
And, whylest she doth her dight,
Doe ye to her of joy and solace sing,
That all the woods may answer, and your eccho ring.

Bring with you all the Nymphes that you can heare
Both of the rivers and the forrests greene,
And of the sea that neighbours to her neare:
Al with gay girlands goodly wel beseene.
And let them also with them bring in hand
Another gay girland
For my fayre love, of lillyes and of roses,
Bound truelove wize, with a blew silke riband.
And let them make great store of bridale poses,
And let them eeke bring store of other flowers,
To deck the bridale bowers.
And let the ground whereas her foot shall tread,
For feare the stones her tender foot should wrong,
Be strewed with fragrant flowers all along,
And diapred lyke the discolored mead.
Which done, doe at her chamber dore awayt,
For she will waken strayt;
The whiles doe ye this song unto her sing,
The woods shall to you answer, and your Eccho ring.

Ye Nymphes of Mulla, which with carefull heed
The silver scaly trouts doe tend full well,
And greedy pikes which use therein to feed;
(Those trouts and pikes all others doo excell;)
And ye likewise, which keepe the rushy lake,
Where none doo fishes take;

Bynd up the locks the which hang scatterd light,
And in his waters, which your mirror make,
Behold your faces as the christall bright,
That when you come whereas my love doth lie,
No blemish she may spie.
And eke, ye lightfoot mayds, which keepe the deere,
That on the hoary mountayne used to towre;
And the wylde wolves, which seeke them to devoure,
With your steele darts doo chace from comming neer;
Be also present heere,
To helpe to decke her, and to help to sing,
That all the woods may answer, and your eccho ring.

Wake now, my love, awake! for it is time;
The Rosy Morne long since left Tithones bed,
All ready to her silver coche to clyme;
And Phœbus gins to shew his glorious hed.
Hark! how the cheerefull birds do chaunt theyr laies
And carroll of Loves praise.
The merry Larke hir mattins sings aloft;
The Thrush replyes; the Mavis descant playes;
The Ouzell shrills; the Ruddock warbles soft;
So goodly all agree, with sweet consent,
To this dayes merriment.
Ah! my deere love, why doe ye sleepe thus long?
When meeter were that ye should now awake,
T' awayt the comming of your joyous make,
And hearken to the birds love-learned song,
The deawy leaves among!
Nor they of joy and pleasance to you sing,
That all the woods them answer, and theyr eccho ring.

My love is now awake out of her dreames,
And her fayre eyes, like stars that dimmèd were
With darksome cloud, now shew theyr goodly beams
More bright then Hesperus his head doth rere.
Come now, ye damzels, daughters of delight,

Helpe quickly her to dight:
But first come ye fayre houres, which were begot
In Joves sweet paradice of Day and Night;
Which doe the seasons of the yeare allot,
And al, that ever in this world is fayre,
Doe make and still repayre:
And ye three handmayds of the Cyprian Queene,
The which doe still adorne her beauties pride,
Helpe to addorne my beautifullest bride:
And, as ye her array, still throw betweene
Some graces to be seene;
And, as ye use to Venus, to her sing,
The whiles the woods shal answer, and your eccho ring.

Now is my love all ready forth to come:
Let all the virgins therefore well awayt:
And ye fresh boyes, that tend upon her groome,
Prepare your selves; for he is comming strayt.
Set all your things in seemely good aray,
Fit for so joyfull day:
The joyfulst day that ever sunne did see.
Faire Sun! shew forth thy favourable ray,
And let thy lifull heat not fervent be,
For feare of burning her sunshyny face,
Her beauty to disgrace.
O fayrest Phoebus! father of the Muse!
If ever I did honour thee aright,
Or sing the thing that mote thy mind delight,
Doe not thy servants simple boone refuse;
But let this day, let this one day, be myne;
Let all the rest be thine.
Then I thy soverayne prayses loud wil sing,
That all the woods shal answer, and theyr eccho ring.

Harke! how the Minstrils gin to shrill aloud
Their merry Musick that resounds from far,
The pipe, the tabor, and the trembling Croud,

That well agree withouten breach or jar.
But, most of all, the Damzels doe delite
When they their tymbrels smyte,
And thereunto doe daunce and carrol sweet,
That all the sences they doe ravish quite;
The whyles the boyes run up and downe the street,
Crying aloud with strong confusèd noyce,
As if it were one voyce,
Hymen, iö Hymen, Hymen, they do shout;
That even to the heavens theyr shouting shrill
Doth reach, and all the firmament doth fill:
To which the people standing all about,
As in approvance, doe thereto applaud,
And loud advaunce her laud;
And evermore they Hymen, Hymen sing,
That al the woods them answer, and theyr eccho ring.

Loe! where she comes along with portly pace,
Lyke Phœbe, from her chamber of the East,
Arysing forth to run her mighty race,
Clad all in white, that seemes a virgin best.
So well it her beseemes, that ye would weene
Some angell she had beene.
Her long loose yellow locks lyke golden wyre,
Sprinckled with perle, and perling flowres atweene,
Doe lyke a golden mantle her attyre;
And, being crownèd with a girland greene,
Seeme lyke some mayden Queene.
Her modest eyes, abashèd to behold
So many gazers as on her do stare,
Upon the lowly ground affixèd are;
Ne dare lift up her countenance too bold,
But blush to heare her prayses sung so loud,
So farre from being proud.
Nathlesse doe ye still loud her prayses sing,
That all the woods may answer, and your eccho ring.

Tell me, ye merchants daughters, did ye see
So fayre a creature in your towne before;
So sweet, so lovely, and so mild as she,
Adornd with beautyes grace and vertues store?
Her goodly eyes lyke Saphyres shining bright,
Her forehead yvory white,
Her cheekes lyke apples which the sun hath rudded,
Her lips lyke cherryes charming men to byte,
Her brest like to a bowle of creame uncrudded,
Her paps lyke lyllies budded,
Her snowie necke lyke to a marble towre;
And all her body like a pallace fayre,
Ascending up, with many a stately stayre,
To honors seat and chastities sweet bowre.
Why stand ye still ye virgins in amaze,
Upon her so to gaze,
Whiles ye forget your former lay to sing,
To which the woods did answer, and your eccho ring?

But if ye saw that which no eyes can see,
The inward beauty of her lively spright,
Garnisht with heavenly guifts of high degree,
Much more then would ye wonder at that sight,
And stand astonisht lyke to those which red
Medusaes mazeful hed.
There dwels sweet love, and constant chastity,
Unspotted fayth, and comely womanhood,
Regard of honour, and mild modesty;
There vertue raynes as Queene in royal throne,
And giveth lawes alone,
The which the base affections doe obay,
And yeeld theyr services unto her will;
Ne thought of thing uncomely ever may
Thereto approch to tempt her mind to ill.
Had ye once scene these her celestial threasures,
And unrevealèd pleasures,

Then would ye wonder, and her prayses sing,
That al the woods should answer, and your echo ring.

Open the temple gates unto my love,
Open them wide that she may enter in,
And all the postes adorne as doth behove,
And all the pillours deck with girlands trim,
For to receyve this Saynt with honour dew,
That commeth in to you.
With trembling steps, and humble reverence,
She commeth in, before th' Almighties view;
Of her ye virgins learne obedience,
When so ye come into those holy places,
To humble your proud faces:
Bring her up to th' high altar, that she may
The sacred ceremonies there partake,
The which do endlesse matrimony make;
And let the roring Organs loudly play
The praises of the Lord in lively notes;
The whiles, with hollow throates,
The Choristers the joyous Antheme sing,
That al the woods may answere, and their eccho ring.

Behold, whiles she before the altar stands,
Hearing the holy priest that to her speakes,
And blesseth her with his two happy hands,
How the red roses flush up in her cheekes,
And the pure snow, with goodly vermill stayne
Like crimsin dyde in grayne:
That even th' Angels, which continually
About the sacred Altare doe remaine,
Forget their service and about her fly,
Ofte peeping in her face, that seems more fayre,
The more they on it stare.
But her sad eyes, still fastened on the ground,
Are governèd with goodly modesty,
That suffers not one looke to glaunce awry,

Which may let in a little thought unsownd.
Why blush ye, love, to give to me your hand,
The pledge of all our band!
Sing, ye sweet Angels, Alleluya sing,
That all the woods may answere, and your eccho ring.

Now al is done: bring home the bride againe;
Bring home the triumph of our victory:
Bring home with you the glory of her gaine;
With joyance bring her and with jollity.
Never had man more joyfull day then this,
Whom heaven would heape with blis,
Make feast therefore now all this live-long day;
This day for ever to me holy is.
Poure out the wine without restraint or stay,
Poure not by cups, but by the belly full,
Poure out to all that wull,
And sprinkle all the postes and wals with wine,
That they may sweat, and drunken be withall.
Crowne ye God Bacchus with a coronall,
And Hymen also crowne with wreathes of vine;
And let the Graces daunce unto the rest,
For they can doo it best:
The whiles the maydens doe theyr carroll sing,
To which the woods shall answer, and theyr eccho ring.

Ring ye the bels, ye yong men of the towne,
And leave your wonted labors for this day:
This day is holy; doe ye write it downe,
That ye for ever it remember may.
This day the sunne is in his chiefest hight,
With Baraby the bright,
From whence declining daily by degrees,
He somewhat loseth of his heat and light,
When once the Crab behind his back he sees.
But for this time it ill ordainèd was,
To chose the longest day in all the yeare,

And shortest night, when longest fitter weare:
Yet never day so long, bat late would passe.
Ring ye the bels, to make it weare away,
And bonefiers make all day;
And daunce about them, and about them sing,
That all the woods may answer, and your eccho ring.

Ah! when will this long weary day have end,
And lende me leave to come unto my love?
How slowly do the houres theyr numbers spend?
How slowly does sad Time his feathers move?
Hast thee, O fayrest Planet, to thy home,
Within the Westerne fome:
Thy tyrèd steedes long since have need of rest.
Long though it be, at last I see it gloome,
And the bright evening-star with golden creast
Appeare out of the East.
Fayre childe of beauty! glorious lampe of love!
That all the host of heaven in rankes doost lead,
And guydest lovers through the nights sad dread,
How chearefully thou lookest from above,
And seemst to laugh atweene thy twinkling light,
As joying in the sight
Of these glad many, which for joy doe sing,
That all the woods them answer, and their echo ring!

Now ceasse, ye damsels, your delights fore-past;
Enough it is that all the day was youres:
Now day is doen, and night is nighing fast,
Now bring the Bryde into the brydall boures.
The night is come, now soon her disaray,
And in her bed her lay;
Lay her in lillies and in violets,
And silken courteins over her display,
And odourd sheetes, and Arras coverlets.
Behold how goodly my faire love does ly,
In proud humility!

Like unto Maia, when as Jove her took
In Tempe, lying on the flowry gras,
Twixt sleepe and wake, after she weary was,
With bathing in the Acidalian brooke.
Now it is night, ye damsels may be gon,
And leave my love alone,
And leave likewise your former lay to sing:
The woods no more shall answere, nor your echo ring.

Now welcome, night! thou night so long expected,
That long daies labour doest at last defray,
And all my cares, which cruell Love collected,
Hast sumd in one, and cancellèd for aye:
Spread thy broad wing over my love and me,
That no man may us see;
And in thy sable mantle us enwrap,
From feare of perrill and foule horror free.
Let no false treason scckc us to entrap,
Nor any dread disquiet once annoy
The safety of our joy;
But let the night be calme, and quietsome,
Without tempestuous storms or sad afray:
Lyke as when Jove with fayre Alcmena lay,
When he begot the great Tirynthian groome:
Or lyke as when he with thy selfe did lie
And begot Majesty.
And let the mayds and yong men cease to sing;
Ne let the woods them answer nor theyr eccho ring.

Let no lamenting cryes, nor dolefull teares,
Be heard all night within, nor yet without:
Ne let false whispers, breeding hidden feares,
Breake gentle sleepe with misconceivèd dout.
Let no deluding dreames, nor dreadfull sights,
Make sudden sad affrights;
Ne let house-fyres, nor lightnings helpelesse harmes,
Ne let the Pouke, nor other evill sprights,

Ne let mischivous witches with theyr charmes,
Ne let hob Goblins, names whose sence we see not,
Fray us with things that be not:
Let not the shriech Oule nor the Storke be heard,
Nor the night Raven, that still deadly yels;
Nor damnèd ghosts, cald up with mighty spels,
Nor griesly vultures, make us once affeard:
Ne let th' unpleasant Quyre of Frogs still croking
Make us to wish theyr choking.
Let none of these theyr drery accents sing;
Ne let the woods them answer, nor theyr eccho ring.

But let stil Silence trew night-watches keepe,
That sacred Peace may in assurance rayne,
And tymely Sleep, when it is tyme to sleepe,
May poure his limbs forth on your pleasant playne;
The whiles an hundred little wingèd loves,
Like divers-fethered doves,
Shall fly and flutter round about your bed,
And in the secret darke, that none reproves,
Their prety stealthes shal worke, and snares shal spread
To filch away sweet snatches of delight,
Conceald through covert night.
Ye sonnes of Venus, play your sports at will!
For greedy pleasure, carelesse of your toyes,
Thinks more upon her paradise of joyes,
Then what ye do, albe it good or ill.
All night therefore attend your merry play,
For it will soone be day:
Now none doth hinder you, that say or sing;
Ne will the woods now answer, nor your Eccho ring.

Who is the same, which at my window peepes?
Or whose is that faire face that shines so bright?
Is it not Cinthia, she that never sleepes,
But walkes about high heaven al the night?
O! fayrest goddesse, do thou not envy

My love with me to spy:
For thou likewise didst love, though now unthought,
And for a fleece of wooll, which privily
The Latmian shepherd once unto thee brought,
His pleasures with thee wrought.
Therefore to us be favorable now;
And sith of wemens labours thou hast charge,
And generation goodly dost enlarge,
Encline thy will t'effect our wishfull vow,
And the chast wombe informe with timely seed,
That may our comfort breed:
Till which we cease our hopefull hap to sing;
Ne let the woods us answere, nor our Eccho ring.

And thou, great Juno! which with awful might
The lawes of wedlock still dost patronize;
And the religion of the faith first plight
With sacred rites hast taught to solemnize;
And eeke for comfort often callèd art
Of women in their smart;
Eternally bind thou this lovely band,
And all thy blessings unto us impart.
And thou, glad Genius! in whose gentle hand
The bridale bowre and geniall bed remaine,
Without blemish or staine;
And the sweet pleasures of theyr loves delight
With secret ayde doest succour and supply,
Till they bring forth the fruitfull progeny;
Send us the timely fruit of this same night.
And thon, fayre Hebe! and thou, Hymen free!
Grant that it may so be.
Til which we cease your further prayse to sing;
Ne any woods shall answer, nor your Eccho ring.

And ye high heavens, the temple of the gods,
In which a thousand torches flaming bright
Doe burne, that to us wretched earthly clods

In dreadful darknesse lend desirèd light;
And all ye powers which in the same remayne,
More then we men can fayne!
Poure out your blessing on us plentiously,
And happy influence upon us raine,
That we may raise a large posterity,
Which from the earth, which they may long possesse
With lasting happinesse,
Up to your haughty pallaces may mount;
And, for the guerdon of theyr glorious merit,
May heavenly tabernacles there inherit,
Of blessèd Saints for to increase the count.
So let us rest, sweet love, in hope of this,
And cease till then our tymely joyes to sing:
The woods no more us answer, nor our eccho ring!

*Song! made in lieu of many ornaments,*
*With which my love should duly have been dect,*
*Which cutting off through hasty accidents,*
*Ye would not stay your dew time to expect,*
*But promist both to recompens;*
*Be unto her a goodly ornament,*
*And for short time an endlesse moniment.*

# CHRISTOPHER MARLOWE
## (1564–1593)

## The Passionate Shepherd to His Love

Come live with me and be my Love,
And we will all the pleasures prove
That hills and valleys, dales and fields,
Or woods or steepy mountain yields.

And we will sit upon the rocks,
And see the shepherds feed their flocks
By shallow rivers, to whose falls
Melodious birds sing madrigals.

And I will make thee beds of roses
And a thousand fragrant posies;
A cap of flowers, and a kirtle
Embroider'd all with leaves of myrtle.

A gown made of the finest wool
Which from our pretty lambs we pull;
Fair-linèd slippers for the cold,
With buckles of the purest gold.

A belt of straw and ivy-buds
With coral clasps and amber studs:
And if these pleasures may thee move,
Come live with me and be my Love.

The shepherd swains shall dance and sing
For thy delight each May morning:
If these delights thy mind may move,
Then live with me and be my Love.

# WILLIAM SHAKESPEARE
## (1563–1616)

### SONNET I

From fairest creatures we desire increase,
That thereby beauty's rose might never die,
But as the riper should by time decease,
His tender heir might bear his memory:
But thou contracted to thine own bright eyes,
Feed'st thy light's flame with self-substantial fuel,
Making a famine where abundance lies,
Thy self thy foe, to thy sweet self too cruel.
Thou that art now the world's fresh ornament
And only herald to the gaudy spring,
Within thine own bud buriest thy content
And tender churl mak'st waste in niggarding.
  Pity the world, or else this glutton be,
    To eat the world's due, by the grave and thee.

### SONNET III

Look in thy glass and tell the face thou viewest
Now is the time that face should form another;
Whose fresh repair if now thou not renewest,
Thou dost beguile the world, unbless some mother.
For where is she so fair whose unear'd womb
Disdains the tillage of thy husbandry?
Or who is he so fond will be the tomb
Of his self-love, to stop posterity?
Thou art thy mother's glass, and she in thee
Calls back the lovely April of her prime;

So thou through windows of thine age shalt see,
Despite of wrinkles this, thy golden time.
  But if thou live, remember'd not to be,
  Die single, and thine image dies with thee.


### SONNET XII

When I do count the clock that tells the time,
And see the brave day sunk in hideous night;
When I behold the violet past prime,
And sable curls, all silvered o'er with white;
When lofty trees I see barren of leaves,
Which erst from heat did canopy the herd,
And summer's green all girded up in sheaves
Borne on the bier with white and bristly beard,
Then of thy beauty do I question make,
That thou among the wastes of time must go,
Since sweets and beauties do themselves forsake
And die as fast as they see others grow;
  And nothing 'gainst Time's scythe can make defence
  Save breed, to brave him when he takes thee hence.


### SONNET XVIII

Shall I compare thee to a summer's day?
Thou art more lovely and more temperate:
Rough winds do shake the darling buds of May,
And summer's lease hath all too short a date:
Sometime too hot the eye of heaven shines,
And often is his gold complexion dimm'd,
And every fair from fair sometime declines,
By chance, or nature's changing course untrimm'd:
But thy eternal summer shall not fade,
Nor lose possession of that fair thou ow'st,
Nor shall death brag thou wander'st in his shade,
When in eternal lines to time thou grow'st,
  So long as men can breathe, or eyes can see,
  So long lives this, and this gives life to thee.

### SONNET XX

A woman's face with nature's own hand painted
Hast thou the master-mistress of my passion;
A woman's gentle heart, but not acquainted
With shifting change, as is false women's fashion,
An eye more bright than theirs, less false in rolling,
Gilding the object whereupon it gazeth;
A man in hue all hues in his controlling,
Which steals men's eyes and women's souls amazeth.
And for a woman wert thou first created;
Till Nature, as she wrought thee, fell a-doting,
And by addition me of thee defeated,
By adding one thing to my purpose nothing.
    But since she prick'd thee out for women's pleasure,
    Mine be thy love, and thy love's use their treasure.

### SONNET XXIX

When in disgrace with fortune and men's eyes,
I all alone beweep my outcast state,
And trouble deaf heaven with my bootless cries,
And look upon myself, and curse my fate,
Wishing me like to one more rich in hope,
Featur'd like him, like him with friends possess'd,
Desiring this man's art, and that man's scope,
With what I most enjoy contented least,
Yet in these thoughts my self almost despising,
Haply I think on thee,—and then my state,
Like to the lark at break of day arising
From sullen earth, sings hymns at heaven's gate;
    For thy sweet love remember'd such wealth brings
    That then I scorn to change my state with kings.

### SONNET XXX

When to the sessions of sweet silent thought
I summon up remembrance of things past,
I sigh the lack of many a thing I sought,
And with old woes new wail my dear times' waste:

Then can I drown an eye, unus'd to flow,
For precious friends hid in death's dateless night,
And weep afresh love's long since cancell'd woe,
And moan the expense of many a vanish'd sight:
Then can I grieve at grievances foregone,
And heavily from woe to woe tell o'er
The sad account of fore-bemoaned moan,
Which I new pay as if not paid before.
　　But if the while I think on thee, dear friend,
　　All losses are restor'd and sorrows end.

### SONNET XXXIII

Full many a glorious morning have I seen
Flatter the mountain-tops with sovereign eye,
Kissing with golden face the meadows green,
Gliding pale streams with heavenly alchemy;
Anon permit the basest clouds to ride
With ugly rack on his celestial face,
And from the forlorn world his visage hide,
Stealing unseen to west with this disgrace:
Even so my sun one early morn did shine,
With all triumphant splendour on my brow;
But, out! alack! he was but one hour mine,
The region cloud hath mask'd him from me now.
　　Yet him for this, my love no whit disdaineth;
　　Suns of the world may stain, when heaven's sun staineth.

### SONNET LV

Not marble, nor the gilded monuments
Of princes, shall outlive this powerful rime;
But you shall shine more bright in these contents
Than unswept stone, besmear'd with sluttish time
When wasteful war shall statues overturn,
And broils root out the work of masonry,
Nor Mars his sword nor war's quick fire shall burn
The living record of your memory.
'Gainst death and all-oblivious enmity

Shall you pace forth; your praise shall still find room
Even in the eyes of all posterity
That wear this world out to the ending doom.
    So, till the judgment that your self arise,
    You live in this, and dwell in lovers' eyes.


## SONNET LXV

Since brass, nor stone, nor earth, nor boundless sea,
But sad mortality o'ersways their power,
How with this rage shall beauty hold a plea,
Whose action is no stronger than a flower?
O, how shall summer's honey breath hold out
Against the wrackful siege of battering days,
When rocks impregnable are not so stout,
Nor gates of steel so strong, but Time decays?
O fearful meditation! where, alack,
Shall Time's best jewel from Time's chest lie hid?
Or what strong hand can hold his swift foot back?
Or who his spoil of beauty can forbid?
    O, none, unless this miracle have might,
    That in black ink my love may still shine bright.


## SONNET LXXI

No longer mourn for me when I am dead
Than you shall hear the surly sullen bell
Give warning to the world that I am fled
From this vile world, with vilest worms to dwell:
Nay if you read this line, remember not
The hand that writ it; for I love you so,
That I in your sweet thoughts would be forgot,
If thinking on me then should make you woe.
O, if , I say, you look upon this verse,
When I perhaps compounded am with clay,
Do not so much as my poor name rehearse,
But let your love even with my life decay;
    Lest the wise world should look into your moan,
    And mock you with me after I am gone.

## SONNET LXXIII

That time of year thou mayst in me behold
When yellow leaves, or none, or few, do hang
Upon those boughs which shake against the cold,
Bare ruin'd choirs, where late the sweet birds sang.
In me thou see'st the twilight of such day
As after sunset fadeth in the west;
Which by and by black night doth take away,
Death's second self that seals up all in rest.
In me thou see'st the glowing of such fire,
That on the ashes of his youth doth lie,
As the death-bed, whereon it must expire,
Consum'd with that which it was nourish'd by.
   This thou perceiv'st, which makes thy love more strong,
   To love that well, which thou must leave ere long.

## SONNET XCIV

They that have power to hurt and will do none,
That do not do the thing they most do show,
Who, moving others, are themselves as stone,
Unmoved, cold, and to temptation slow;
They rightly do inherit heaven's graces,
And husband nature's riches from expense;
They are the lords and owners of their faces,
Others but stewards of their excellence.
The summer's flower is to the summer sweet,
Though to itself it only live and die,
But if that flower with base infection meet,
The basest weed outbraves his dignity:
   For sweetest things turn sourest by their deeds;
   Lilies that fester, smell far worse than weeds.

## SONNET CVI

When in the chronicle of wasted time
I see descriptions of the fairest wights,
And beauty making beautiful old rime,
In praise of ladies dead, and lovely knights,

Then, in the blazon of sweet beauty's best,
Of hand, of foot, of lip, of eye, of brow,
I see their antique pen would have express'd
Even such a beauty as you master now.
So all their praises are but prophecies
Of this our time, all you prefiguring;
And, for they look'd but with divining eyes,
They had not skill enough your worth to sing:
    For we, which now behold these present days,
    Have eyes to wonder, but lack tongues to praise.

### SONNET CVII

Not mine own fears, nor the prophetic soul
Of the wide world dreaming on things to come,
Can yet the lease of my true love control,
Suppos'd as forfeit to a confin'd doom.
The mortal moon hath her eclipse endur'd,
And the sad augurs mock their own presage;
Incertainties now crown themselves assur'd,
And peace proclaims olives of endless age.
Now with the drops of this most balmy time
My love looks fresh, and Death to me subscribes,
Since, spite of him, I'll live in this poor rime,
While he insults o'er dull and speechless tribes:
    And thou in this shalt find thy monument,
    When tyrants' crests and tombs of brass are spent.

### SONNET CXVI

Let me not to the marriage of true minds
Admit impediments. Love is not love
Which alters when it alteration finds,
Or bends with the remover to remove:
O, no! it is an ever-fixed mark,
That looks on tempests and is never shaken;
It is the star to every wandering bark,
Whose worth's unknown, although his height be taken.
Love's not Time's fool, though rosy lips and cheeks

Within his bending sickle's compass come;
Love alters not with his brief hours and weeks,
But bears it out even to the edge of doom.
   If this be error and upon me prov'd,
   I never writ, nor no man ever lov'd.

## SONNET CXXIX

The expense of spirit in a waste of shame
Is lust in action; and till action, lust
Is perjur'd, murderous, bloody, full of blame,
Savage, extreme, rude, cruel, not to trust;
Enjoy'd no sooner but despised straight;
Past reason hunted; and no sooner had,
Past reason hated, as a swallow'd bait,
On purpose laid to make the taker mad:
Mad in pursuit, and in possession so;
Had, having, and in quest to have, extreme;
A bliss in proof, and prov'd, a very woe;
Before, a joy propos'd; behind, a dream.
   All this the world well knows; yet none knows well
   To shun the heaven that leads men to this hell.

## SONNET CXXX

My mistress' eyes are nothing like the sun;
Coral is far more red than her lips' red:
If snow be white, why then her breasts are dun;
If hairs be wires, black wires grow on her head.
I have seen roses damask'd, red and white,
But no such roses see I in her cheeks;
And in some perfumes is there more delight
Than in the breath that from my mistress reeks.
I love to hear her speak, yet well I know
That music hath a far more pleasing sound:
I grant I never saw a goddess go;
My mistress, when she walks, treads on the ground:
   And yet, by heaven, I think my love as rare
   As any she belied with false compare.

## SONNET CXXXVIII

When my love swears that she is made of truth,
I do believe her, though I know she lies,
That she might think me some untutor'd youth,
Unlearned in the world's false subtleties.
Thus vainly thinking that she thinks me young,
Although she knows my days are past the best,
Simply I credit her false-speaking tongue:
On both sides thus is simple truth supprest.
But wherefore says she not she is unjust?
And wherefore say not I that I am old?
O, love's best habit is in seeming trust,
And age in love loves not to have years told:
    Therefore I lie with her, and she with me,
    And in our faults by lies we flattered be.

## SONNET CXLVI

Poor soul, the centre of my sinful earth,
Fool'd by these rebel powers that thee array,
Why dost thou pine within and suffer dearth,
Painting thy outward walls so costly gay?
Why so large cost, having so short a lease,
Dost thou upon thy fading mansion spend?
Shall worms, inheritors of this excess,
Eat up thy charge? Is this thy body's end?
Then, soul live thou upon thy servant's loss,
And let that pine to aggravate thy store;
Buy terms divine in selling hours of dross;
Within be fed, without be rich no more:
    So shall thou feed on Death, that feeds on men,
    And Death once dead, there's no more dying then.

# JOHN DONNE
## (1572–1631)

## Death

Death, be not proud, though some have callèd thee
Mighty and dreadful, for thou art not so:
For those whom thou think'st thou dost overthrow
Die not, poor Death; nor yet canst thou kill me.
From Rest and Sleep, which but thy picture be,
Much pleasure, then from thee much more must flow;
And soonest our best men with thee do go—
Rest of their bones and souls' delivery!
Thou'rt slave to fate, chance, kings, and desperate men,
And dost with poison, war, and sickness dwell;
And poppy or charms can make us sleep as well
And better than thy stroke. Why swell'st thou then?
   One short sleep past, we wake eternally,
   And Death shall be no more: Death, thou shalt die!

## The Flea

Mark but this flea, and mark in this,
How little that which thou deny'st me is;
It suck'd me first, and now sucks thee,
And in this flea our two bloods mingled be.
Thou know'st that this cannot be said
A sin, nor shame, nor loss of maidenhead;
   Yet this enjoys before it woo,
   And pamper'd swells with one blood made of two;
   And this, alas! is more than we could do.

O stay, three lives in one flea spare,
Where we almost, yea, more than married are.
This flea is you and I, and this
Our marriage bed, and marriage temple is.
Though parents grudge, and you, we're met,
And cloister'd in these living walls of jet.
 Though use make you apt to kill me,
 Let not to that self-murder added be,
 And sacrilege, three sins in killing three.

Cruel and sudden, hast thou since
Purpled thy nail in blood of innocence?
Wherein could this flea guilty be,
Except in that drop which it suck'd from thee?
Yet thou triumph'st, and say'st that thou
Find'st not thyself nor me the weaker now.
 'Tis true; then learn how false fears be;
 Just so much honour, when thou yield'st to me,
 Will waste, as this flea's death took life from thee.

## Woman's Constancy

Now thou hast loved me one whole day,
To-morrow when thou leavest, what wilt thou say?
Wilt thou then antedate some new-made vow?
  Or say that now
We are not just those persons which we were?
Or that oaths made in reverential fear
Of Love, and his wrath, any may forswear?
Or, as true deaths true marriages untie,
So lovers' contracts, images of those,
Bind but till sleep, death's image, them unloose?
  Or, your own end to justify,
For having purposed change and falsehood, you
Can have no way but falsehood to be true?

Vain lunatic, against these 'scapes I could
　　　Dispute, and conquer, if I would;
　　　Which I abstain to do,
For by to-morrow I may think so too.

## The Sun Rising

　　　Busy old fool, unruly Sun,
　　　　Why dost thou thus,
Through windows, and through curtains, call on us?
Must to thy motions lovers' seasons run?
　　　Saucy pedantic wretch, go chide
　　　Late school-boys, or sour prentices,
　　Go tell court-huntsmen, that the king will ride,
　　Call country ants to harvest offices;
Love, all alike, no season knows nor clime,
No hours, days, months, which are the rags of time.

　　　Thy beams so reverend and strong,
　　　　Why shouldst thou think?
I could eclipse, and cloud them with a wink,
But that I would not lose her sight so long.
　　　If her eyes have not blinded thine,
　　　Look, and to-morrow late tell me,
　　Whether both th' Indias of spice and mine
　　Be where thou left'st them, or lie here with me.
Ask for those kings whom thou saw'st yesterday,
And thou shalt hear, "All here in one bed lay."

　　　She's all states, and all princes I;
　　　　Nothing else is;
Princes do but play us; compared to this,
All honour's mimic, all wealth alchymy.
　　　Thou, Sun, art half as happy as we,
　　　In that the world's contract thus;

Thine age asks ease, and since thy duties be
To warm the world, that's done in warming us.
Shine here to us, and thou art everywhere;
This bed thy centre is, these walls thy sphere.

## Love's Usury

For every hour that thou wilt spare me now,
I will allow,
Usurious god of love, twenty to thee,
When with my brown my grey hairs equal be.
Till then, Love, let my body range, and let
Me travel, sojourn, snatch, plot, have, forget,
Resume my last year's relict; think that yet
We had never met.

Let me think any rival's letter mine,
And at next nine
Keep midnight's promise; mistake by the way
The maid, and tell the lady of that delay;
Only let me love none; no not the sport
From country grass to comfitures of court,
Or city's *quelque-choses*; let not report
My mind transport.

This bargain's good; if, when I'm old, I be
Inflamed by thee,
If thine own honour, or my shame and pain,
Thou covet most, at that age thou shalt gain.
Do thy will then; then subject and degree
And fruit of love, Love, I submit to thee.
Spare me till then; I'll bear it, though she be
One that love me.

# The Canonization

For God's sake hold your tongue, and let me love;
   Or chide my palsy, or my gout;
   My five grey hairs, or ruin'd fortune flout;
With wealth your state, your mind with arts improve;
     Take you a course, get you a place,
     Observe his Honour, or his Grace;
Or the king's real, or his stamp'd face
   Contemplate; what you will, approve,
   So you will let me love.

Alas! alas! who's injured by my love?
   What merchant's ships have my sighs drown'd?
   Who says my tears have overflow'd his ground?
When did my colds a forward spring remove?
     When did the heats which my veins fill
     Add one more to the plaguy bill?
Soldiers find wars, and lawyers find out still
   Litigious men, whom quarrels move,
   Though she and I do love.

Call's what you will, we are made such by love;
   Call her one, me another fly,
   We're tapers too, and at our own cost die,
And we in us find th' eagle and the dove.
     The phoenix riddle hath more wit
     By us; we two being one, are it;
So, to one neutral thing both sexes fit.
   We die and rise the same, and prove
   Mysterious by this love.

We can die by it, if not live by love,
   And if unfit for tomb or hearse
   Our legend be, it will be fit for verse;
And if no piece of chronicle we prove,
     We'll build in sonnets pretty rooms;
     As well a well-wrought urn becomes

The greatest ashes, as half-acre tombs,
    And by these hymns all shall approve
    Us canonized for love;

And thus invoke us, "You, whom reverend love
    Made one another's hermitage;
    You, to whom love was peace, that now is rage;
Who did the whole world's soul contract, and drove
      Into the glasses of your eyes;
      So made such mirrors, and such spies,
That they did all to you epitomize—
    Countries, towns, courts beg from above
    A pattern of your love."

## Break of Day

Stay, O sweet, and do not rise;
The light that shines comes from thine eyes;
The day breaks not, it is my heart,
Because that you and I must part.
    Stay, or else my joys will die
    And perish in their infancy.

'Tis true, 'tis day; what though it be?
O, wilt thou therefore rise from me?
Why should we rise because 'tis light?
Did we lie down, because 'twas night?
Love, which in spite of darkness brought us hither,
Should in despite of light keep us together.

Light hath no tongue, but is all eye;
If it could speak as well as spy,
This were the worst that it could say,
That being well I fain would stay,
And that I loved my heart and honour so,
That I would not from him, that had them, go.

Must business thee from hence remove?
O! that's the worst disease of love,
The poor, the foul, the false, love can
Admit, but not the busied man.
He which hath business, and makes love, doth do
Such wrong, as when a married man doth woo.

## A Nocturnal upon St. Lucy's Day, Being the Shortest Day

'Tis the year's midnight, and it is the day's,
Lucy's, who scarce seven hours herself unmasks;
   The sun is spent, and now his flasks
    Send forth light squibs, no constant rays;
      The world's whole sap is sunk;
The general balm th' hydroptic earth hath drunk,
Whither, as to the bed's-feet, life is shrunk,
Dead and interr'd; yet all these seem to laugh,
Compared with me, who am their epitaph.

Study me then, you who shall lovers be
At the next world, that is, at the next spring;
   For I am a very dead thing,
    In whom Love wrought new alchemy.
      For his art did express
A quintessence even from nothingness,
From dull privations, and lean emptiness;
He ruin'd me, and I am re-begot
Of absence, darkness, death—things which are not.

All others, from all things, draw all that's good,
Life, soul, form, spirit, whence they being have;
   I, by Love's limbec, am the grave
    Of all, that's nothing. Oft a flood
      Have we two wept, and so
Drown'd the whole world, us two; oft did we grow,

To be two chaoses, when we did show
Care to aught else; and often absences
Withdrew our souls, and made us carcasses.

But I am by her death—which word wrongs her—
Of the first nothing the elixir grown;
    Were I a man, that I were one
    I needs must know; I should prefer,
        If I were any beast,
Some ends, some means; yea plants, yea stones detest,
And love; all, all some properties invest.
If I an ordinary nothing were,
As shadow, a light, and body must be here.

But I am none; nor will my sun renew.
You lovers, for whose sake the lesser sun
    At this time to the Goat is run
    To fetch new lust, and give it you,
        Enjoy your summer all,
Since she enjoys her long night's festival.
Let me prepare towards her, and let me call
This hour her vigil, and her eve, since this
Both the year's and the day's deep midnight is.

## A Valediction Forbidding Mourning

As virtuous men pass mildly away,
    And whisper to their souls to go,
Whilst some of their sad friends do say,
    "Now his breath goes," and some say, "No."

So let us melt, and make no noise,
    No tear-floods, nor sigh-tempests move;
'Twere profanation of our joys
    To tell the laity our love.

Moving of th' earth brings harms and fears;
   Men reckon what it did, and meant;
But trepidation of the spheres,
   Though greater far, is innocent.

Dull sublunary lovers' love
   —Whose soul is sense—cannot admit
Of absence, 'cause it doth remove
   The thing which elemented it.

But we by a love so far refined,
   That ourselves know not what it is,
Inter-assurèd of the mind,
   Care less eyes, lips and hands to miss.

Our two souls therefore, which are one,
   Though I must go, endure not yet
A breach, but an expansion,
   Like gold to airy thinness beat.

If they be two, they are two so
   As stiff twin compasses are two;
Thy soul, the fix'd foot, makes no show
   To move, but doth, if th' other do.

And though it in the centre sit,
   Yet, when the other far doth roam,
It leans, and hearkens after it,
   And grows erect, as that comes home.

Such wilt thou be to me, who must,
   Like th' other foot, obliquely run;
Thy firmness makes my circle just,
   And makes me end where I begun.

# The Ecstacy

Where, like a pillow on a bed,
　A pregnant bank swell'd up, to rest
The violet's reclining head,
　Sat we two, one another's best.

Our hands were firmly cemented
　By a fast balm, which thence did spring;
Our eye-beams twisted, and did thread
　Our eyes upon one double string.

So to engraft our hands, as yet
　Was all the means to make us one;
And pictures in our eyes to get
　Was all our propagation.

As, 'twixt two equal armies, Fate
　Suspends uncertain victory,
Our souls—which to advance their state,
　Were gone out—hung 'twixt her and me.

And whilst our souls negotiate there,
　We like sepulchral statues lay;
All day, the same our postures were,
　And we said nothing, all the day.

If any, so by love refined,
　That he soul's language understood,
And by good love were grown all mind,
　Within convenient distance stood,

He—though he knew not which soul spake,
　Because both meant, both spake the same—
Might thence a new concoction take,
　And part far purer than he came.

This ecstacy doth unperplex
　(We said) and tell us what we love;
We see by this, it was not sex;
　We see, we saw not, what did move;

But as all several souls contain
　Mixture of things they know not what,
Love these mix'd souls doth mix again,
　And makes both one, each this, and that.

A single violet transplant,
　The strength, the colour, and the size—
All which before was poor and scant—
　Redoubles still, and multiplies.

When love with one another so
　Interanimates two souls,
That abler soul, which thence doth flow,
　Defects of loneliness controls.

We then, who are this new soul, know,
　Of what we are composed, and made,
For th' atomies of which we grow
　Are souls, whom no change can invade.

But, O alas! so long, so far,
　Our bodies why do we forbear?
They are ours, though not we; we are
　Th' intelligences, they the spheres.

We owe them thanks, because they thus
　Did us, to us, at first convey,
Yielded their senses' force to us,
　Nor are dross to us, but allay.

On man heaven's influence works not so,
    But that it first imprints the air;
For soul into the soul may flow,
    Though it to body first repair.

As our blood labours to beget
    Spirits, as like souls as it can;
Because such fingers need to knit
    That subtle knot, which makes us man;

So must pure lovers' souls descend
    To affections, and to faculties,
Which sense may reach and apprehend,
    Else a great prince in prison lies.

To our bodies turn we then, that so
    Weak men on love reveal'd may look;
Love's mysteries in souls do grow,
    But yet the body is his book.

And if some lover, such as we,
    Have heard this dialogue of one,
Let him still mark us, he shall see
    Small change when we're to bodies gone.

# BEN JONSON

## (1572–1637)

## Song to Celia

Drink to me only with thine eyes,
    And I will pledge with mine;
Or leave a kiss but in the cup,
    And I'll not look for wine.
The thirst, that from the soul doth rise,
    Doth ask a drink divine:
But might I of Jove's nectar sup,
    I would not change for thine.

I sent thee late a rosy wreath,
    Not so much honouring thee
As giving it a hope, that there
    It could not wither'd be.
But thou thereon didst only breathe,
    And sent'st it back to me:
Since when it grows, and smells, I swear,
    Not of itself, but thee.

## To the Memory of My Beloved Master, William Shakespeare

To draw no envy, SHAKESPEARE, on thy name,
Am I thus ample to thy book and fame;
While I confess thy writings to be such,
As neither man, nor Muse, can praise too much.
'Tis true, and all men's suffrage. But these ways
Were not the paths I meant unto thy praise;
For silliest ignorance on these may light,
Which, when it sounds at best, but echoes right;
Or blind affection, which doth ne'er advance
The truth, but gropes, and urgeth all by chance;
Or crafty malice might pretend this praise,
And think to ruin, where it seemed to raise.
These are, as some infamous bawd or whore,
Should praise a matron; what could hurt her more?
But thou art proof against them, and, indeed,
Above the ill fortune of them, or the need.
I therefore will begin: Soul of the age!
The applause! delight! the wonder of our stage!
My SHAKESPEARE rise! I will not lodge thee by
Chaucer, or Spenser, or bid Beaumont lie
A little further off, to make thee room:
Thou art a monument without a tomb,
And art alive still, while thy book doth live,
And we have wits to read and praise to give.
That I not mix thee so, my brain excuses,
I mean with great, but disproportioned Muses:
For if I thought my judgment were of years,
I should commit thee surely with thy peers,
And tell how far thou didst our Lily outshine,
Or sporting Kyd, or Marlowe's mighty line.
And though thou hadst small Latin and less Greek,
From thence to honour thee, I will not seek
For names: but call forth thundering Æschylus,
Euripides, and Sophocles to us.
Pacuvius, Accius, him of Cordoua dead,

To live again, to hear thy buskin tread,
And shake a stage: or when thy socks were on,
Leave thee alone for the comparison
Of all, that insolent Greece, or haughty Rome
Sent forth, or since did from their ashes come.
Triumph, my Britain, thou hast one to show,
To whom all scenes of Europe homage owe.
He was not of an age, but for all time!
And all the Muses still were in their prime,
When, like Apollo, he came forth to warm
Our ears, or like a Mercury to charm!
Nature herself was proud of his designs,
And joyed to wear the dressing of his lines!
Which were so richly spun, and woven so fit,
As, since, she will vouchsafe no other wit.
The merry Greek, tart Aristophanes,
Neat Terence, witty Plautus, now not please;
But antiquated and deserted lie,
As they were not of nature's family.
Yet must I not give nature all; thy art,
My gentle Shakespeare, must enjoy a part.
For though the poet's matter nature be,
His art doth give the fashion: and, that he
Who casts to write a living line, must sweat,
(Such as thine are) and strike the second heat
Upon the Muses' anvil; turn the same,
And himself with it, that he thinks to fame;
Or for the laurel, he may gain a scorn;
For a good poet's made, as well as born.
And such wert thou! Look how the father's face
Lives in his issue, even so the race
Of Shakespeare's mind and manners brightly shines
In his well turnéd, and true filéd lines;
In each of which he seems to shake a lance,
As brandished at the eyes of ignorance.
Sweet Swan of Avon! what a sight it were
To see thee in our water yet appear,

And make those flights upon the banks of Thames,
That so did take Eliza, and our James!
But stay, I see thee in the hemisphere
Advanced, and made a constellation there!
Shine forth, thou Star of poets, and with rage,
Or influence, chide, or cheer the drooping stage,
Which, since thy flight from hence, hath mourned like night,
And despairs day, but for thy volume's light.

## An Elegy

Though beauty be the mark of praise,
    And yours of whom I sing, be such,
    As not the world can praise too much,
Yet 'tis your virtue now I raise.

A virtue, like allay, so gone
    Throughout your form; as though that move,
    And draw, and conquer all men's love,
This subjects you to love of one,

Wherein you triumph yet; because
    'Tis of yourself, and that you use
    The noblest freedom, not to choose
Against or faith, or honour's laws.

But who could less expect from you,
    In whom alone Love lives agen?
    By whom he is restored to men;
And kept, and bred, and brought up true?

His falling temples you have reared,
    The withered garlands ta'en away;
    His altars kept from the decay
That envy wished and nature feared:

And on them burn so chaste a flame,
   With so much loyalty's expense,
   As Love t' acquit such excellence,
Is gone himself into your name.

And you are he; the deity
   To whom all lovers are designed,
   That would their better objects find;
Among which faithful troop am I.

Who, as an offering at your shrine,
   Have sung this hymn, and here entreat
   One spark of your diviner heat
To light upon a love of mine.

Which, if it kindle not, but scant
   Appear, and that to shortest view,
   Yet give me leave t' adore in you
What I, in her, am grieved to want.

## Of Life and Death

The ports of death are sins; of life, good deeds;
Through which our merit leads us to our meeds.
How wilful blind is he, then, that would stray,
And hath it in his powers to make his way!
This world death's region is, the other life's;
And here, it should be one of our first strifes,
So to front death, as men might judge us past it:
For good men but see death, the wicked taste it.

## Clerimont's Song

Still to be neat, still to be drest,
As you were going to a feast;
Still to be powdered, still perfumed:
Lady, it is to be presumed,
Though art's hid causes are not found,
All is not sweet, all is not sound.

Give me a look, give me a face,
That makes simplicity a grace;
Robes loosely flowing, hair as free;
Such sweet neglect more taketh me
Than all the adulteries of art:
They strike mine eyes, but not my heart.

## To Penshurst

Thou art not, PENSHURST, built to envious show
Of touch or marble; nor canst boast a row
Of polish'd pillars, or a roof of gold:
Thou hast no lantern, whereof tales are told;
Or stair, or courts; but stand'st an ancient pile,
And these grudg'd at, art reverenced the while.
Thou joy'st in better marks, of soil, of air,
Of wood, of water; therein thou art fair.
Thou hast thy walks for health, as well as sport:
Thy mount, to which thy Dryads do resort,
Where Pan and Bacchus their high feasts have made,
Beneath the broad beech, and the chestnut shade;
That taller tree, which of a nut was set,
At his great birth, where all the Muses met.
There, in the writhed bark, are cut the names
Of many a sylvan, taken with his flames;
And thence the ruddy satyrs oft provoke
The lighter fauns, to reach thy lady's oak.
Thy copse too, named of Gamage, thou hast there,

That never fails to serve thee season'd deer,
When thou wouldst feast, or exercise thy friends.
The lower land, that to the river bends,
Thy sheep, thy bullocks, kine, and calves do feed;
The middle grounds thy mares and horses breed.
Each bank doth yield thee conies; and the tops
Fertile of wood, Ashore and Sydneys copp's,
To crown thy open table, doth provide
The purpled pheasant, with the speckled side:
The painted partridge lies in ev'ry field,
And for thy mess is willing to be kill'd.
And if the high-swoln Medway fail thy dish,
Thou hast thy ponds, that pay thee tribute fish,
Fat aged carps that run into thy net,
And pikes, now weary their own kind to eat,
As loth the second draught or cast to stay,
Officiously at first themselves betray.
Bright eels that emulate them, and leap on land,
Before the fisher, or into his hand.
Then hath thy orchard fruit, thy garden flowers,
Fresh as the air, and new as are the hours.
The early cherry, with the later plum,
Fig, grape, and quince, each in his time doth come:
The blushing apricot, and woolly peach
Hang on thy walls, that every child may reach.
And though thy walls be of the country stone,
They're rear'd with no man's ruin, no man's groan;
There's none, that dwell about them, wish them down;
But all come in, the farmer and the clown;
And no one empty-handed, to salute
Thy lord and lady, though they have no suit.
Some bring a capon, some a rural cake,
Some nuts, some apples; some that think they make
The better cheeses, bring them; or else send
By their ripe daughters, whom they would commend
This way to husbands; and whose baskets bear
An emblem of themselves in plum, or pear.

But what can this (more than express their love)
Add to thy free provisions, far above
The need of such? whose liberal board doth flow,
With all that hospitality doth know!
Where comes no guest, but is allow'd to eat,
Without his fear, and of thy lord's own meat:
Where the same beer and bread, and self-same wine,
That is his lordship's, shall be also mine.
And I not fain to sit (as some this day,
At great men's tables) and yet dine away.
Here no man tells my cups; nor standing by,
A waiter, doth my gluttony envy:
But gives me what I call, and lets me eat,
He knows, below, he shall find plenty of meat;
Thy tables hoard not up for the next day,
Nor, when I take my lodging, need I pray
For fire, or lights, or livery; all is there ;
As if thou then wert mine, or I reign'd here:
There's nothing I can wish, for which I stay.
That found king JAMES, when hunting late, this way,
With his brave son, the prince; they saw thy fires
Shine bright on every hearth, as the desires
Of thy Penates had been set on flame,
To entertain them; or the country came,
With all their zeal, to warm their welcome here.
What (great, I will not say, but) sudden chear
Didst thou then make 'em! and what praise was heap'd
On thy good lady, then! who therein reap'd
The just reward of her high huswifry;
To have her linen, plate, and all things nigh,
When she was far; and not a room, but drest,
As if it had expected such a guest!
These, Penshurst, are thy praise, and yet not all.
Thy lady's noble, fruitful, chaste withal.
His children thy great lord may call his own;
A fortune, in this age, but rarely known.

They are, and have been taught religion; thence
Their gentler spirits have suck'd innocence.
Each morn, and even, they are taught to pray,
With the whole household, and may, every day,
Read in their virtuous parents' noble parts,
The mysteries of manners, arms, and arts.
Now, Penshurst, they that will proportion thee
With other edifices, when they see
Those proud ambitious heaps, and nothing else,
May say, their lords have built, but thy lord dwells.

## To the World

### A Farewell for a Gentlewoman, Virtuous and Noble

False world, good-night! since thou hast brought
   That hour upon my morn of age,
Henceforth I quit thee from my thought,
   My part is ended on thy stage.

Do not once hope that thou canst tempt
   A spirit so resolv'd to tread
Upon thy throat, and live exempt
   From all the nets that thou canst spread.

I know thy forms are studied arts,
   Thy subtle ways be narrow straits;
Thy courtesy but sudden starts,
   And what thou call'st thy gifts are baits.

I know too, though thou strut and paint,
   Yet art thou both shrunk up, and old;
That only fools make thee a saint,
   And all thy good is to be sold.

I know thou whole art but a shop
   Of toys and trifles, traps and snares,
To take the weak, or make them stop:
   Yet art thou falser than thy wares.

And knowing this should I yet stay,
   Like such as blow away their lives,
And never will redeem a day,
   Enamour'd of their golden gyves?

Or having 'scaped shall I return,
   And thrust my neck into the noose,
From whence so lately, I did burn,
   With all my powers, my self to loose?

What bird, or beast is known so dull,
   That fled his cage, or broke his chain,
And tasting air and freedom, wull
   Render his head in there again?

If these who have but sense, can shun
   The engines, that have them annoy'd;
Little for me had reason done,
   If I could not thy gins avoid.

Yes, threaten, do. Alas, I fear
   As little, as I hope from thee:
I know thou canst nor shew, nor bear
   More hatred, than thou hast to me.

My tender, first, and simple years
   Thou didst abuse, and then betray;
Since stirr'dst up jealousies and fears,
   When all the causes were away.

Then in a soil hast planted me,
  Where breathe the basest of thy fools;
Where envious arts professed be,
  And pride and ignorance the schools:

Where nothing is examin'd, weigh'd,
  But as 'tis rumour'd, so believed;
Where every freedom is betray'd,
  And every goodness tax'd or grieved.

But what we're born for, we must bear:
  Our frail condition it is such,
That what to all may happen here,
  If 't chance to me, I must not grutch.

Else I my state should much mistake,
  To harbour a divided thought
From all my kind; that for my sake,
  There should a miracle be wrought.

No, I do know that I was born
  To age, misfortune, sickness, grief:
But I will bear these with that scorn,
  As shall not need thy false relief.

Nor for my peace will I go far,
  As wanderers do, that still do roam;
But make my strengths, such as they are,
  Here in my bosom, and at home.

# ROBERT HERRICK
## (1591–1674)

## Corinna's Going a-Maying

Get up, get up for shame! The blooming morn
Upon her wings presents the god unshorn.
  See how Aurora throws her fair
  Fresh-quilted colours through the air:
  Get up, sweet slug-a-bed, and see
  The dew bespangling herb and tree!
Each flower has wept and bow'd toward the east
Above an hour since, yet you not drest;
  Nay! not so much as out of bed?
  When all the birds have matins said
  And sung their thankful hymns, 'tis sin,
  Nay, profanation, to keep in,
Whereas a thousand virgins on this day
Spring sooner than the lark, to fetch in May.

Rise and put on your foliage, and be seen
To come forth, like the spring-time, fresh and green,
  And sweet as Flora. Take no care
  For jewels for your gown or hair:
  Fear not; the leaves will strew
  Gems in abundance upon you:
Besides, the childhood of the day has kept,
Against you come, some orient pearls unwept.
  Come, and receive them while the light
  Hangs on the dew-locks of the night:
  And Titan on the eastern hill
  Retires himself, or else stands still

Till you come forth! Wash, dress, be brief in praying.
Few beads are best when once we go a-Maying.

Come, my Corinna, come; and coming, mark
How each field turns a street, each street a park,
      Made green and trimm'd with trees! see how
      Devotion gives each house a bough
      Or branch! each porch, each door, ere this,
      An ark, a tabernacle is,
Made up of white-thorn neatly interwove,
As if here were those cooler shades of love.
      Can such delights be in the street
      And open fields, and we not see't?
      Come, we'll abroad: and let's obey
      The proclamation made for May,
And sin no more, as we have done, by staying;
But, my Corinna, come, let's go a-Maying.

There's not a budding boy or girl this day
But is got up and gone to bring in May.
      A deal of youth ere this is come
      Back, and with white-thorn laden home.
      Some have despatch'd their cakes and cream,
      Before that we have left to dream:
And some have wept and woo'd, and plighted troth,
And chose their priest, ere we can cast off sloth:
      Many a green-gown has been given,
      Many a kiss, both odd and even:
      Many a glance, too, has been sent
      From out the eye, love's firmament:
Many a jest told of the keys betraying
This night, and locks pick'd: yet we're not a-Maying!

Come, let us go, while we are in our prime,
And take the harmless folly of the time!
      We shall grow old apace, and die
      Before we know our liberty.

Our life is short, and our days run
As fast away as does the sun.
And, as a vapour or a drop of rain,
Once lost, can ne'er be found again,
So when or you or I are made
A fable, song, or fleeting shade,
All love, all liking, all delight
Lies drown'd with us in endless night.
Then, while time serves, and we are but decaying,
Come, my Corinna, come, let's go a-Maying.

## To the Virgins, to Make Much of Time

Gather ye rosebuds while ye may,
Old Time is still a-flying:
And this same flower that smiles to-day
To-morrow will be dying.

The glorious lamp of heaven, the sun,
The higher he's a-getting,
The sooner will his race be run,
And nearer he's to setting.

That age is best which is the first,
When youth and blood are warmer;
But being spent, the worse, and worst
Times still succeed the former.

Then be not coy, but use your time,
And while ye may, go marry:
For having lost but once your prime,
You may for ever tarry.

## To Violets

Welcome, maids of honour!
　　You do bring
　　In the spring,
And wait upon her.

She has virgins many,
　　Fresh and fair;
　　Yet you are
More sweet than any.

You're the maiden posies,
　　And so graced
　　To be placed
'Fore damask roses.

Yet, though thus respected,
　　By-and-by
　　Ye do lie,
Poor girls, neglected.

## To Daffodils

Fair Daffodils, we weep to see
　　You haste away so soon;
As yet the early-rising sun
　　Has not attain'd his noon.
　　　　Stay, stay
　　Until the hasting day
　　　　Has run
　　But to the evensong;
And, having pray'd together, we
　　Will go with you along.

We have short time to stay, as you,
We have as short a spring;
As quick a growth to meet decay,
As you, or anything.
We die
As your hours do, and dry
Away
Like to the summer's rain;
Or as the pearls of morning's dew,
Ne'er to be found again.

———

## To Blossoms

Fair pledges of a fruitful tree,
Why do ye fall so fast?
Your date is not so past
But you may stay yet here awhile
To blush and gently smile,
And go at last.

What! were ye born to be
An hour or half's delight,
And so to bid good night?
'Twas pity Nature brought you forth
Merely to show your worth
And lose you quite.

But you are lovely leaves, where we
May read how soon things have
Their end, though ne'er so brave:
And after they have shown their pride
Like you awhile, they glide
Into the grave.

## The Primrose

Ask me why I send you here
This sweet Infanta of the year?
Ask me why I send to you
This primrose, thus bepearl'd with dew?
I will whisper to your ears:—
The sweets of love are mix'd with tears.

Ask me why this flower does show
So yellow-green, and sickly too?
Ask me why the stalk is weak
And bending (yet it doth not break)?
I will answer:—These discover
What fainting hopes are in a lover.

## The Funeral Rites of the Rose

The Rose was sick and smiling died;
And, being to be sanctified,
About the bed there sighing stood
The sweet and flowery sisterhood:
Some hung the head, while some did bring,
To wash her, water from the spring;
Some laid her forth, while others wept,
But all a solemn fast there kept:
The holy sisters, some among,
The sacred dirge and trental sung.
But ah! what sweets smelt everywhere,
As Heaven had spent all perfumes there.
At last, when prayers for the dead
And rites were all accomplishèd,
They, weeping, spread a lawny loom,
And closed her up as in a tomb.

## Delight in Disorder

A sweet disorder in the dress
Kindles in clothes a wantonness:
A lawn about the shoulders thrown
Into a fine distraction:
An erring lace, which here and there
Enthrals the crimson stomacher:
A cuff neglectful, and thereby
Ribbands to flow confusedly:
A winning wave, deserving note,
In the tempestuous petticoat:
A careless shoe-string, in whose tie
I see a wild civility:
Do more bewitch me than when art
Is too precise in every part.

## Upon Julia's Clothes

Whenas in silks my Julia goes,
Then, then, methinks, how sweetly flows
The liquefaction of her clothes!

Next, when I cast mine eyes and see
That brave vibration each way free,
—O how that glittering taketh me!

## The Night-Piece: To Julia

Her eyes the glow-worm lend thee,
The shooting stars attend thee;
    And the elves also,
    Whose little eyes glow
Like the sparks of fire, befriend thee.

No Will-o'-the-wisp mislight thee,
Nor snake or slow-worm bite thee;
    But on, on thy way
    Not making a stay,
Since ghost there's none to affright thee.

Let not the dark thee cumber:
What though the moon does slumber?
    The stars of the night
    Will lend thee their light
Like tapers clear without number.

Then, Julia, let me woo thee,
Thus, thus to come unto me;
    And when I shall meet
    Thy silv'ry feet,
My soul I'll pour into thee.

## His Winding-Sheet

Come thou, who art the wine and wit
    Of all I've writ:
The grace, the glory, and the best
    Piece of the rest.
Thou art of what I did intend
    The all and end;
And what was made, was made to meet
    Thee, thee, my sheet.
Come then and be to my chaste side
    Both bed and bride:
We two, as reliques left, will have
    One rest, one grave:
And hugging close, we will not fear
    Lust entering here:

Where all desires are dead and cold
        As is the mould;
And all affections are forgot,
        Or trouble not.
Here, here, the slaves and prisoners be
        From shackles free:
And weeping widows long oppress'd
        Do here find rest.
The wrongèd client ends his laws
        Here, and his cause.
Here those long suits of Chancery lie
        Quiet, or die:
And all Star-Chamber bills do cease
        Or hold their peace.
Here needs no Court for our Request
        Where all are best,
All wise, all equal, and all just
        Alike i' th' dust.
Nor need we here to fear the frown
        Of court or crown:
Where fortune bears no sway o'er things,
        There all are kings.
In this securer place we'll keep
        As lull'd asleep;
Or for a little time we'll lie
        As robes laid by;
To be another day re-worn,
        Turn'd, but not torn:
Or like old testaments engross'd,
        Lock'd up, not lost.
And for a while lie here conceal'd,
        To be reveal'd
Next at the great Platonick year,
        And then meet here.

# ANDREW MARVELL
## (1621–1678)

## To His Coy Mistress

Had we but world enough and time,
This coyness, lady, were no crime.
We would sit down and think which way
To walk, and pass our long love's day.
Thou by the Indian Ganges' side
Shouldst rubies find: I by the tide
Of Humber would complain. I would
Love you ten years before the Flood,
And you should, if you please, refuse
Till the conversion of the Jews.
My vegetable love should grow
Vaster than empires and more slow.
An hundred years should go to praise
Thine eyes, and on thy forehead gaze;
Two hundred to adore each breast,
But thirty thousand to the rest;
An age at least to every part,
And the last age should show your heart.
For, lady, you deserve this state,
Nor would I love at lower rate.

   But at my back I always hear
Time's wingèd chariot hurrying near,
And yonder all before us lie
Deserts of vast eternity.

Thy beauty shall no more be found,
Nor in thy marble vault shall sound
My echoing song; then worms shall try
That long-preserved virginity,
And your quaint honour turn to dust,
And into ashes all my lust.
The grave's a fine and private place,
But none, I think, do there embrace.
    Now, therefore, while the youthful hue
Sits on thy skin like morning dew,
And while thy willing soul transpires
At every pore with instant fires,
Now, let us sport us while we may;
And now, like amorous birds of prey,
Rather at once our time devour,
Than languish in his slow-chapt power!
Let us roll all our strength, and all
Our sweetness up into one ball;
And tear our pleasures with rough strife,
Thorough the iron gates of life!
Thus, though we cannot make our sun
Stand still, yet we will make him run.

# The Garden

### I

How vainly men themselves amaze
To win the palm, the oak, or bays;
And their uncessant labours see
Crowned from some single herb or tree,
Whose short and narrow-vergèd shade
Does prudently their toils upbraid;
While all the flowers and trees do close,
To weave the garlands of Repose!

### II

Fair Quiet, have I found thee here,
And Innocence, thy sister dear?
Mistaken long, I sought you then
In busy companies of men.
Your sacred plants, if here below,
Only among the plants will grow;
Society is all but rude
To this delicious solitude.

### III

No white nor red was ever seen
So amorous as this lovely green.
Fond lovers, cruel as their flame,
Cut in these trees their mistress' name:
Little, alas, they know or heed,
How far these beauties hers exceed!
Fair trees! wheres'e'er your barks I wound,
No name shall but your own be found.

### IV

When we have run our passion's heat,
Love hither makes his best retreat.
The Gods, that mortal beauty chase,
Still in a tree did end their race;
Apollo hunted Daphne so,
Only that she might laurel grow;
And Pan did after Syrinx speed,
Not as a nymph, but for a reed.

### V

What wondrous life is this I lead!
Ripe apples drop about my head;
The luscious clusters of the vine
Upon my mouth do crush their wine;
The nectarine and curious peach,
Into my hands themselves do reach;
Stumbling on melons as I pass,
Insnared with flowers, I fall on grass.

### VI

Meanwhile the mind, from pleasure less,
Withdraws into its happiness;
The mind, that ocean where each kind
Does straight its own resemblance find;
Yet it creates, transcending these,
Far other worlds, and other seas,
Annihilating all that's made
To a green thought in a green shade.

### VII

Here at the fountain's sliding foot,
Or at some fruit-tree's mossy root,
Casting the body's vest aside,
My soul into the boughs does glide:
There, like a bird, it sits and sings,
Then whets and combs its silver wings,
And, till prepared for longer flight,
Waves in its plumes the various light.

### VIII

Such was that happy Garden-state,
While man there walked without a mate:
After a place so pure and sweet,
What other help could yet be meet?
But 'twas beyond a mortal's share

To wander solitary there:
Two paradises 'twere in one,
To live in Paradise alone.

IX

How well the skilful gardener drew
Of flowers and herbs, this dial new;
Where, from above, the milder sun
Does through a fragrant zodiac run;
And as it works, the industrious bee
Computes its time as well as we.
How could such sweet and wholesome hours
Be reckoned but with herbs and flowers!

## The Mower Against Gardens

Luxurious man to bring his vice in use,
    Did after him the world seduce.
And from the fields the flowers and plants allure,
    Where Nature was most plain and pure.
He first enclosed within the gardens square
    A dead and standing pool of air;
And a more luscious earth for them did knead
    Which stupefied them while it fed.
The pink grew then as double as his mind,
    The nutriment did change the kind.
With strange perfumes he did the roses taint;
    And flowers themselves were taught to paint.
The tulip white did for complexion seek
    And learned to interline its cheek;
Its onion root they then so high did hold,
    That one was for a meadow sold.
Another world was searched through oceans new,
    To find the Marvel of Peru;

And yet these rarities might be allowed
　　To man, that sovereign thing and proud,
Had he not dealt between the bark and tree,
　　Forbidden mixtures there to see;
No plant now knew the stock from which it came,
　　He grafts upon the wild the tame,
That the uncertain and adulterate fruit
　　Might put the palate in dispute.
His green seraglio has its eunuchs too,
　　Lest any tyrant him outdo;
And in the cherry he does Nature vex,
　　To procreate without a sex.
'Tis all enforced, the fountain and the grot,
　　While the sweet fields do lie forgot,
Where willing Nature does to all dispense
　　A wild and fragrant innocence;
And fauns and fairies do the meadows till
　　More by their presence than their skill.
Their statues polished by some ancient hand,
　　May to adorn the gardens stand;
But, howsoe'er the figures do excel,
　　The Gods themselves with us do dwell.

## The Mower's Song

### I

My mind was once the true survey
Of all these meadows fresh and gay,
And in the greenness of the grass
Did see its hopes as in a glass;
When Juliana came, and she,
What I do to the grass, does to my thoughts and me.

## II

But these, while I with sorrow pine,
Grew more luxuriant still and fine,
That not one blade of grass you spied,
But had a flower on either side—
When Juliana came, and she,
What I do to the grass, does to my thoughts and me.

## III

Unthankful meadows, could you so
A fellowship so true forego,
And in your gaudy May-games meet,
While I lay trodden under feet,
When Juliana came?—and she,
What I do to the grass, does to my thoughts and me.

## IV

But what you in compassion ought,
Shall now by my revenge be wrought;
And flowers, and grass, and I, and all,
Will in one common ruin fall—
For Juliana comes, and she,
What I do to the grass, does to my thoughts and me.

## V

And thus, ye meadows which have been
Companions of my thoughts more green,
Shall now the heraldry become
With which I shall adorn my tomb—
For Juliana comes, and she,
What I do to the grass, does to my thoughts and me.

# Damon the Mower

### I

Hark! how the mower Damon sung,
With love of Juliana stung,
While everything did seem to paint
The scene more fit for his complaint.
Like her fair eyes the day was fair,
But scorching like his amorous care;
Sharp, like his scythe, his sorrow was,
And withered, like his hopes, the grass.

### II

Oh what unusual heats are here,
Which thus our sun-burned meadows sear!
The grasshopper its pipe gives o'er,
And hamstringed frogs can dance no more:
But in the brook the green frog wades,
And grasshoppers seek out the shades,
Only the snake that kept within,
Now glitters in its second skin.

### III

This heat the sun could never raise,
Nor dog-star so inflame the days.
It from an higher beauty grow'th,
Which burns the fields and mower both;
Which made the Dog and makes the Sun
Hotter than his own Phaeton.
Not July causeth these extremes,
But Juliana's scorching beams.

### IV

Tell me where I may pass the fires,
Of the hot day, or hot desires;
To what cool cave shall I descend,
Or to what gelid fountain bend?

Alas! I look for ease in vain,
When remedies themselves complain;
No moisture but my tears do rest,
No cold but in her icy breast.

### V

How long wilt thou, fair shepherdess,
Esteem me and my presents less?
To thee the harmless snake I bring,
Disarmèd of its teeth and sting;
To thee chameleons, changing hue,
And oak-leaves tipt with honey dew;
Yet thou ungrateful hast not sought
Nor what they are, nor who them brought.

### VI

I am the mower Damon, known
Through all the meadows I have mown.
On me the morn her dew distils
Before her darling daffodils;
And if at noon my toil me heat,
The sun himself licks off my sweat;
While, going home, the evening sweet
In cowslip-water bathes my feet.

### VII

What though the piping shepherd stock
The plains with an unnumbered flock,
This scythe of mine discovers wide
More ground than all his sheep do hide.
With this the golden fleece I shear
Of all these closes every year,
And though in wool more poor than they,
Yet am I richer far in hay.

### VIII

Nor am I so deformed to sight,
If in my scythe I lookèd right;
In which I see my picture done,
As in a crescent moon the sun.
The deathless fairies take me oft
To lead them in their dances soft;
And when I tune myself to sing,
About me they contract their ring.

### IX

How happy might I still have mowed,
Had not Love here his thistles sowed!
But now I all the day complain,
Joining my labour to my pain,
And with my scythe cut down the grass,
Yet still my grief is where it was;
But, when the iron blunter grows,
Sighing I whet my scythe and woes.

### X

While thus he drew his elbow round
Depopulating all the ground,
And with his whistling scythe does cut
Each stroke between the earth and root,
The edgèd steel, by careless chance,
Did into his own ankle glance,
And there among the grass fell down,
By his own scythe, the mower mown.

### XI

Alas! said he, these hurts are slight
To those that die by Love's despite.
With shepherd's purse, and clown's all-heal,
The blood I stanch and wound I seal.

Only for him no cure is found,
Whom Juliana's eyes do wound;
'Tis Death alone that this must do;
For, Death, thou art a Mower too.

## The Mower to the Glow-Worms

### I

Ye living lamps by whose dear light
The nightingale does sit so late,
And studying all the summer-night,
Her matchless songs does meditate;

### II

Ye country comets that portend
No war nor prince's funeral,
Shining unto no higher end
Than to presage the grass's fall;

### III

Ye glow-worms, whose officious flame
To wandering mowers shows the way,
That in the night have lost their aim,
And after foolish fires do stray;

### IV

Your courteous lights in vain you waste,
Since Juliana here is come,
For she my mind hath so displaced,
That I shall never find my home.

# The Definition of Love

### I

My Love is of a birth as rare
  As 'tis, for object, strange and high:
It was begotten by Despair,
  Upon Impossibility.

### II

Magnanimous Despair alone
  Could show me so divine a thing,
Where feeble Hope could ne'er have flown,
  But vainly flapped its tinsel wing.

### III

And yet I quickly might arrive
  Where my extended soul is fixed;
But Fate does iron wedges drive,
  And always crowds itself betwixt.

### IV

For Fate with jealous eye does see
  Two perfect loves, nor lets them close;
Their union would her ruin be,
  And her tyrannic power depose.

### V

And therefore her decrees of steel
  Us, as the distant poles, have placed,
Though Love's whole world on us doth wheel,
  Not by themselves to be embraced.

### VI

Unless the giddy heaven fall,
  And earth some new convulsion tear,
And, us to join, the world should all
  Be cramped into a planisphere.

VII

As lines, so loves oblique, may well
   Themselves in every angle greet:
But ours, so truly parallel,
   Though infinite, can never meet.


VIII

Therefore the love which us doth bind,
   But Fate so enviously debars,
Is the conjunction of the mind,
   And opposition of the stars.


# The Coronet

When for the thorns with which I long, too long,
      With many a piercing wound,
      My Saviour's head have crowned,
I seek with garlands to redress that wrong;
      Through every garden, every mead
I gather flowers (my fruits are only flowers),
      Dismantling all the fragrant towers
That once adorned my shepherdess's head:
And now, when I have summed up all my store,
      Thinking (so I myself deceive)
      So rich a chaplet thence to weave
As never yet the King of Glory wore,
      Alas! I find the Serpent old,
      That, twining in his speckled breast
      About the flowers disguised, does fold,
      With wreaths of fame and interest.
Ah, foolish man, that wouldst debase with them
And mortal glory, Heaven's diadem!
But Thou who only couldst the Serpent tame,
Either his slippery knots at once untie,
And disentangle all his winding snare.

Or shatter too with him my curious frame,
And let these wither—so that he may die—
Though set with skill, and chosen out with care;
That they, while Thou on both their spoils dost tread,
May crown Thy feet, that could not crown Thy head.

# GEORGE HERBERT

## (1593–1633)

## Affliction

When first Thou didst entice to Thee my heart,
        I thought the service brave:
So many joys I writ down for my part,
        Besides what I might have
Out of my stock of natural delights,
Augmented with Thy gracious benefits.

I lookèd on Thy furniture so fine,
        And made it fine to me,
Thy glorious household-stuff did me entwine,
        And 'tice me unto Thee.
Such stars I counted mine: both heaven and earth
Paid me my wages in a world of mirth.

What pleasures could I want, whose King I served,
        Where joys my fellows were?
Thus argued into hopes, my thoughts reserved
        No place for grief or fear;
Therefore my sudden soul caught at the place,
And made her youth and fierceness seek Thy face:

At first Thou gav'st me milk and sweetnesses;
        I had my wish and way:
My days were strewed with flowers and happiness:
        There was no month but May.
But with my years sorrow did twist and grow,
And made a party unawares for woe.

My flesh began unto my soul in pain,
           Sicknesses cleave my bones,
Consuming agues dwell in every vein,
           And tune my breath to groans:
Sorrow was all my soul; I scarce believed,
Till grief did tell me roundly, that I lived.

When I got health, Thou took'st away my life,
           And more; for my friends die;
My mirth and edge was lost; a blunted knife
           Was of more use than I.
Thus thin and lean without a fence or friend,
I was blown through with every storm and wind.

Whereas my birth and spirit rather took
           The way that takes the town;
Thou didst betray me to a lingering book,
           And wrap me in a gown.
I was entangled in the world of strife,
Before I had the power to change my life.

Yet, for I threatened oft the siege to raise,
           Not simpering all mine age,
Thou often didst with academic praise
           Melt and disolve my rage.
I took Thy sweetened pill, till I came near;
I could not go away, nor persevere.

Yet lest perchance I should too happy be
           In my unhappiness,
Turning my purge to food, Thou throwest me
           Into more sicknesses.
Thus doth Thy power cross-bias me, not making
Thine own gift good, yet me from my ways taking.

Now I am here, what Thou wilt do with me
        None of my books will show:
I read, and sigh, and wish I were a tree;
        For sure then I should grow
To fruit or shade: at least some bird would trust
Her household to me, and I should be just.

Yet, though Thou troublest me, I must be meek;
        In weakness must be stout;
Well, I will change the service, and go seek
        Some other master out.
Ah, my dear God! though I am clean forgot,
Let me not love Thee, if I love Thee not.

## Sin

Lord, with what care hast Thou begirt us round!
      Parents first season us: then schoolmasters
      Deliver us to laws; they send us bound
To rules of reason, holy messengers,

Pulpits and Sundays, sorrow dogging sin,
      Afflictions sorted, anguish of all sizes,
      Fine nets and stratagems to catch us in,
Bibles laid open, millions of surprises,

Blessings beforehand, ties of gratefulness,
      The sound of glory ringing in our ears;
      Without, our shame; within, our consciences;
Angels and grace, eternal hopes and fears.

      Yet all these fences and their whole array
      One cunning bosom-sin blows quite away.

# Vanity

The fleet astronomer can bore
And thread the spheres with his quick-piercing mind:
He views their stations, walks from door to door,
        Surveys, as if he had designed
To make a purchase there: he sees their dances,
        And knoweth long before,
Both their full-eyed aspects, and secret glances.

        The nimble diver with his side
Cuts through the working waves, that he may fetch
His dearly-earned pearl, which God did hide
        On purpose from the venturous wretch;
That He might save his life, and also hers,
        Who with excessive pride
Her own destruction and his danger wears.

        The subtile chymic can divest
And strip the creature naked, till he find
        The callow principles within their nest:
        There he imparts to them his mind,
Admitted to their bed-chamber, before
        They appear trim and drest
To ordinary suitors at the door.

        What hath not man sought out and found,
But his dear God? who yet His glorious law
        Embosoms in us, mellowing the ground
        With showers and frosts, with love and awe;
So that we need not say, where's this command?
        Poor man! thou searchest round
To find out death, but missest life at hand.

# Virtue

Sweet day, so cool, so calm, so bright,
The bridal of the earth and sky,
The dew shall weep thy fall to-night;
        For thou must die.

Sweet rose, whose hue angry and brave
Bids the rash gazer wipe his eye,
Thy root is ever in its grave,
        And thou must die.

Sweet spring, full of sweet days and roses,
A box where sweets compacted lie,
My music shows ye have your closes,
        And all must die.

Only a sweet and virtuous soul,
Like seasoned timber, never gives;
But though the whole world turn to coal,
        Then chiefly lives.

# Discipline

Throw away Thy rod,
Throw away Thy wrath:
    O my God,
Take the gentle path.

For my heart's desire
Unto Thine is bent:
    I aspire
To a full consent.

Not a word or look
I affect to own,
    But by book,
And Thy book alone.

Though I fail, I weep:
Though I halt in pace,
    Yet I creep
To the throne of grace.

Then let wrath remove;
Love will do the deed:
    For with love
Stony hearts will bleed

Love is swift of foot;
Love's a man of war,
    And can shoot,
And can hit from far.

Who can 'scape his bow?
That which wrought on Thee,
    Brought Thee low,
Needs must work on me.

Throw away Thy rod;
Though man frailties hath,
    Thou art God:
Throw away Thy wrath.

## The Pulley

When God at first made man,
Having a glass of blessing standing by;
Let us (said He) pour on him all we can:
Let the world's riches, which dispersed lie,
    Contract into a span.

So strength first made a way;
Then beauty flowed, then wisdom, honour, pleasure:
When almost all was out, God made a stay,
Perceiving that alone of all His treasure,
    Rest, in the bottom lay.

    For if I should (said He)
Bestow this jewel also on My creature,
He would adore My gifts instead of Me,
And rest in nature, not the God of nature:
    So both should losers be.

    Yet let him keep the rest,
But keep them with repining restlessness:
Let him be rich and weary, that at least,
If goodness lead him not, yet weariness
    May toss him to My breast.

## The Collar

I struck the board, and cried, no more;
      I will abroad.
What? shall I ever sigh and pine?
My lines and life are free; free as the road,
Loose as the wind, as large as store.
        Shall I be still in suit?
Have I no harvest but a thorn
To let me blood, and not restore
What I have lost with cordial fruit?
        Sure there was wine,
Before my sighs did dry it: there was corn,
    Before my tears did drown it.
Is the year only lost to me?
    Have I no bays to crown it?

No flowers, no garlands gay? all blasted?
All wasted?
Not so, my heart: but there is fruit,
And thou hast hands.
Recover all thy sigh-blown age
On double pleasures: leave thy cold dispute
Of what is fit, and not: forsake thy cage,
Thy rope of sands,
Which petty thoughts have made, and made to thee
Good cable, to enforce and draw,
And be thy law,
While thou didst wink and wouldst not see.
Away; take heed:
I will abroad.
Call in thy death's-head there: tie up thy fears.
He that forbears
To suit and serve his need,
Deserves his load.
But as I raved and grew more fierce and wild
At every word,
Methought I heard one calling, "Child":
And I replied, "My Lord!"

# Love

Love bade me welcome: yet my soul drew back,
  Guilty of dust and sin.
But quick-eyed Love, observing me grow slack
  From my first entrance in,
Drew nearer to me, sweetly questioning,
  If I lacked anything.

A guest, I answered, worthy to be here:
  Love said, You shall be he.
I the unkind, ungrateful? Ah my dear,
  I cannot look on thee.
Love took my hand, and smiling did reply,
  Who made the eyes but I?

Truth, Lord, but I have marred them: let my shame
  Go where it doth deserve.
And know you not, says Love, who bore the blame?
  My dear, then I will serve.
You must sit down, says Love, and taste my meat:
  So I did sit and eat.

# RICHARD CRASHAW

## (1612–1649)

## A Hymn, to the Name and Honour of the Admirable Saint Teresa

Love, thou art absolute sole lord
Of life and death. To prove the word
We'll now appeal to none of all
Those thy old soldiers, great and tall,
Ripe men of martyrdom, that could reach down,
With strong arms, their triumphant crown;
Such as could with lusty breath,
Speak loud into the face of Death
Their great Lord's glorious Name, to none
Of those whose spacious bosoms spread a throne
For Love at large to fill; spare blood and sweat:
And see him take a private seat,
Making his mansion in the mild
And milky soul of a soft child.

 Scarce has she learnt to lisp the name
Of martyr; yet she thinks it shame
Life should so long play with that breath
Which spent can buy so brave a death.
She never undertook to know
What Death with Love should have to do;
Nor has she e'er yet understood
Why to show love, she should shed blood,
Yet though she cannot tell you why,
She can love, and she can die.

Scarce has she blood enough to make
A guilty sword blush for her sake;
Yet has she a heart dares hope to prove
How much less strong is Death than Love.
  Be Love but there, let poor six years
Be posed with the maturest fears
Man trembles at, you straight shall find
Love knows no nonage, nor the mind;
'Tis love, not years or limbs that can
Make the martyr, or the man.
Love touched her heart, and lo it beats
High, and burns with such brave heats;
Such thirsts to die, as dares drink up
A thousand cold deaths in one cup.
Good reason; for she breathes all fire;
Her white breast heaves with strong desire
Of what she may, with fruitless wishes,
Seek for amongst her mother's kisses.
  Since 'tis not to be had at home
She'll travel to a martyrdom.
No home for hers confesses she
But where she may a martyr be.
  She'll to the Moors; and trade with them
For this unvalued diadem:
She'll offer them her dearest breath,
With Christ's name in't, in change for death:
She'll bargain with them, and will give
Them God, teach them how to live
In Him; or, if they this deny,
For Him she'll teach them how to die.
So shall she leave amongst them sown
Her Lord's blood, or at least her own.
  Farewell then, all the World adieu;
Teresa is no more for you.
Farewell, all pleasures, sports, and joys
(Never till now esteemèd toys)

Farewell, whatever dear may be,
Mother's arms, or father's knee:
Farewell house, and farewell home!
She's for the Moors, and martyrdom.

Sweet, not so fast! lo, thy fair Spouse
Whom thou seek'st with so swift vows;
Calls thee back, and bids thee come
T' embrace a milder martyrdom.

Blest powers forbid, thy tender life
Should bleed upon a barbarous knife:
Or some base hand have power to rase
Thy breast's chaste cabinet, and uncase
A soul kept there so sweet: O no,
Wise Heaven will never have it so.
Thou art Love's victim; and must die
A death more mystical and high:
Into Love's arms thou shalt let fall
A still-surviving funeral.
His is the dart must make the death
Whose stroke shall taste thy hallowed breath;
A dart thrice dipp'd in that rich flame
Which writes thy Spouse's radiant Name
Upon the roof of Heaven, where aye
It shines; and with a sovereign ray
Beats bright upon the burning faces
Of souls which in that Name's sweet graces
Find everlasting smiles: so rare,
So spiritual, pure, and fair
Must be th' immortal instrument
Upon whose choice point shall be sent
A life so loved: and that there be
Fit executioners for thee,
The fairest and first-born sons of fire.
Blest seraphim, shall leave their quire,
And turn Love's soldiers, upon thee
To exercise their archery.

O how oft shalt thou complain
Of a sweet and subtle pain:
Of intolerable joys:
Of a death, in which who dies
Loves his death, and dies again,
And would for ever so be slain.
And lives, and dies; and knows not why
To live, but that he thus may never leave to die.
  How kindly will thy gentle heart
Kiss the sweetly-killing dart,
And close in his embraces keep
Those delicious wounds, that weep
Balsam to heal themselves with; thus
When these thy deaths, so numerous,
Shall all at last die into one,
And melt thy soul's sweet mansion;
Like a soft lump of incense, hasted
By too hot a fire, and wasted
Into perfuming clouds, so fast
Shalt thou exhale to Heaven at last
In a resolving sight and then
O what? Ask not the tongues of men;
Angels cannot tell; suffice
Thyself shalt feel thine own full joys,
And hold them fast for ever there.
So soon as thou shalt first appear,
The moon of maiden stars, thy white
Mistress, attended by such bright
Souls as thy shining self, shall come
And in her first ranks make thee room;
Where 'mongst her snowy family
Immortal welcomes wait for thee.
  O what delight, when revealed Life shall stand.
And teach thy lips Heaven with His hand;
On which thou now may'st to thy wishes
Heap up thy consecrated kisses.

What joys shall seize thy soul, when She,
Bending her blessed eyes on Thee,
(Those second smiles of Heaven,) shall dart
Her mild rays through Thy melting heart.
　　Angels, thy old friends, there shall greet thee,
Glad at their own home now to meet thee.
　　All thy good works which went before
And waited for thee, at the door,
Shall own thee there; and all in one
Weave a constellation
Of crowns, with which the King thy Spouse
Shall build up thy triumphant brows.
　　All thy old woes shall now smile on thee,
And thy pains sit bright upon thee,
All thy sorrows here shall shine,
All thy sufferings be divine:
Tears shall take comfort, and turn gems,
And wrongs repent to diadems.
Even thy death shall live; and new
Dress the soul, that erst he slew.
Thy wounds shall blush to such bright scars
As keep account of the Lamb's wars.
　　Those rare works where thou shalt leave writ
Love's noble history, with wit
Taught thee by none but Him, while here
They feed our souls, shall clothe thine there.
Each heavenly word, by whose hid flame
Our hard hearts shall strike fire, the same
Shall flourish on thy brows, and be
Both fire to us and flame to thee;
Whose light shall live bright in thy face
By glory, in our hearts by grace.
　　Thou shalt look round about, and see
Thousands of crown'd souls throng to be
Themselves thy crown: sons of thy vows,
The virgin-births with which thy sovereign Spouse
Made fruitful thy fair soul. Go now

And with them all about thee, bow
To Him; put on, (He'll say,) put on
(My rosy love) that thy rich zone
Sparkling with the sacred flames
Of thousand souls, whose happy names
Heaven keep upon thy score: (Thy bright
Life brought them first to kiss the light,
That kindled them to stars,) and so
Thou with the Lamb, thy Lord, shalt go,
And wheresoe'er He sets His white
Steps, walk with Him those ways of light,
Which who in death would live to see,
Must learn in life to die like thee.

## Music's Duel

Now westward Sol had spent the richest beams
Of Noon's high glory, when, hard by the streams
Of Tiber, on the scene of a green plat,
Under protection of an oak, there sat
A sweet lute's-master, in whose gentle airs
He lost the day's heat, and his own hot cares.
   Close in the covert of the leaves there stood
A Nightingale, come from the neighbouring wood,
(The sweet inhabitant of each glad tree,
Their Muse, their Syren—harmless Syren she,)
There stood she list'ning, and did entertain
The music's soft report, and mould the same
In her own murmurs, that whatever mood
His curious fingers lent, her voice made good.
The man perceived his rival and her art;
Disposed to give the light-foot lady sport,
Awakes his lute, and 'gainst the fight to come
Informs it, in a sweet præludium
Of closer strains, and, ere the war begin,
He lightly skirmishes on every string

Charged with a flying touch; and straightway she
Carves out her dainty voice as readily,
Into a thousand sweet distinguish'd tones,
And reckons up in soft divisions
Quick volumes of wild notes, to let him know,
By that shrill taste, she could do something too.
    His nimble hands' instinct then taught each string
A cap'ring cheerfulness, and made them sing
To their own dance; now negligently rash
He throws his arm, and with a long-drawn dash
Blends all together; then distinctly trips
From this to that, then quick returning skips
And snatches this again, and pauses there.
She measures every measure, everywhere
Meets art with art; sometimes, as if in doubt,
Not perfect yet, and fearing to be out,
Trails her plain ditty in one long-spun note,
Through the sleek passage of her open throat,
A clear unwrinkled song; then doth she point it
With tender accents, and severely joint it
By short diminutives, that being rear'd
In controverting warbles evenly shared,
With her sweet self she wrangles. He, amazed
That from so small a channel should be raised
The torrent of a voice whose melody
Could melt into such sweet variety,
Strains higher yet, that tickled with rare art
The tattling strings (each breathing in his part),
Most kindly do fall out; the grumbling base
In surly groans disdains the treble's grace;
The high-perch'd treble chirps at this, and chides,
Until his finger (Moderator) hides
And closes the sweet quarrel, rousing all,
Hoarse, shrill, at once, as when the trumpets call
Hot Mars to th' harvest of death's field, and woo
Men's hearts into their hands; this lesson too
She gives him back; her supple breast thrills out

Sharp airs, and staggers in a warbling doubt
Of dallying sweetness, hovers o'er her skill,
And folds in wav'd notes with a trembling bill
The pliant series of her slippery song;
Then starts she suddenly into a throng
Of short thick sobs, whose thundering volleys float,
And roll themselves over her lubric throat
In panting murmurs, 'still'd out of her breast,
That ever-bubbling spring, the sugar'd nest
Of her delicious soul, that there does lie
Bathing in streams of liquid melody;
Music's best seed-plot; when in ripen'd airs
A golden-headed harvest fairly rears
His honey-dropping tops, plough'd by her breath,
Which there reciprocally laboureth
In that sweet soil; it seems a holy choir
Founded to th' name of great Apollo's lyre;
Whose silver-roof rings with the sprightly notes
Of sweet-lipp'd angel-imps, that swill their throats
In cream of morning Helicon, and then
Prefer soft anthems to the ears of men,
To woo them from their beds, still murmuring
That men can sleep while they their matins sing:
(Most divine service) whose so early lay
Prevents the eyelids of the blushing Day.
There might you hear her kindle her soft voice
In the close murmur of a sparkling noise,
And lay the ground-work of her hopeful song,
Still keeping in the forward stream, so long,
Till a sweet whirlwind (striving to get out)
Heaves her soft bosom, wanders round about,
And makes a pretty earthquake in her breast,
Till the fledged notes at length forsake their nest,
Fluttering in wanton shoals, and to the sky,
Wing'd with their own wild echoes, prattling fly.
She opes the floodgate, and lets loose a tide
Of streaming sweetness, which in state doth ride

On the waved back of every swelling strain,
Rising and falling in a pompous train;
And while she thus discharges a shrill peal
Of flashing airs, she qualifies their zeal
With the cool epode of a graver note,
Thus high, thus low, as if her silver throat
Would reach the brazen voice of War's hoarse bird.
Her little soul is ravish'd, and so pour'd
Into loose ecstasies, that she is placed
Above herself, Music's Enthusiast.

    Shame now and anger mixed a double stain
In the Musician's face; "Yet once again
(Mistress) I come; now reach a strain, my lute,
Above her mock, or be for ever mute;
Or tune a song of victory to me,
Or to thyself sing thine own obsequy";
So said, his hands sprightly as fire he flings,
And with a quavering coyness tastes the strings.
The sweet-lipp'd sisters, musically frighted,
Singing their fears, are fearfully delighted,
Trembling as when Apollo's golden hairs
Are fann'd and frizzled in the wanton airs
Of his own breath, which married to his lyre
Doth tune the spheres, and make Heaven's self look higher.
From this to that, from that to this he flies,
Feels Music's pulse in all her arteries;
Caught in a net which there Apollo spreads,
His fingers struggle with the vocal threads.
Following those little rills, he sinks into
A sea of Helicon; his hand does go
Those paths of sweetness which with nectar drop,
Softer than that which pants in Hebe's cup.
The humorous strings expound his learnèd touch
By various glosses; now they seem to grutch,
And murmur in a buzzing din, then gingle
In shrill-tongued accents, striving to be single.
Every smooth turn, every delicious stroke

Gives life to some new grace; thus doth he invoke
Sweetness by all her names; thus, bravely thus,
(Fraught with a fury so harmonious)
The Lute's light genius now does proudly rise,
Heaved on the surges of swollen rhapsodies,
Whose flourish (meteor-like) doth curl the air
With flash of high-born fancies; here and there
Dancing in lofty measures, and anon
Creeps on the soft touch of a tender tone;
Whose trembling murmurs melting in wild airs
Runs to and fro, complaining his sweet cares,
Because those precious mysteries that dwell
In Music's ravish'd soul he dares not tell,
But whisper to the world: thus do they vary
Each string his note, as if they meant to carry
Their Master's blest soul (snatch'd out at his ears
By a strong ecstasy) through all the spheres
Of Music's heaven; and seat it there on high
In th' empyrean of pure harmony.
At length (after so long, so loud a strife
Of all the strings, still breathing the best life
Of blest variety, attending on
His fingers' fairest revolution,
In many a sweet rise, many as sweet a fall)
A full-mouth'd diapason swallows all.

   This done, he lists what she would say to this,
And she (although her breath's late exercise
Had dealt too roughly with her tender throat),
Yet summons all her sweet powers for a note.
Alas! in vain, (for while sweet soul) she tries
To measure all those wild diversities
Of chatt'ring strings, by the small size of one
Poor simple voice, raised in a natural tone;
She fails, and failing grieves, and grieving dies.
She dies: and leaves her life the Victor's prize,
Falling upon his lute: O, fit to have
(That lived so sweetly) dead, so sweet a grave.

# HENRY VAUGHAN
## (1621–1695)

## The Retreate

Happy those early dayes, when I
Shin'd in my angell-infancy!
Before I understood this place
Appointed for my second race,
Or taught my soul to fancy ought
But a white, celestiall thought;
When yet I had not walkt above
A mile or two from my first love,
And looking back, at that short space,
Could see a glimpse of his bright face;
When on some gilded cloud or flowre
My gazing soul would dwell an houre,
And in those weaker glories spy
Some shadows of eternity;
Before I taught my tongue to wound
My conscience with a sinfull sound,
Or had the black art to dispence
A sev'rall sinne to ev'ry sence,
But felt through all this fleshly dresse
Bright shootes of everlastingnesse.
    O how I long to travell back,
And tread again that ancient track!
That I might once more reach that plaine,
Where first I left my glorious traine;
From whence th' inlightned spirit sees
That shady city of palme-trees.

But ah! my soul with too much stay
Is drunk, and staggers in the way!
Some men a forward motion love,
But I by backward steps would move;
And when this dust falls to the urn,
In that state I came return.

## The World

### I

I saw eternity the other night,
Like a great ring of pure and endless light,
    All calm, as it was bright;
And round beneath it, time, in hours, days, years,
        Driv'n by the spheres
Like a vast shadow mov'd, in which the world
    And all her train were hurl'd.
The doting lover, in his queintest strain,
        Did there complain;
Neer him, his lute, his fancy, and his flights,
        Wit's sour delights;
With gloves and knots, the silly snares of pleasure,
        Yet his dear treasure
All scatter'd lay, while he his eyes did pour
        Upon a flowr.

### II

The darksome statesman hung with weights and woe,
Like a thick midnight fog, mov'd there so slow,
    He did nor stay nor go;
Condemning thoughts, like mad ecclipses, scowl
        Upon his soul,
And clouds of crying witnesses without
    Pursued him with one shout.
Yet digg'd the mole, and, lest his ways be found,
        Workt under ground,

Where he did clutch his prey; but one did see
        That policie;
Churches and altars fed him; perjuries
        Were gnats and flies;
It rain'd about him bloud and tears; but he
        Drank them as free.

### III

The fearfull miser, on a heap of rust,
Sate pining all his life there; did scarce trust
        His own hands with the dust;
Yet would not place one peece above, but lives
        In feare of theeves.
Thousands there were, as frantick as himself,
        And hugg'd each one his pelf;
The downright epicure plac'd heav'n in sense,
        And scorn'd pretence;
While others, slipt into a wide excesse,
        Said little lesse;
The weaker sort, slight, triviall wares inslave,
        Who think them brave,
And poor, despised truth sate counting by
        Their victory.

### IV

Yet some, who all this while did weep and sing,
And sing and weep, soar'd up into the ring;
        But most would use no wing.
"O fools," said I, "thus to prefer dark night
        Before true light!
To live in grots and caves, and hate the day
        Because it shews the way,
The way, which, from this dead and dark abode,
        Leads up to God;
A way where you might tread the sun, and be
        More bright than he!"

But, as I did their madnes so discusse,
    One whisper'd thus,
"This ring the bridegroome did for none provide,
    But for his bride."

## They Are All Gone

They are all gone into the world of light,
    And I alone sit lingring here!
Their very memory is fair and bright,
    And my sad thoughts doth clear.

It glows and glitters in my cloudy brest,
    Like stars upon some gloomy grove,
Or those faint beams in which this hill is drest
    After the sun's remove.

I see them walking in an air of glory,
    Whose light doth trample on my days;
My days, which are at best but dull and hoary,
    Meer glimering and decays.

O holy hope! and high humility!
    High as the heavens above!
These are your walks, and you have shew'd them me
    To kindle my cold love.

Dear, beauteous death; the jewel of the just!
    Shining nowhere but in the dark;
What mysteries do lie beyond thy dust,
    Could man outlook that mark!

He that hath found some fledg'd bird's nest may know
    At first sight if the bird be flown;
But what fair dell or grove he sings in now,
    That is to him unknown.

And yet, as angels in some brighter dreams,
    Call to the soul when man doth sleep,
So some strange thoughts transcend our wonted theams,
      And into glory peep.

If a star were confin'd into a tomb,
    Her captive flames must needs burn there;
But, when the hand that lockt her up gives room,
      She'll shine through all the sphære.

O Father of eternal life, and all
    Created glories under thee!
Resume thy spirit from this world of thrall
      Into true liberty.

Either disperse these mists, which blot and fill
    My perspective still as they pass;
Or else remove me hence unto that hill
      Where I shall need no glass.

# JOHN MILTON

## (1608–1674)

## On the Morning of Christ's Nativity

### I

This is the month, and this the happy morn,
   Wherein the Son of Heaven's eternal King,
Of wedded Maid and Virgin-Mother born,
   Our great redemption from above did bring;
   For so the holy sages once did sing,
That he our deadly forfeit should release,
And with his Father work us a perpetual peace.

### II

That glorious form, that light unsufferable,
   And that far-beaming blaze of majesty,
Wherewith he wont at Heaven's high council-table
   To sit the midst of Trinal Unity,
   He laid aside; and, here with us to be,
Forsook the courts of everlasting day,
And chose with us a darksome house of mortal clay.

### III

Say, heavenly Muse, shall not thy sacred vein
   Afford a present to the Infant God?
Hast thou no verse, no hymn, or solemn strain,
   To welcome him to this his new abode,
   Now, while the heaven, by the Sun's team untrod,
Hath took no print of the approaching light,
And all the spangled host keep watch in squadrons bright?

### IV

See how from far upon the eastern road
   The star-led wizards haste with odours sweet!
Oh! run, prevent them with thy humble ode,
   And lay it lowly at his blessed feet;
   Have thou the honour first thy Lord to greet,
  And join thy voice unto the angel quire,
From out his secret altar touched with hallowed fire.

### THE HYMN

#### I

   It was the winter wild,
   While the heaven-born child
All meanly wrapt in the rude manger lies;
   Nature in awe to him
   Had doffed her gaudy trim,
With her great Master so to sympathize.
   It was no season then for her
To wanton with the Sun her lusty paramour.

#### II

   Only with speeches fair
   She woos the gentle air
To hide her guilty front with innocent snow,
   And on her naked shame,
   Pollute with sinful blame,
The saintly veil of maiden-white to throw,
   Confounded, that her Maker's eyes
Should look so near upon her foul deformities.

#### III

   But he, her fears to cease,
   Sent down the meek-eyed Peace;
She, crowned with olive green, came softly sliding
   Down through the turning sphere,
   His ready harbinger,
With turtle wing the amorous clouds dividing;

And, waving wide her myrtle wand,
She strikes an universal peace through sea and land.

IV

No war or battle's sound
Was heard the world around;
The idle spear and shield were high up hung;
The hooked chariot stood,
Unstained with hostile blood;
The trumpet spake not to the armed throng;
And kings sat still with awful eye,
As if they surely knew their sovran Lord was by.

V

But peaceful was the night,
Wherein the Prince of Light
His reign of peace upon the earth began.
The winds, with wonder whist,
Smoothly the waters kissed,
Whispering new joys to the mild oceän,
Who now hath quite forgot to rave,
While birds of calm sit brooding on the charmed wave.

VI

The stars, with deep amaze,
Stand fixed in steadfast gaze,
Bending one way their precious influence,
And will not take their flight,
For all the morning-light,
Or Lucifer that often warned them thence;
But in their glimmering orbs did glow,
Until their Lord himself bespake, and bid them go.

VII

And, though the shady gloom
Had given day her room,
The sun himself withheld his wonted speed;

And hid his head for shame,
As his inferior flame
The new-enlightened world no more should need;
He saw a greater sun appear
Than his bright throne or burning axletree could bear.

### VIII

The shepherds on the lawn,
Or ere the point of dawn,
Sat simply chatting in a rustic row;
Full little thought they than
That the mighty Pan
Was kindly come to live with them below.
Perhaps their loves, or else their sheep,
Was all that did their silly thoughts so busy keep.

### IX

When such music sweet
Their hearts and ears did greet,
As never was by mortal finger strook;
Divinely-warbled voice
Answering the stringed noise,
As all their souls in blissful rapture took.
The air, such pleasure loth to lose,
With thousand echoes still prolongs each heavenly close.

### X

Nature, that heard such sound,
Beneath the hollow round
Of Cynthia's seat, the airy region thrilling,
Now was almost won
To think her part was done,
And that her reign had here its last fulfilling.
She knew such harmony alone
Could hold all Heaven and Earth in happier uniön.

### XI

At last surrounds their sight
A globe of circular light,
That with long beams the shame-faced Night arrayed.
The helmed Cherubim,
And sworded Seraphim,
Are seen, in glittering ranks with wings displayed,
Harping, in loud and solemn quire,
With unexpressive notes to Heaven's new-born Heir.

### XII

Such music—as 'tis said—
Before was never made,
But when of old the Sons of Morning sung;
While the Creator great
His constellations set,
And the well-balanced World on hinges hung,
And cast the dark foundations deep,
And bid the weltering waves their oozy channel keep.

### XIII

Ring out, ye crystal spheres!
Once bless our human ears,
—If ye have power to touch our senses so—
And let your silver-chime
Move in melodious time,
And let the base of heaven's deep organ blow;
And with your ninefold harmony
Make up full consort to the angelic symphony.

### XIV

For if such holy song
Enwrap our fancy long,
Time will run back, and fetch the Age of Gold;
And speckled Vanity
Will sicken soon and die,

And leprous Sin will melt from earthly mould;
 And Hell itself will pass away,
And leave her dolorous mansions to the peering day.

### XV

 Yea Truth and Justice then
 Will down return to men,
Orbed in a rainbow, and like glories wearing;
 Mercy will sit between,
 Throned in celestial sheen,
With radiant feet the tissued clouds down steering;
 And Heaven, as at some festival,
Will open wide the gates of her high palace-hall.

### XVI

 But wisest Fate says No,
 This must not yet be so,
The Babe lies yet in smiling infancy,
 That, on the bitter cross,
 Must redeem our loss;
So both himself and us to glorify:
 Yet first, to those ychained in sleep,
The wakeful trump of doom must thunder through the deep.

### XVII

 With such a horrid clang
 As on mount Sinai rang,
While the red fire and smouldering clouds outbrake.
 The aged earth aghast,
 With terror of that blast,
Shall from the surface to the centre shake;
 When, at the world's last sessiön,
The dreadful Judge in middle air shall spread his throne.

### XVIII

 And then at last our bliss
 Full and perfect is,

But now begins; for from this happy day
    The Old Dragon under ground,
    In straiter limits bound,
  Not half so far casts his usurped sway,
    And, wroth to see his kingdom fail,
Swinges the scaly horror of his folded tail.

### XIX

    The oracles are dumb,
    No voice or hideous hum
Runs through the arched roof in words deceiving.
    Apollo from his shrine
    Can no more divine,
With hollow shriek the steep of Delphos leaving.
    No nightly trance, or breathed spell,
Inspires the pale-eyed priest from the prophetic cell.

### XX

    The lonely mountains o'er,
    And the resounding shore,
A voice of weeping heard and loud lament;
    From haunted spring, and dale
    Edged with poplar pale,
The parting Genius is with sighing sent;
    With flower-inwoven tresses torn
The Nymphs in twilight shade of tangled thickets mourn.

### XXI

    In consecrated earth,
    And on the holy hearth,
The Lars and Lemures moan with midnight plaint;
    In urns and altars round,
    A drear and dying sound
Affrights the Flamens at their service quaint;
    And the chill marble seems to sweat,
While each peculiar power forgoes his wonted seat.

### XXII

Peor and Baälim
Forsake their temples dim,
With that twice battered god of Palestine;
And mooned Ashtaroth,
Heaven's queen and mother both,
Now sits not girt with tapers' holy shine;
The Lybic Hammon shrinks his horn;
In vain the Tyrian maids their wounded Thammuz mourn.

### XXIII

And sullen Moloch, fled,
Hath left in shadows dread
His burning idol all of blackest hue;
In vain with cymbals' ring
They call the grisly king,
In dismal dance about the furnace blue;
The brutish gods of Nile as fast,
Isis, and Orus, and the dog Anubis hast.

### XXIV

Nor is Osiris seen
In Memphian grove or green,
Trampling the unshowered grass with lowings loud;
Nor can he be at rest
Within his sacred chest,
Nought but profoundest hell can be his shroud;
In vain, with timbreled anthems dark,
The sable-stoled sorcerers bear his worshiped ark.

### XXV

He feels, from Juda's land,
The dreaded Infant's hand,
The rays of Bethlehem blind his dusky eyn;
Nor all the gods beside
Longer dare abide,
Nor Typhon huge ending in snaky twine.

Our Babe, to shew his Godhead true,
Can in his swaddling-bands control the damned crew.

### XXVI

So when the sun in bed,
Curtained with cloudy red,
Pillows his chin upon an orient wave,
The flocking shadows pale
Troop to the infernal jail,
Each fettered ghost slips to his several grave,
And the yellow-skirted fayes
Fly after the Night steeds, leaving their moon-loved maze.

### XXVII

But see! the Virgin blest
Hath laid her Babe to rest,
Time is our tedious song should here have ending;
Heaven's youngest-teemed star
Hath fixed her polished car,
Her sleeping Lord with handmaid-lamp attending;
And all about the courtly stable
Bright-harnessed angels sit in order serviceable.

## L' Allegro

Hence, loathed Melancholy!
Of Cerberus and blackest Midnight born,
In Stygian cave forlorn,
'Mongst horrid shapes, and shrieks, and sights unholy.
Find out some uncouth cell,
Where brooding Darkness spreads his jealous wings,
And the night-raven sings;
There, under ebon shades and low-browed rocks
As ragged as thy locks.
In dark Cimmerian desert ever dwell.

But come, thou Goddess fair and free,
In Heaven yclept Euphrosynè,
And by men, heart-easing Mirth;
Whom lovely Venus, at a birth
With two sister Graces more,
To ivy-crowned Bacchus bore;
Or whether, as some sager sing,
The frolic wind that breathes the spring,
Zephyr, with Aurora playing,
As he met her once a-maying,
There, on beds of violets blue,
And fresh-blown roses washed in dew,
Filled her with thee, a daughter fair,
So buxom, blithe, and debonair.
　　Haste thee, Nymph, and bring with thee
Jest and youthful Jollity,
Quips and Cranks, and wanton Wiles,
Nods and Becks, and wreathed Smiles—
Such as hang on Hebe's cheek,
And love to live in dimple sleek;
Sport, that wrinkled Care derides,
And Laughter, holding both his sides:
Come, and trip it as you go
On the light fantastic toe;
And in thy right hand lead with thee
The mountain-nymph, sweet Liberty;
And, if I give thee honour due,
Mirth, admit me of thy crew,
To live with her and live with thee,
In unreproved pleasures free;
To hear the lark begin his flight,
And singing startle the dull night
From his watch-tower in the skies,
Till the dappled dawn doth rise;
Then to come, in spite of sorrow,
And at my window bid good morrow,
Through the sweet-briar, or the vine,

Or the twisted eglantine;
While the cock, with lively din,
Scatters the rear of darkness thin,
And, to the stack or the barn-door,
Stoutly struts his dames before:
Oft listening how the hounds and horn
Cheerly rouse the slumbering Morn,
From the side of some hoar hill,
Through the high wood echoing shrill.
Sometime walking, not unseen,
By hedgerow elms, on hillocks green,
Right against the eastern gate,
Where the great Sun begins his state,
Robed in flames and amber light,
The clouds in thousand liveries dight;
While the ploughman, near at hand,
Whistles o'er the furrowed land,
And the milkmaid singeth blithe,
And the mower whets his scythe,
And every shepherd tells his tale,
Under the hawthorn in the dale.
Straight mine eye hath caught new pleasures,
Whilst the landskip round it measures;
Russet lawns, and fallows grey,
Where the nibbling flocks do stray,
Mountains on whose barren breast
The labouring clouds do often rest,
Meadows trim with daisies pied,
Shallow brooks, and rivers wide,
Towers and battlements it sees,
Bosomed high in tufted trees,
Where perhaps some Beauty lies,
The Cynosure of neighbouring eyes.
Hard by a cottage-chimney smokes
From betwixt two aged oaks,
Where Corydon and Thyrsis, met,
Are at their savoury dinner set

Of herbs and other country messes,
Which the neat-handed Phillis dresses;
And then in haste her bower she leaves,
With Thestylis to bind the sheaves;
Or, if the earlier season lead,
To the tanned haycock in the mead.

    Sometimes, with secure delight,
The upland hamlets will invite,
When the merry bells ring round,
And the jocund rebecks sound,
To many a youth and many a maid,
Dancing in the chequered shade,
And young and old come forth to play
On a sunshine holiday,
Till the live-long daylight fail;
Then to the spicy nut-brown ale,
With stories told of many a feat,
How faery Mab the junkets eat;
She was pinched and pulled, she said;
And he, by Friar's lantern led,
Tells how the drudging goblin sweat,
To earn his cream-bowl duly set,
When in one night, ere glimpse of morn,
His shadowy flail hath threshed the corn
That ten day-labourers could not end;
Then lies him down, the lubbar-fiend,
And, stretched out all the chimney's length,
Basks at the fire his hairy strength,
And crop-full out of doors he flings,
Ere the first cock his matin rings.
Thus done the tales, to bed they creep,
By whispering winds soon lulled asleep.

    Towered cities please us then,
And the busy hum of men,
Where throngs of knights and barons bold,
In weeds of peace, high triumphs hold,

With store of ladies, whose bright eyes
Rain influence, and judge the prize
Of wit or arms, while both contend
To win her grace, whom all commend.
There let Hymen oft appear
In saffron robe, with taper clear,
And pomp, and feast, and revelry,
With mask and antique pageantry;
Such sights as youthful poets dream,
On summer-eves by haunted stream.
Then to the well-trod stage anon,
If Jonson's learned sock be on,
Or sweetest Shakespeare, Fancy's child,
Warble his native wood-notes wild.

And ever, against eating cares,
Lap me in soft Lydian airs,
Married to immortal verse,
Such as the meeting soul may pierce,
In notes with many a winding bout
Of linked sweetness long drawn out,
With wanton heed and giddy cunning
The melting voice through mazes running,
Untwisting all the chains that tie
The hidden soul of harmony;
That Orpheus' self may heave his head,
From golden slumber on a bed
Of heaped Elysian flowers, and hear
Such strains as would have won the ear
Of Pluto, to have quite set free
His half-regained Eurydicè.

These delights if thou canst give,
Mirth, with thee I mean to live.

## Il Penseroso

Hence, vain deluding Joys,
The brood of Folly without father bred!
How little you bested,
Or fill the fixed mind with all your toys!
Dwell in some idle brain,
And fancies fond with gaudy shapes possess,
As thick and numberless
As the gay motes that people the sunbeams,
Or likest hovering dreams,
The fickle pensioners of Morpheus' train.
But hail, thou Goddess sage and holy!
Hail, divinest Melancholy,
Whose saintly visage is too bright
To hit the sense of human sight,
And therefore to our weaker view
O'erlaid with black, staid Wisdom's hue;
Black, but such as in esteem
Prince Memnon's sister might beseem,
Or that starred Ethiop queen that strove
To set her beauty's praise above
The Sea-Nymphs', and their powers offended:
Yet thou art higher far descended.
Thee bright-haired Vesta long of yore
To solitary Saturn bore;
His daughter she; in Saturn's reign
Such mixture was not held a stain.
Oft in glimmering bowers and glades
He met her, and in secret shades
Of woody Ida's inmost grove,
While yet there was no fear of Jove.
Come, pensive Nun, devout and pure,
Sober, steadfast, and demure,
All in a robe of darkest grain,
Flowing with majestic train,
And sable stole of cypres-lawn

Over thy decent shoulders drawn.
Come, but keep thy wonted state,
With even step, and musing gait,
And looks commercing with the skies,
Thy rapt soul sitting in thine eyes;
There, held in holy passion still,
Forget thyself to marble, till
With a sad, leaden, downward cast
Thou fix them on the earth as fast.
And join with thee calm Peace and Quiet,
Spare Fast, that oft with gods doth diet,
And hears the Muses in a ring
Aye round about Jove's altar sing;
And add to these retired Leisure,
That in trim gardens takes his pleasure.
But, first and chiefest, with thee bring
Him that yon soars on golden wing,
Guiding the fiery-wheeled throne,
The Cherub Contemplatiön;
And the mute Silence hist along,
'Less Philomel will deign a song,
In her sweetest, saddest plight,
Smoothing the rugged brow of Night;
While Cynthia cheeks her dragon-yoke,
Gently o'er the accustomed oak.
Sweet bird, that shunnest the noise of folly,
Most musical, most melancholy!
Thee, chantress, oft the woods among
I woo to hear thy even-song;
And missing thee I walk unseen,
On the dry, smooth-shaven green,
To behold the wandering moon,
Riding near her highest noon,
Like one that has been led astray
Through the heaven's wide pathless way,
And oft, as if her head she bowed,
Stooping through a fleecy cloud.

    Oft, on a plat of rising ground,
I hear the far-off curfew sound,
Over some wide-watered shore.
Swinging slow with sullen roar;
Or, if the air will not permit,
Some still, removed place will fit,
Where glowing embers through the room
Teach light to counterfeit a gloom,
Far from all resort of mirth,
Save the cricket on the hearth,
Or the bellman's drowsy charm,
To bless the doors from nightly harm;
Or let my lamp, at midnight-hour,
Be seen in some high, lonely tower,
Where I may oft out-watch the Bear,
With thrice great Hermes, or unsphere
The spirit of Plato, to unfold
What worlds or what vast regions hold
The immortal mind, that hath forsook
Her mansion in this fleshly nook;
And of those demons that are found
In fire, air, flood, or underground,
Whose power hath a true consent
With planet, or with element.
Sometime let gorgeous Tragedy
In sceptred pall come sweeping by,
Presenting Thebes, or Pelops' line,
Or the tale of Troy divine,
Or what, though rare, of later age
Ennobled hath the buskined stage.

    But, O sad Virgin! that thy power
Might raise Musæus from his bower,
Or bid the soul of Orpheus sing
Such notes as warbled to the string
Drew iron tears down Pluto's cheek,
And made Hell grant what love did seek;
Or call up him that left half-told

The story of Cambuscan bold,
Of Camball, and of Algarsife,
And who had Canacè to wife,
That owned the virtuous ring and glass;
And of the wondrous horse of brass,
On which the Tartar king did ride;
And if aught else great bards beside
In sage and solemn tunes have sung,
Of turneys and of trophies hung,
Of forests and enchantments drear,
Where more is meant than meets the ear.
　　Thus, Night, oft see me in thy pale career,
Till civil-suited Morn appear,
Not tricked and frounced, as she was wont
With the Attic boy to hunt,
But kerchiefed in a comely cloud,
While rocking winds are piping loud,
Or ushered with a shower still,
When the gust hath blown his fill,
Ending on the rustling leaves,
With minute-drops from off the eaves.
　　And when the sun begins to fling
His flaring beams, me, Goddess, bring
To arched walks of twilight groves,
And shadows brown, that Sylvan loves,
Of pine, or monumental oak,
Where the rude axe with heaved stroke
Was never heard the Nymphs to daunt,
Or fright them from their hallowed haunt.
There, in close covert by some brook,
Where no profaner eye may look,
Hide me from day's garish eye,
While the bee with honeyed thigh,
That at her flowery work doth sing,
And the waters murmuring,
With such consort as they keep,
Entice the dewy-feathered Sleep.

And let some strange, mysterious dream
Wave at his wings, in aery stream
Of lively portraiture displayed,
Softly on my eyelids laid;
And, as I wake, sweet music breathe
Above, about, or underneath,
Sent by some Spirit to mortals good,
Or the unseen Genius of the wood.

But let my due feet never fail
To walk the studious cloisters pale,
And love the high embowed roof,
With antic pillars massy-proof
And storied windows richly dight,
Casting a dim religious light.
There let the pealing organ blow,
To the full-voiced quire below,
In service high, and anthems clear,
As may with sweetness, through mine ear,
Dissolve me into ecstasies,
And bring all Heaven before mine eyes.

And may at last my weary age
Find out the peaceful hermitage,
The hairy gown and mossy cell,
Where I may sit, and rightly spell
Of every star that heaven doth shew,
And every herb that sips the dew;
Till old experience do attain
To something like prophetic strain.

These pleasures, Melancholy, give,
And I with thee will choose to live.

# Lycidas

*A lament for a friend drowned in his passage from
Chester on the Irish Seas,* 1637

Yet once more, O ye laurels, and once more
Ye myrtles brown, with ivy never-sere,
I come to pluck your berries harsh and crude,
And with forced fingers rude
Shatter your leaves before the mellowing year.
Bitter constraint, and sad occasion dear,
Compels me to disturb your season due;
For Lycidas is dead, dead ere his prime,
Young Lycidas, and hath not left his peer.
Who would not sing for Lycidas? he knew
Himself to sing, and build the lofty rime.
He must not float upon his watery bier
Unwept, and welter to the parching wind,
Without the meed of some melodious tear.
    Begin then, Sisters of the sacred well,
That from beneath the seat of Jove doth spring;
Begin, and somewhat loudly sweep the string.
Hence with denial vain, and coy excuse—
So may some gentle Muse
With lucky words favour my destined urn,
And as he passes turn,
And bid fair peace be to my sable shroud—
For we were nursed upon the self-same hill,
Fed the same flock by fountain, shade, and rill;
Together both, ere the high lawns appeared
Under the opening eyelids of the Morn,
We drove a-field, and both together heard
What time the grey-fly winds her sultry horn,
Battening our flocks with the fresh dews of night,
Oft till the star that rose at evening, bright,
Toward heaven's descent had sloped his westering wheel.
Meanwhile the rural ditties were not mute.
Tempered to the oaten flute;

Rough Satyrs danced, and Fauns with cloven heel
From the glad sound would not be absent long,
And old Damœtas loved to hear our song.

    But oh! the heavy change, now thou art gone,
Now thou art gone, and never must return!
Thee, Shepherd, thee the woods and desert caves,
With wild thyme and the gadding vine o'ergrown,
And all their echoes mourn.
The willows, and the hazel-copses green,
Shall now no more be seen
Fanning their joyous leaves to thy soft lays.
As killing as the canker to the rose,
Or taint-worm to the weanling herds that graze,
Or frost to flowers, that their gay wardrobe wear,
When first the white-thorn blows;
Such, Lycidas, thy loss to shepherds' ear.

    Where were ye, Nymphs, when the remorseless deep
Closed o'er the head of your loved Lycidas?
For neither were ye playing on the steep,
Where your old bards, the famous Druids, lie,
Nor on the shaggy top of Mona high,
Nor yet where Deva spreads her wizard stream.
Ay me, I fondly dream!
Had ye been there . . . for what could that have done?
What could the Muse herself that Orpheus bore,
The Muse herself for her enchanting son,
Whom universal Nature did lament,
When, by the rout that made the hideous roar,
His gory visage down the stream was sent,
Down the swift Hebrus to the Lesbian shore?

    Alas! what boots it with incessant care
To tend the homely, slighted shepherd's trade,
And strictly meditate the thankless Muse?
Were it not better done, as others use,
To sport with Amaryllis in the shade,
Or with the tangles of Neæra's hair?
Fame is the spur that the clear spirit doth raise.

—That last infirmity of noble mind—
To scorn delights, and live laborious days;
But the fair guerdon when we hope to find,
And think to burst out into sudden blaze,
Comes the blind Fury with the abhorred shears,
And slits the thin-spun life. "But not the praise,"
Phœbus replied, and touched my trembling ears.
"Fame is no plant that grows on mortal soil,
Nor in the glistering foil
Set-off to the world, nor in broad rumour lies,
But lives and spreads aloft by those pure eyes,
And perfect witness of all-judging Jove;
As he pronounces lastly on each deed,
Of so much fame in Heaven expect thy meed."
    O fountain Arethuse, and thou honoured flood,
Smooth-sliding Mincius, crowned with vocal reeds,
That strain I heard was of a higher mood.
But now my oat proceeds,
And listens to the herald of the sea,
That came in Neptune's plea.
He asked the waves, and asked the felon winds,
What hard mishap hath doomed this gentle swain?
And questioned every gust of rugged wings,
That blows from off each beaked promontory.
They knew not of his story;
And sage Hippotades their answer brings,
That not a blast was from his dungeon strayed;
The air was calm, and on the level brine
Sleek Panopè with all her sisters played.
It was that fatal and perfidious bark,
Built in the eclipse, and rigged with curses dark,
That sunk so low that sacred head of thine.
    Next Camus, reverend sire, went footing slow,
His mantle hairy and his bonnet sedge,
Inwrought with figures dim, and on the edge
Like to that sanguine flower inscribed with woe.
"Ah! who hath reft," quoth he, "my dearest pledge?"

Last came, and last did go,
The pilot of the Galilean lake;
Two massy keys he bore of metals twain—
The golden opes, the iron shuts amain.
He shook his mitred locks, and stern bespake:
"How well could I have spared for thee, young swain,
Enow of such as, for their bellies' sake,
Creep, and intrude, and climb into the fold!
Of other care they little reckoning make,
Than how to scramble at the shearers' feast,
And shove away the worthy bidden guest.
Blind mouths! that scarce themselves know how to hold
A sheep-hook, or have learned aught else the least
That to the faithful herdman's art belongs!
What reeks it them? What need they? They are sped;
And, when they list, their lean and flashy songs
Grate on their scrannel pipes of wretched straw;
The hungry sheep look up, and are not fed,
But, swollen with wind and the rank mist they draw,
Rot inwardly, and foul contagion spread;
Beside what the grim wolf with privy paw
Daily devours apace, and nothing said.
But that two-handed engine at the door
Stands ready to smite once, and smite no more."
    Return, Alpheüs, the dread voice is past,
That shrunk thy streams; return, Sicilian Muse,
And call the vales, and bid them hither cast
Their bells, and flowerets of a thousand hues.
Ye valleys low, where the mild whispers use
Of shades, and wanton winds, and gushing brooks,
On whose fresh lap the swart-star sparely looks,
Throw hither all your quaint-enamelled eyes,
That on the green turf suck the honeyed showers,
And purple all the ground with vernal flowers.
Bring the rathe primrose that forsaken dies,
The tufted crow-toe, and pale jessamine,
The white pink, and the pansy freaked with jet,

The glowing violet,
The musk-rose, and the well-attired woodbine,
With cowslips wan that hang the pensive head,
And every flower that sad embroidery wears;
Bid amaranthus all his beauty shed,
And daffadillies fill their cups with tears,
To strew the laureate hearse where Lycid lies.
For so, to interpose a little ease,
Let our frail thoughts dally with false surmise,
Ay me! whilst thee the shores and sounding seas
Wash far away, where'er thy bones are hurled;
Whether beyond the stormy Hebrides,
Where thou perhaps under the whelming tide
Visitest the bottom of the monstrous world;
Or whether thou, to our moist vows denied,
Sleepest by the fable of Bellerus old,
Where the great Vision of the guarded mount
Looks toward Namancos and Bayona's hold . . .
Look homeward, Angel, now, and melt with ruth;
And, O ye dolphins, waft the hapless youth.

    Weep no more, woful shepherds, weep no more,
For Lycidas, your sorrow, is not dead,
Sunk though he be beneath the watery floor.
So sinks the day-star in the ocean-bed,
And yet anon repairs his drooping head,
And tricks his beams, and with new-spangled ore
Flames in the forehead of the morning sky:
So Lycidas sunk low, but mounted high,
Through the dear might of Him that walked the waves,
Where, other groves and other streams along,
With nectar pure his oozy locks he laves,
And hears the unexpressive nuptial song,
In the blest kingdoms meek of joy and love.
There entertain him all the saints above,
In solemn troops, and sweet societies,
That sing, and singing in their glory move,
And wipe the tears for ever from his eyes.

Now, Lycidas, the shepherds weep no more;
Henceforth thou art the Genius of the shore,
In thy large recompense, and shalt be good
To all that wander in that perilous flood.
    Thus sang the uncouth swain to the oaks and rills,
While the still Morn went out with sandals gray;
He touched the tender stops of various quills,
With eager thought warbling his Doric lay;
And now the sun had stretched out all the hills,
And now was dropped into the western bay.
At last he rose, and twitched his mantle blue;
Tomorrow to fresh woods, and pastures new.

SONNET XVIII

# On the Late Massacre in Piemont

Avenge, O Lord, thy slaughtered saints, whose bones
    Lie scattered on the Alpine mountains cold;
    Even them who kept thy truth so pure of old,
    When all our fathers worshiped stocks and stones,
Forget not; in thy book record their groans
    Who were thy sheep, and in their ancient fold
    Slain by the bloody Piemontese, that rolled
    Mother with infant down the rocks; their moans
The vales redoubled to the hills, and they
    To heaven. Their martyred blood and ashes sow
    O'er all the Italian fields, where still doth sway
The triple tyrant; that from these may grow
    A hundredfold, who having learned thy way
    Early may fly the Babylonian woe.

SONNET XIX

# On His Blindness

When I consider how my light is spent
   Ere half my days, in this dark world and wide,
   And that one talent, which is death to hide,
   Lodged with me useless, though my soul more bent
To serve therewith my Maker, and present
   My true account, lest He, returning, chide;
   "Doth God exact day-labour, light denied?"
   I fondly ask. But Patience, to prevent
That murmur, soon replies: "God doth not need
   Either man's work or his own gifts. Who best
   Bear his mild yoke, they serve him best. His state
Is kingly. Thousands, at his bidding, speed
   And post o'er land and ocean, without rest;
   They also serve who only stand and wait."

SONNET XXIII

# On His Deceased Wife

Methought I saw my late-espoused saint,
   Brought to me like Alcestis from the grave,
   Whom Jove's great son to her glad husband gave,
   Rescued from Death by force, though pale and faint.
Mine, as whom washed from spot of childbed-taint
   Purification in the Old Law did save,
   And such, as yet once more I trust to have
   Full sight of her in Heaven without restraint,
Came vested all in white, pure as her mind.
   Her face was veiled, yet to my fancied sight
   Love, sweetness, goodness, in her person shined
So clear, as in no face with more delight.
   But oh! as to embrace me she inclined,
   I waked, she fled, and day brought back my night.

# JOHN DRYDEN
## (1631–1700)

## A Song for St. Cecilia's Day

### 22d November, 1687

### I

From harmony, from heavenly harmony,
   This universal frame began:
  When nature underneath a heap
    Of jarring atoms lay,
  And could not heave her head,
The tuneful voice was heard from high,
   "Arise, ye more than dead."
Then cold, and hot, and moist, and dry,
In order to their stations leap,
   And Music's power obey.
From harmony, from heavenly harmony,
This universal frame began;
From harmony to harmony
Through all the compass of the notes it ran,
The diapason closing full in man.

### II

What passion cannot music raise and quell?
  When Jubal struck the chorded shell,
   His listening brethren stood around,
  And, wondering, on their faces fell
   To worship that celestial sound:

Less than a God they thought there could not dwell
    Within the hollow of that shell,
    That spoke so sweetly, and so well.
What passion cannot music raise and quell?

### III

    The trumpet's loud clangor
        Excites us to arms,
    With shrill notes of anger,
        And mortal alarms.
    The double, double, double beat
        Of the thundering drum,
        Cries, hark! the foes come:
Charge, charge! 'tis too late to retreat.

### IV

    The soft complaining flute,
        In dying notes, discovers
        The woes of hopeless lovers;
Whose dirge is whispered by the warbling lute.

### V

    Sharp violins proclaim
    Their jealous pangs, and desperation,
    Fury, frantic indignation,
    Depth of pains, and height of passion,
        For the fair, disdainful dame.

### VI

    But, oh! what art can teach,
        What human voice can reach,
    The sacred organs praise?
        Notes inspiring holy love,
    Notes that wing their heavenly ways
        To mend the choirs above.

### VII

Orpheus could lead the savage race;
And trees uprooted left their place,
Sequacious of the lyre:
But bright Cecilia raised the wonder higher;
When to her organ vocal breath was given,
An angel heard, and straight appeared,
Mistaking earth for heaven.

### GRAND CHORUS

As from the power of sacred lays
The spheres began to move,
And sung the great Creators praise
To all the blessed above;
So when the last and dreadful hour
This crumbling pageant shall devour,
The trumpet shall be heard on high,
The dead shall live, the living die,
And Music shall untune the sky.

## Mac-Flecknoe

All human things are subject to decay,
And, when fate summons, monarchs must obey.
This Flecknoe found, who, like Augustus, young
Was called to empire, and had governed long;
In prose and verse was owned, without dispute,
Through all the realms of Nonsense, absolute.
This aged prince, now flourishing in peace,
And blest with issue of a large increase,
Worn out with business, did at length debate
To settle the succession of the state;
And, pondering which of all his sons was fit
To reign, and wage immortal war with wit,
Cried,—"'Tis resolved! for nature pleads, that he
Should only rule, who most resembles me.

Shadwell alone my perfect image bears,
Mature in dulness from his tender years;
Shadwell alone, of all my sons, is he,
Who stands confirmed in full stupidity.
The rest to some faint meaning make pretence,
But Shadwell never deviates into sense;
Some beams of wit on other souls may fall,
Strike through, and make a lucid interval;
But Shadwell's genuine night admits no ray,
His rising fogs prevail upon the day.
Besides, his goodly fabric fills the eye,
And seems designed for thoughtless majesty;
Thoughtless as monarch oaks, that shade the plain,
And, spread in solemn state, supinely reign.
Heywood and Shirley were but types of thee,
Thou last great prophet of tautology!
Even I, a dunce of more renown than they,
Was sent before but to prepare thy way;
And, coarsely clad in Norwich drugget, came
To teach the nations in thy greater name.
My warbling lute,—the lute I whilom strung,
When to King John of Portugal I sung,—
Was but the prelude to that glorious day,
When thou on silver Thames didst cut thy way,
With well-timed oars, before the royal barge,
Swelled with the pride of thy celestial charge;
And big with hymn, commander of an host,—
The like was ne'er in Epsom blankets tost.
Methinks I see the new Arion sail,
The lute still trembling underneath thy nail.
At thy well-sharpened thumb, from shore to shore,
The trebles squeak for fear, the basses roar;
Echoes, from Pissing-Alley, Shadwell call,
And Shadwell they resound from Aston Hall.
About thy boat the little fishes throng,
As at the morning toast that floats along.
Sometimes, as prince of thy harmonious band,

Thou wield'st thy papers in thy threshing hand;
St. André's feet ne'er kept more equal time,
Not even the feet of thy own Psyche's rhyme,
Though they in number as in sense excel;
So just, so like tautology, they fell,
That, pale with envy, Singleton forswore
The lute and sword, which he in triumph bore,
And vowed he ne'er would act Villerius more."
   Here stopt the good old sire, and wept for joy,
In silent raptures of the hopeful boy.
All arguments, but most his plays, persuade,
That for anointed dulness he was made.
   Close to the walls which fair Augusta bind,
(The fair Augusta much to fears inclined,)
An ancient fabric raised to inform the sight,
There stood of yore, and Barbican it hight;
A watch-tower once, but now, so fate ordains,
Of all the pile an empty name remains;
From its old ruins brothel-houses rise,
Scenes of lewd loves, and of polluted joys;
Where their vast courts the mother-strumpets keep,
And, undisturbed by watch, in silence sleep.
Near these a Nursery erects its head,
Where queens are formed, and future heroes bred;
Where unfledged actors learn to laugh and cry;
Where infant punks their tender voices try,
And little Maximins the gods defy.
Great Fletcher never treads in buskins here,
Nor greater Jonson dares in socks appear;
But gentle Simkin just reception finds
Amidst this monument of vanished minds;
Pure clinches the suburban muse affords,
And Panton waging harmless war with words.
Here Flecknoe, as a place to fame well known,
Ambitiously designed his Shadwell's throne.
For ancient Decker prophesied long since,
That in this pile should reign a mighty prince,

Born for a scourge of wit, and flail of sense;
To whom true dulness should some Psyches owe,
But worlds of Misers from his pen should flow;
Humorists, and Hypocrites, it should produce,
Whole Raymond families, and tribes of Bruce.
   Now empress Fame had published the renown
Of Shadwell's coronation through the town.
Roused by report of fame, the nations meet,
From near Bunhill, and distant Watling Street.
No Persian carpets spread the imperial way,
But scattered limbs of mangled poets lay;
From dusty shops neglected authors come,
Martyrs of pies, and relics of the bum;
Much Heywood, Shirley, Ogleby there lay,
But loads of Shadwell almost choked the way;
Bilked stationers for yeomen stood prepared,
And Herringman was captain of the guard.
The hoary prince in majesty appeared,
High on a throne of his own labours reared.
At his right hand our young Ascanius sate,
Rome's other hope, and pillar of the state;
His brows thick fogs, instead of glories, grace,
And lambent dulness played around his face.
As Hannibal did to the altars come,
Sworn by his sire, a mortal foe to Rome,
So Shadwell swore, nor should his vow be vain,
That he till death true dulness would maintain;
And, in his father's right, and realm's defence,
Ne'er to have peace with wit, nor truce with sense.
The king himself the sacred unction made,
As king by office, and as priest by trade.
In his sinister hand, instead of ball,
He placed a mighty mug of potent ale;
"Love's kingdom" to his right he did convey,
At once his sceptre, and his rule of sway;
Whose righteous lore the prince had practised young,
And from whose loins recorded Psyche sprung.

His temples, last, with poppies were o'erspread,
That nodding seemed to consecrate his head.
Just at the point of time, if fame not lie,
On his left hand twelve reverend owls did fly;—
So Romulus, 'tis sung, by Tiber's brook,
Presage of sway from twice six vultures took.
The admiring throng loud acclamations make,
And omens of his future empire take.
The sire then shook the honours of his head,
And from his brows damps of oblivion shed
Full on the filial dulness: long he stood,
Repelling from his breast the raging god;
At length burst out in this prophetic mood:—

    "Heavens bless my son! from Ireland let him reign,
To far Barbadoes on the western main;
Of his dominion may no end be known,
And greater than his father's be his throne;
Beyond love's kingdom let him stretch his pen!"
He paused, and all the people cried, "Amen."
Then thus continued he: "My son, advance
Still in new impudence, new ignorance.
Success let others teach, learn thou from me
Pangs without birth, and fruitless industry.
Let Virtuosos in five years be writ,
Yet not one thought accuse thy toil of wit.
Let gentle George in triumph tread the stage,
Make Dorimant betray, and Loveit rage;
Let Cully, Cockwood, Fopling, charm the pit,
And in their folly show the writer's wit;
Yet still thy fools shall stand in thy defence,
And justify their author's want of sense.
Let them be all by thy own model made
Of dulness, and desire no foreign aid;
That they to future ages may be known,
Not copies drawn, but issue of thy own:
Nay, let thy men of wit too be the same,
All full of thee, and differing but in name;

But let no alien Sedley interpose,
To lard with wit thy hungry Epsom prose.
And when false flowers of rhetoric thou wouldst cull,
Trust nature; do not labour to be dull,
But write thy best, and top; and, in each line,
Sir Formal's oratory will be thine:
Sir Formal, though unsought, attends thy quill,
And does thy northern dedications fill.
Nor let false friends seduce thy mind to fame,
By arrogating Jonson's hostile name;
Let father Flecknoe fire thy mind with praise,
And uncle Ogleby thy envy raise.
Thou art my blood, where Jonson has no part:
What share have we in nature, or in art?
Where did his wit on learning fix a brand,
And rail at arts he did not understand?
Where made he love in Prince Nicander's vein,
Or swept the dust in Psyche's humble strain?
Where sold he bargains, 'whip-stitch, kiss my arse,'
Promised a play, and dwindled to a farce?
When did his muse from Fletcher scenes purloin,
As thou whole Etherege dost transfuse to thine?
But so transfused, as oil and waters flow,
His always floats above, thine sinks below.
This is thy province, this thy wondrous way,
New humours to invent for each new play:
This is that boasted bias of thy mind,
By which one way to dulness 'tis inclined;
Which makes thy writings lean on one side still,
And, in all changes, that way bends thy will.
Nor let thy mountain-belly make pretence
Of likeness; thine's a tympany of sense
A tun of man in thy large bulk is writ,
But sure thou'rt but a kilderkin of wit.
Like mine, thy gentle numbers feebly creep;
Thy tragic muse gives smiles, thy comic sleep.
With whate'er gall thou sett'st thyself to write,

Thy inoffensive satires never bite;
In thy felonious heart though venom lies,
It does but touch thy Irish pen, and dies.
Thy genius call thee not to purchase fame
In keen iambics, but mild anagram.
Leave writing plays, and choose for thy command,
Some peaceful province in Acrostic land.
There thou may'st wings display, and altars raise,
And torture one poor word ten thousand ways;
Or, if thou wouldst thy different talents suit,
Set thy own songs, and sing them to thy lute."

    He said:—but his last words were scarcely heard;
For Bruce and Longvil had a trap prepared,
And down they sent the yet declaiming bard.
Sinking he left his drugget robe behind,
Borne upwards by a subterranean wind.
The mantle fell to the young prophet's part,
With double portion of his father's art.

# ALEXANDER POPE

## (1688–1744)

## The Rape of the Lock

*A Heroi-Comical Poem*

### CANTO I

What dire offence from am'rous causes springs,
What mighty contests rise from trivial things,
I sing—This verse to CARYL, Muse! is due:
This, ev'n Belinda may vouchsafe to view:
Slight is the subject, but not so the praise,
If she inspire, and he approve my lays.
 Say what strange motive, Goddess! could compel
A well-bred lord t'assault a gentle belle?
O say what stranger cause, yet unexplored,
Could make a gentle belle reject a lord?
In tasks so bold, can little men engage,
And in soft bosoms dwells such mighty rage?
 Sol thro' white curtains shot a tim'rous ray,
And oped those eyes that must eclipse the day:
Now lap-dogs give themselves the rousing shake,
And sleepless lovers, just at twelve, awake:
Thrice rung the bell, the slipper knocked the ground,
And the pressed watch return'd a silver sound.
Belinda still her downy pillow prest,
Her guardian sylph prolong'd the balmy rest:
'Twas he had summon'd to her silent bed
The morning-dream that hovered o'er her head;
A youth more glitt'ring than a birth-night beau,

(That ev'n in slumber caused her cheek to glow)
Seemed to her ear his winning lips to lay,
And thus in whispers said, or seemed to say.

    Fairest of mortals, thou distinguish'd care
Of thousand bright inhabitants of air!
If e'er one vision touched thy infant thought,
Of all the nurse and all the priest have taught;
Of airy elves by moonlight shadows seen,
The silver token, and the circled green,
Or virgins visited by angel-pow'rs,
With golden crowns and wreaths of heav'nly flow'rs;
Hear and believe! thy own importance know,
Nor bound thy narrow views to things below.
Some secret truths, from learned pride concealed,
To maids alone and children are reveal'd:
What tho' no credit doubting wits may give!
The fair and innocent shall still believe.
Know, then, unnumber'd spirits round thee fly,
The light militia of the lower sky:
These, tho' unseen, are ever on the wing,
Hang o'er the box, and hover round the ring.
Think what an equipage thou hast in air,
And view with scorn two pages and a chair.
As now your own, our beings were of old,
And once inclosed in woman's beauteous mould;
Thence, by a soft transition, we repair
From earthly vehicles to these of air.
Think not, when woman's transient breath is fled,
That all her vanities at once are dead;
Succeeding vanities she still regards,
And tho' she plays no more, o'erlooks the cards.
Her joy in gilded chariots, when alive,
And love of ombre, after death survive.
For when the fair in all their pride expire,
To their first elements their souls retire:
The sprites of fiery termagants in flame
Mount up, and take a salamander's name.

Soft yielding minds to water glide away,
And sip, with nymphs, their elemental tea.
The graver prude sinks downward to a gnome,
In search of mischief still on earth to roam.
The light coquettes in sylphs aloft repair,
And sport and flutter in the fields of air.

    Know further yet; whoever fair and chaste
Rejects mankind, is by some sylph embraced:
For spirits, freed from mortal laws, with ease
Assume what sexes and what shapes they please.
What guards the purity of melting maids,
In courtly balls, and midnight masquerades,
Safe from the treach'rous friend, the daring spark,
The glance by day, the whisper in the dark,
When kind occasion prompts their warm desires,
When music softens, and when dancing fires?
'Tis but their sylph, the wise celestials know,
Tho' honour is the word with men below.

    Some nymphs there are, too conscious of their face,
For life predestined to the gnomes' embrace.
These swell their prospects and exalt their pride,
When offers are disdain'd, and love denied:
Then gay ideas crowd the vacant brain,
While peers, and dukes, and all their sweeping train,
And garters, stars, and coronets appear,
And in soft sounds, "Your Grace" salutes their ear.
'Tis these that early taint the female soul,
Instruct the eyes of young coquettes to roll,
Teach infant-cheeks a bidden blush to know,
And little hearts to flutter at a beau.

    Oft, when the world imagine women stray,
The sylphs thro' mystic mazes guide their way,
Thro' all the giddy circle they pursue,
And old impertinence expel by new.
What tender maid but must a victim fall
To one man's treat, but for another's ball?
When Florio speaks what virgin could withstand,

If gentle Damon did not squeeze her hand?
With varying vanities, from ev'ry part,
They shift the moving toyshop of their heart;
Where wigs with wigs, with sword-knots sword-knots strive,
Beaux banish beaux, and coaches coaches drive.
This erring mortals levity may call;
Oh blind to truth! the sylphs contrive it all.

   Of these am I, who thy protection claim,
A watchful sprite, and Ariel is my name.
Late, as I rang'd the crystal wilds of air,
In the clear mirror of thy ruling star
I saw, alas! some dread event impend,
Ere to the main this morning sun descend,
But heav'n reveals not what, or how, or where:
Warn'd by the sylph, oh pious maid, beware!
This to disclose is all thy guardian can:
Beware of all, but most beware of man!

   He said; when Shock, who thought she slept too long,
Leap'd up, and wak'd his mistress with his tongue.
'Twas then, Belinda, if report say true,
Thy eyes first open'd on a billet-doux;
Wounds, charms, and ardours were no sooner read,
But all the vision vanished from thy head.

   And now, unveiled, the toilet stands display'd,
Each silver vase in mystic order laid.
First, robed in white, the nymph intent adores,
With head uncovered, the cosmetic pow'rs.
A heav'nly image in the glass appears,
To that she bends, to that her eyes she rears;
Th' inferior priestess, at her altar's side,
Trembling begins the sacred rites of pride.
Unnumbered treasures ope at once, and here
The various off'rings of the world appear;
From each she nicely culls with curious toil,
And decks the Goddess with the glitt'ring spoil.
This casket India's glowing gems unlocks,
And all Arabia breathes from yonder box.

The tortoise here and elephant unite,
Transform'd to combs, the speckled, and the white.
Here files of pins extend their shining rows,
Puffs, powders, patches, bibles, billet-doux.
Now awful beauty puts on all its arms;
The fair each moment rises in her charms,
Repairs her smiles, awakens ev'ry grace,
And calls forth all the wonders of her face;
Sees by degrees a purer blush arise,
And keener lightnings quicken in her eyes.
The busy sylphs surround their darling care,
These set the head, and those divide the hair,
Some fold the sleeve, whilst others plait the gown;
And Betty's prais'd for labours not her own.

### CANTO II

Not with more glories, in th' etherial plain,
The sun first rises o'er the purpled main,
Than, issuing forth, the rival of his beams
Launched on the bosom of the silver Thames.
Fair nymphs, and well-drest youths around her shone,
But ev'ry eye was fixed on her alone.
On her white breast a sparkling cross she wore,
Which Jews might kiss, and infidels adore.
Her lively looks a sprightly mind disclose,
Quick as her eyes, and as unfixed as those:
Favours to none, to all she smiles extends;
Oft she rejects, but never once offends.
Bright as the sun, her eyes the gazers strike,
And, like the sun, they shine on all alike.
Yet graceful ease, and sweetness void of pride,
Might hide her faults, if belles had faults to hide:
If to her share some female errors fall,
Look on her face, and you'll forget 'em all.

This nymph, to the destruction of mankind,
Nourished two locks, which graceful hung behind
In equal curls, and well conspired to deck

With shining ringlets the smooth iv'ry neck.
Love in these labyrinths his slaves detains,
And mighty hearts are held in slender chains.
With hairy springes we the birds betray,
Slight lines of hair surprise the finny prey,
Fair tresses man's imperial race ensnare,
And beauty draws us with a single hair.

　　Th' advent'rous baron the bright locks admired;
He saw, he wish'd, and to the prize aspir'd.
Resolved to win, he meditates the way,
By force to ravish, or by fraud betray;
For when success a lover's toil attends,
Few ask, if fraud or force attained his ends.

　　For this, ere Phœbus rose, he had implored
Propitious heav'n, and ev'ry pow'r ador'd,
But chiefly love—to love an altar built,
Of twelve vast French romances, neatly gilt.
There lay three garters, half a pair of gloves;
And all the trophies of his former loves;
With tender billet-doux he lights the pyre,
And breathes three am'rous sighs to raise the fire.
Then prostrate falls, and begs with ardent eyes
Soon to obtain, and long possess the prize:
The pow'rs gave ear, and granted half his pray'r,
The rest, the winds dispersed in empty air.

　　But now secure the painted vessel glides,
The sun-beams trembling on the floating tides:
While melting music steals upon the sky,
And softened sounds along the waters die;
Smooth flow the waves, the zephyrs gently play,
Belinda smil'd, and all the world was gay.
All but the sylph—with careful thoughts opprest,
Th' impending woe sat heavy on his breast.
He summons strait his denizens of air;
The lucid squadrons round the sails repair:
Soft o'er the shrouds aërial whispers breathe,
That seem'd but zephyrs to the train beneath.

Some to the sun their insect-wings unfold,
Waft on the breeze, or sink in clouds of gold;
Transparent forms, too fine for mortal sight,
Their fluid bodies half dissolved in light,
Loose to the wind their airy garments flew,
Thin glitt'ring textures of the filmy dew,
Dipt in the richest tincture of the skies,
Where light disports in ever-mingling dyes,
While ev'ry beam new transient colours flings,
Colours that change whene'er they wave their wings.
Amid the circle, on the gilded mast,
Superior by the head, was Ariel plac'd;
His purple pinions op'ning to the sun,
He raised his azure wand, and thus begun.
    Ye sylphs and sylphids, to your chief give ear!
Fays, fairies, genii, elves, and demons, hear!
Ye know the spheres and various tasks assigned
By laws eternal to th' aërial kind.
Some in the fields of purest æther play,
And bask and whiten in the blaze of day.
Some guide the course of wand'ring orbs on high,
Or roll the planets thro' the boundless sky.
Some less refined, beneath the moon's pale light
Pursue the stars that shoot athwart the night,
Or suck the mists in grosser air below,
Or dip their pinions in the painted bow,
Or brew fierce tempests on the wintry main,
Or o'er the glebe distil the kindly rain.
Others on earth o'er human race preside,
Watch all their ways, and all their actions guide:
Of these the chief the care of nations own,
And guard with arms divine the British throne.
    Our humbler province is to tend the Fair,
Not a less pleasing, tho' less glorious care;
To save the powder from too rude a gale,
Nor let th' imprisoned essences exhale;
To draw fresh colours from the vernal flow'rs;

To steal from rainbows e'er they drop in show'rs
A brighter wash; to curl their waving hairs,
Assist their blushes, and inspire their airs;
Nay oft, in dreams, invention we bestow,
To change a flounce, or add a furbelow.

    This day, black omens threat the brightest fair,
That e'er deserved a watchful spirit's care;
Some dire disaster, or by force, or slight;
But what, or where, the fates have wrapt in night.
Whether the nymph shall break Diana's law,
Or some frail china jar receive a flaw;
Or stain her honour or her new brocade;
Forget her pray'rs, or miss a masquerade;
Or lose her heart, or necklace, at a ball;
Or whether Heav'n has doom'd that Shock must fall.
Haste, then, ye spirits! to your charge repair:
The flutt'ring fan be Zephyretta's care;
The drops to thee, Brillante, we consign;
And, Momentilla, let the watch be thine;
Do thou, Crispissa, tend her fav'rite lock;
Ariel himself shall be the guard of Shock.

    To fifty chosen sylphs, of special note,
We trust th' important charge, the petticoat:
Oft have we known that seven-fold fence to fail,
Tho' stiff with hoops, and armed with ribs of whale;
Form a strong line about the silver bound,
And guard the wide circumference around.

    Whatever spirit, careless of his charge,
His post neglects, or leaves the fair at large,
Shall feel sharp vengeance soon o'ertake his sins,
Be stopped in vials, or transfix'd with pins;
Or plunged in lakes of bitter washes lie,
Or wedged whole ages in a bodkin's eye:
Gums and pomatums shall his flight restrain,
While clogg'd he beats his silken wings in vain;
Or alum styptics with contracting pow'r
Shrink his thin essence like a rivel'd flow'r:

Or, as Ixion fix'd, the wretch shall feel
The giddy motion of the whirling mill,
In fumes of burning chocolate shall glow,
And tremble at the sea that froths below!
    He spoke; the spirits from the sails descend;
Some, orb in orb, around the nymph extend;
Some thrid the mazy ringlets of her hair;
Some hang upon the pendants of her ear:
With beating hearts the dire event they wait,
Anxious, and trembling for the birth of fate.

## CANTO III

Close by those meads, for ever crown'd with flow'rs,
Where Thames with pride surveys his rising tow'rs,
There stands a structure of majestic frame,
Which from the neighb'ring Hampton takes its name.
Here Britain's statesmen oft the fall foredoom
Of forcign Tyrants and of Nymphs at home;
Here thou, great ANNA! whom three realms obey,
Dost sometimes counsel take—and sometimes tea.
    Hither the heroes and the nymphs resort,
To taste awhile the pleasures of a court;
In various talk th' instructive hours they passed,
Who gave the ball, or paid the visit last;
One speaks the glory of the British queen,
And one describes a charming Indian screen;
A third interprets motions, looks, and eyes;
At ev'ry word a reputation dies.
Snuff, or the fan, supply each pause of chat,
With singing, laughing, ogling, and all that.
    Mcanwhile, declining from the noon of day,
The sun obliquely shoots his burning ray;
The hungry judges soon the sentence sign,
And wretches hang that jury-men may dine;
The merchant from th' Exchange returns in peace,
And the long labours of the toilet cease.
Belinda now, whom thirst of fame invites,

Burns to encounter two advent'rous knights,
At ombre singly to decide their doom;
And swells her breast with conquests yet to come.
Straight the three bands prepare in arms to join,
Each band the number of the sacred nine.
Soon as she spreads her hand, th' aërial guard
Descend, and sit on each important card:
First Ariel perched upon a Matadore,
Then each, according to the rank they bore;
For sylphs, yet mindful of their ancient race,
Are, as when women, wondrous fond of place.

    Behold, four kings in majesty rever'd,
With hoary whiskers and a forky beard;
And four fair queens whose hands sustain a flow'r,
Th' expressive emblem of their softer pow'r;
Four knaves in garbs succinct, a trusty band,
Caps on their heads, and halberts in their hand;
And particoloured troops, a shining train,
Draw forth to combat on the velvet plain.

    The skilful nymph reviews her force with care:
Let spades be trumps! she said, and trumps they were.

    Now move to war her sable Matadores,
In show like leaders of the swarthy Moors.
Spadillio first, unconquerable lord!
Led off two captive trumps, and swept the board.
As many more Manillio forced to yield,
And marched a victor from the verdant field.
Him Basto follow'd, but his fate more hard
Gain'd but one trump and one plebeian card.
With his broad sabre next, a chief in years,
The hoary Majesty of Spades appears,
Puts forth one manly leg, to sight revealed,
The rest, his many-colour'd robe concealed.
The rebel knave, who dares his prince engage,
Proves the just victim of his royal rage.
Ev'n mighty Pam, that kings and queens o'erthrew
And mow'd down armies in the fights of loo,

Sad chance of war! now destitute of aid,
Falls undistinguished by the victor spade!
   Thus far both armies to Belinda yield;
Now to the baron fate inclines the field.
His warlike Amazon her host invades,
Th' imperial consort of the crown of spades.
The club's black tyrant first her victim died,
Spite of his haughty mien, and barb'rous pride:
What boots the regal circle on his head,
His giant limbs, in state unwieldy spread;
That long behind he trails his pompous robe,
And, of all monarch's, only grasps the globe?
   The baron now his diamonds pours apace;
Th' embroider'd king who shows but half his face,
And his refulgent queen, with pow'rs combined
Of broken troops an easy conquest find.
Clubs, diamonds, hearts, in wild disorder seen,
With throngs promiscuous strow the level green.
Thus when dispersed a routed army runs,
Of Asia's troops, and Afric's sable sons,
With like confusion different nations fly,
Of various habit, and of various dye,
The pierc'd battalions dis-united fall,
In heaps on heaps; one fate o'erwhelms them all.
   The knave of diamonds tries his wily arts,
And wins (oh shameful chance!) the queen of hearts.
At this, the blood the virgin's cheek forsook,
A livid paleness spreads o'er all her look;
She sees, and trembles at th' approaching ill,
Just in the jaws of ruin, and codille.
And now (as oft in some distemper'd state)
On one nice trick depends the gen'ral fate.
An ace of hearts steps forth: The king unseen
Lurk'd in her hand, and mourn'd his captive queen:
He springs to vengeance with an eager pace,
And falls like thunder on the prostrate ace.
The nymph exulting fills with shouts the sky;

The walls, the woods, and long canals reply.

   Oh thoughtless mortals! ever blind to fate,

Too soon dejected, and too soon elate.

Sudden, these honours shall be snatch'd away,

And cursed for ever this victorious day.

   For lo! the board with cups and spoons is crown'd,

The berries crackle, and the mill turns round;

On shining altars of Japan they raise

The silver lamp; the fiery spirits blaze:

From silver spouts the grateful liquors glide,

While China's earth receives the smoking tide:

At once they gratify their scent and taste,

And frequent cups prolong the rich repast.

Straight hover round the Fair her airy band;

Some, as she sipped, the fuming liquor fanned,

Some o'er her lap their careful plumes displayed,

Trembling, and conscious of the rich brocade.

Coffee, (which makes the politician wise,

And see thro' all things with his half-shut eyes)

Sent up in vapours to the baron's brain

New stratagems, the radiant lock to gain.

Ah cease, rash youth! desist ere 'tis too late,

Fear the just Gods, and think of Scylla's Fate!

Chang'd to a bird, and sent to flit in air,

She dearly pays for Nisus' injur'd hair!

   But when to mischief mortals bend their will,

How soon they find fit instruments of ill!

Just then, Clarissa drew with tempting grace

A two-edged weapon from her shining case:

So ladies in romance assist their knight,

Present the spear, and arm him for the fight.

He takes the gift with rev'rence, and extends

The little engine on his fingers' ends;

This just behind Belinda's neck he spread,

As o'er the fragrant steams she bends her head.

Swift to the lock a thousand sprites repair,

A thousand wings, by turns, blow back the hair;

And thrice they twitched the diamond in her ear;
Thrice she looked back, and thrice the foe drew near.
Just in that instant, anxious Ariel sought
The close recesses of the virgin's thought;
As on the nosegay in her breast reclined,
He watched th' ideas rising in her mind,
Sudden he viewed, in spite of all her art,
An earthly lover lurking at her heart.
Amazed, confused, he found his pow'r expired,
Resigned to fate, and with a sigh retired.

    The peer now spreads the glitt'ring forfex wide,
T' inclose the lock; now joins it, to divide.
Ev'n then, before the fatal engine closed,
A wretched sylph too fondly interposed;
Fate urged the shears, and cut the sylph in twain,
(But airy substance soon unites again)
The meeting points the sacred hair dissever
From the fair head, for ever, and for ever!

    Then flashed the living lightning from her eyes,
And screams of horror rend th' affrighted skies.
Not louder shrieks to pitying heav'n are cast,
When husbands, or when lap-dogs breathe their last;
Or when rich China vessels fall'n from high,
In glitt'ring dust and painted fragments lie!

    Let wreaths of triumph now my temples twine,
(The victor cried) the glorious prize is mine!
While fish in streams, or birds delight in air,
Or in a coach and six the British fair,
As long as Atalantis shall be read,
Or the small pillow grace a lady's bed,
While visits shall be paid on solemn days,
When num'rous wax-lights in bright order blaze,
While nymphs take treats, or assignations give,
So long my honour, name, and praise shall live!
What time would spare, from steel receives its date,
And monuments, like men, submit to fate!
Steel could the labour of the Gods destroy,

And strike to dust th' imperial tow'rs of Troy;
Steel could the works of mortal pride confound,
And hew triumphal arches to the ground.
What wonder then, fair nymph! thy hairs should feel,
The conqu'ring force of unresisted steel?

## CANTO IV

But anxious cares the pensive nymph oppressed,
And secret passions labour'd in her breast.
Not youthful kings in battle seized alive,
Not scornful virgins who their charms survive,
Not ardent lovers robbed of all their bliss,
Not ancient ladies when refused a kiss,
Not tyrants fierce that unrepenting die,
Not Cynthia when her manteau's pinned awry,
E'er felt such rage, resentment, and despair,
As thou, sad virgin! for thy ravish'd hair.

For that sad moment, when the sylphs withdrew
And Ariel weeping from Belinda flew,
Umbriel, a dusky, melancholy sprite,
As ever sullied the fair face of light,
Down, to the central earth, his proper scene,
Repaired to search the gloomy cave of spleen.

Swift on his sooty pinions flits the gnome,
And in a vapour reached the dismal dome.
No cheerful breeze this sullen region knows,
The dreaded east is all the wind that blows.
Here in a grotto, sheltered close from air,
And screened in shades from day's detested glare,
She sighs for ever on her pensive bed,
Pain at her side, and Megrim at her head.

Two handmaids wait the throne: alike in place,
But diff'ring far in figure and in face.
Here stood Ill-nature like an ancient maid,
Her wrinkled form in black and white arrayed;
With store of pray'rs, for mornings, nights, and noons,
Her hand is filled; her bosom with lampoons.

There Affectation, with a sickly mien,
Shows in her cheek the roses of eighteen,
Practised to lisp, and hang the head aside,
Faints into airs, and languishes with pride,
On the rich quilt sinks with becoming woe,
Wrapt in a gown, for sickness, and for show.
The fair ones feel such maladies as these,
When each new night-dress gives a new disease.

    A constant vapour o'er the palace flies;
Strange phantoms rising as the mists arise;
Dreadful, as hermit's dreams in haunted shades,
Or bright, as visions of expiring maids.
Now glaring fiends, and snakes on rolling spires,
Pale spectres, gaping tombs, and purple fires:
Now lakes of liquid gold, Elysian scenes,
And crystal domes, and angels in machines.

    Unnumber'd throngs on every side are seen,
Of bodies chang'd to various forms by spleen.
Here living tea-pots stand, one arm held out,
One bent; the handle this, and that the spout:
A pipkin there, like Homer's tripod walks;
Here sighs a jar, and there a goose-pie talks;
Men prove with child, as pow'rful fancy works,
And maids turn'd bottles, call aloud for corks.

    Safe past the gnome thro' this fantastic band,
A branch of healing spleenwort in his hand.
Then thus address'd the pow'r: "Hail, wayward Queen!
Who rule the sex to fifty from fifteen:
Parent of vapours and of female wit,
Who give th' hysteric, or poetic fit,
On various tempers act by various ways,
Make some take physic, others scribble plays;
Who cause the proud their visits to delay,
And send the godly in a pet to pray.
A nymph there is, that all thy pow'r disdains,
And thousands more in equal mirth maintains.
But oh! if e'er thy gnome could spoil a grace,

Or raise a pimple on a beauteous face,
Like citron-waters matrons cheeks inflame,
Or change complexions at a losing game;
If e'er with airy horns I planted heads,
Or rumpled petticoats, or tumbled beds,
Or caused suspicion when no soul was rude,
Or discompos'd the head-dress of a Prude,
Or e'er to costive lap-dog gave disease,
Which not the tears of brightest eyes could ease:
Hear me, and touch Belinda with chagrin,
That single act gives half the world the spleen."
    The Goddess with a discontented air
Seems to reject him, tho' she grants his pray'r.
A wondrous bag with both her hands she binds,
Like that where once Ulysses held the winds;
There she collects the force of female lungs,
Sighs, sobs, and passions, and the war of tongues.
A vial next she fills with fainting fears,
Soft sorrows, melting griefs, and flowing tears.
The gnome rejoicing bears her gifts away,
Spreads his black wings, and slowly mounts to day.
    Sunk in Thalestris' arms the nymph he found,
Her eyes dejected and her hair unbound.
Full o'er their heads the swelling bag he rent,
And all the Furies issu'd at the vent.
Belinda burns with more than mortal ire,
And fierce Thalestris fans the rising fire.
"O wretched maid!" she spread her hands, and cried,
(While Hampton's echoes, "Wretched maid!" replied)
"Was it for this you took such constant care
The bodkin, comb, and essence to prepare?
For this your locks in paper durance bound,
For this with tort'ring irons wreathed around?
For this with fillets strained your tender head,
And bravely bore the double loads of lead?
Gods! shall the ravisher display your hair,
While the fops envy, and the ladies stare!

Honour forbid! at whose unrivalled shrine
Ease, pleasure, virtue, all our sex resign.
Methinks already I your tears survey,
Already hear the horrid things they say,
Already see you a degraded toast,
And all your honour in a whisper lost!
How shall I, then, your helpless fame defend?
'Twill then be infamy to seem your friend!
And shall this prize, th' inestimable prize,
Exposed thro' crystal to the gazing eyes,
And heightened by the diamond's circling rays,
On that rapacious hand for ever blaze?
Sooner shall grass in Hyde-park Circus grow,
And wits take lodgings in the sound of Bow;
Sooner let earth, air, sea, to chaos fall,
Men, monkeys, lap-dogs, parrots, perish all!"

    She said; then raging to Sir Plume repairs,
And bids her beau demand the precious hairs:
(Sir Plume of amber snuff-box justly vain,
And the nice conduct of a clouded cane)
With earnest eyes, and round unthinking face,
He first the snuff-box open'd, then the case,
And thus broke out    "My Lord, why, what the devil?
Z—ds! damn the lock! 'fore Gad, you must be civil!
Plague on't! 'tis past a jest—nay prithee, pox!
Give her the hair"—he spoke, and rapp'd his box.

    "It grieves me much" (replied the Peer again)
"Who speaks so well should ever speak in vain.
But by this lock, this sacred lock I swear,
(Which never more shall join its parted hair;
Which never more its honours shall renew,
Clipped from the lovely head where late it grew)
That while my nostrils draw the vital air,
This hand, which won it, shall for ever wear."
He spoke, and speaking, in proud triumph spread
The long-contended honours of her head.

    But Umbriel, hateful gnome! forbears not so;

He breaks the vial whence the sorrows flow.
Then see! the nymph in beauteous grief appears,
Her eyes half-languishing, half-drowned in tears;
On her heaved bosom hung her drooping head,
Which, with a sigh, she raised; and thus she said.
   "For ever cursed be this detested day,
Which snatched my best, my fav'rite curl away!
Happy! ah ten times happy had I been,
If Hampton-Court these eyes had never seen!
Yet am not I the first mistaken maid,
By love of courts to num'rous ills betrayed.
Oh had I rather un-admir'd remain'd
In some lone isle, or distant Northern land;
Where the gilt chariot never marks the way,
Where none learn ombre, none e'er taste bohea!
There kept my charms concealed from mortal eye,
Like roses, that in deserts bloom and die.
What mov'd my mind with youthful lords to roam?
Oh had I stayed, and said my pray'rs at home!
'Twas this, the morning omens seemed to tell,
Thrice from my trembling hand the patch-box fell;
The tott'ring China shook without a wind,
Nay, Poll sat mute, and Shock was most unkind!
A sylph too warned me of the threats of fate,
In mystic visions, now believed too late!
See the poor remnants of these slighted hairs!
My hands shall rend what ev'n thy rapine spares:
These in two sable ringlets taught to break,
Once gave new beauties to the snowy neck;
The sister-lock now sits uncouth, alone,
And in its fellow's fate foresees its own;
Uncurled it hangs, the fatal shears demands,
And tempts once more, thy sacrilegious hands.
Oh hadst thou, cruel! been content to seize
Hairs less in sight, or any hairs but these!"

## CANTO V

She said: the pitying audience melt in tears.
But fate and Jove had stopp'd the baron's ears.
In vain Thalestris with reproach assails,
For who can move when fair Belinda fails?
Not half so fixed the Trojan could remain,
While Anna begg'd and Dido raged in vain.
Then grave Clarissa graceful waved her fan;
Silence ensued, and thus the nymph began.

"Say why are beauties praised and honoured most,
The wise man's passion, and the vain man's toast?
Why decked with all that land and sea afford,
Why Angels called, and Angel-like adored?
Why round our coaches crowd the white-gloved beaux,
Why bows the side-box from its inmost rows;
How vain are all these glories, all our pains,
Unless good sense preserve what beauty gains:
That men may say, when we the front-box grace:
'Behold the first in virtue as in face!'
Oh! if to dance all night, and dress all day,
Charmed the small-pox, or chased old-age away;
Who would not scorn what housewife's cares produce,
Or who would learn one earthly thing of use?
To patch, nay ogle, might become a saint,
Nor could it sure be such a sin to paint,
But since, alas! frail beauty must decay,
Curled or uncurled, since locks will turn to grey;
Since painted, or not painted, all shall fade,
And she who scorns a man, must die a maid;
What then remains but well our pow'r to use,
And keep good-humour still whate'er we lose?
And trust me, dear! good-humour can prevail,
When airs, and flights, and screams, and scolding fail.
Beauties in vain their pretty eyes may roll;
Charms strike the sight, but merit wins the soul."

So spoke the dame, but no applause ensued;
Belinda frowned, Thalestris called her prude.

"To arms, to arms!" the fierce virago cries,
And swift as lightning to the combat flies.
All side in parties, and begin th' attack;
Fans clap, silks rustle, and tough whalebones crack;
Heroes' and heroines' shouts confus'dly rise,
And bass, and treble voices strike the skies.
No common weapons in their hands are found,
Like gods they fight, nor dread a mortal wound.

So when bold Homer makes the gods engage,
And heav'nly breasts with human passions rage;
'Gainst Pallas, Mars; Latona, Hermes arms;
And all Olympus rings with loud alarms:
Jove's thunder roars, heav'n trembles all around,
Blue Neptune storms, the bellowing deeps resound:
Earth shakes her nodding tow'rs, the ground gives way,
And the pale ghosts start at the flash of day!

Triumphant Umbriel on a sconce's height
Clapp'd his glad wings, and sate to view the fight:
Propped on their bodkin spears, the sprites survey
The growing combat, or assist the fray.

While thro' the press enraged Thalestris flies,
And scatters death around from both her eyes,
A beau and witling perished in the throng,
One died in metaphor, and one in song.
"O cruel nymph! a living death I bear,"
Cry'd Dapperwit, and sunk beside his chair,
A mournful glance Sir Fopling upwards cast,
"Those eyes are made so killing"—was his last.
Thus on Mæander's flow'ry margin lies
Th' expiring Swan, and as he sings he dies.

When bold Sir Plume had drawn Clarissa down,
Chloe stepp'd in, and kill'd him with a frown;
She smiled to see the doughty hero slain,
But, at her smile, the beau revived again.

Now Jove suspends his golden scales in air,
Weighs the men's wits against the lady's hair;
The doubtful beam long nods from side to side;

At length the wits mount up, the hairs subside.
  See, fierce Belinda on the baron flies,
With more than usual lightning in her eyes:
Nor feared the chief th' unequal fight to try,
Who sought no more than on his foe to die.
But this bold Lord with manly strength endued,
She with one finger and a thumb subdued:
Just where the breath of life his nostrils drew,
A charge of snuff the wily virgin threw;
The gnomes direct, to ev'ry atom just,
The pungent grains of titillating dust.
Sudden, with starting tears each eye o'erflows,
And the high dome re-echoes to his nose.
  Now meet thy fate, incensed Belinda cried,
And drew a deadly bodkin from her side.
(The same, his ancient personage to deck,
Her great great grandsire wore about his neck,
In three seal-rings; which after, melted down,
Formed a vast buckle for his widow's gown:
Her infant grandame's whistle next it grew,
The bells she jingled, and the whistle blew;
Then in a bodkin graced her mother's hairs,
Which long she wore, and now Belinda wears.)
  "Boast not my fall" (he cried) "insulting foe!
Thou by some other shalt be laid as low,
Nor think, to die dejects my lofty mind:
All that I dread is leaving you behind!
Rather than so, ah let me still survive,
And burn in Cupid's flames—but burn alive."
  "Restore the lock!" she cries; and all around
"Restore the lock!" the vaulted roofs rebound.
Not fierce Othello in so loud a strain
Roared for the handkerchief that caused his pain.
But see how oft ambitious aims are crossed,
And chiefs contend 'till all the prize is lost!
The lock, obtained with guilt, and kept with pain,
In ev'ry place is sought, but sought in vain:

With such a prize no mortal must be blest,
So heav'n decrees! with heav'n who can contest?
    Some thought it mounted to the Lunar sphere,
Since all things lost on earth are treasur'd there.
There Hero's wits are kept in pond'rous vases,
And beau's in snuff-boxes and tweezer-cases.
There broken vows and death-bed alms are found,
And lovers' hearts with ends of riband bound,
The courtier's promises, and sick man's pray'rs,
The smiles of harlots, and the tears of heirs,
Cages for gnats, and chains to yoke a flea,
Dried butterflies, and tomes of casuistry.
    But trust the muse—she saw it upward rise,
Tho' mark'd by none but quick, poetic eyes:
(So Rome's great founder to the heav'ns withdrew,
To Proculus alone confess'd in view)
A sudden star, it shot thro' liquid air,
And drew behind a radiant trail of hair.
Not Berenice's locks first rose so bright,
The heav'ns bespangling with dishevelled light.
The sylphs behold it kindling as it flies,
And pleased pursue its progress thro' the skies.
    This the beau monde shall from the Mall survey,
And hail with music its propitious ray.
This the blest lover shall for Venus take,
And send up vows from Rosamonda's lake.
This Partridge soon shall view in cloudless skies,
When next he looks thro' Galileo's eyes;
And hence th' egregious wizard shall foredoom
The fate of Louis, and the fall of Rome.
    Then cease, bright nymph! to mourn thy ravished hair,
Which adds new glory to the shining sphere!
Not all the tresses that fair head can boast,
Shall draw such envy as the lock you lost.
For, after all the murders of your eye,
When, after millions slain, yourself shall die:

When those fair suns shall set, as set they must,
And all those tresses shall be laid in dust,
This lock, the muse shall consecrate to fame,
And 'midst the stars inscribe Belinda's name.

# SAMUEL JOHNSON
## (1709–1784)

## The Vanity of Human Wishes

### In Imitation of the Tenth Satire of Juvenal

Let observation, with extensive view,
Survey mankind, from China to Peru;
Remark each anxious toil, each eager strife,
And watch the busy scenes of crowded life;
Then say, how hope and fear, desire and hate
O'erspread with snares the clouded maze of fate;
Where wav'ring man, betray'd by vent'rous pride
To tread the dreary paths, without a guide,
As treach'rous phantoms in the mist delude,
Shuns fancied ills, or chases airy good;
How rarely reason guides the stubborn choice,
Rules the bold hand, or prompts the suppliant voice;
How nations sink, by darling schemes oppress'd,
When vengeance listens to the fool's request.
Fate wings with ev'ry wish th' afflictive dart,
Each gift of nature, and each grace of art;
With fatal heat impetuous courage glows,
With fatal sweetness elocution flows,
Impeachment stops the speaker's pow'rful breath,
And restless fire precipitates on death.
    But, scarce observ'd, the knowing and the bold
Fall in the gen'ral massacre of gold;
Wide wasting pest! that rages unconfin'd,
And crowds with crimes the records of mankind;
For gold his sword the hireling ruffian draws,

For gold the hireling judge distorts the laws;
Wealth heap'd on wealth, nor truth nor safety buys,
The dangers gather as the treasures rise.
   Let hist'ry tell where rival kings command,
And dubious title shakes the madded land,
When statutes glean the refuse of the sword,
How much more safe the vassal than the lord;
Low sculks the hind beneath the rage of power,
And leaves the wealthy traitor in the Tower,
Untouch'd his cottage, and his slumbers sound,
Though confiscation's vultures hover round.
   The needy traveller, serene and gay,
Walks the wild heath, and sings his toil away.
Does envy seize thee? crush th' upbraiding joy;
Increase his riches, and his peace destroy;
Now fears, in dire vicissitude, invade,
The rustling brake alarms, and quiv'ring shade;
Nor light nor darkness bring his pain relief,
One shows the plunder, and one hides the thief.
   Yet still one gen'ral cry the skies assails,
And gain and grandeur load the tainted gales:
Few know the toiling statesman's fear or care,
Th' insidious rival, and the gaping heir.
Once more, Democritus, arise on earth,
With cheerful wisdom and instructive mirth,
See motley life in modern trappings dress'd,
And feed with varied fools th' eternal jest:
Thou, who could'st laugh where want enchain'd caprice,
Toil crush'd conceit, and man was of a piece;
Where wealth, unlov'd, without a mourner died;
And scarce a sycophant was fed by pride;
Where ne'er was known the form of mock debate,
Or seen a new-made mayor's unwieldy state;
Where change of fav'rites made no change of laws,
And senates heard, before they judg'd a cause;
How would'st thou shake at Britain's modish tribe,
Dart the quick taunt, and edge the piercing gibe?

Attentive truth and nature to descry,
And pierce each scene with philosophick eye;
To thee were solemn toys, or empty show,
The robes of pleasure, and the veils of woe:
All aid the farce, and all thy mirth maintain,
Whose joys are causeless, or whose griefs are vain.

    Such was the scorn that fill'd the sage's mind,
Renew'd at ev'ry glance on human kind;
How just that scorn, ere yet thy voice declare,
Search ev'ry state, and canvass ev'ry pray'r.

    Unnumber'd suppliants crowd preferment's gate,
Athirst for wealth, and burning to be great;
Delusive fortune hears th' incessant call,
They mount, they shine, evaporate, and fall.
On ev'ry stage the foes of peace attend,
Hate dogs their flight, and insult mocks their end.
Love ends with hope, the sinking statesman's door
Pours in the morning worshipper no more;
For growing names the weekly scribbler lies,
To growing wealth the dedicator flies;
From ev'ry room descends the painted face,
That hung the bright palladium of the place;
And, smok'd in kitchens, or in auctions sold,
To better features yields the frame of gold;
For now no more we trace in ev'ry line
Heroick worth, benevolence divine:
The form, distorted, justifies the fall,
And detestation rids th' indignant wall.

    But will not Britain hear the last appeal,
Sign her foes' doom, or guard her fav'rites' zeal?
Through freedom's sons no more remonstrance rings,
Degrading nobles and controling kings;
Our supple tribes repress their patriot throats,
And ask no questions but the price of votes;
With weekly libels and septennial ale,
Their wish is full to riot and to rail.

In full-blown dignity, see Wolsey stand,
Law in his voice, and fortune in his hand;
To him the church, the realm their pow'rs consign,
Through him the rays of regal bounty shine;
Turn'd by his nod the stream of honour flows,
His smile alone security bestows.
Still to new heights his restless wishes tow'r,
Claim leads to claim, and pow'r advances pow'r;
Till conquest, unresisted, ceas'd to please,
And rights, submitted, left him none to seize.
At length his sov'reign frowns—the train of state
Mark the keen glance, and watch the sign to hate.
Where'er he turns, he meets a stranger's eye,
His suppliants scorn him, and his followers fly;
Now drops, at once, the pride of awful state,
The golden canopy, the glitt'ring plate,
The regal palace, the luxurious board,
The liv'ried army, and the menial lord.
With age, with cares, with maladies oppress'd,
He seeks the refuge of monastick rest:
Grief aids disease, remember'd folly stings,
And his last sighs reproach the faith of kings.
    Speak thou, whose thoughts at humble peace repine,
Shall Wolsey's wealth, with Wolsey's end, be thine?
Or liv'st thou now, with safer pride content,
The wisest justice on the banks of Trent?
For, why did Wolsey, near the steeps of fate,
On weak foundations raise th' enormous weight?
Why but to sink beneath misfortune's blow,
With louder ruin to the gulfs below?
    What gave great Villiers to th' assassin's knife,
And fix'd disease on Harley's closing life?
What murder'd Wentworth, and what exil'd Hyde,
By kings protected, and to kings allied?
What but their wish indulg'd in courts to shine,
And pow'r too great to keep, or to resign?

When first the college rolls receive his name,
The young enthusiast quits his ease for fame;
Through all his veins the fever of renown
Spreads from the strong contagion of the gown;
O'er Bodley's dome his future labours spread,
And Bacon's mansion trembles o'er his head.
Are these thy views? Proceed, illustrious youth,
And virtue guard thee to the throne of truth!
Yet, should thy soul indulge the gen'rous heat
Till captive science yields her last retreat;
Should reason guide thee with her brightest ray,
And pour on misty doubt resistless day;
Should no false kindness lure to loose delight,
Nor praise relax, nor difficulty fright;
Should tempting novelty thy cell refrain,
And sloth effuse her opiate fumes in vain;
Should beauty blunt on fops her fatal dart,
Nor claim the triumph of a letter'd heart;
Should no disease thy torpid veins invade,
Nor melancholy's phantoms haunt thy shade;
Yet hope not life, from grief or danger free,
Nor think the doom of man revers'd for thee:
Deign on the passing world to turn thine eyes,
And pause awhile from letters, to be wise;
There mark what ills the scholar's life assail,
Toil, envy, want, the patron, and the gaol.
See nations, slowly wise and meanly just,
To buried merit raise the tardy bust.
If dreams yet flatter, once again attend,
Hear Lydiat's life, and Galileo's end.
   Nor deem, when learning her last prize bestows,
The glitt'ring eminence exempt from woes;
See, when the vulgar scape, despis'd or aw'd,
Rebellion's vengeful talons seize on Laud.
From meaner minds though smaller fines content,
The plunder'd palace, or sequester'd rent;

Mark'd out by dang'rous parts, he meets the shock,
And fatal learning leads him to the block:
Around his tomb let art and genius weep,
But hear his death, ye blockheads, hear and sleep.

    The festal blazes, the triumphal show,
The ravish'd standard, and the captive foe,
The senate's thanks, the gazette's pompous tale,
With force resistless o'er the brave prevail.
Such bribes the rapid Greek o'er Asia whirl'd;
For such the steady Romans shook the world;
For such, in distant lands, the Britons shine,
And stain with blood the Danube or the Rhine;
This pow'r has praise, that virtue scarce can warm,
Till fame supplies the universal charm.
Yet reason frowns on war's unequal game,
Where wasted nations raise a single name;
And mortgag'd states, their grandsires' wreaths regret,
From age to age in everlasting debt;
Wreaths which, at last, the dear-bought right convey
To rust on medals, or on stones decay.

    On what foundation stands the warriour's pride,
How just his hopes, let Swedish Charles decide;
A frame of adamant, a soul of fire,
No dangers fright him, and no labours tire;
O'er love, o'er fear, extends his wide domain,
Unconquer'd lord of pleasure and of pain;
No joys to him pacifick sceptres yield,
War sounds the trump, he rushes to the field;
Behold surrounding kings their pow'rs combine,
And one capitulate, and one resign;
Peace courts his hand, but spreads her charms in vain;
"Think nothing gain'd," he cries, "till nought remain,
On Moscow's walls till Gothick standards fly,
And all be mine beneath the polar sky."
The march begins in military state,
And nations on his eye suspended wait;

Stern famine guards the solitary coast,
And winter barricades the realm of frost;
He comes, nor want nor cold his course delay;—
Hide, blushing glory, hide Pultowa's day:
The vanquish'd hero leaves his broken bands,
And shows his miseries in distant lands;
Condemn'd a needy supplicant to wait,
While ladies interpose, and slaves debate.
But did not chance, at length, her errour mend?
Did no subverted empire mark his end?
Did rival monarchs give the fatal wound?
Or hostile millions press him to the ground?
His fall was destin'd to a barren strand,
A petty fortress, and a dubious hand;
He left the name, at which the world grew pale,
To point a moral, or adorn a tale.

    All times their scenes of pompous woes afford,
From Persia's tyrant to Bavaria's lord.
In gay hostility and barb'rous pride,
With half mankind embattl'd at his side,
Great Xerxes comes to seize the certain prey,
And starves exhausted regions in his way;
Attendant flatt'ry counts his myriads o'er,
Till counted myriads sooth his pride no more;
Fresh praise is try'd till madness fires his mind,
The waves he lashes, and enchains the wind,
New pow'rs are claimed, new pow'rs are still bestow'd,
Till rude resistance lops the spreading god;
The daring Greeks deride the martial show,
And heap their valleys with the gaudy foe;
Th' insulted sea, with humbler thoughts, he gains;
A single skiff to speed his flight remains;
Th' incumber'd oar scarce leaves the dreaded coast
Through purple billows and a floating host.

    The bold Bavarian, in a luckless hour,
Tries the dread summits of Cæsarean pow'r,

With unexpected legions bursts away,
And sees defenceless realms receive his sway;—
Short sway! fair Austria spreads her mournful charms,
The queen, the beauty, sets the world in arms;
From hill to hill the beacon's rousing blaze
Spreads wide the hope of plunder and of praise;
The fierce Croatian, and the wild Hussar,
With all the sons of ravage, crowd the war;
The baffled prince, in honour's flatt'ring bloom
Of hasty greatness, finds the fatal doom,
His foes' derision, and his subjects' blame,
And steals to death from anguish and from shame.
    Enlarge my life with multitude of days!
In health, in sickness, thus the suppliant prays;
Hides from himself his state, and shuns to know,
That life protracted is protracted woe.
Time hovers o'er, impatient to destroy,
And shuts up all the passages of joy;
In vain their gifts the bounteous seasons pour,
The fruit autumnal, and the vernal flow'r;
With listless eyes the dotard views the store,
He views, and wonders that they please no more;
Now pall the tasteless meats, and joyless wines,
And luxury with sighs her slave resigns.
Approach, ye minstrels, try the soothing strain,
Diffuse the tuneful lenitives of pain:
No sounds, alas! would touch th' impervious ear,
Though dancing mountains witness'd Orpheus near;
Nor lute nor lyre his feeble pow'rs attend,
Nor sweeter musick of a virtuous friend;
But everlasting dictates crowd his tongue,
Perversely grave, or positively wrong.
The still returning tale, and ling'ring jest,
Perplex the fawning niece and pamper'd guest,
While growing hopes scarce awe the gath'ring sneer,
And scarce a legacy can bribe to hear;

The watchful guests still hint the last offence;
The daughter's petulance, the son's expense,
Improve his heady rage with treach'rous skill,
And mould his passions till they make his will.

Unnumber'd maladies his joints invade,
Lay siege to life, and press the dire blockade;
But unextinguished av'rice still remains,
And dreaded losses aggravate his pains;
He turns, with anxious heart and crippled hands,
His bonds of debt, and mortgages of lands;
Or views his coffers with suspicious eyes,
Unlocks his gold, and counts it till he dies.

But grant, the virtues of a temp'rate prime
Bless with an age exempt from scorn or crime;
An age that melts with unperceiv'd decay,
And glides in modest innocence away;
Whose peaceful day benevolence endears,
Whose night congratulating conscience cheers;
The gen'ral fav'rite as the gen'ral friend;
Such age there is, and who shall wish its end?

Yet e'en on this her load misfortune flings,
To press the weary minutes' flagging wings;
New sorrow rises as the day returns,
A sister sickens, or a daughter mourns.
Now kindred merit fills the sable bier,
Now lacerated friendship claims a tear;
Year chases year, decay pursues decay,
Still drops some joy from with'ring life away;
New forms arise, and diff'rent views engage,
Superfluous lags the vet'ran on the stage,
Till pitying nature signs the last release,
And bids afflicted worth retire to peace.

But few there are whom hours like these await,
Who set unclouded in the gulfs of fate.
From Lydia's monarch should the search descend,
By Solon caution'd to regard his end,

In life's last scene what prodigies surprise,
Fears of the brave, and follies of the wise!
From Marlb'rough's eyes the streams of dotage flow,
And Swift expires a driv'ller and a show.

    The teeming mother, anxious for her race,
Begs for each birth the fortune of a face;
Yet Vane could tell what ills from beauty spring;
And Sedley curs'd the form that pleas'd a king.
Ye nymphs of rosy lips and radiant eyes,
Whom pleasure keeps too busy to be wise;
Whom joys with soft varieties invite,
By day the frolick, and the dance by night;
Who frown with vanity, who smile with art,
And ask the latest fashion of the heart;
What care, what rules, your heedless charms shall save,
Each nymph your rival, and each youth your slave?
Against your fame with fondness hate combines,
The rival batters, and the lover mines.
With distant voice neglected virtue calls,
Less heard and less, the faint remonstrance falls;
Tir'd with contempt, she quits the slipp'ry reign,
And pride and prudence take her seat in vain.
In crowd at once, where none the pass defend,
The harmless freedom, and the private friend.
The guardians yield, by force superiour ply'd:
To int'rest, prudence; and to flatt'ry, pride.
Here beauty falls, betray'd, despis'd, distress'd,
And hissing infamy proclaims the rest.

    Where then shall hope and fear their objects find?
Must dull suspense corrupt the stagnant mind?
Must helpless man, in ignorance sedate,
Roll darkling down the torrent of his fate?
Must no dislike alarm, no wishes rise,
No cries invoke the mercies of the skies?
Inquirer, cease; petitions yet remain
Which heav'n may hear; nor deem religion vain.

Still raise for good the supplicating voice,
But leave to heav'n the measure and the choice.
Safe in his pow'r, whose eyes discern afar
The secret ambush of a specious pray'r;
Implore his aid, in his decisions rest,
Secure, whate'er he gives, he gives the best.
Yet, when the sense of sacred presence fires,
And strong devotion to the skies aspires,
Pour forth thy fervours for a healthful mind,
Obedient passions, and a will resign'd;
For love, which scarce collective man can fill;
For patience, sov'reign o'er transmuted ill;
For faith, that, panting for a happier seat,
Counts death kind nature's signal of retreat:
These goods for man the laws of heav'n ordain;
These goods he grants, who grants the pow'r to gain;
With these celestial wisdom calms the mind,
And makes the happiness she does not find.

# THOMAS GRAY
## (1716–1771)

## Elegy Written in a Country Church-Yard

The Curfew tolls the knell of parting day,
  The lowing herd wind slowly o'er the lea,
The plowman homeward plods his weary way,
  And leaves the world to darkness and to me.

Now fades the glimmering landscape on the sight,
  And all the air a solemn stillness holds,
Save where the beetle wheels his droning flight,
  And drowsy tinklings lull the distant folds:

Save that from yonder ivy-mantled tow'r
  The mopeing owl does to the moon complain
Of such as, wand'ring near her secret bow'r,
  Molest her ancient solitary reign.

Beneath those rugged elms, that yew-tree's shade,
  Where heaves the turf in many a mould'ring heap,
Each in his narrow cell for ever laid,
  The rude Forefathers of the hamlet sleep.

The breezy call of incense-breathing Morn,
  The swallow twitt'ring from the straw-built shed,
The cock's shrill clarion, or the echoing horn,
  No more shall rouse them from their lowly bed.

For them no more the blazing hearth shall burn,
   Or busy housewife ply her evening care:
No children run to lisp their sire's return,
   Or climb his knees the envied kiss to share.

Oft did the harvest to their sickle yield,
   Their furrow oft the stubborn glebe has broke:
How jocund did they drive their team afield!
   How bow'd the woods beneath their sturdy stroke!

Let not Ambition mock their useful toil,
   Their homely joys, and destiny obscure;
Nor Grandeur hear with a disdainful smile
   The short and simple annals of the poor.

The boast of heraldry, the pomp of pow'r,
   And all that beauty, all that wealth e'er gave,
Awaits alike th' inevitable hour.
   The paths of glory lead but to the grave.

Nor you, ye Proud, impute to These the fault,
   If Mem'ry o'er their Tomb no Trophies raise,
Where through the long-drawn isle and fretted vault
   The pealing anthem swells the note of praise.

Can storied urn or animated bust
   Back to its mansion call the fleeting breath?
Can Honour's voice provoke the silent dust,
   Or Flatt'ry soothe the dull cold ear of death?

Perhaps in this neglected spot is laid
   Some heart once pregnant with celestial fire;
Hands, that the rod of empire might have sway'd,
   Or wak'd to extasy the living lyre.

But Knowledge to their eyes her ample page
   Rich with the spoils of time did ne'er unroll;
Chill Penury repress'd their noble rage,
   And froze the genial current of the soul.

Full many a gem of purest ray serene,
   The dark unfathom'd caves of ocean bear:
Full many a flower is born to blush unseen,
   And waste its sweetness on the desert air.

Some village-Hampden that with dauntless breast
   The little Tyrant of his fields withstood,
Some mute inglorious Milton here may rest,
   Some Cromwell guiltless of his country's blood.

Th' applause of list'ning senates to command,
   The threats of pain and ruin to despise,
To scatter plenty o'er a smiling land,
   And read their hist'ry in a nation's eyes,

Their lot forbad: nor circumscrib'd alone
   Their growing virtues, but their crimes confin'd;
Forbad to wade through slaughter to a throne,
   And shut the gates of mercy on mankind,

The struggling pangs of conscious truth to hide,
   To quench the blushes of ingenuous shame,
Or heap the shrine of Luxury and Pride
   With incense kindled at the Muse's flame.

Far from the madding crowd's ignoble strife,
   Their sober wishes never learn'd to stray;
Along the cool sequester'd vale of life
   They kept the noiseless tenor of their way.

Yet ev'n these bones from insult to protect
   Some frail memorial still erected nigh,
With uncouth rhimes and shapeless sculpture deck'd,
   Implores the passing tribute of a sigh.

Their name, their years, spelt by th' unletter'd muse,
   The place of fame and elegy supply:
And many a holy text around she strews,
   That teach the rustic moralist to die.

For who to dumb Forgetfulness a prey,
   This pleasing anxious being e'er resign'd,
Left the warm precincts of the chearful day,
   Nor cast one longing ling'ring look behind?

On some fond breast the parting soul relies,
   Some pious drops the closing eye requires;
E'en from the tomb the voice of Nature cries,
   E'en in our Ashes live their wonted Fires.

For thee, who mindful of th' unhonour'd Dead,
   Dost in these lines their artless tale relate;
If chance, by lonely contemplation led,
   Some kindred Spirit shall inquire thy fate,—

Haply some hoary-headed Swain may say,
   "Oft have we seen him at the peep of dawn
Brushing with hasty steps the dews away
   To meet the sun upon the upland lawn.

"There at the foot of yonder nodding beech,
   That wreathes its old fantastic roots so high,
His listless length at noontide would he stretch,
   And pore upon the brook that babbles by.

"Hard by yon wood, now smiling as in scorn,
  Mutt'ring his wayward fancies he would rove,
Now drooping, woeful-wan, like one forlorn,
  Or craz'd with care, or cross'd in hopeless love.

"One morn I miss'd him on the custom'd hill,
  Along the heath, and near his fav'rite tree;
Another came; nor yet beside the rill,
  Nor up the lawn, nor at the wood was he:

"The next, with dirges due in sad array
  Slow thro' the church-way path we saw him born.
Approach and read (for thou cans't read) the lay,
  Grav'd on the stone beneath yon aged thorn."

### THE EPITAPH

*Here rests his head upon the lap of Earth*
  *A Youth, to Fortune and to Fame unknown.*
*Fair Science frown'd not on his humble birth,*
  *And Melancholy mark'd him for her own.*

*Large was his bounty, and his soul sincere,*
  *Heav'n did a recompence as largely send:*
*He gave to Mis'ry all he had, a tear,*
  *He gain'd from Heav'n ('twas all he wish'd) a friend.*

*No farther seek his merits to disclose,*
  *Or draw his frailties from their dread abode,*
*(There they alike in trembling hope repose,)*
  *The bosom of his Father and his God.*

# ROBERT BURNS
## (1759–1796)

## To a Mouse

*On Turning up Her Nest with the Plough,*
*November 1785*

Wee, sleekit, cowrin, tim'rous beastie,
O, what a panic's in thy breastie!
Thou need na start awa sae hasty,
    Wi' bickering brattle!
I wad be laith to rin an' chase thee,
    Wi' murd'ring pattle!

I'm truly sorry man's dominion,
Has broken nature's social union,
An' justifies that ill opinion,
    Which makes thee startle
At me, thy poor, earth-born companion,
    An' fellow-mortal!

I doubt na, whiles, but thou may thieve;
What then? poor beastie, thou maun live!
A daimen icker in a thrave
    'S a sma' request;
I'll get a blessin wi' the lave,
    An' never miss't!

Thy wee bit housie, too, in ruin!
It's silly wa's the win's are strewin!
An' naething, now, to big a new ane,
          O' foggage green!
An' bleak December's winds ensuin,
            Baith snell an' keen!

Thou saw the fields laid bare an' waste,
An' weary winter comin fast,
An' cozie here, beneath the blast,
          Thou thought to dwell—
Till crash! the cruel coulter past
           Out thro' thy cell.

That wee bit heap o' leaves an' stibble,
Has cost thee mony a weary nibble!
Now thou's turn'd out, for a' thy trouble,
          But house or hald,
To thole the winter's sleety dribble,
           An' cranreuch cauld!

But Mousie, thou art no thy lane,
In proving foresight may be vain;
The best-laid schemes o' mice an' men
          Gang aft agley,
An' lea'e us nought but grief an' pain,
           For promis'd joy!

Still thou art blest, compar'd wi' me
The present only toucheth thee:
But och! I backward cast my e'e,
          On prospects drear!
An' forward, tho' I canna see,
           I guess an' fear!

# To a Louse

## *On seeing one on a Lady's Bonnet at Church*

Ha! whaur ye gaun, ye crowlin ferlie?
Your impudence protects you sairly;
I canna say but ye strunt rarely,
      Owre gauze and lace;
Tho', faith ! I fear ye dine but sparely
      On sic a place.

Ye ugly, creepin, blastit wonner,
Detested, shunn'd by saunt an' sinner,
How daur ye set your fit upon her—
      Sae fine a lady?
Gae somewhere else and seek your dinner
      On some poor body.

Swith! in some beggar's haffet squattle;
There ye may creep, and sprawl, and sprattle,
Wi' ither kindred, jumping cattle,
      In shoals and nations;
Whaur horn nor bane ne'er daur unsettle
      Your thick plantations.

Now haud you there, ye're out o' sight,
Below the fatt'rels, snug and tight;
Na, faith ye yet! ye'll no be right,
      Till ye've got on it—
The verra tapmost, tow'rin height
      O' Miss's bonnet.

My sooth! right bauld ye set your nose out,
As plump an' grey as ony groset:
O for some rank, mercurial rozet,
      Or fell, red smeddum,
I'd gie you sic a hearty dose o't,
      Wad dress your droddum.

I wad na been surpris'd to spy
You on an auld wife's flainen toy;
Or aiblins some bit duddie boy,
      On's wyliecoat;
But Miss's fine Lunardi! fye!
      How daur ye do't?

O Jeany, dinna toss your head,
An' set your beauties a' abread!
Ye little ken what cursed speed
      The blastie's makin:
Thae winks an' finger-ends, I dread,
      Are notice takin.

O wad some Power the giftie gie us
To see oursels as ithers see us!
It wad frae mony a blunder free us,
      An' foolish notion:
What airs in dress an' gait wad lea'e us,
      An' ev'n devotion!

## A Red, Red Rose

O my Luve's like a red, red rose,
  That's newly sprung in June:
O my Luve's like the melodie,
  That's sweetly play'd in tune.

As fair art thou, my bonie lass,
  So deep in luve am I;
And I will luve thee still, my dear,
  Till a' the seas gang dry.

Till a' the seas gang dry, my dear,
  And the rocks melt wi' the sun;
And I will luve thee still, my dear,
  While the sands o' life shall run.

And fare-thee-weel, my only Luve!
And fare-thee-weel, a while!
And I will come again, my Luve,
Tho' 'twere ten thousand mile!

---

# Tam O' Shanter

## A Tale

"Of Brownyis and of Bogillis full is this Buke."
—GAWIN DOUGLAS

When chapman billies leave the street,
And drouthy neibors, neibors meet;
As market days are wearing late,
And folk begin to tak the gate,
While we sit bousing at the nappy,
An' getting fou and unco happy,
We think na on the lang Scots miles,
The mosses, waters, slaps and stiles,
That lie between us and our hame,
Where sits our sulky, sullen dame,
Gathering her brows like gathering storm,
Nursing her wrath to keep it warm.

    This truth fand honest TAM O' SHANTER,
As he frae Ayr ae night did canter:
(Auld Ayr, wham ne'er a town surpasses,
For honest men and bonie lasses).

    O Tam! had'st thou but been sae wise,
As taen thy ain wife Kate's advice!
She tauld thee weel thou was a skellum,
A blethering, blustering, drunken blellum;
That frae November till October,
Ae market-day thou was na sober;
That ilka melder wi' the Miller,

Thou sat as lang as thou had siller;
That ev'ry naig was ca'd a shoe on
The Smith and thee gat roarin fou on;
That at the L—d's house, ev'n on Sunday,
Thou drank wi' Kirkton Jean till Monday,
She prophesied that late or soon,
Thou wad be found, deep drown'd in Doon,
Or catch'd wi' warlocks in the mirk,
By Alloway's auld, haunted kirk

Ah, gentle dames! it gars me greet,
To think how mony counsels sweet,
How mony lengthen'd, sage advices,
The husband frae the wife despises!

But to our tale:—Ae market night,
Tam had got planted unco right,
Fast by an ingle, bleezing finely,
Wi reaming swats that drank divinely;
And at his elbow, Souter Johnie,
His ancient, trusty, drouthy crony;
Tam lo'ed him like a very brither;
They had been fou for weeks thegither.
The night drave on wi' sangs an' clatter;
And aye the ale was growing better:
The Landlady and Tam grew gracious,
Wi' favours secret, sweet and precious:
The Souter tauld his queerest stories;
The Landlord's laugh was ready chorus:
The storm without might rair and rustle,
Tam did na mind the storm a whistle.

Care, mad to see a man sae happy,
E'en drown'd himsel amang the nappy.
As bees flee hame wi' lades o' treasure,
The minutes wing'd their way wi' pleasure:
Kings may be blest, but Tam was glorious,
O'er a' the ills o' life victorious!

But pleasures are like poppies spread,
You seize the flow'r, its bloom is shed;
Or like the snow falls in the river,
A moment white—then melts for ever;
Or like the Borealis race,
That flit ere you can point their place;
Or like the Rainbow's lovely form
Evanishing amid the storm.—
Nae man can tether Time nor Tide,
The hour approaches Tam maun ride;
That hour, o' night's black arch the key-stane,
That dreary hour he mounts his beast in;
And sic a night he taks the road in,
As ne'er poor sinner was abroad in.

The wind blew as 'twad blawn its last;
The rattling showers rose on the blast;
The speedy gleams the darkness swallow'd;
Loud, deep, and lang the thunder bellow'd:
That night, a child might understand,
The deil had business on his hand.

Weel-mounted on his grey mare Meg,
A better never lifted leg,
Tam skelpit on thro' dub and mire,
Despising wind, and rain, and fire;
Whiles holding fast his gude blue bonnet,
Whiles crooning o'er some auld Scots sonnet,
Whiles glow'rin round wi' prudent cares,
Lest bogles catch him unawares;
Kirk-Alloway was drawing nigh,
Where ghaists and houlets nightly cry.

By this time he was cross the ford,
Where in the snaw the chapman smoor'd;
And past the birks and meikle stane,
Where drunken Charlie brak's neck-bane;

And thro' the whins, and by the cairn,
Where hunters fand the murder'd bairn;
And near the thorn, aboon the well,
Where Mungo's mither hang'd hersel'.
Before him Doon pours all his floods,
The doubling storm roars thro' the woods,
The lightings flash from pole to pole,
Near and more near the thunders roll,
When, glimmering thro' the groaning trees.
Kirk-Alloway seem'd in a bleeze,
Thro' ilka bore the beams were glancing,
And loud resounded mirth and dancing.

Inspiring bold John Barleycorn!
What dangers thou canst make us scorn!
Wi' tippenny, we fear nae evil;
Wi' usquabae, we'll face the devil!
The swats sae ream'd in Tammie's noddle,
Fair play, he car'd na deils a boddle,
But Maggie stood, right sair astonish'd,
Till, by the heel and hand admonish'd,
She ventur'd forward on the light;
And, wow! Tam saw an unco sight!

Warlocks and witches in a dance:
Nae cotillon, brent new frae France,
But hornpipes, jigs, strathspeys, and reels,
Put life and mettle in their heels.
A winnock-bunker in the east,
There sat auld Nick, in shape o' beast;
A towzie tyke, black, grim, and large,
To gie them music was his charge:
He screw'd the pipes and gart them skirl,
Till roof and rafters a' did dirl.—
Coffins stood round, like open presses,
That shaw'd the Dead in their last dresses;
And (by some devilish cantraip sleight)

Each in its cauld hand held a light.
By which heroic Tam was able
To note upon the haly table,
A murderer's banes, in gibbet-airns;
Twa span-lang, wee, unchristened bairns;
A thief, new-cutted frae a rape,
Wi' his last gasp his gab did gape;
Five tomahawks, wi' blude red-rusted:
Five scimitars, wi' murder crusted;
A garter which a babe had strangled:
A knife, a father's throat had mangled.
Whom his ain son of life bereft,
The grey-hairs yet stack to the heft;
Wi' mair of horrible and awfu',
Which even to name wad be unlawfu'.

As Tammie glowr'd, amaz'd, and curious,
The mirth and fun grew fast and furious;
The Piper loud and louder blew,
The dancers quick and quicker flew,
They reel'd, they set, they cross'd, they cleekit,
Till ilka carlin swat and reekit,
And coost her duddies to the wark,
And linkit at it in her sark!

Now Tam, O Tam! had they been queans,
A' plump and strapping in their teens!
Their sarks, instead o' creeshie flainen,
Been snaw-white seventeen hunder linen!—
Thir breeks o' mine, my only pair,
That ance were plush o' guid blue hair,
I wad hae gien them off my hurdies,
For ae blink o' the bonie burdies!
But wither'd beldams, auld and droll,
Rigwoodie hags wad spean a foal,
Louping an' flinging on a crummock,
I wonder did na turn thy stomach.

But Tam kent what was what fu' brawlie:
There was ae winsome wench and waulie
That night enlisted in the core,
Lang after ken'd on Carrick shore;
(For mony a beast to dead she shot,
And perish'd mony a bonie boat,
And shook baith meikle corn and bear,
And kept the country-side in fear);
Her cutty sark, o' Paisley harn,
That while a lassie she had worn,
In longitude tho' sorely scanty,
It was her best, and she was vauntie.
Ah! little ken'd thy reverend grannie,
That sark she coft for her wee Nannie,
Wi' twa pund Scots ('twas a' her riches),
Wad ever grac'd a dance of witches!

But here my Muse her wing maun cour,
Sic flights are far beyond her power;
To sing how Nannie lap and flang,
(A souple jade she was and strang),
And how Tam stood, like ane bewitch'd,
And thought his very een enrich'd:
Even Satan glowr'd, and fidg'd fu' fain,
And hotch'd and blew wi' might and main:
Till first ae caper, syne anither,
Tam tint his reason a' thegither,
And roars out, "Weel done, Cutty-sark!"
And in an instant all was dark:
And scarcely had he Maggie rallied,
When out the hellish legion sallied.

As bees bizz out wi' angry fyke,
When plundering herds assail their byke;
As open pussie's mortal foes,
When, pop! she starts before their nose;
As eager runs the market-crowd,

When "Catch the thief!" resounds aloud;
So Maggie runs, the witches follow,
Wi' mony an eldritch skreich and hollow.

    Ah, Tam! Ah, Tam! thou'll get thy fairin!
In hell, they'll roast thee like a herrin!
In vain thy Kate awaits thy comin!
Kate soon will be a woefu' woman!
Now, do thy speedy-utmost, Meg,
And win the key-stone o' the brig;
There, at them thou thy tail may toss,
A running stream they dare na cross.
But ere the keystane she could make,
The fient a tail she had to shake!
For Nannie, far before the rest,
Hard upon noble Maggie prest,
And flew at Tam wi' furious ettle;
But little wist she Maggie's mettle!
Ae spring brought off her master hale,
But left behind her ain grey tail:
The carlin claught her by the rump,
And left poor Maggie scarce a stump.

    Now, wha this tale o' truth shall read,
Ilk man, and mother's son, take heed:
Whene'er to Drink you are inclin'd,
Or Cutty-sarks rin in your mind,
Think ye may buy the joys o'er dear;
Remember Tam o' Shanter's mare.

# WILLIAM BLAKE
## (1757–1827)

## SONGS OF INNOCENCE

### Introduction

Piping down the valleys wild,
Piping songs of pleasant glee,
On a cloud I saw a child,
And he laughing said to me:—

"Pipe a song about a lamb":
So I piped with merry cheer.
"Piper, pipe that song again":
So I piped; he wept to hear.

"Drop thy pipe, thy happy pipe,
Sing thy songs of happy cheer":
So I sung the same again,
While he wept with joy to hear.

"Piper, sit thee down and write
In a book that all may read—"
So he vanish'd from my sight;
And I pluck'd a hollow reed,

And I made a rural pen,
And I stain'd the water clear,
And I wrote my happy songs
Every child may joy to hear.

## The Shepherd

How sweet is the shepherd's sweet lot;
From the morn to the evening he strays;
He shall follow his sheep all the day,
And his tongue shall be filled with praise.

For he hears the lambs' innocent call,
And he hears the ewes' tender reply;
He is watchful while they are in peace,
For they know when their shepherd is nigh.

## The Echoing Green

The sun does arise
And make happy the skies;
The merry bells ring
To welcome the spring;
The skylark and thrush,
The birds of the bush,
Sing louder around
To the bells' cheerful sound,
While our sports shall be seen
On the echoing green.

Old John with white hair
Does laugh away care,
Sitting under the oak
Among the old folk.
They laugh at our play,
And soon they all say:
"Such, such were the joys
When we, all girls and boys,
In our youth-time were seen
On the echoing green."

Till the little ones, weary,
No more can be merry;
The sun does descend,
And our sports have an end.
Round the laps of their mothers
Many sisters and brothers,
Like birds in their nest,
Are ready for rest;
And sport no more seen
On the darkening green.

## The Lamb

Little lamb, who made thee?
Dost thou know who made thee,
Gave thee life and bid thee feed
By the stream and o'er the mead;
Gave thee clothing of delight,
Softest clothing, woolly, bright;
Gave thee such a tender voice
Making all the vales rejoice;
 Little lamb, who made thee?
 Dost thou know who made thee?

Little lamb, I'll tell thee,
Little lamb, I'll tell thee.
He is called by thy name,
For he calls himself a Lamb:
He is meek and he is mild,
He became a little child.
I a child and thou a lamb,
We are called by his name.
 Little lamb, God bless thee,
 Little lamb, God bless thee.

# The Little Black Boy

My mother bore me in the southern wild,
And I am black, but oh! my soul is white;
White as an angel is the English child,
But I am black, as if bereaved of light.

My mother taught me underneath a tree,
And sitting down before the heat of day,
She took me on her lap, and kissed me,
And, pointing to the east, began to say:—

"Look on the rising sun,—there God does live,
And gives his light, and gives his heat away;
And flowers, and trees, and beast, and men receive
Comfort in morning, joy in the noon-day.

"And we are put on earth a little space,
That we may learn to bear the beams of love;
And these black bodies and this sun-burnt face
Are but a cloud, and like a shady grove.

"For when our souls have learnt the heat to bear,
The clouds will vanish, we shall hear his voice,
Saying, 'Come out from the grove, my love and care,
And round my golden tent like lambs rejoice.'"

Thus did my mother say, and kissed me;
And thus I say to little English boy,—
"When I from black, and he from white cloud free,
And round the tent of God like lambs we joy,

"I'll shade him from the heat, till he can bear
To lean in joy upon our Father's knee;
And then I'll stand, and stroke his silver hair,
And be like him, and he will then love me."

# The Blossom

Merry, merry sparrow,
Under leaves so green,
    A happy blossom
Sees you, swift as arrow
Seek your cradle narrow
    Near my bosom.

Pretty, pretty robin,
Under leaves so green,
    A happy blossom
Hears you sobbing, sobbing,
Pretty, pretty robin,
    Near my bosom.

# The Chimney-Sweeper

When my mother died I was very young,
And my father sold me while yet my tongue
Could scarcely cry "'weep, 'weep, 'weep, 'weep!"
So your chimneys I sweep and in soot I sleep.

There's little Tom Dacre, who cried when his head,
That curl'd like a lamb's back, was shaved: so I said:
"Hush, Tom, never mind it, for when your head's bare
You know that the soot cannot spoil your white hair."

And so he was quiet; and that very night,
As Tom was a-sleeping, he had such a sight;
That thousands of sweepers, Dick, Joe, Ned, and Jack,
Were all of them lock'd up in coffins of black.

And by came an angel who had a bright key,
And he open'd the coffins and set them all free;
Then down a green plain, leaping, laughing they run,
And wash in a river and shine in the sun.

Then naked and white, all their bags left behind,
They rise upon clouds and sport in the wind;
And the angel told Tom if he'd be a good boy,
He'd have God for his father and never want joy.

And so Tom awoke; and we rose in the dark,
And got with our bags and our brushes to work.
Though the morning was cold Tom was happy and warm:
So if all do their duty they need not fear harm.

## The Little Boy Lost

Father! father! where are you going?
   O, do not walk so fast.
Speak, father, speak to your little boy,
   Or else I shall be lost.

The night was dark, no father was there;
   The child was wet with dew;
The mire was deep and the child did weep,
   And away the vapour flew.

## The Little Boy Found

The little boy lost in the lonely fen,
   Led by the wandering light,
Began to cry; but God, ever nigh,
   Appear'd like his father in white;

He kiss'd the child, and by the hand led,
   And to his mother brought,
Who, in sorrow pale, thro' the lonely dale,
   Her little boy weeping sought.

# A Cradle Song

Sweet dreams, form a shade
O'er my lovely infant's head;
Sweet dreams of pleasant streams
By happy, silent, moony beams.

Sweet sleep, with soft down
Weave thy brows an infant crown.
Sweet sleep, angel mild,
Hover o'er my happy child.

Sweet smiles in the night
Hover over my delight;
Sweet smiles, mother's smiles,
All the livelong night beguiles.

Sweet moans, dove-like sighs,
Chase not slumber from thy eyes.
Sweet moans, sweeter smiles,
All the dove-like moans beguiles.

Sleep, sleep, happy child,
All creation slept and smiled;
Sleep, sleep, happy sleep,
While o'er thee thy mother weep.

Sweet babe, in thy face
Holy image I can trace.
Sweet babe, once like thee
Thy Maker lay and wept for me.

Wept for me, for thee, for all
When he was an infant small.
Thou his image ever see,
Heavenly face that smiles on thee.

Smiles on thee, on me, on all;
Who became an infant small.
Infant smiles are his own smiles;
Heaven and earth to peace beguiles.

## The Divine Image

To mercy, pity, peace, and love
 All pray in their distress;
And to these virtues of delight
 Return their thankfulness.

For mercy, pity, peace, and love
 Is God, our Father dear;
And mercy, pity, peace, and love
 Is man His child and care.

For mercy has a human heart,
 Pity, a human face;
And love, the human form divine,
 And peace, the human dress.

Then every man of every clime
 That prays in his distress,
Prays to the human form divine,
 Love, Mercy, Pity, Peace.

And all must love the human form
 In heathen, Turk, or Jew;
Where mercy, love, and pity dwell,
 There God is dwelling too.

# Holy Thursday

'Twas on a Holy Thursday, their innocent faces clean,
The children walking two and two, in red and blue and green,
Grey-headed beadles walk'd before, with wands as white as snow,
Till into the high dome of Paul's they like Thames' waters flow.

O what a multitude they seem'd, these flowers of London town;
Seated in companies, they sit with radiance all their own.
The hum of multitudes was there, but multitudes of lambs,
Thousands of little boys and girls raising their innocent hands.

Now like a mighty wind they raise to heaven the voice of song,
Or like harmonious thunderings the seats of heaven among.
Beneath them sit the aged men, wise guardians of the poor;
Then cherish pity, lest you drive an angel from your door.

# Night

The sun descending in the west,
The evening star does shine;
The birds are silent in their nest,
And I must seek for mine.
The moon, like a flower,
In heaven's high bower,
With silent delight
Sits and smiles on the night.

Farewell, green fields and happy groves,
Where flocks have took delight;
Where lambs have nibbled, silent moves
The feet of angels bright.
Unseen they pour blessing,
And joy without ceasing,
On each bud and blossom
And each sleeping bosom.

They look in every thoughtless nest,
Where birds are cover'd warm;
They visit caves of every beast,
To keep them all from harm.
If they see any weeping
That should have been sleeping,
They pour sleep on their head,
And sit down by their bed.

When wolves and tigers howl for prey
They pitying stand and weep,
Seeking to drive their thirst away,
And keep them from the sheep.
But if they rush dreadful,
The angels most heedful
Receive each mild spirit,
New worlds to inherit.

And there the lion's ruddy eyes
Shall flow with tears of gold,
And pitying the tender cries,
And walking round the fold,
Saying, "Wrath, by his meekness
And by his health, sickness
Is driven away
From our immortal day.

"And now beside thee, bleating lamb,
I can lie down and sleep;
Or think on him who bore thy name,
Graze after thee, and weep.
For, wash'd in life's river,
My bright mane for ever
Shall shine like the gold
As I guard o'er the fold."

# Spring

Sound the flute!
Now it's mute.
Birds delight
Day and night;
Nightingale
In the dale,
Lark in sky,
Merrily,
Merrily, merrily, to welcome in the year.

Little boy,
Full of joy;
Little girl,
Sweet and small;
Cock does crow,
So do you.
Merry voice,
Infant noise,
Merrily, merrily to welcome in the year.

Little lamb,
Here I am;
Come and lick
My white neck;
Let me pull
Your soft wool;
Let me kiss
Your soft face:
Merrily, merrily, we welcome in the year.

## Nurse's Song

When the voices of children are heard on the green
And laughing is heard on the hill,
My heart is at rest within my breast,
And everything else is still.

Then come home, my children, the sun is gone down,
And the dews of night arise;
Come, come, leave off play, and let us away
Till the morning appears in the skies.

No, no, let us play, for it is yet day,
And we cannot go to sleep;
Besides in the sky the little birds fly,
And the hills are all cover'd with sheep.

Well, well, go and play till the light fades away,
And then go home to bed.
The little ones leap'd and shouted and laugh'd
And all the hills echoed.

## Infant Joy

I have no name,
I am but two days old.
What shall I call thee?
I happy am,
Joy is my name.—
Sweet joy befall thee!

Pretty joy!
Sweet joy but two days old.
Sweet joy I call thee.
Thou dost smile,
I sing the while,
Sweet joy befall thee!

# A Dream

Once a dream did weave a shade
O'er my angel-guarded bed,
That an emmet lost its way
Where on grass methought I lay.

Troubled, wilder'd, and forlorn,
Dark, benighted, travel-worn,
Over many a tangled spray,
All heart-broke I heard her say:

"O my children! do they cry?
Do they hear their father sigh?
Now they look abroad to see,
Now return and weep for me."

Pitying I dropp'd a tear;
But I saw a glow-worm near:
Who replied, "What wailing wight
Calls the watchman of the night?

"I am set to light the ground
While the beetle goes his round:
Follow now the beetle's hum;
Little wanderer, hie thee home."

# Laughing Song

When the green woods laugh with the voice of joy,
And the dimpling stream runs laughing by,
When the air does laugh with our merry wit,
And the green hill laughs with the noise of it;

When the meadows laugh with lively green,
And the grasshopper laughs in the merry scene,
When Mary and Susan and Emily
With their sweet round mouths sing Ha, ha, he!

When the painted birds laugh in the shade,
When our table with cherries and nuts is spread,
Come live and be happy and join with me
To sing the sweet chorus of Ha, ha, he!

## The School-Boy

I love to rise in a summer morn
    When the birds sing on every tree;
The distant huntsman winds his horn,
    And the sky-lark sings with me.
    O! what sweet company.

But to go to school in a summer morn,
    O! it drives all joy away;
Under a cruel eye outworn,
    The little ones spend the day
    In sighing and dismay.

Ah! then at times I drooping sit,
    And spend many an anxious hour;
Nor in my book can I take delight
    Nor sit in learning's bower,
    Worn thro' with the dreary shower.

How can the bird, that is born for joy,
    Sit in a cage and sing?
How can a child, when fears annoy,
    But droop his tender wing,
    And forget his youthful spring?

O father and mother, if buds are nipp'd,
    And blossoms blown away,
And if the tender plants are stripp'd
    Of their joy in the springing day,
    By sorrow and care's dismay,

How shall the summer arise in joy,
   Or the summer fruits appear?
Or how shall we gather what griefs destroy,
   Or bless the mellowing year,
   When the blasts of winter appear?

## On Another's Sorrow

Can I see another's woe,
And not be in sorrow too?
Can I see another's grief,
And not seek for kind relief?

Can I see a falling tear,
And not feel my sorrow's share?
Can a father see his child
Weep, nor be with sorrow fill'd?

Can a mother sit and hear
An infant groan, an infant fear?
No, no, never can it be,
Never, never can it be.

And can he who smiles on all
Hear the wren with sorrows small,
Hear the small bird's grief and care
Hear the woes that infants bear,

And not sit beside the nest,
Pouring pity in their breast;
And not sit the cradle near,
Weeping tear on infant's tear;

And not sit both night and day,
Wiping all our tears away?
O! no, never can it be,
Never, never can it be.

He doth give his joy to all;
He becomes an infant small;
He becomes a man of woe;
He doth feel the sorrow too.

Think not thou canst sigh a sigh
And thy Maker is not by;
Think not thou canst weep a tear
And thy Maker is not near.

O ! he gives to us his joy
That our grief he may destroy:
Till our grief is fled and gone
He doth sit by us and moan.

## The Voice of the Ancient Bard

Youth of delight, come hither,
And see the opening morn,
Image of truth new-born.
Doubt is fled and clouds of reason,
Dark disputes and artful teasing.
Folly is an endless maze,
Tangled roots perplex her ways,
How many have fallen there!
They stumble all night over bones of the dead,
And feel they know not what but care,
And wish to lead others when they should be led.

## Songs of Experience

### Introduction

Hear the voice of the Bard,
Who present, past, and future sees;
Whose ears have heard
The Holy Word
That walk'd among the ancient trees.

Calling the lapsed soul,
And weeping in the evening dew;
That might control
The starry pole,
And fallen, fallen light renew!

O Earth, O Earth, return!
Arise from out the dewy grass;
Night is worn;
And the morn
Rises from the slumbrous mass.

Turn away no more:
Why wilt thou turn away?
The starry floor,
The watery shore,
Is given thee till the break of day.

### Earth's Answer

Earth raised up her head
From the darkness dread and drear.
Her light fled,
Stony dread!
And her locks cover'd with grey despair.

Prison'd on watery shore,
Starry Jealousy does keep my den:
Cold and hoar,
Weeping o'er,
I hear the father of the ancient men.

Selfish father of men,
Cruel, jealous, selfish fear,
Can delight,
Chain'd in night,
The virgins of youth and morning bear?

Does spring hide its joy
When buds and blossoms grow?
Does the sower
Sow by night,
Or the ploughman in darkness plough?

Break this heavy chain
That does freeze my bones around.
Selfish! vain!
Eternal bane!
That free love with bondage bound.

———

## Infant Sorrow

My mother groan'd, my father wept,
Into the dangerous world I leapt;
Helpless, naked, piping loud,
Like a fiend hid in a cloud.

Struggling in my father's hands,
Striving against my swaddling-bands,
Bound and weary, I thought best
To sulk upon my mother's breast.

## My Pretty Rose-Tree

A flower was offer'd to me,
Such a flower as May never bore;
But I said, I've a pretty rose-tree,
And I pass'd the sweet flower o'er.

Then I went to my pretty rose-tree,
To tend her by day and by night;
But my rose turn'd away with jealousy,
And her thorns were my only delight.

## Ah! Sun-Flower

Ah, Sunflower! weary of time,
Who countest the steps of the sun;
Seeking after that sweet golden clime,
Where the traveller's journey is done;

Where the youth pined away with desire,
And the pale virgin shrouded in snow,
Arise from their graves and aspire
Where my sunflower wishes to go.

## The Lily

The modest rose puts forth a thorn,
The humble sheep a threatening horn;
While the lily white shall in love delight,
Nor a thorn nor a threat stain her beauty bright.

# The Sick Rose

O rose, thou art sick:
The invisible worm,
That flies in the night
In the howling storm,

Has found out thy bed
Of crimson joy;
And his dark secret love
Does thy life destroy.

# Nurse's Song

When the voices of children are heard on the green,
    And whisperings are in the dale,
The days of my youth rise fresh in my mind,
    My face turns green and pale.

Then come home, my children, the sun is gone down,
    And the dews of night arise;
Your spring and your day are wasted in play
    And your winter and night in disguise.

# The Clod and the Pebble

Love seeketh not itself to please,
Nor for itself hath any care;
But for another gives its ease,
And builds a heaven in hell's despair.

So sung a little clod of clay,
Trodden with the cattle's feet;
But a pebble of the brook
Warbled out these metres meet:

Love seeketh only self to please,
To bind another to its delight,
Joys in another's loss of ease,
And builds a hell in heaven's despite.

## The Garden of Love

I went to the garden of Love,
And saw what I never had seen:
A Chapel was built in the midst,
Where I used to play on the green.

And the gates of this chapel were shut,
And "Thou shalt not" writ over the door;
So I turn'd to the garden of Love
That so many sweet flowers bore;

And I saw it was filled with graves
And tombstones where flowers should be:
And priests in black gowns were walking their rounds,
And binding with briars my joys and desires.

## The Fly

Little fly,
Thy summer's play
My thoughtless hand
Has brush'd away.

Am not I
A fly like thee?
Or art not thou
A man like me?

For I dance,
And drink, and sing,
Till some blind hand
Shall brush my wing.

If thought is life
And strength and breath,
And the want
Of thought is death;

Then am I
A happy fly,
If I live
Or if I die.

## The Tiger

Tiger, tiger, burning bright
In the forests of the night,
What immortal hand or eye
Could frame thy fearful symmetry?

In what distant deeps or skies
Burnt the fire of thine eyes?
On what wings dare he aspire?
What the hand dare seize the fire?

And what shoulder, and what art,
Could twist the sinews of thy heart
And when thy heart began to beat,
What dread hand? and what dread feet

What the hammer? what the chain?
In what furnace was thy brain?
What the anvil? what dread grasp
Dare its deadly terrors clasp?

When the stars threw down their spears,
And water'd heaven with their tears,
Did he smile his work to see?
Did he who made the lamb make thee?

Tiger, tiger, burning bright
In the forests of the night,
What immortal hand or eye
Dare frame thy fearful symmetry?

## A Little Boy Lost

Nought loves another as itself,
    Nor venerates another so,
Nor is it possible to thought
    A greater than itself to know:

And, father, how can I love you
    Or any of my brothers more?
I love you like the little bird
    That picks up crumbs around the door.

The priest sat by and heard the child,
    In trembling zeal he seized his hair:
He led him by his little coat,
    And all admired the priestly care.

And standing on the altar high:
    "Lo! what a fiend is here!" said he:
"One who sets reason up for judge
    Of our most holy mystery."

The weeping child could not be heard,
    The weeping parents wept in vain;
They stripp'd him to his little shirt
    And bound him in an iron chain;

And burn'd him in a holy place
   Where many had been burn'd before:
The weeping parents wept in vain.
   Are such things done on Albion's shore?

## Holy Thursday

Is this a holy thing to see
   In a rich and fruitful land,
Babes reduced to misery,
   Fed with cold and usurous hand?

Is that trembling cry a song?
   Can it be a song of joy?
And so many children poor?
   It is a land of poverty!

And their sun does never shine,
   And their fields are bleak and bare.
And their ways are fill'd with thorns:
   It is eternal winter there.

For where'er the sun does shine,
   And where'er the rain does fall,
Babe can never hunger there,
   Nor poverty the mind appal.

## The Angel

I dreamt a dream! what can it mean?
And that I was a maiden queen,
Guarded by an angel mild:
Witless woe was ne'er beguiled.

And I wept both night and day,
And he wiped my tears away,
And I wept both day and night,
And hid from him my heart's delight.

So he took his wings and fled;
Then the morn blush'd rosy red;
I dried my tears and arm'd my fears
With ten thousand shields and spears.

Soon my angel came again:
I was arm'd, he came in vain;
For the time of youth was fled,
And grey hairs were on my head.

## The Little Girl Lost

In futurity
I prophetic see
That the earth from sleep
(Grave the sentence deep)

Shall arise and seek
For her maker meek;
And the desert wild
Become a garden mild.

In the southern clime,
Where the summer's prime
Never fades away,
Lovely Lyca lay.

Seven summers old
Lovely Lyca told;
She had wander'd long
Hearing wild birds' song.

Sweet sleep, come to me
Underneath this tree.
Do father, mother weep?
Where can Lyca sleep?

Lost in desert wild
Is your little child.
How can Lyca sleep
If her mother weep?

If her heart does ache,
Then let Lyca wake;
If my mother sleep,
Lyca shall not weep.

Frowning, frowning night,
O'er this desert bright,
Let thy moon arise
While I close my eyes.

Sleeping Lyca lay:
While the beasts of prey,
Come from caverns deep,
View'd the maid asleep.

The kingly lion stood,
And the virgin view'd,
Then he gamboll'd round
O'er the hallow'd ground.

Leopards, tigers play
Round her as she lay,
While the lion old
Bow'd his mane of gold,

And her bosom lick,
And upon her neck
From his eyes of flame
Ruby tears there came.

While the lioness
Loosed her slender dress,
And naked they convey'd
To caves the sleeping maid.

## The Little Girl Found

All the night in woe
Lyca's parents go
Over valleys deep,
While the deserts weep.

Tired and woe-begone,
Hoarse with making moan,
Arm in arm seven days
They traced the desert ways.

Seven nights they sleep
Among shadows deep,
And dream they see their child
Starved in desert wild.

Pale, through pathless ways
The fancied image strays,
Famish'd, weeping, weak,
With hollow piteous shriek.

Rising from unrest
The trembling woman press'd
With feet of weary woe:
She could no further go.

In his arms he bore
Her, arm'd with sorrow sore;
Till before their way
A couching lion lay.

Turning back was vain:
Soon his heavy mane
Bore them to the ground;
Then he stalk'd around,

Smelling to his prey;
But their fears allay
When he licks their hands,
And silent by them stands.

They look upon his eyes
Fill'd with deep surprise;
And, wondering, behold
A spirit arm'd in gold—

On his head a crown;
On his shoulders down
Flow'd his golden hair;
Gone was all their care.

"Follow me," he said;
"Weep not for the maid;
In my palace deep
Lyca lies asleep."

Then they followed
Where the vision led;
And saw their sleeping child
Among tigers wild.

To this day they dwell
In a lonely dell;
Nor fear the wolvish howl,
Nor the lion's growl.

## London

I wander thro' each charter'd street
    Near where the charter'd Thames does flow,
And mark in every face I meet
    Marks of weakness, marks of woe.

In every cry of every man,
    In every infant's cry of fear,
In every voice, in every ban,
    The mind-forged manacles I hear.

How the chimney-sweeper's cry
    Every blackening church appals;
And the hapless soldier's sigh
    Runs in blood down palace-walls.

But most thro' midnight streets I hear
    How the youthful harlot's curse
Blasts the new-born infant's tear,
    And blights with plagues the marriage hearse.

## To Tirzah

Whate'er is born of mortal birth
Must be consumed with the earth,
To rise from generation free:
Then what have I to do with thee?

The sexes sprung from shame and pride
Blow'd in the morn; in evening died.
But mercy changed death into sleep:
The sexes rose to work and weep.

Thou mother of my mortal part
With cruelty didst mould my heart,
And with false, self-deceiving tears
Didst bind my nostrils, eyes and ears;

Didst close my tongue in senseless clay
And me to mortal life betray:
The death of Jesus set me free:
Then what have I to do with thee?

*IT IS RAISED A SPIRITUAL BODY.*

## The Human Abstract

Pity would be no more
If we did not make somebody poor;
And mercy no more could be
If all were as happy as we.

And mutual fear brings peace,
Till the selfish loves increase;
Then cruelty knits a snare
And spreads his baits with care.

He sits down with holy fears,
And waters the ground with tears;
Then humility takes its root
Underneath his foot.

Soon spreads the dismal shade
Of mystery over his head;
And the caterpillar and fly
Feed on the mystery.

And it bears the fruit of deceit,
Ruddy and sweet to eat;
And the raven his nest has made
In its thickest shade.

The gods of the earth and sea
Sought through Nature to find this tree;
But their search was all in vain.
There grows one in the human brain.

## The Chimney-Sweeper

A little black thing among the snow,
   Crying, " 'weep! 'weep!" in notes of woe:
Where are thy father and mother, say?
   —They are both gone up to the church to pray.

Because I was happy upon the heath,
   And smiled among the winter's snow,
They clothed me in the clothes of death,
   And taught me to sing the notes of woe.

And because I am happy, and dance and sing,
   They think they have done me no injury,
And are gone to praise God and his Priest and King
   Who make up a heaven of our misery.

## A Poison-Tree

I was angry with my friend;
I told my wrath, my wrath did end.
I was angry with my foe;
I told it not, my wrath did grow.

And I water'd it in fears,
Night and morning with my tears;
And I sunned it with smiles
And with soft deceitful wiles.

And it grew both day and night,
Till it bore an apple bright;
And my foe beheld it shine,
And he knew that it was mine,

And into my garden stole
When the night had veil'd the pole:
In the morning glad I see
My foe outstretch'd beneath the tree.

## A Little Girl Lost

Children of the future age,
Reading this indignant page,
Know that in a former time,
Love, sweet love, was thought a crime!

In the Age of Gold,
Free from winter's cold,
Youth and maiden bright,
To the holy light,
Naked in the sunny beams delight.

Once a youthful pair,
Fill'd with softest care,
Met in garden bright,
Where the holy light
Had just removed the curtains of the night.

There in rising day,
On the grass they play;
Parents were afar,
Strangers came not near;
And the maiden soon forgot her fear.

Tired with kisses sweet,
They agree to meet
When the silent sleep
Waves o'er heaven's deep,
And the weary tired wanderers weep.

To her father white
Came the maiden bright;
But his loving look,
Like the holy book,
All her tender limbs with terror shook.

Ona, pale and weak,
To thy father speak!
O the trembling fear,
O the dismal care
That shakes the blossoms of my hoary hair!

# A Divine Image

Cruelty has a human heart
    And Jealousy a human face;
Terror the human form divine,
    And Secrecy the human dress.

The human dress is forged iron,
    The human form a fiery forge,
The human face a furnace seal'd,
    The human heart its hungry gorge.

# The Little Vagabond

Dear mother, dear mother, the church is cold,
But the ale-house is pleasant and healthy and warm;
Besides I can tell where I am used well,
Such usage in heaven will never do well.

But if at the church they would give us some ale
And a pleasant fire our souls to regale,
We'd sing and we'd pray all the livelong day:
Nor ever once wish from the church to stray.

Then the parson might preach and drink and sing,
And we'd be as happy as birds in the spring:
And modest Dame Lurch, who is always at church,
Would not have bandy children nor fasting nor birch.

And God like a Father rejoicing to see
His children as pleasant and happy as He,
Would have no more quarrel with the devil or the barrel,
But kiss him and give him both drink and apparel.

# WILLIAM WORDSWORTH
## (1770–1850)

## Resolution and Independence

### I

There was a roaring in the wind all night;
The rain came heavily and fell in floods;
But now the sun is rising calm and bright;
The birds are singing in the distant woods;
Over his own sweet voice the Stock-dove broods;
The Jay makes answer as the Magpie chatters;
And all the air is filled with pleasant noise of waters.

### II

All things that love the sun are out of doors;
The sky rejoices in the morning's birth;
The grass is bright with rain-drops;—on the moors
The hare is running races in her mirth;
And with her feet she from the plashy earth
Raises a mist; that, glittering in the sun,
Suns with her all the way, wherever she doth run.

### III

I was a Traveller then upon the moor;
I saw the hare that raced about with joy;
I heard the woods and distant waters roar;
Or heard them not, as happy as a boy:
The pleasant season did my heart employ:
My old remembrances went from me wholly;
And all the ways of men, so vain and melancholy.

### IV

But, as it sometimes chanceth, from the might
Of joy in minds that can no further go,
As high as we have mounted in delight
In our dejection do we sink as low;
To me that morning did it happen so;
And fears and fancies thick upon me came;
Dim sadness—and blind thoughts, I knew not, nor could name.

### V

I heard the skylark warbling in the sky;
And I bethought me of the playful hare:
Even such a happy Child of earth am I;
Even as these blissful creatures do I fare;
Far from the world I walk, and from all care;
But there may come another day to me—
Solitude, pain of heart, distress, and poverty.

### VI

My whole life I have lived in pleasant thought,
As if life's business were a summer mood;
As if all needful things would come unsought
To genial faith, still rich in genial good;
But how can He expect that others should
Build for him, sow for him, and at his call
Love him, who for himself will take no heed at all?

### VII

I thought of Chatterton, the marvellous Boy,
The sleepless Soul that perished in his pride;
Of Him who walked in glory and in joy
Following his plough, along the mountain-side:
By our own spirits are we deified:
We Poets in our youth begin in gladness;
But thereof come in the end despondency and madness.

### VIII

Now, whether it were by peculiar grace,
A leading from above, a something given,
Yet it befell that, in this lonely place,
When I with these untoward thoughts had striven.
Beside a pool bare to the eye of heaven
I saw a Man before me unawares:
The oldest man he seemed that ever wore grey hairs.

### IX

As a huge stone is sometimes seen to lie
Couched on the bald top of an eminence;
Wonder to all who do the same espy.
By what means it could thither come, and whence;
So that it seems a thing endued with sense:
Like a sea-beast crawled forth, that on a shelf
Of rock or sand reposeth, there to sun itself;

### X

Such seemed this Man, not all alive nor dead,
Nor all asleep—in his extreme old age:
His body was bent double, feet and head
Coming together in life's pilgrimage;
As if some dire constraint of pain, or rage
Of sickness felt by him in times long past,
A more than human weight upon his frame had cast.

### XI

Himself he propped, limbs, body, and pale face,
Upon a long grey staff of shaven wood:
And, still as I drew near with gentle pace,
Upon the margin of that moorish flood
Motionless as a cloud the old Man stood.
That heareth not the loud winds when they call;
And moveth all together, if it move at all.

### XII

At length, himself unsettling, he the pond
Stirred with his staff, and fixedly did look
Upon the muddy water, which he conned,
As if he had been reading in a book:
And now a stranger's privilege I took;
And, drawing to his side, to him did say,
"This morning gives us promise of a glorious day."

### XIII

A gentle answer did the old Man make,
In courteous speech which forth he slowly drew:
And him with further words I thus bespake,
"What occupation do you there pursue?
This is a lonesome place for one like you."
Ere he replied, a flash of mild surprise
Broke from the sable orbs of his yet-vivid eyes.

### XIV

His words came feebly, from a feeble chest,
But each in solemn order followed each.
With something of a lofty utterance drest—
Choice word and measured phrase, above the reach
Of ordinary men; a stately speech;
Such as grave Livers do in Scotland use,
Religious men, who give to God and man their dues.

### XV

He told, that to these waters he had come
To gather leeches, being old and poor:
Employment hazardous and wearisome!
And he had many hardships to endure:
From pond to pond he roamed, from moor to moor;
Housing, with God's good help, by choice or chance:
And in this way he gained an honest maintenance.

## XVI

The old Man still stood talking by my side;
But now his voice to me was like a stream
Scarce heard; nor word from word could I divide;
And the whole body of the Man did seem
Like one whom I had met with in a dream;
Or like a man from some far region sent
To give me human strength, by apt admonishment.

## XVII

My former thoughts returned: the fear that kills;
And hope that is unwilling to be fed;
Cold, pain, and labour, and all fleshly ills;
And mighty Poets in their misery dead.
—Perplexed, and longing to be comforted,
My question eagerly did I renew,
"How is it that you live, and what is it you do?"

## XVIII

He with a smile did then his words repeat;
And said that, gathering leeches, far and wide
He travelled; stirring thus about his feet
The waters of the pools where they abide.
"Once I could meet with them on every side;
But they have dwindled long by slow decay;
Yet still I persevere, and find them where I may."

## XIX

While he was talking thus, the lonely place.
The old Man's shape, and speech—all troubled me:
In my mind's eye I seemed to see him pace
About the weary moors continually,
Wandering about alone and silently.
While I these thoughts within myself pursued.
He, having made a pause, the same discourse renewed.

## XX

And soon with this he other matter blended,
Cheerfully uttered, with demeanour kind.
But stately in the main; and, when he ended,
I could have laughed myself to scorn to find
In that decrepit Man so firm a mind.
"God," said I, "be my help and stay secure;
I'll think of the Leech-gatherer on the lonely moor!"

# Lines

*Composed a few miles above Tintern Abbey, on revisiting the banks of the Wye during a tour. July 13, 1798*

Five years have past; five summers, with the length
Of five long winters! and again I hear
These waters, rolling from their mountain-springs
With a soft inland murmur.—Once again
Do I behold these steep and lofty cliffs,
That on a wild secluded scene impress
Thoughts of more deep seclusion; and connect
The landscape with the quiet of the sky.
The day is come when I again repose
Here, under this dark sycamore, and view
These plots of cottage-ground, these orchard-tufts,
Which at this season, with their unripe fruits.
Are clad in one green hue, and lose themselves
'Mid groves and copses. Once again I see
These hedge-rows, hardly hedge-rows, little lines
Of sportive wood run wild: these pastoral farms,
Green to the very door; and wreaths of smoke
Sent up, in silence, from among the trees!
With some uncertain notice as might seem
Of vagrant dwellers in the houseless woods,
Or of some Hermit's cave, where by his fire
The Hermit sits alone.

These beauteous forms,
Through a long absence, have not been to me
As is a landscape to a blind man's eye:
But oft, in lonely rooms, and 'mid the din
Of towns and cities, I have owed to them,
In hours of weariness, sensations sweet,
Felt in the blood, and felt along the heart;
And passing even into my purer mind,
With tranquil restoration:—feelings too
Of unremembered pleasure: such, perhaps,
As have no slight or trivial influence
On that best portion of a good man's life,
His little, nameless, unremembered, acts
Of kindness and of love. Nor less, I trust,
To them I may have owed another gift,
Of aspect more sublime; that blessed mood.
In which the burthen of the mystery,
In which the heavy and the weary weight
Of all this unintelligible world,
Is lightened:—that serene and blessed mood.
In which the affections gently lead us on,—
Until, the breath of this corporeal frame
And even the motion of our human blood
Almost suspended, we are laid asleep
In body, and become a living soul:
While with an eye made quiet by the power
Of harmony, and the deep power of joy,
We see into the life of things.
                                        If this
Be but a vain belief, yet, oh! how oft—
In darkness and amid the many shapes
Of joyless daylight; when the fretful stir
Unprofitable, and the fever of the world,
Have hung upon the beatings of my heart—
How oft, in spirit, have I turned to thee,
O sylvan Wye! thou wanderer thro' the woods,
How often has my spirit turned to thee!

And now, with gleams of half-extinguished thought.
With many recognitions dim and faint.
And somewhat of a sad perplexity,
The picture of the mind revives again:
While here I stand, not only with the sense
Of present pleasure, but with pleasing thoughts.
That in this moment there is life and food
For future years. And so I dare to hope,
Though changed, no doubt, from what I was when first
I came among these hills; when like a roe
I bounded o'er the mountains by the sides
Of the deep rivers, and the lonely streams.
Wherever nature led: more like a man
Flying from something that he dreads than one
Who sought the thing he loved. For nature then
(The coarser pleasures of my boyish days,
And their glad animal movements all gone by)
To me was all in all.—I cannot paint
What then I was. The sounding cataract
Haunted me like a passion: the tall rock.
The mountain, and the deep and gloomy wood,
Their colours and their forms, were then to me
An appetite; a feeling and a love,
That had no need of a remoter charm,
By thought supplied, nor any interest
Unborrowed from the eye.—That time is past,
And all its aching joys are now no more.
And all its dizzy raptures. Not for this
Faint I, nor mourn nor murmur; other gifts
Have followed; for such loss, I would believe,
Abundant recompense. For I have learned
To look on nature, not as in the hour
Of thoughtless youth; but hearing oftentimes
The still, sad music of humanity.
Nor harsh nor grating, though of ample power
To chasten and subdue. And I have felt
A presence that disturbs me with the joy

Of elevated thoughts; a sense sublime
Of something far more deeply interfused,
Whose dwelling is the light of setting suns,
And the round ocean and the living air,
And the blue sky, and in the mind of man:
A motion and a spirit, that impels
All thinking things, all objects of all thought,
And rolls through all things. Therefore am I still
A lover of the meadows and the woods,
And mountains; and of all that we behold
From this green earth; of all the mighty world
Of eye, and ear,—both what they half create,
And what perceive; well pleased to recognise
In nature and the language of the sense
The anchor of my purest thoughts, the nurse,
The guide, the guardian of my heart, and soul
Of all ray moral being.
                    Nor perchance,
If I were not thus taught, should I the more
Suffer my genial spirits to decay:
For thou art with me here upon the banks
Of this fair river; thou my dearest Friend,
My dear, dear Friend; and in thy voice I catch
The language of my former heart, and read
My former pleasures in the shooting lights
Of thy wild eyes. Oh! yet a little while
May I behold in thee what I was once,
My dear, dear Sister! and this prayer I make,
Knowing that Nature never did betray
The heart that loved her; 'tis her privilege,
Through all the years of this our life, to lead
From joy to joy: for she can so inform
The mind that is within us, so impress
With quietness and beauty, and so feed
With lofty thoughts, that neither evil tongues,
Rash judgments, nor the sneers of selfish men.
Nor greetings where no kindness is, nor all

The dreary intercourse of daily life,
Shall e'er prevail against us, or disturb
Our cheerful faith, that all which we behold
Is full of blessings. Therefore let the moon
Shine on thee in thy solitary walk;
And let the misty mountain-winds be free
To blow against thee: and, in after years.
When these wild ecstasies shall be matured
Into a sober pleasure; when thy mind
Shall be a mansion for all lovely forms,
Thy memory be as a dwelling-place
For all sweet sounds and harmonies; oh! then,
If solitude, or fear, or pain, or grief,
Should be thy portion, with what healing thoughts
Of tender joy wilt thou remember me,
And these my exhortations! Nor, perchance—
If I should be where I no more can hear
Thy voice, nor catch from thy wild eyes these gleams
Of past existence—wilt thou then forget
That on the banks of this delightful stream
We stood together; and that I, so long
A worshipper of Nature, hither came
Unwearied in that service: rather say
With warmer love—oh! with far deeper zeal
Of holier love. Nor wilt thou then forget
That after many wanderings, many years
Of absence, these steep woods and lofty cliffs,
And this green pastoral landscape, were to me
More dear, both for themselves and for thy sake!

# Ode: Intimations of Immortality
# from Recollections of Early Childhood

*The Child is father of the Man;*
*And I could wish my days to be*
*Bound each to each by natural piety.*

## I

There was a time when meadow, grove, and stream,
The earth, and every common sight,
    To me did seem
    Apparelled in celestial light,
The glory and the freshness of a dream.
It is not now as it hath been of yore; —
    Turn wheresoe'er I may,
      By night or day,
The things which I have seen I now can see no more.

## II

    The Rainbow comes and goes,
    And lovely is the Rose,
    The Moon doth with delight
Look round her when the heavens are bare,
    Waters on a starry night
    Are beautiful and fair;
    The sunshine is a glorious birth;
    But yet I know, where'er I go,
That there hath past away a glory from the earth.

## III

Now, while the birds thus sing a joyous song,
    And while the young lambs bound
    As to the tabor's sound,
To me alone there came a thought of grief:
A timely utterance gave that thought relief,
    And I again am strong:
The cataracts blow their trumpets from the steep;

No more shall grief of mine the season wrong;
I hear the Echoes through the mountains throng,
The Winds come to me from the fields of sleep,
  And all the earth is gay;
   Land and sea
  Give themselves up to jollity.
  And with the heart of May
  Doth every Beast keep holiday;—
  Thou Child of Joy,
Shout round me, let me hear thy shouts, thou happy Shepherd-boy!


IV

Ye blessèd Creatures, I have heard the call
 Ye to each other make; I see
The heavens laugh with you in your jubilee;
 My heart is at your festival,
  My head hath its coronal,
The fulness of your bliss, I feel—I feel it all.
   Oh evil day! if I were sullen
   While Earth herself is adorning,
    This sweet May-morning,
   And the Children are culling
    On every side.
   In a thousand valleys far and wide,
   Fresh flowers; while the sun shines warm,
And the Babe leaps up on his Mother's arm:—
   I hear, I hear, with joy I hear!
   —But there's a Tree, of many, one,
A single Field, which I have looked upon,
Both of them speak of something that is gone:
   The Pansy at my feet
   Doth the same tale repeat:
Whither is fled the visionary gleam?
Where is it now, the glory and the dream?

### V

Our birth is but a sleep and a forgetting:
The Soul that rises with us, our life's Star,
  Hath had elsewhere its setting,
   And cometh from afar:
  Not in entire forgetfulness,
  And not in utter nakedness,
But trailing clouds of glory do we come
  From God, who is our home:
Heaven lies about us in our infancy!
Shades of the prison-house begin to close
  Upon the growing Boy,
But He beholds the light, and whence it flows,
  He sees it in his joy;
The Youth, who daily farther from the east
  Must travel, still is Nature's Priest,
  And by the vision splendid
  Is on his way attended;
At length the Man perceives it die away,
And fade into the light of common day.

### VI

Earth fills her lap with pleasures of her own;
Yearnings she hath in her own natural kind.
And, even with something of a Mother's mind,
  And no unworthy aim,
  The homely Nurse doth all she can
To make her Foster-child, her Inmate Man,
  Forget the glories he hath known.
And that imperial palace whence he came.

### VII

Behold the Child among his new-born blisses,
A six years' Darling of a pigmy size!
See, where 'mid work of his own hand he lies,
Fretted by sallies of his mother's kisses,
With light upon him from his father's eyes!

See, at his feet, some little plan or chart,
Some fragment from his dream of human life,
Shaped by himself with newly-learned art;
  A wedding or a festival,
  A mourning or a funeral;
   And this hath now his heart,
   And unto this he frames his song:
    Then will he fit his tongue
To dialogues of business, love, or strife;
   But it will not be long
   Ere this be thrown aside,
   And with new joy and pride
The little Actor cons another part;
Filling from time to time his "humorous stage"
With all the Persons, down to palsied Age,
That Life brings with her in her equipage;
   As if his whole vocation
   Were endless imitation.

VIII

Thou, whose exterior semblance doth belie
   Thy Soul's immensity;
Thou best Philosopher, who yet dost keep
Thy heritage, thou Eye among the blind,
That, deaf and silent, read'st the eternal deep,
Haunted for ever by the eternal mind,—
   Mighty Prophet! Seer blest!
   On whom those truths do rest,
Which we are toiling all our lives to find,
In darkness lost, the darkness of the grave;
Thou, over whom thy Immortality
Broods like the Day, a Master o'er a Slave,
A Presence which is not to be put by;
Thou little child, yet glorious in the might
Of heaven-born freedom on thy being's height,
Why with such earnest pains dost thou provoke
The years to bring the inevitable yoke,

Thus blindly with thy blessedness at strife?
Full soon thy Soul shall have thy earthly freight,
And custom lie upon thee with a weight,
Heavy as frost, and deep almost as life!

IX

O joy! that in our embers
Is something that doth live,
That nature yet remembers
What was so fugitive!
The thought of our past years in me doth breed
Perpetual benediction: not indeed
For that which is most worthy to be blest;
Delight and liberty, the simple creed
Of Childhood, whether busy or at rest,
With new-fledged hope still fluttering in his breast:—
Not for these I raise
The song of thanks and praise;
But for those obstinate questionings
Of sense and outward things,
Fallings from us, vanishings;
Blank misgivings of a Creature
Moving about in worlds not realised.
High instincts before which our mortal Nature
Did tremble like a guilty Thing surprised:
But for those first affections,
Those shadowy recollections,
Which, be they what they may,
Are yet the fountain-light of all our day,
Are yet a master-light of all our seeing;
Uphold us, cherish, and have power to make
Our noisy years seem moments in the being
Of the eternal Silence: truths that wake,
To perish never:
Which neither listlessness, nor mad endeavour,
Nor Man nor Boy,
Nor all that is at enmity with joy,

Can utterly abolish or destroy!
  Hence in a season of calm wather
  Though inland far we be,
Our souls have sight of that immortal sea
   Which brought us hither,
  Can such a moment travel thither,
And see the children sport upon the shore,
And hear the mighty waters rolling evermore.

X

Then sing, ye Birds, sing, sing a joyous song!
  And let the young Lambs bound
  As to the tabor's sound!
We in thought will join your throng,
  Ye that pipe and ye that play,
  Ye that through your hearts today
  Feel the gladness of the May!
What though the radiance which was once so bright
Be now for ever taken from my sight,
  Though nothing can bring back the hour
Of splendour in the grass, of glory in the flower;
  We will grieve not, rather find
  Strength in what remains behind;
  In the primal sympathy
  Which having been must ever be;
  In the soothing thoughts that spring
  Out of human suffering;
  In the faith that looks through death,
In years that bring the philosophic mind.

XI

And O, ye Fountains, Meadows, Hills, and Groves,
Forebode not any severing of our loves
Yet in my heart of hearts I feel your might;
I only have relinquished one delight
To live beneath your more habitual sway

I love the Brooks which down their channels fret,
Even more than when I tripped lightly as they;
The innocent brightness of a new-born Day
                    Is lovely yet;
The Clouds that gather round the setting sun
Do take a sober colouring from an eye
That hath kept watch o'er man's mortality;
Another race hath been, and other palms are won.
Thanks to the human heart by which we live,
Thanks to its tenderness, its joys, and fears,
To me the meanest flower that blows can give
Thoughts that do often lie too deep for tears.

## "Strange fits of passion I have known"

Strange fits of passion have I known:
And I will dare to tell.
But in the Lover's ear alone,
What once to me befell.

When she I loved looked every day
Fresh as a rose in June,
I to her cottage bent my way,
Beneath an evening-moon.

Upon the moon I fixed my eye.
All over the wide lea;
With quickening pace my horse drew nigh
Those paths so dear to me.

And now we reached the orchard-plot;
And, as we climbed the hill,
The sinking moon to Lucy's cot
Came near, and nearer still.

In one of those sweet dreams I slept,
Kind Nature's gentlest boon!
And all the while my eyes I kept
On the descending moon.

My horse moved on; hoof after hoof
He raised, and never stopped:
When down behind the cottage roof,
At once, the bright moon dropped.

What fond and wayward thoughts will slide
Into a Lover's head!
"O mercy!" to myself I cried,
"If Lucy should be dead!"

## "She dwelt among untrodden ways"

She dwelt among the untrodden ways
    Beside the springs of Dove,
A Maid whom there were none to praise
    And very few to love:

A violet by a mossy stone
    Half hidden from the eye!
—Fair as a star, when only one
    Is shining in the sky.

She lived unknown, and few could know
    When Lucy ceased to be;
But she is in her grave, and, oh,
    The difference to me!

## "I travelled among unknown men"

I travelled among unknown men,
    In lands beyond the sea;
Nor, England! did I know till then
    What love I bore to thee.

'Tis past, that melancholy dream!
    Nor will I quit thy shore
A second time; for still I seem
    To love thee more and more.

Among thy mountains did I feel
    The joy of my desire;
And she I cherished turned her wheel
    Beside an English fire.

Thy mornings showed, thy nights concealed,
    The bowers where Lucy played;
And thine too is the last green field
    That Lucy's eyes surveyed.

## "Three years she grew in sun and shower"

Three years she grew in sun and shower,
Then Nature said, "A lovelier flower
On earth was never sown;
This Child I to myself will take;
She shall be mine, and I will make
A Lady of my own.

"Myself will to my darling be
Both law and impulse: and with me
The Girl in rock and plain.
In earth and heaven, in glade and bower,
Shall feel an overseeing power ,
To kindle or restrain.

"She shall be sportive as the fawn
That wild with glee across the lawn
Or up the mountain springs;
And hers shall be the breathing balm.
And hers the silence and the calm
Of mute insensate things.

"The floating clouds their state shall lend
To her; for her the willow bend;
Nor shall she fail to see
Even in the motions of the Storm
Grace that shall mould the Maiden's form
By silent sympathy.

"The stars of midnight shall be dear
To her; and she shall lean her ear
In many a secret place
Where rivulets dance their wayward round,
And beauty born of murmuring sound
Shall pass into her face.

"And vital feelings of delight
Shall rear her form to stately height,
Her virgin bosom swell;
Such thoughts to Lucy I will give
While she and I together live
Here in this happy dell."

Thus Nature spake—The work was done—
How soon my Lucy's race was run!
She died, and left to me
This heath, this calm, and quiet scene;
The memory of what has been,
And never more will be.

## "A slumber did my spirit seal"

A slumber did my spirit seal;
   I had no human fears:
She seemed a thing that could not feel
   The touch of earthly years.

No motion has she now, no force;
   She neither hears nor sees;
Rolled round in earth's diurnal course,
   With rocks, and stones, and trees.

## "I wandered lonely as a cloud"

I wandered lonely as a cloud
That floats on high o'er vales and hills,
When all at once I saw a crowd,
A host, of golden daffodils;
Beside the lake, beneath the trees,
Fluttering and dancing in the breeze.

Continuous as the stars that shine
And twinkle on the milky way,
They stretched in never-ending line
Along the margin of a bay:
Ten thousand saw I at a glance,
Tossing their heads in sprightly dance.

The waves beside them danced; but they
Out-did the sparkling waves in glee:
A poet could not but be gay,
In such a jocund company:
I gazed—and gazed—but little thought
What wealth the show to me had brought:

For oft, when on my couch I lie
In vacant or in pensive mood,
They flash upon that inward eye
Which is the bliss of solitude;
And then my heart with pleasure fills,
And dances with the daffodils.

## "The world is too much with us"

The world is too much with us; late and soon,
Getting and spending, we lay waste our powers:
Little we see in Nature that is ours;
We have given our hearts away, a sordid boon!
This Sea that bares her bosom to the moon;
The winds that will be howling at all hours,
And are up-gathered now like sleeping flowers;
For this, for everything, we are out of tune;
It moves us not.—Great God! I'd rather be
A Pagan suckled in a creed outworn;
So might I, standing on this pleasant lea,
Have glimpses that would make me less forlorn;
Have sight of Proteus rising from the sea;
Or hear old Triton blow his wreathèd horn.

## To a Skylark

Ethereal minstrel! pilgrim of the sky!
Dost thou despise the earth where cares abound?
Or, while the wings aspire, are heart and eye
Both with thy nest upon the dewy ground?
Thy nest which thou canst drop into at will,
Those quivering wings composed, that music still!

Leave to the nightingale her shady wood;
A privacy of glorious light is thine;
Whence thou dost pour upon the world a flood
Of harmony, with instinct more divine;
Type of the wise who soar, but never roam;
True to the kindred points of Heaven and Home!

## The Solitary Reaper

Behold her, single in the field.
Yon solitary Highland Lass!
Reaping and singing by herself;
Stop here, or gently pass!
Alone she cuts and binds the grain,
And sings a melancholy strain;
O listen! for the Vale profound
Is overflowing with the sound.

No Nightingale did ever chaunt
More welcome notes to weary bands
Of travellers in some shady haunt,
Among Arabian sands:
A voice so thrilling ne'er was heard
In spring-time from the Cuckoo-bird,
Breaking the silence of the seas
Among the farthest Hebrides.

Will no one tell me what she sings ?—
Perhaps the plaintive numbers flow
For old, unhappy, far-off things,
And battles long ago:
Or is it some more humble lay,
Familiar matter of to-day?
Some natural sorrow, loss, or pain,
That has been, and may be again?

Whate'er the theme, the Maiden sang
As if her song could have no ending;
I saw her singing at her work.
And o'er the sickle bending;—
I listened, motionless and still;
And, as I mounted up the hill,
The music in my heart I bore,
Long after it was heard no more.

## Mutability

From low to high doth dissolution climb,
And sink from high to low, along a scale
Of awful notes, whose concord shall not fail;
A musical but melancholy chime,
Which they can hear who meddle not with crime,
Nor avarice, nor over-anxious care.
Truth fails not; but her outward forms that bear
The longest date do melt like frosty rime,
That in the morning whitened hill and plain
And is no more; drop like the tower sublime
Of yesterday, which royally did wear
His crown of weeds, but could not even sustain
Some casual shout that broke the silent air,
Or the unimaginable touch of Time.

# Ode to Duty

*Jam non consilio bonus, sed more èo perductus,*
*ut non tantum rectè facere possim, sed nisi*
*rectè facere non possim.*

Stern Daughter of the Voice of God!
O Duty! if that name thou love
Who art a light to guide, a rod
To check the erring, and reprove;
Thou, who art victory and law
When empty terrors overawe;
From vain temptations dost set free;
And calm'st the weary strife of frail humanity!

There are who ask not if thine eye
Be on them; who, in love and truth,
Where no misgiving is, rely
Upon the genial sense of youth:
Glad Hearts! without reproach or blot;
Who do thy work, and know it not:
Oh! if through confidence misplaced
They fail, thy saving arms, dread Power! around them cast.

Serene will be our days and bright,
And happy will our nature be,
When love is an unerring light,
And joy its own security.
And they a blissful course may hold
Even now, who, not unwisely bold,
Live in the spirit of this creed;
Yet seek thy firm support, according to their need.

Loving freedom, and untried;
No sport of every random gust,
Yet being to myself a guide,
Too blindly have reposed my trust:

And oft, when in my heart was heard
Thy timely mandate, I deferred
The task, in smoother walks to stray;
But thee I now would serve more strictly, if I may.

Through no disturbance of my soul,
Or strong compunction in me wrought,
I supplicate for thy control;
But in the quietness of thought:
Me this unchartered freedom tires;
I feel the weight of chance-desires:
My hopes no more must change their name,
I long for a repose that ever is the same.

Stern Lawgiver! yet thou dost wear
The Godhead's most benignant grace;
Nor know we anything so fair
As is the smile upon thy face:
Flowers laugh before thee on their beds
And fragrance in thy footing treads;
Thou dost preserve the stars from wrong;
And the most ancient heavens, through
  Thee, are fresh and strong.

To humbler functions, awful Power!
I call thee: I myself commend
Unto thy guidance from this hour;
Oh, let my weakness have an end!
Give unto me, made lowly wise,
The spirit of self-sacrifice;
The confidence of reason give;
And in the light of truth thy Bondman let me live!

# SAMUEL TAYLOR COLERIDGE

## (1772–1834)

## The Rime of the Ancient Mariner

### IN SEVEN PARTS

*Facile credo, plures esse Naturas invisibiles quam visibiles in rerum universitate. Sed horum omnium familiam quis nobis enarrabit? et gradus et cognationes et discrimina et singulorum munera? Quid agunt? quae loca habitant? Harum rerum notitiam semper ambivit ingenium humanum, nunquam attigit. Juvat, interea, non diffiteor, quandoque in animo, tanquam in tabula, majoris et melioris mundi imaginem contemplari: ne mens assuefacta hodiernae vitae minutiis se contrahat nimis, et tota subsidat in pusillas cogitationes. Sed veritati interea invigilandum est, modusque servandus, ut certa ab incertis, diem a nocte, distingunamus.*

— T. BURNET, *Archaeol. Phil.* p. 68.

### ARGUMENT

*How a Ship having passed the Line was driven by storms to the cold Country towards the South Pole; and how from thence she made her course to the tropical Latitude of the Great Pacific Ocean; and of the strange things that befell; and in what manner the Ancyent Marinere came back to his own Country.*

PART I

*An ancient Mariner meeteth three Gallants bidden to a wedding feast, and detaineth one.*

It is an ancient Mariner,
And he stoppeth one of three.
"By thy long grey beard and glittering eye,
Now wherefore stopp'st thou me?

The Bridegroom's doors are opened wide,
And I am next of kin;
The guests are met, the feast is set:
May'st hear the merry din."

He holds him with his skinny hand,
"There was a ship," quoth he.
"Hold off! unhand me, grey-beard loon!"
Eftsoons his hand dropt he.

*The Wedding Guest is*
*spellbound by the eye*
*of the old seafaring*
*man and constrained to*
*hear his tale.*

He holds him with his glittering eye—
The Wedding-Guest stood still,
And listens like a three years' child:
The Mariner hath his will.

The Wedding-Guest sat on a stone:
He cannot choose but hear;
And thus spake on that ancient man,
The bright-eyed Mariner.

"The ship was cheered, the harbour cleared,
Merrily did we drop
Below the kirk, below the hill,
Below the lighthouse top.

*The Mariner tells how*
*the ship sailed*
*southward with a good*
*wind and fair weather,*
*till it reached the line.*

The Sun came up upon the left,
Out of the sea came he!
And he shone bright, and on the right
Went down into the sea.

"Higher and higher every day,
Till over the mast at noon—"
The Wedding-Guest here beat his breast,
For he heard the loud bassoon.

*The Wedding-Guest
heareth the bridal
music; but the Mariner
continueth his tale.*

The bride hath paced into the hall,
Red as a rose is she;
Nodding their heads before her goes
The merry minstrelsy.

The Wedding-Guest he beat his breast,
Yet he cannot choose but hear;
And thus spake on that ancient man,
The bright-eyed Mariner.

*The ship driven by
a storm toward the
south pole.*

"And now the STORM-BLAST came, and he
Was tyrannous and strong:
He struck with his o'ertaking wings,
And chased us south along.

"With sloping masts and dipping prow,
As who pursued with yell and blow
Still treads the shadow of his foe,
And forward bends his head,
The ship drove fast, loud roared the blast,
And southward aye we fled.

"And now there came both mist and snow,
And it grew wondrous cold:
And ice, mast-high, came floating by,
As green as emerald.

*The land of ice, and of
fearful sounds where
no living thing was to
be seen.*

"And through the drifts the snowy clifts
Did send a dismal sheen:
Nor shapes of men nor beasts we ken—
The ice was all between.

"The ice was here, the ice was there,
The ice was all around:
It cracked and growled, and roared and howled,
Like noises in a swound!

*Till a great sea-bird,*
*called the Albatross,*
*came through the*
*snow-fog, and was*
*received with great joy*
*and hospitality.*

"At length did cross an Albatross,
Thorough the fog it came;
As if it had been a Christian soul,
We hailed it in God's name.

"It ate the food it ne'er had eat,
And round and round it flew.
The ice did split with a thunder-fit;
The helmsman steered us through!

*And lo! the Albatross*
*proveth a bird of good*
*omen, and followeth*
*the ship as it returned*
*northward through fog*
*and floating ice.*

"And a good south wind sprung up behind;
The Albatross did follow,
And every day, for food or play,
Came to the mariner's hollo!

"In mist or cloud, on mast or shroud,
It perched for vespers nine;
Whiles all the night, through fog-smoke white.
Glimmered the white Moon-shine."

*The ancient Mariner*
*inhospitably killeth the*
*pious bird of good*
*omen.*

"God save thee, ancient Mariner!
From the fiends, that plague thee thus!—
Why look'st thou so?"—"With my cross-bow
I shot the ALBATROSS."


PART II
The Sun now rose upon the right:
Out of the sea came he,
Still hid in mist, and on the left
Went down into the sea.

And the good south wind still blew behind,
But no sweet bird did follow,
Nor any day for food or play
Came to the mariners' hollo!

*His shipmates cry out against the ancient Mariner, for killing the bird of good luck.*

And I had done a hellish thing,
And it would work 'em woe:
For all averred, I had killed the bird
That made the breeze to blow.
Ah wretch! said they, the bird to slay,
That made the breeze to blow!

*But when the fog cleared off they justify the name and thus make themselves accomplices in the crime.*

Nor dim nor red, like God's own head,
The glorious Sun uprist:
Then all averred, I had killed the bird
That brought the fog and mist.
'Twas right, said they, such birds to slay,
That bring the fog and mist.

*The fair breeze continues; the ship enters the Pacific Ocean, and sails northward, even till it reaches the Line.*

The fair breeze blew, the white foam flew,
The furrow followed free;
We were the first that ever burst
Into that silent sea.

Down dropt the breeze, the sails dropt down,
'Twas sad as sad could be;
And we did speak only to break
The silence of the sea!

*The ship hath been suddenly becalmed.*

All in a hot and copper sky,
The bloody Sun, at noon,
Right up above the mast did stand,
No bigger than the Moon.

Day after day, day after day,
We stuck, nor breath nor motion;
As idle as a painted ship
Upon a painted ocean.

*And the Albatross
begins to be avenged.*

Water, water, every where,
And all the boards did shrink;
Water, water, every where,
Nor any drop to drink.

The very deep did rot: O Christ!
That ever this should be!
Yea, slimy things did crawl with legs
Upon the slimy sea.

About, about, in reel and rout
The death-fires danced at night;
The water, like a witch's oils,
Burnt green, and blue and white.

*A Spirit had followed
them; one of the
invisible inhabitants
of this planet, neither
departed souls nor
angels; concerning*

And some in dreams assuréd were
Of the Spirit that plagued us so;
Nine fathom deep he had followed us
From the land of mist and snow.

*whom the learned Jew, Josephus, and the Platonic Constantinopolitan, Michael Psellus, may be
consulted. They are very numerous, and there is no climate or element without one or more.*

And every tongue, through utter drought,
Was withered at the root;
We could not speak, no more than if
We had been choked with soot.

*The shipmates in their
sore distress, would
fain throw the whole
guilt on the ancient
Mariner: in sign
whereof they hang
the dead sea-bird
around his neck.*

Ah! well a-day! what evil looks
Had I from old- and young!
Instead of the cross, the Albatross
About my neck was hung.

PART III

There passed a weary time. Each throat
Was parched, and glazed each eye.
A weary time! a weary time!
How glazed each weary eye,
When looking westward, I beheld
A something in the sky.

*The ancient Mariner beholdeth a sign in the element afar off.*

At first it seemed a little speck
And then it seemed a mist;
It moved and moved, and took at last
A certain shape, I wist.

A speck, a mist, a shape, I wist!
And still it neared and neared:
As if it dodged a water-sprite,
It plunged and tacked and veered.

*At its nearer approach, it seemeth him to be a ship; and at a dear ransom he freeth his speech from the bonds of thirst.*

With throats unslaked, with black lips baked,
We could nor laugh nor wail;
Through utter drought all dumb we stood!
I bit my arm, I sucked the blood,
And cried, A sail! a sail!

*A flash of joy;*

With throats unslaked, with black lips baked,
Agape they heard me call:
Gramercy! they for joy did grin,
And all at once their breath drew in,
As they were drinking all.

*And horror follows. For can it be a ship that comes onward without wind or tide?*

See! see! (I cried) she tacks no more!
Hither to work us weal;
Without a breeze, without a tide,
She steadies with upright keel!

The western wave was all a-flame.
The day was well nigh done!
Almost upon the western wave
Rested the broad bright Sun;
When that strange shape drove suddenly
Betwixt us and the Sun.

*It seemeth him but the*
*skeleton of a ship.*

And straight the Sun was necked with bars,
  (Heaven's Mother send us grace!)
As if through a dungeon-grate he peered
With broad and burning face.

*And its ribs are seen as*
*bars on the face of the*
*setting Sun.*

Alas! (thought I, and my heart beat loud)
How fast she nears and nears!
Are those *her* sails that glance in the Sun,
Like restless gossameres?

*The Spectre-Woman*
*and her Death-mate*
*and no other on board*
*the skeleton ship.*

Are those *her* ribs through which the Sun
Did peer, as through a grate?
And is that Woman all her crew?
Is that a DEATH? and are there two?
Is DEATH that woman's mate?

*Like vessel, like crew!*

*Death and Life-in-*
*Death have diced for*
*the ship's crew, and she*
*(the latter) winneth the*
*ancient Mariner.*

*Her* lips were red, *her* looks were free,
Her locks were yellow as gold:
Her skin was as white as leprosy,
The Night-mare LIFE-IN-DEATH was she,
Who thicks man's blood with cold.

The naked hulk alongside came,
And the twain were casting dice;
"The game is done! I've won! I've won!"
Quoth she, and whistles thrice.

*No twilight within the courts of the Sun.*

The Sun's rim dips; the stars rush out:
At one stride comes the dark:
With far-heard whisper, o'er the sea,
Off shot the spectre-bark.

*At the rising of the Moon,*

We listened and looked sideways up!
Fear at my heart, as at a cup,
My life-blood seemed to sip!
The stars were dim, and thick the night,
The steersman's face by his lamp gleamed white;
From the sails the dew did drip—

Till clomb above the eastern bar
The hornéd Moon, with one bright star
Within the nether tip.

*One after another,*

One after one, by the star-dogged Moon,
Too quick for groan or sigh,
Each turned his face with a ghastly pang,
And cursed me with his eye.

*His shipmates drop down dead.*

Four times fifty living men,
(And I heard nor sigh nor groan)
With heavy thump, a lifeless lump,
They dropped down one by one.

*But Life-in-Death begins her work on the ancient Mariner.*

The souls did from their bodies fly,—
They fled to bliss or woe!
And every soul, it passed me by,
Like the whizz of my cross-bow!

## PART IV

*The Wedding-Guest feareth that a Spirit is talking to him;*

"I fear thee, ancient Mariner!
I fear thy skinny hand!
And thou art long, and lank, and brown,
As is the ribbed sea-sand.

"I fear thee and thy glittering eye,
And thy skinny hand, so brown."—
Fear not, fear not, thou Wedding-Guest!
This body dropt not down.

*But the ancient Mariner assureth him of his bodily life, and proceedeth to relate his horrible penance.*

Alone, alone, all, all alone,
Alone on a wide wide sea!
And never a saint took pity on
My soul in agony.

*He despiseth the creatures of the calm,*

The many men, so beautiful!
And they all dead did lie:
And a thousand thousand slimy things
Lived on; and so did I.

*And envieth that they should live and so many lie dead.*

I looked upon the rotting sea,
And drew my eyes away;
I looked upon the rotting deck,
And there the dead men lay.

I looked to heaven, and tried to pray;
But or ever a prayer had gusht,
A wicked whisper came, and made
My heart as dry as dust.

I closed my lids, and kept them close,
And the balls like pulses beat;
For the sky and the sea, and the sea and the sky
Lay like a load on my weary eye,
And the dead were at my feet.

*But the curse liveth for him in the eye of the dead men.*

The cold sweat melted from their limbs,
Nor rot nor reek did they:
The look with which they looked on me
Had never passed away.

An orphan's curse would drag to hell
A spirit from on high;
 But oh! more horrible than that
Is the curse in a dead man's eye!
Seven days, seven nights, I saw that curse,
And yet I could not die.

*In his loneliness and*
*fixedness he yearneth*
*towards the journeying*
*Moon, and the stars*
*that still sojourn,*
*yet still move onward;*
*and every where the*
*blue sky belongs to*
*them, and is their*
*appointed rest, and*
*their native country*
*and their own natural*
*homes, which they*
*enter unannounced,*

The moving Moon went up the sky,
And no where did abide:
Softly she was going up,
And a star or two beside—

Her beams bemocked the sultry main,
 Like April hoar-frost spread;
But where the ship's huge shadow lay,
 The charmèd water burnt alway
A still and awful red.

*as lords that are certainly expected and yet there is a silent joy at their arrival.*

*By the light of the*
*Moon he beholdeth*
*God's creatures of the*
*great calm.*

Beyond the shadow of the ship,
I watched the water-snakes:
They moved in tracks of shining white,
And when they reared, the elfish light
Fell off in hoary flakes.

Within the shadow of the ship
I watched their rich attire:
Blue, glossy green, and velvet black,
They coiled and swam; and every track
Was a flash of golden fire.

*Their beauty and their*
*happiness.*

O happy living things! no tongue
Their beauty might declare:
A spring of love gushed from my heart,

*He blesseth them in*
*his heart.*

And I blessed them unaware:
Sure my kind saint took pity on me,
And I blessed them unaware.

*The spell begins to break.*

The self-same moment I could pray;
And from my neck so free
The Albatross fell off, and sank
Like lead into the sea.

PART V

Oh sleep! it is a gentle thing,
Beloved from pole to pole!
To Mary Queen the praise be given!
She sent the gentle sleep from Heaven,
That slid into my soul.

*By grace of the holy Mother, the ancient Mariner is refreshed with rain.*

The silly buckets on the deck,
That had so long remained,
I dreamt that they were filled with dew;
And when I awoke, it rained.

My lips were wet, my throat was cold,
My garments all were dank;
Sure I had drunken in my dreams,
And still my body drank.

I moved, and could not feel my limbs:
I was so light—almost
I thought that I had died in sleep,
And was a blesséd ghost.

*He heareth sounds and seeth strange sights and commotions in the sky and the element.*

And soon I heard a roaring wind:
 It did not come anear;
But with its sound it shook the sails,
That were so thin and sere.

The upper air burst into life!
And a hundred fire-flags sheen,
To and fro they were hurried about!
And to and fro, and in and out,
The wan stars danced between.

And the coming wind did roar more loud,
And the sails did sigh like sedge;
And the rain poured down from one black cloud;
The Moon was at its edge.

The thick black cloud was cleft, and still
The Moon was at its side:
Like waters shot from some high crag,
The lightning fell with never a jag,
A river steep and wide.

*The bodies of the ship's crew are inspired and the ship moves on;*

The loud wind never reached the ship,
Yet now the ship moved on!
Beneath the lightning and the Moon
The dead men gave a groan.

They groaned, they stirred, they all uprose,
Nor spake, nor moved their eyes;
It had been strange, even in a dream,
To have seen those dead men rise.

The helmsman steered, the ship moved on;
Yet never a breeze up-blew;
The mariners all 'gan work the ropes,
Where they were wont to do;
They raised their limbs like lifeless tools—
We were a ghastly crew.

The body of my brother's son
Stood by me, knee to knee:
The body and I pulled at one rope,
But he said nought to me.

*But not by the souls of the men, nor by dæmons of earth or middle air, but by a blessed troop of angelic spirits, sent down by the invocation of the guardian saint.*

"I fear thee, ancient Mariner!"
Be calm, thou Wedding-Guest!
'Twas not those souls that fled in pain,
Which to their corses came again
But a troop of spirits blest:

For when it dawned—they dropped their arms,
And clustered round the mast;
Sweet sounds rose slowly through their mouths,
And from their bodies passed.

Around, around, flew each sweet sound,
Then darted to the Sun;
Slowly the sounds came back again,
Now mixed, now one by one.

Sometimes a-dropping from the sky
I heard the sky-lark sing;
Sometimes all little birds that are,
How they seemed to fill the sea and air
With their sweet jargoning!

And now 'twas like all instruments,
Now like a lonely flute;
And now it is an angel's song,
That makes the heavens be mute.

It ceased; yet still the sails made on
A pleasant noise till noon,
A noise like of a hidden brook
In the leafy month of June,
That to the sleeping woods all night
Singeth a quiet tune.

Till noon we quietly sailed on,
Yet never a breeze did breathe:
Slowly and smoothly went the ship,
Moved onward from beneath.

*The lonesome Spirit*
*from the south-pole*
*carries on the ship*
*as far as the Line,*
*in obedience to the*
*angelic troop, but still*
*requireth vengeance.*

Under the keel nine fathom deep,
From the land of mist and snow,
The spirit slid: and it was he
That made the ship to go.
The sails at noon left off their tune,
And the ship stood still also.

The Sun, right up above the mast,
Had fixed her to the ocean:
But in a minute she 'gan stir,
With a short uneasy motion—
Backwards and forwards half her length
With a short uneasy motion.

Then like a pawing horse let go,
She made a sudden bound:
It flung the blood into my head,
And I fell down in a swound.

*The Polar Spirit's*
*fellow-dæmons, the*
*invisible inhabitants of*
*the element, take part*
*in his wrong; and two*
*of them relate, one to*
*the other, that penance*
*long and heavy for the*
*ancient Mariner hath*
*been accorded to the*
*Polar Spirit, who*
*returneth southward.*

How long in that same fit I lay,
I have not to declare;
But ere my living life returned,
I heard and in my soul discerned
Two voices in the air.

"Is it he?" quoth one, "Is this the man?
By him who died on cross,
With his cruel bow he laid full low
The harmless Albatross.

"The spirit who bideth by himself
In the land of mist and snow,
He loved the bird that loved the man
Who shot him with his bow."

The other was a softer voice.
 As soft as honey-dew:
Quoth he, "The man hath penance done,
And penance more will do."


PART VI

FIRST VOICE

"But tell me, toll me! speak again,
Thy soft response renewing—
What makes that ship drive on so fast?
What is the ocean doing?"


SECOND VOICE

"Still as a slave before his lord,
The ocean hath no blast;
His great bright eye most silently
Up to the Moon is cast—


"If he may know which way to go;
For she guides him smooth or grim.
See, brother, see! how graciously
She looketh down on him."


FIRST VOICE

*The Mariner hath been cast into a trance; for the angelic power causeth the vessel to drive northward faster than human life could endure.*

"But why drives on that ship so fast,
Without or wave or wind?"


SECOND VOICE

"The air is cut away before,
And closes from behind.


"Fly, brother, fly! more high, more high!
Or we shall be belated:
For slow and slow that ship will go,
When the Mariner's trance is abated."

*The supernatural motion is retarded; the Mariner awakes, and his penance begins anew.*

I woke, and we were sailing on
As in a gentle weather:
'Twas night, calm night, the moon was high;
The dead men stood together.

All stood together on the deck,
For a charnel-dungeon fitter:
All fixed on me their stony eyes,
That in the Moon did glitter.

The pang, the curse, with which they died,
Had never passed away:
I could not draw my eyes from theirs,
Nor turn them up to pray.

*The curse is finally expiated.*

And now this spell was snapt: once more
I viewed the ocean green,
And looked far forth, yet little saw
Of what had else been seen—

Like one, that on a lonesome road
Doth walk in fear and dread,
And having once turned round walks on,
And turns no more his head;
Because he knows, a frightful fiend
Doth close behind him tread.

But soon there breathed a wind on me,
Nor sound nor motion made:
Its path was not upon the sea,
In ripple or in shade.

It raised my hair, it fanned my cheek
Like a meadow-gale of spring—
It mingled strangely with my fears,
Yet it felt like a welcoming.

Swiftly, swiftly flew the ship,
Yet she sailed softly too:
Sweetly, sweetly blew the breeze—
On me alone it blew.

*And the Mariner beholdeth his native country.*

Oh! dream of joy! is this indeed
The light-house top I see?
Is this the hill? is this the kirk?
Is this mine own countree?

We drifted o'er the harbour-bar,
And I with sobs did pray—
O let me be awake, my God!
Or let me sleep alway.

The harbour-bay was clear as glass,
So smoothly it was strewn
And on the bay the moonlight lay,
And the shadow of the Moon.

The rock shone bright, the kirk no less,
That stands above the rock:
The moonlight steeped in silentness
The steady weathercock.

And the bay was white with silent light,
Till rising from the same,

*The angelic spirits leave the dead bodies,*

Full many shapes, that shadows were,
In crimson colours came.

A little distance from the prow
Those crimson shadows were:

*And appear in their own forms of light.*

I turned my eyes upon the deck—
Oh, Christ! what saw I there!

Each corse lay flat, lifeless and flat,
And, by the holy rood!
A man all light, a seraph-man,
On every corse there stood.

This seraph-band, each waved his hand:
It was a heavenly sight!
They stood as signals to the land,
Each one a lovely light;

This seraph-band, each waved his hand:
No voice did they impart—
No voice; but oh! the silence sank
Like music on my heart.

But soon I heard the dash of oars,
I heard the Pilot's cheer;
My head was turned perforce away
And I saw a boat appear.

The Pilot and the Pilot's boy,
I heard them coming fast:
Dear Lord in Heaven! it was a joy
The dead men could not blast.

I saw a third—I heard his voice:
It is the Hermit good!
He singeth loud his godly hymns
That he makes in the wood.
He'll shrieve my soul, he'll wash away
The Albatross's blood.

PART VII

*The Hermit of the*
*Wood,*

This Hermit good lives in that wood
Which slopes down to the sea.
How loudly his sweet voice he rears!
 He loves to talk with marineres
That come from a far countree.

He kneels at morn, and noon, and eve—
He hath a cushion plump:
It is the moss that wholly hides
The rotted old oak-stump.

The skiff-boat neared: I heard them talk,
"Why, this is strange, I trow!
Where are those lights so many and fair,
That signal made but now?"

*Approacheth the ship*
*with wonder.*

"Strange, by my faith!" the Hermit said—
"And they answered not our cheer!
The planks looked warped! and see those sails,
 How thin they are and sere!
I never saw aught like to them,
Unless perchance it were

Brown skeletons of leaves that lag
My forest-brook along;
When the ivy-tod is heavy with snow,
And the owlet whoops to the wolf below,
That eats the she-wolfs young."

"Dear Lord! it hath a fiendish look—
(The Pilot made reply)
I am a-feared"—"Push on, push on!"
Said the Hermit cheerily.

The boat came closer to the ship,
But I nor spake nor stirred;
The boat came close beneath the ship,
And straight a sound was heard.

*The ship suddenly sinketh.*

Under the water it rumbled on,
Still louder and more dread:
It reached the ship, it split the bay;
The ship went down like lead.

*The ancient Mariner is saved in the Pilot's boat.*

Stunned by that loud and dreadful sound,
Which sky and ocean smote,
Like one that hath been seven days drowned
My body lay afloat;
But swift as dreams, myself I found
Within the Pilot's boat.

Upon the whirl, where sank the ship,
The boat spun round and round;
And all was still, save that the hill
Was telling of the sound.

I moved my lips—the Pilot shrieked
And fell down in a fit;
The holy Hermit raised his eyes,
And prayed where he did sit.

I took the oars: the Pilot's boy,
Who now doth crazy go,
Laughed loud and long, and all the while
His eyes went to and fro.
"Ha! ha!" quoth he, "full plain I see,
The Devil knows how to row."

And now, all in my own countree,
I stood on the firm land!
The Hermit stepped forth from the boat,
And scarcely he could stand.

*The ancient Mariner*
*earnestly entreateth*
*the Hermit to shrieve*
*him; and the penance*
*of life falls on him.*

"O shrieve me, shrieve me, holy man!"
The Hermit crossed his brow.
"Say quick," quoth he, "I bid thee say—
What manner of man art thou?"

Forthwith this frame of mine was wrenched
With a woful agony,
Which forced me to begin my tale;
And then it left me free.

*And ever and anon*
*through out his*
*future life an agony*
*constraineth him*
*to travel from*
*land to land;*

Since then, at an uncertain hour,
That agony returns:
And till my ghastly tale is told,
This heart within me burns.

I pass, like night, from land to land;
I have strange power of speech;
That moment that his face I see,
I know the man that must hear me:
To him my tale I teach.

What loud uproar bursts from that door!
The wedding-guests are there:
But in the garden-bower the bride
And bride-maids singing are:
And hark the little vesper bell,
Which biddeth me to prayer!

O Wedding-Guest! this soul hath been
Alone on a wide wide sea:
So lonely 'twas, that God himself
Scarce seeméd there to be.

O sweeter than the marriage-feast,
'Tis sweeter far to me,
To walk together to the kirk
With a goodly company!—

To walk together to the kirk,
And all together pray,
While each to his great Father bends,
Old men, and babes, and loving friends
And youths and maidens gay!

*And to teach, by his own example, love and reverence to all things that God made and loveth.*

Farewell, farewell! but this I tell
To thee, thou Wedding-Guest!
He prayeth well, who loveth well
Both man and bird and beast.

He prayeth best, who loveth best
All things both great and small;
For the dear God who loveth us,
He made and loveth all.

The Mariner, whose eye is bright,
Whose beard with age is hoar,
Is gone: and now the Wedding-Guest
Turned from the bridegroom's door.

He went like one that hath been stunned,
And is of sense forlorn:
A sadder and a wiser man,
He rose the morrow morn.

## Frost at Midnight

The Frost performs its secret ministry,
Unhelped by any wind. The owlet's cry
Came loud—and hark, again! loud as before.
The inmates of my cottage, all at rest,
Have left me to that solitude, which suits
Abstruser musings: save that at my side
My cradled infant slumbers peacefully.
'Tis calm indeed! so calm, that it disturbs
And vexes meditation with its strange
And extreme silentness. Sea, hill, and wood,
This populous village! Sea, and hill, and wood,
With all the numberless goings-on of life,
Inaudible as dreams! the thin blue flame
Lies on my low-burnt fire, and quivers not;
Only that film, which fluttered on the grate,
Still flutters there, the sole unquiet thing.
Methinks, its motion in this hush of nature
Gives it dim sympathies with me who live,
Making it a companionable form,
Whose puny flaps and freaks the idling Spirit
By its own moods interprets, every where
Echo or mirror seeking of itself,
And makes a toy of Thought.

But O! how oft,
How oft, at school, with most believing mind,
Presageful, have I gazed upon the bars,
To watch that fluttering *stranger*! and as oft
With unclosed lids, already had I dreamt
Of my sweet birth-place, and the old church-tower,
Whose bells, the poor man's only music, rang
From morn to evening, all the hot Fair-day,
So sweetly, that they stirred and haunted me
With a wild pleasure, falling on mine ear
Most like articulate sounds of things to come!
So gazed I, till the soothing things, I dreamt,

Lulled me to sleep, and sleep prolonged my dreams!
And so I brooded all the following morn,
Awed by the stern preceptor's face, mine eye
Fixed with mock study on my swimming book:
Save if the door half opened, and I snatched
A hasty glance, and still my heart leaped up,
For still I hoped to see the *stranger's* face,
Townsman, or aunt, or sister more beloved,
My play-mate when we both were clothed alike!

   Dear Babe, that sleepest cradled by my side,
Whose gentle breathings, heard in this deep calm,
Fill up the interspersèd vacancies
And momentary pauses of the thought!
My babe so beautiful! it thrills my heart
With tender gladness, thus to look at thee,
And think that thou shalt learn far other lore,
And in far other scenes! For I was reared
In the great city, pent 'mid cloisters dim,
And saw nought lovely but the sky and stars.
But *thou,* my babe! shalt wander like a breeze
By lakes and sandy shores, beneath the crags
Of ancient mountain, and beneath the clouds,
Which image in their bulk both lakes and shores
And mountain crags: so shalt thou see and hear
The lovely shapes and sounds intelligible
Of that eternal language, which thy God
Utters, who from eternity doth teach
Himself in all, and all things in himself.
Great universal Teacher! he shall mould
Thy spirit, and by giving make it ask.

   Therefore all seasons shall be sweet to thee,
Whether the summer clothe the general earth
With greenness, or the redbreast sit and sing
Betwixt the tufts of snow on the bare branch
Of mossy apple-tree, while the nigh thatch

Smokes in the sun-thaw; whether the eave-drops fall
Heard only in the trances of the blast,
Or if the secret ministry of frost
Shall hang them up in silent icicles,
Quietly shining to the quiet Moon.

## Kubla Khan

### Or, A Vision in a Dream. A Fragment.

In Xanadu did Kubla Khan
A stately pleasure-dome decree:
Where Alph, the sacred river, ran
Through caverns measureless to man
    Down to a sunless sea.
So twice five miles of fertile ground
With walls and towers were girdled round:
And there were gardens bright with sinuous rills,
Where blossomed many an incense-bearing tree;
And here were forests ancient as the hills,
Enfolding sunny spots of greenery.

But oh! that deep romantic chasm which slanted
Down the green hill athwart a cedarn cover!
A savage place! as holy and enchanted
As e'er beneath a waning moon was haunted
By woman wailing for her demon-lover!
And from this chasm, with ceaseless turmoil seething,
As if this earth in fast thick pants were breathing,
A mighty fountain momently was forced:
Amid whose swift half-intermitted burst
Huge fragments vaulted like rebounding hail,
Or chaffy grain beneath the thresher's flail:
And 'mid these dancing rocks at once and ever
It flung up momently the sacred river.

Five miles meandering with a mazy motion
Through wood and dale the sacred river ran,
Then reached the caverns measureless to man.
And sank in tumult to a lifeless ocean:
And 'mid this tumult Kubla heard from far
Ancestral voices prophesying war!
 The shadow of the dome of pleasure
 Floated midway on the waves;
 Where was heard the mingled measure
 From the fountain and the caves.
It was a miracle of rare device,
A sunny pleasure-dome with caves of ice!

 A damsel with a dulcimer
 In a vision once I saw:
 It was an Abyssinian maid,
 And on her dulcimer she played,
 Singing of Mount Abora.
 Could I revive within me
 Her symphony and song,
 To such a deep delight 'twould win me,
That with music loud and long.
I would build that dome in air,
That sunny dome! those caves of ice!
And all who heard should see them there,
And all should cry, Beware! Beware!
His flashing eyes, his floating hair!
Weave a circle round him thrice,
And close your eyes with holy dread,
For he on honey-dew hath fed,
And drunk the milk of Paradise.

# Dejection: An Ode

Late, late yestreen I saw the new Moon,
With the old Moon in her arms;
And I fear, I fear, my Master dear!
We shall have a deadly storm.
*Ballad of Sir Patrick Spence.*

### I

Well! If the Bard was weather-wise, who made
  The grand old ballad of Sir Patrick Spence,
  This night, so tranquil now, will not go hence
Unroused by winds, that ply a busier trade
Than those which mould yon cloud in lazy flakes,
Or the dull sobbing draft, that moans and rakes
Upon the strings of this Æolian lute,
    Which better far were mute.
  For lo! the New-moon winter-bright!
  And overspread with phantom light,
  (With swimming phantom light o'erspread
  But rimmed and circled by a silver thread)
I see the old Moon in her lap, foretelling
  The coming-on of rain and squally blast.
And oh! that even now the gust were swelling,
  And the slant night-shower driving loud and fast!
Those sounds which oft have raised me, whilst they awed,
    And sent my soul abroad,
Might now perhaps their wonted impulse give,
Might startle this dull pain, and make it move and live!

### II

A grief without a pang, void, dark, and drear,
  A stifled, drowsy, unimpassioned grief,
  Which finds no natural outlet, no relief,
    In word, or sigh, or tear—
O Lady! in this wan and heartless mood,
To other thoughts by yonder throstle woo'd,
  All this long eve, so balmy and serene,

Have I been gazing on the western sky,
And its peculiar tint of yellow green:
And still I gaze—and with how blank an eye!
And those thin clouds above, in flakes and bars,
That give away their motion to the stars;
Those stars, that glide behind them or between,
Now sparkling, now bedimmed, but always seen:
Yon crescent Moon, as fixed as if it grew
In its own cloudless, starless lake of blue;
I see them all so excellently fair,
I see, not feel, how beautiful they are!

### III

My genial spirits fail;
And what can these avail
To lift the smothering weight from off my breast?
It were a vain endeavour,
Though I should gaze for ever
On that green light that lingers in the west:
I may not hope from outward forms to win
The passion and the life, whose fountains are within.

### IV

O Lady! we receive but what we give,
And in our life alone does Nature live:
Ours is her wedding garment, ours her shroud!
And would we aught behold, of higher worth,
Than that inanimate cold world allowed
To the poor loveless ever-anxious crowd,
Ah! from the soul itself must issue forth
A light, a glory, a fair luminous cloud
Enveloping the Earth—
And from the soul itself must there be sent
A sweet and potent voice, of its own birth,
Of all sweet sounds the life and element!

### V

O pure of heart! thou need'st not ask of me
What this strong music in the soul may be!
What, and wherein it doth exist,
This light, this glory, this fair luminous mist,
This beautiful and beauty-making power.
   Joy, virtuous Lady! Joy that ne'er was given,
Save to the pure, and in their purest hour,
Life, and Life's effluence, cloud at once and shower,
Joy, Lady! is the spirit and the power,
Which wedding Nature to us gives in dower
   A new Earth and new Heaven,
Undreamt of by the sensual and the proud—
Joy is the sweet voice, Joy the luminous cloud—
    We in ourselves rejoice!
And thence flows all that charms or ear or sight,
   All melodies the echoes of that voice,
All colours a suffusion from that light.

### VI

There was a time when, though my path was rough,
   This joy within me dallied with distress,
And all misfortunes were but as the stuff
   Whence Fancy made me dreams of happiness:
For hope grew round me, like the twining vine,
And fruits, and foliage, not my own, seemed mine.
But now afflictions bow me down to earth:
Nor care I that they rob me of my mirth;
   But oh! each visitation
Suspends what nature gave me at my birth,
   My shaping spirit of Imagination.
For not to think of what I needs must feel,
   But to be still and patient, all I can;
And haply by abstruse research to steal
   From my own nature all the natural man—
   This was my sole resource, my only plan:

Till that which suits a part infects the whole,
And now is almost grown the habit of my soul.

### VII

Hence, viper thoughts, that coil around my mind,
Reality's dark dream!
I turn from you, and listen to the wind,
Which long has raved unnoticed. What a scream
Of agony by torture lengthened out
That lute sent forth! Thou Wind, that rav'st without,
Bare crag, or mountain-tairn, or blasted tree,
Or pine-grove whither woodman never clomb,
Or lonely house, long held the witches home,
Methinks were fitter instruments for thee,
Mad Lutanist! who in this month of showers,
Of dark-brown gardens, and of peeping flowers,
Mak'st Devils' yule, with worse than wintry song,
The blossoms, buds, and timorous leaves among.
Thou Actor, perfect in all tragic sounds!
Thou mighty Poet, e'en to frenzy bold!
What tell'st thou now about?
'Tis of the rushing of an host in rout,
With groans, of trampled men, with smarting wounds—
At once they groan with pain, and shudder with the cold!
But hush! there is a pause of deepest silence!
And all that noise, as of a rushing crowd,
With groans, and tremulous shudderings—all is over—
It tells another tale, with sounds less deep and loud!
A tale of less affright,
And tempered with delight,
As Otway's self had framed the tender lay,—
'Tis of a little child
Upon a lonesome wild,
Not far from home, but she hath lost her way:
And now moans low in bitter grief and fear,
And now screams loud, and hopes to make her mother hear.

## VIII

'Tis midnight, but small thoughts have I of sleep:
Full seldom may my friend such vigils keep!
Visit her, gentle Sleep! with wings of healing,
　　And may this storm be but a mountain-birth,
May all the stars hang bright above her dwelling,
　　　Silent as though they watched the sleeping Earth!
　　　　With light heart may she rise,
　　　　Gay fancy, cheerful eyes,
　　Joy lift her spirit, joy attune her voice;
To her may all things live, from pole to pole,
Their life the eddying of her living soul!
　　O simple spirit, guided from above,
Dear Lady! friend devoutest of my choice,
Thus mayest thou ever, evermore rejoice.

# LORD BYRON
## (1788–1824)

## "When we two parted"

When we two parted
  In silence and tears,
Half broken-hearted
  To sever for years,
Pale grew thy cheek and cold,
  Colder thy kiss;
Truly that hour foretold
  Sorrow to this.

The dew of the morning
  Sunk chill on my brow—
It felt like the warning
  Of what I feel now.
Thy vows are all broken,
  And light is thy fame;
I hear thy name spoken,
  And share in its shame.

They name thee before me,
  A knell to mine ear;
A shudder comes o'er me—
  Why wert thou so dear?
They know not I knew thee,
  Who knew thee too well:—
Long, long shall I rue thee,
  Too deeply to tell.

In secret we met—
   In silence I grieve
That thy heart could forget,
   Thy spirit deceive.
If I should meet thee
   After long years,
How should I greet thee?—
   With silence and tears.

## "She walks in beauty"

She walks in beauty, like the night
   Of cloudless climes and starry skies;
And all that's best of dark and bright
   Meet in her aspect and her eyes:
Thus mellow'd to that tender light
   Which heaven to gaudy day denies.

One shade the more, one ray the less,
   Had half impair'd the nameless grace
Which waves in every raven tress,
   Or softly lightens o'er her face;
Where thoughts serenely sweet express
   How pure, how dear their dwelling-place.

And on that cheek, and o'er that brow,
   So soft, so calm, yet eloquent,
The smiles that win, the tints that glow,
   But tell of days in goodness spent,
A mind at peace with all below,
   A heart whose love is innocent!

# The Destruction of Sennacherib

The Assyrian came down like the wolf on the fold,
And his cohorts were gleaming in purple and gold;
And the sheen of their spears was like stars on the sea,
When the blue wave rolls nightly on deep Galilee.

Like the leaves of the forest when Summer is green,
That host with their banners at sunset were seen:
Like the leaves of the forest when Autumn hath blown,
That host on the morrow lay wither'd and strown.

For the Angel of Death spread his wings on the blast,
And breathed in the face of the foe as he pass'd;
And the eyes of the sleepers wax'd deadly and chill,
And their hearts but once heaved, and for ever grew still!

And there lay the steed with his nostril all wide,
But through it there roll'd not the breath of his pride:
And the foam of his gasping lay white on the turf,
And cold as the spray of the rock-beating surf.

And there lay the rider distorted and pale,
With the dew on his brow and the rust on his mail;
And the tents were all silent, the banners alone,
The lances unlifted, the trumpet unblown.

And the widows of Ashur are loud in their wail,
And the idols are broke in the temple of Baal;
And the might of the Gentile, unsmote by the sword,
Hath melted like snow in the glance of the Lord!

## "So we'll go no more a roving"

So we'll go no more a roving
    So late into the night,
Though the heart be still as loving,
    And the moon be still as bright.

For the sword outwears its sheath,
    And the soul wears out the breast,
And the heart must pause to breathe,
    And Love itself have rest.

Though the night was made for loving,
    And the day returns too soon,
Yet we'll go no more a roving
    By the light of the moon.

## The Prisoner of Chillon

### A Fable

#### SONNET ON CHILLON

Eternal Spirit of the chainless Mind!
    Brightest in dungeons, Liberty! thou art,
    For there thy habitation is the heart—
The heart which love of thee alone can bind;
And when thy sons to fetters are consign'd—
    To fetters, and the damp vault's dayless gloom,
    Their country conquers with their martyrdom,
And Freedom's fame finds wings on every wind.
Chillon! thy prison is a holy place,
    And thy sad floor an altar; for 'twas trod,
Until his very steps have left a trace
    Worn, as if thy cold pavement were a sod,
By Bonnivard!—May none those marks efface!
    For they appeal from tyranny to God.

### I

My hair is grey, but not with years,
   Nor grew it white
   In a single night,
As men's have grown from sudden fears.
My limbs are bow'd, though not with toil,
  But rusted with a vile repose,
For they have been a dungeon's spoil,
  And mine has been the fate of those
To whom the goodly earth and air
Are bann'd, and barr'd—forbidden fare.
But this was for my father's faith,
I suffer'd chains and courted death;
That father perish'd at the stake
For tenets he would not forsake;
And for the same his lineal race
In darkness found a dwelling-place.
We were seven—who now are one,
  Six in youth, and one in age,
Finish'd as they had begun,
  Proud of Persecution's rage;
One in fire, and two in field,
Their belief with blood have seal'd,
Dying as their father died,
For the God their foes denied;
Three were in a dungeon cast,
Of whom this wreck is left the last.

### II

There are seven pillars of Gothic mould
In Chillon's dungeons deep and old,
There are seven columns, massy and grey,
Dim with a dull imprison'd ray,
A sunbeam which hath lost its way,
And through the crevice and the cleft
Of the thick wall is fallen and left;
Creeping o'er the floor so damp,

Like a marsh's meteor lamp.
And in each pillar there is a ring,
 And in each ring there is a chain;
That iron is a cankering thing,
 For in these limbs its teeth remain,
With marks that will not wear away,
Till I have done with this new day,
Which now is painful to these eyes,
Which have not seen the sun so rise
For years—I cannot count them o'er,
I lost their long and heavy score
When my last brother droop'd and died,
And I lay living by his side.

### III

They chain'd us each to a column stone,
And we were three—yet, each alone;
We could not move a single pace,
We could not see each other's face,
But with that pale and livid light
That made us strangers in our sight.
And thus together, yet apart,
Fetter'd in hand, but join'd in heart,
'Twas still some solace, in the dearth
Of the pure elements of earth,
To hearken to each other's speech,
And each turn comforter to each.
With some new hope or legend old,
Or song heroically bold;
But even these at length grew cold.
Our voices took a dreary tone,
An echo of the dungeon stone,
 A grating sound—not full and free
 As they of yore were wont to be:
 It might be fancy, but to me
They never sounded like our own.

### IV

I was the eldest of the three,
   And to uphold and cheer the rest
   I ought to do—and did my best;
And each did well in his degree.
   The youngest, whom my father loved,
Because our mother's brow was given
To him, with eyes as blue as heaven—
   For him my soul was sorely moved.
And truly might it be distress'd
To see such bird in such a nest;
For he was beautiful as day
   (When day was beautiful to me
   As to young eagles being free)—
   A polar day, which will not see
A sunset till its summer's gone,
   Its sleepless summer of long light,
The snow-clad offspring of the sun:
   And thus he was as pure and bright,
And in his natural spirit gay,
With tears for nought but others' ills;
And then they flow'd like mountain rills,
Unless he could assuage the woe
Which he abhorr'd to view below.

### V

The other was as pure of mind,
But form'd to combat with his kind;
Strong in his frame, and of a mood
Which 'gainst the world in war had stood,
And perish'd in the foremost rank
   With joy:—but not in chains to pine:
His spirit wither'd with their clank,
   I saw it silently decline—
   And so perchance in sooth did mine:
But yet I forced it on to cheer

Those relics of a home so dear.
He was a hunter of the hills,
 Had follow'd there the deer and wolf;
 To him this dungeon was a gulf,
And fetter'd feet the worst of ills.

### VI

 Lake Leman lies by Chillon's walls:
A thousand feet in depth below
Its massy waters meet and flow;
Thus much the fathom-line was sent
From Chillon's snow-white battlement
 Which round about the wave inthrals:
A double dungeon wall and wave
Have made—and like a living grave.
Below the surface of the lake
The dark vault lies wherein we lay:
We heard it ripple night and day;
 Sounding o'er our heads it knock'd;
And I have felt the winter's spray
Wash through the bars when winds were high
And wanton in the happy sky;
 And then the very rock hath rock'd,
 And I have felt it shake, unshock'd,
Because I could have smiled to see
The death that would have set me free.

### VII

I said my nearer brother pined,
I said his mighty heart declined,
He loathed and put away his food;
It was not that 't was coarse and rude,
For we were used to hunters' fare,
And for the like had little care.
The milk drawn from the mountain goat
Was changed for water from the moat,
Our bread was such as captives' tears

Have moisten'd many a thousand years,
Since man first pent his fellow men
Like brutes within an iron den;
But what were these to us or him?
These wasted not his heart or limb;
My brother's soul was of that mould
Which in a palace had grown cold,
Had his free breathing been denied
The range of the steep mountain's side.
But why delay the truth?—he died.
I saw, and could not hold his head,
Nor reach his dying hand—nor dead,—
Though hard I strove, but strove in vain,
To rend and gnash my bonds in twain.
He died—and they unlock'd his chain,
And scoop'd for him a shallow grave
Even from the cold earth of our cave.
I begg'd them, as a boon, to lay
His corse in dust whereon the day
Might shine—it was a foolish thought,
But then within my brain it wrought,
That even in death his freeborn breast
In such a dungeon could not rest.
I might have spared my idle prayer;
They coldly laugh'd—and laid him there:
The flat and turfless earth above
The being we so much did love;
His empty chain above it leant,
Such murder's fitting monument!

## VIII

But he, the favourite and the flower,
Most cherish'd since his natal hour,
His mother's image in fair face,
The infant love of all his race,
His martyr'd father's dearest thought,
My latest care, for whom I sought

To hoard my life, that his might be
Less wretched now, and one day free;
He, too, who yet had held untired
A spirit natural or inspired—
He, too, was struck, and day by day
Was wither'd on the stalk away.
Oh, God! it is a fearful thing
To see the human soul take wing
In any shape, in any mood:—
I've seen it rushing forth in blood,
I've seen it on the breaking ocean
Strive with a swoln convulsive motion,
I've seen the sick and ghastly bed
Of Sin delirious with its dread:
But these were horrors—this was woe
Unmix'd with such—but sure and slow.
He faded, and so calm and meek,
So softly worn, so sweetly weak,
So tearless, yet so tender—kind,
And grieved for those he left behind;
With all the while a cheek whose bloom
Was as a mockery of the tomb,
Whose tints as gently sunk away
As a departing rainbow's ray;
An eye of most transparent light,
That almost made the dungeon bright;
And not a word of murmur, not
A groan o'er his untimely lot,—
A little talk of better days,
A little hope my own to raise,
For I was sunk in silence—lost
In this last loss, of all the most;
And then the sighs he would suppress
Of fainting nature's feebleness,
More slowly drawn, grew less and less.
I listen'd, but I could not hear—
I call'd, for I was wild with fear;

I knew't was hopeless, but my dread
Would not be thus admonishèd.
I call'd, and thought I heard a sound—
I burst my chain with one strong bound,
And rush'd to him:—I found him not,
*I* only stirr'd in this black spot,
*I* only lived—*I* only drew
The accursèd breath of dungeon-dew;
The last—the sole—the dearest link
Between me and the eternal brink,
Which bound me to my failing race,
Was broken in this fatal place.
One on the earth, and one beneath—
My brothers—both had ceased to breathe:
I took that hand which lay so still,
Alas! my own was full as chill,
I had not strength to stir, or strive,
But felt that I was still alive—
A frantic feeling, when we know
That what we love shall ne'er be so.
    I know not why
      I could not die,
I had no earthly hope—but faith,
And that forbade a selfish death.

IX

What next befell me then and there
    I know not well—I never knew;
First came the loss of light, and air,
    And then of darkness too.
I had no thought, no feeling—none—
Among the stones I stood a stone,
And was, scarce conscious what I wist,
As shrubless crags within the mist;
For all was blank, and bleak, and grey,
It was not night—it was not day,
It was not even the dungeon-light

So hateful to my heavy sight,
But vacancy absorbing space,
And fixedness—without a place;
There were no stars, no earth, no time,
No check, no change, no good, no crime—
But silence, and a stirless breath
Which neither was of life nor death;
A sea of stagnant idleness,
Blind, boundless, mute, and motionless!

X

A light broke in upon my brain,—
    It was the carol of a bird;
It ceased, and then it came again,
    The sweetest song ear ever heard,
And mine was thankful till my eyes
Ran over with the glad surprise,
And they that moment could not see
I was the mate of misery.
But then by dull degrees came back
My senses to their wonted track;
I saw the dungeon walls and floor
Close slowly round me as before,
I saw the glimmer of the sun
Creeping as it before had done,
But through the crevice where it came
That bird was perch'd, as fond and tame,
    And tamer than upon the tree;
A lovely bird, with azure wings,
And song that said a thousand things,
    And seem'd to say them all for me!
I never saw its like before,
I ne'er shall see its likeness more:
It seem'd like me to want a mate,
But was not half so desolate,
And it was come to love me when
None lived to love me so again,

And cheering from my dungeon's brink,
Had brought me back to feel and think.
I know not if it late were free,
   Or broke its cage to perch on mine,
But knowing well captivity,
   Sweet bird! I could not wish for thine!
Or if it were, in wingèd guise,
A visitant from Paradise;
For—Heaven forgive that thought! the while
Which made me both to weep and smile—
I sometimes deem'd that it might be
My brother's soul come down to me;
But then at last away it flew,
And then't was mortal—well I knew,
For he would never thus have flown,
And left me twice so doubly lone,—
Lone—as the corse within its shroud,
Lone—as a solitary cloud,
   A single cloud on a sunny day,
While all the rest of heaven is clear,
A frown upon the atmosphere
That hath no business to appear
   When skies are blue and earth is gay.

XI

A kind of change came in my fate,
My keepers grew compassionate;
I know not what had made them so,
They were inured to sights of woe,
But so it was:—my broken chain
With links unfasten'd did remain,
And it was liberty to stride
Along my cell from side to side,
And up and down, and then athwart,
And tread it over every part;
And round the pillars one by one,
Returning where my walk begun,

Avoiding only, as I trod,
My brothers' graves without a sod;
For if I thought with heedless tread
My step profaned their lowly bed,
My breath came gaspingly and thick,
And my crush'd heart fell blind and sick.

### XII

I made a footing in the wall,
　　It was not therefrom to escape,
For I had buried one and all
　　Who loved me in a human shape;
And the whole earth would henceforth be
A wider prison unto me.
No child, no sire, no kin had I,
No partner in my misery;
I thought of this, and I was glad,
For thought of them had made me mad;
But I was curious to ascend
To my barr'd windows, and to bend
Once more, upon the mountains high,
The quiet of a loving eye.

### XIII

I saw them—and they were the same,
They were not changed like me in frame;
I saw their thousand years of snow
On high—their wide long lake below,
And the blue Rhone in fullest flow;
I heard the torrents leap and gush
O'er channell'd rock and broken bush;
I saw the white-wall'd distant town,
And whiter sails go skimming down.
And then there was a little isle,
Which in my very face did smile,
　　The only one in view;
A small green isle, it seem'd no more,

Scarce broader than my dungeon floor,
But in it there were three tall trees,
And o'er it blew the mountain breeze,
And by it there were waters flowing,
And on it there were young flowers growing
    Of gentle breath and hue.
The fish swam by the castle wall,
And they seem'd joyous each and all;
The eagle rode the rising blast,
Methought he never flew so fast
As then to me he seem'd to fly;
And then new tears came in my eye,
And I felt troubled and would fain
I had not left my recent chain.
And when I did descend again,
The darkness of my dim abode
Fell on me as a heavy load;
It was as is a new-dug grave,
Closing o'er one we sought to save;
And yet my glance, too much oppress'd,
Had almost need of such a rest.


                    XIV
It might be months, or years, or days—
    I kept no count, I took no note,
I had no hope my eyes to raise,
    And clear them of their dreary mote.
At last men came to set me free,
    I ask'd not why, and reck'd not where,
It was at length the same to me,
Fetter'd or fetterless to be,
    I learn'd to love despair.
And thus when they appear'd at last,
And all my bonds aside were cast,
These heavy walls to me had grown
A hermitage—and all my own!
And half I felt as they were come

To tear me from a second home.
With spiders I had friendship made,
And watch'd them in their sullen trade,
Had seen the mice by moonlight play,
And why should I feel less than they?
We were all inmates of one place,
And I, the monarch of each race,
Had power to kill—yet, strange to tell!
In quiet we had learn'd to dwell—
My very chains and I grew friends,
So much a long communion tends
To make us what we are:—even I
Regain'd my freedom with a sigh.

## On This Day I Complete My Thirty-Sixth Year

'Tis time this heart should be unmoved,
   Since others it hath ceased to move:
Yet, though I cannot be beloved,
     Still let me love!

My days are in the yellow leaf;
   The flowers and fruits of love are gone;
The worm, the canker, and the grief
     Are mine alone!

The fire that on my bosom preys
   Is lone as some volcanic isle;
No torch is kindled at its blaze—
     A funeral pile.

The hope, the fear, the jealous care,
   The exalted portion of the pain
And power of love, I cannot share,
     But wear the chain.

But 'tis not *thus*—and 'tis not *here*—
 Such thoughts should shake my soul, nor *now*,
Where glory decks the hero's bier,
  Or binds his brow.

The sword, the banner, and the field,
 Glory and Greece, around me see!
The Spartan, borne upon his shield,
  Was not more free.

Awake! (not Greece—she *is* awake!)
 Awake, my spirit! Think through *whom*
Thy life-blood tracks its parent lake,
  And then strike home!

Tread those reviving passions down,
 Unworthy manhood!—unto thee
Indifferent should the smile or frown
  Of beauty be.

If thou regret'st thy youth, *why live?*
 The land of honourable death
Is here:—up to the field, and give
  Away thy breath!

Seek out—less often sought than found—
 A soldier's grave, for thee the best;
Then look around, and choose thy ground,
  And take thy rest.

# PERCY BYSSHE SHELLEY
## (1792–1822)

## Hymn to Intellectual Beauty

### I

The awful shadow of some unseen Power
    Floats though unseen among us,—visiting
    This various world with as inconstant wing
As summer winds that creep from flower to flower,—
Like moonbeams that behind some piny mountain shower,
    It visits with inconstant glance
    Each human heart and countenance;
Like hues and harmonies of evening,—
    Like clouds in starlight widely spread,—
    Like memory of music fled,—
    Like aught that for its grace may be
Dear, and yet dearer for its mystery.

### II

Spirit of BEAUTY, that dost consecrate
    With thine own hues all thou dost shine upon
    Of human thought or form,—where art thou gone?
Why dost thou pass away and leave our state,
This dim vast vale of tears, vacant and desolate?
    Ask why the sunlight not for ever
    Weaves rainbows o'er yon mountain-river,
Why aught should fail and fade that once is shown,
    Why fear and dream and death and birth
    Cast on the daylight of this earth
    Such gloom,—why man has such a scope
For love and hate, despondency and hope?

### III

No voice from some sublimer world hath ever
    To sage or poet these responses given—
    Therefore the names of Demon, Ghost, and Heaven,
Remain the records of their vain endeavour,
Frail spells—whose uttered charm might not avail to sever.
    From all we hear and all we see,
    Doubt, chance, and mutability.
Thy light alone—like mist o'er mountains driven,
    Or music by the night-wind sent
    Through strings of some still instrument,
    Or moonlight on a midnight stream,
Gives grace and truth to life's unquiet dream.

### IV

Love, Hope, and Self-esteem, like clouds depart
    And come, for some uncertain moments lent.
    Man were immortal, and omnipotent,
Didst thou, unknown and awful as thou art,
Keep with thy glorious train firm state within his heart.
    Thou messenger of sympathies,
    That wax and wane in lovers' eyes—
Thou—that to human thought art nourishment,
    Like darkness to a dying flame!
    Depart not as thy shadow came,
    Depart not—lest the grave should be,
Like life and fear, a dark reality.

### V

While yet a boy I sought for ghosts, and sped
    Through many a listening chamber, cave and ruin,
    And starlight wood, with fearful steps pursuing
Hopes of high talk with the departed dead.
I called on poisonous names with which our youth is fed;
    I was not heard—I saw them not —
    When musing deeply on the lot
Of life, at that sweet time when winds are wooing

All vital things that wake to bring
News of birds and blossoming,—
Sudden, thy shadow fell on me;
I shrieked, and clasped my hands in ecstasy!

### VI

I vowed that I would dedicate my powers
    To thee and thine—have I not kept the vow?
    With beating heart and streaming eyes, even now
I call the phantoms of a thousand hours
Each from his voiceless grave: they have in visioned bowers
    Of studious zeal or love's delight
    Outwatched with me the envious night—
They know that never joy illumed my brow
    Unlinked with hope that thou wouldst free
    This world from its dark slavery,
    That thou—O awful LOVELINESS,
Wouldst give whate'er these words cannot express.

### VII

The day becomes more solemn and serene
    When noon is past—there is a harmony
    In autumn, and a lustre in its sky,
Which through the summer is not heard or seen,
As if it could not be, as if it had not been!
    Thus let thy power, which like the truth
    Of nature on my passive youth
Descended, to my onward life supply
    Its calm—to one who worships thee,
    And every form containing thee,
    Whom, SPIRIT fair, thy spells did bind
To fear himself, and love all human kind.

# Mont Blanc

*Lines Written in the Vale of Chamouni*

### I

The everlasting universe of things
Flows through the mind, and rolls its rapid waves,
Now dark—now glittering—now reflecting gloom—
Now lending splendour, where from secret springs
The source of human thought its tribute brings
Of waters,—with a sound but half its own,
Such as a feeble brook will oft assume
In the wild woods, among the mountains lone,
Where waterfalls around it leap for ever,
Where woods and winds contend, and a vast river
Over its rocks ceaselessly bursts and raves.

### II

Thus thou, Ravine of Arve—dark, deep Ravine—
Thou many-coloured, many-voicèd vale,
Over whose pines, and crags, and caverns sail
Fast cloud-shadows and sunbeams: awful scene,
Where Power in likeness of the Arve comes down
From the ice-gulfs that gird his secret throne,
Bursting through these dark mountains like the flame
Of lightning through the tempest;—thou dost lie,
Thy giant brood of pines around thee clinging,
Children of elder time, in whose devotion
The chainless winds still come and ever came
To drink their odours, and their mighty swinging
To hear—an old and solemn harmony;
Thine earthly rainbows stretched across the sweep
Of the aethereal waterfall, whose veil
Robes some unsculptured image; the strange sleep
Which when the voices of the desert fail
Wraps all in its own deep eternity;—
Thy caverns echoing to the Arve's commotion,
A loud, lone sound no other sound can tame;

Thou art pervaded with that ceaseless motion,
Thou art the path of that unresting sound—
Dizzy Ravine! and when I gaze on thee
I seem as in a trance sublime and strange
To muse on my own separate fantasy,
My own, my human mind, which passively
Now renders and receives fast influencings,
Holding an unremitting interchange
With the clear universe of things around;
One legion of wild thoughts, whose wandering wings
Now float above thy darkness, and now rest
Where that or thou art no unbidden guest,
In the still cave of the witch Poesy,
Seeking among the shadows that pass by
Ghosts of all things that are, some shade of thee,
Some phantom, some faint image; till the breast
From which they fled recalls them, thou art there!

### III

Some say that gleams of a remoter world
Visit the soul in sleep,—that death is slumber,
And that its shapes the busy thoughts outnumber
Of those who wake and live.—I look on high;
Has some unknown omnipotence unfurled
The veil of life and death? or do I lie
In dream, and does the mightier world of sleep
Spread far around and inaccessibly
Its circles? For the very spirit fails,
Driven like a homeless cloud from steep to steep
That vanishes among the viewless gales!
Far, far above, piercing the infinite sky,
Mont Blanc appears,—still, snowy, and serene—
Its subject mountains their unearthly forms
Pile around it, ice and rock; broad vales between
Of frozen floods, unfathomable deeps,
Blue as the overhanging heaven, that spread
And wind among the accumulated steeps;

A desert peopled by the storms alone,
Save when the eagle brings some hunter's bone,
And the wolf tracks her there—how hideously
Its shapes are heaped around! rude, bare, and high,
Ghastly, and scarred, and riven.—Is this the scene
Where the old Earthquake-daemon taught her young
Ruin? Were these their toys? or did a sea
Of fire envelop once this silent snow?
None can reply—all seems eternal now.
The wilderness has a mysterious tongue
Which teaches awful doubt, or faith so mild,
So solemn, so serene, that man may be,
But for such faith, with nature reconciled;
Thou hast a voice, great Mountain, to repeal
Large codes of fraud and woe; not understood
By all, but which the wise, and great, and good
Interpret, or make felt, or deeply feel.

IV

The fields, the lakes, the forests, and the streams,
Ocean, and all the living things that dwell
Within the daedal earth; lightning, and rain,
Earthquake, and fiery flood, and hurricane,
The torpor of the year when feeble dreams
Visit the hidden buds, or dreamless sleep
Holds every future leaf and flower;—the bound
With which from that detested trance they leap;
The works and ways of man, their death and birth,
And that of him and all that his may be;
All things that move and breathe with toil and sound
Are born and die; revolve, subside, and swell.
Power dwells apart in its tranquillity,
Remote, serene, and inaccessible:
And *this*, the naked countenance of earth,
On which I gaze, even these primaeval mountains
Teach the adverting mind. The glaciers creep
Like snakes that watch their prey, from their far fountains,

Slow rolling on; there, many a precipice,
Frost and the Sun in scorn of mortal power
Have piled: dome, pyramid, and pinnacle,
A city of death, distinct with many a tower
And wall impregnable of beaming ice.
Yet not a city, but a flood of ruin
Is there, that from the boundaries of the sky
Rolls its perpetual stream; vast pines are strewing
Its destined path, or in the mangled soil
Branchless and shattered stand; the rocks, drawn down
From yon remotest waste, have overthrown
The limits of the dead and living world,
Never to be reclaimed. The dwelling-place
Of insects, beasts, and birds, becomes its spoil;
Their food and their retreat for ever gone.
So much of life and joy is lost. The race
Of man flies far in dread; his work and dwelling
Vanish, like smoke before the tempest's stream,
And their place is not known. Below, vast caves
Shine in the rushing torrents' restless gleam.
Which from those secret chasms in tumult welling
Meet in the vale, and one majestic River,
The breath and blood of distant lands, for ever
Rolls its loud waters to the ocean-waves,
Breathes its swift vapours to the circling air.

V

Mont Blanc yet gleams on high:—the power is there,
The still and solemn power of many sights,
And many sounds, and much of life and death.
In the calm darkness of the moonless nights,
In the lone glare of day, the snows descend
Upon that Mountain; none beholds them there,
Nor when the flakes burn in the sinking sun,
Or the star-beams dart through them:—Winds contend
Silently there, and heap the snow with breath
Rapid and strong, but silently! Its home

The voiceless lightning in these solitudes
Keeps innocently, and like vapour broods
Over the snow. The secret Strength of things
Which governs thought, and to the infinite dome
Of Heaven is as a law, inhabits thee!
And what were thou, and earth, and stars, and sea,
If to the human mind's imaginings
Silence and solitude were vacancy?

## Ozymandias

I met a traveller from an antique land
Who said: Two vast and trunkless legs of stone
Stand in the desert . . . Near them, on the sand,
Half sunk, a shattered visage lies, whose frown,
And wrinkled lip, and sneer of cold command,
Tell that its sculptor well those passions read
Which yet survive, stamped on these lifeless things,
The hand that mocked them, and the heart that fed:
And on the pedestal these words appear:
"My name is Ozymandias, king of kings:
Look on my works, ye Mighty, and despair!"
Nothing beside remains. Round the decay
Of that colossal wreck, boundless and bare
The lone and level sands stretch far away.

## Ode to the West Wind

### I

O wild West Wind, thou breath of Autumn's being,
Thou, from whose unseen presence the leaves dead
Are driven, like ghosts from an enchanter fleeing,

Yellow, and black, and pale, and hectic red,
Pestilence-stricken multitudes: O thou,
Who chariotest to their dark wintry bed

The wingèd seeds, where they lie cold and low,
Each like a corpse within its grave, until
Thine azure sister of the Spring shall blow

Her clarion o'er the dreaming earth, and fill
(Driving sweet buds like flocks to feed in air)
With living hues and odours plain and hill:

Wild Spirit, which art moving everywhere;
Destroyer and preserver; hear, oh, hear!

## II

Thou on whose stream, mid the steep sky's commotion,
Loose clouds like earth's decaying leaves are shed,
Shook from the tangled boughs of Heaven and Ocean,

Angels of rain and lightning: there are spread
On the blue surface of thine aëry surge,
Like the bright hair uplifted from the head

Of some fierce Maenad, even from the dim verge
Of the horizon to the zenith's height,
The locks of the approaching storm. Thou dirge

Of the dying year, to which this closing night
Will be the dome of a vast sepulchre,
Vaulted with all thy congregated might

Of vapours, from whose solid atmosphere
Black rain, and fire, and hail will burst: oh, hear!

## III

Thou who didst waken from his summer dreams
The blue Mediterranean, where he lay,
Lulled by the coil of his crystalline streams,

Beside a pumice isle in Baiae's bay,
And saw in sleep old palaces and towers
Quivering within the wave's intenser day,

All overgrown with azure moss and flowers
So sweet, the sense faints picturing them! Thou
For whose path the Atlantic's level powers

Cleave themselves into chasms, while far below
The sea-blooms and the oozy woods which wear
The sapless foliage of the ocean, know

Thy voice, and suddenly grow gray with fear,
And tremble and despoil themselves: oh, hear!

IV

If I were a dead leaf thou mightest bear;
If I were a swift cloud to fly with thee;
A wave to pant beneath thy power, and share

The impulse of thy strength, only less free
Than thou, O uncontrollable! If even
I were as in my boyhood, and could be

The comrade of thy wanderings over Heaven,
As then, when to outstrip thy skiey speed
Scarce seemed a vision; I would ne'er have striven

As thus with thee in prayer in my sore need.
Oh, lift me as a wave, a leaf, a cloud!
I fall upon the thorns of life! I bleed!

A heavy weight of hours has chained and bowed
One too like thee; tameless, and swift, and proud.

V

Make me thy lyre, even as the forest is:
What if my leaves are falling like its own!
The tumult of thy mighty harmonies

Will take from both a deep autumnal tone,
Sweet though in sadness. Be thou Spirit fierce,
My spirit! Be thou me, impetuous one!

Drive my dead thoughts over the universe
Like withered leaves to quicken a new birth!
And, by the incantation of this verse,

Scatter, as from an unextinguished hearth
Ashes and sparks, my words among mankind!
Be through my lips to unawakened earth

The trumpet of a prophecy! O, Wind,
If Winter comes, can Spring be far behind?

## To a Skylark

Hail to thee, blithe Spirit!
Bird thou never wert,
That from Heaven, or near it,
Pourest thy full heart
In profuse strains of unpremeditated art.

Higher still and higher
From the earth thou springest
Like a cloud of fire;
The blue deep thou wingest,
And singing still dost soar, and soaring ever singest.

In the golden lightning
　　Of the sunken sun,
　O'er which clouds are bright'ning,
　　Thou dost float and run; ·
Like an unbodied joy whose race is just begun.

　　The pale purple even
　　　Melts around thy flight;
　Like a star of Heaven,
　　　In the broad daylight
Thou art unseen, but yet I hear thy shrill delight,

　　Keen as are the arrows
　　　Of that silver sphere,
　Whose intense lamp narrows
　　　In the white dawn clear
Until we hardly see—we feel that it is there.

　　All the earth and air
　　　With thy voice is loud,
　As, when night is bare,
　　　From one lonely cloud
The moon rains out her beams, and Heaven is overflowed.

　　What thou art we know not;
　　　What is most like thee?
　From rainbow clouds there flow not
　　　Drops so bright to see
As from thy presence showers a rain of melody.

　　Like a Poet hidden
　　　In the light of thought,
　Singing hymns unbidden,
　　　Till the world is wrought
To sympathy with hopes and fears it heeded not:

Like a high-born maiden
In a palace-tower,
Soothing her love-laden
Soul in secret hour
With music sweet as love, which overflows her bower:

Like a glow-worm golden
In a dell of dew,
Scattering unbeholden
Its aëreal hue
Among the flowers and grass, which screen it from the view!

Like a rose embowered
In its own green leaves,
By warm winds deflowered,
Till the scent it gives
Makes faint with too much sweet those heavy-wingèd thieves:

Sound of vernal showers
On the twinkling grass,
Rain-awakened flowers,
All that ever was
Joyous, and clear, and fresh, thy music doth surpass:

Teach us, Sprite or Bird,
What sweet thoughts are thine:
I have never heard
Praise of love or wine
That panted forth a flood of rapture so divine.

Chorus Hymeneal,
Or triumphal chant,
Matched with thine would be all
But an empty vaunt,
A thing wherein we feel there is some hidden want.

What objects are the fountains
Of thy happy strain?
What fields, or waves, or mountains?
What shapes of sky or plain?
What love of thine own kind? what ignorance of pain?

With thy clear keen joyance
Languor cannot be:
Shadow of annoyance
Never came near thee:
Thou lovest—but ne'er knew love's sad satiety.

Waking or asleep,
Thou of death must deem
Things more true and deep
Than we mortals dream,
Or how could thy notes flow in such a crystal stream?

We look before and after,
And pine for what is not:
Our sincerest laughter
With some pain is fraught;
Our sweetest songs are those that tell of saddest thought.

Yet if we could scorn
Hate, and pride, and fear;
If we were things born
Not to shed a tear,
I know not how thy joy we ever should come near.

Better than all measures
Of delightful sound,
Better than all treasures
That in books are found,
Thy skill to poet were, thou scorner of the ground!

Teach me half the gladness
That thy brain must know,
Such harmonious madness
From my lips would flow
The world should listen then—as I am listening now.

## Adonais

### I

I weep for Adonais—he is dead!
O, weep for Adonais! though our tears
Thaw not the frost which binds so dear a head!
And thou, sad Hour, selected from all years
To mourn our loss, rouse thy obscure compeers,
And teach them thine own sorrow, say: "With me
Died Adonais; till the Future dares
Forget the Past, his fate and fame shall be
An echo and a light unto eternity!"

### II

Where wert thou, mighty Mother, when he lay,
When thy Son lay, pierced by the shaft which flies
In darkness? where was lorn Urania
When Adonais died? With veilèd eyes,
'Mid listening Echoes, in her Paradise
She sate, while one, with soft enamoured breath,
Rekindled all the fading melodies,
With which, like flowers that mock the corse beneath,
He had adorned and hid the coming bulk of Death.

### III

Oh, weep for Adonais—he is dead!
Wake, melancholy Mother, wake and weep!
Yet wherefore? Quench within their burning bed
Thy fiery tears, and let thy loud heart keep
Like his, a mute and uncomplaining sleep;

For he is gone, where all things wise and fair
　Descend;—oh, dream not that the amorous Deep
　Will yet restore him to the vital air;
Death feeds on his mute voice, and laughs at our despair.

### IV

Most musical of mourners, weep again!
　Lament anew, Urania!—He died,
　Who was the Sire of an immortal strain,
　Blind, old, and lonely, when his country's pride,
　The priest, the slave, and the liberticide,
　Trampled and mocked with many a loathèd rite
　Of lust and blood; he went, unterrified,
　Into the gulf of death; but his clear Sprite
Yet reigns o'er earth; the third among the sons of light.

### V

Most musical of mourners, weep anew!
　Not all to that bright station dared to climb;
　And happier they their happiness who knew,
　Whose tapers yet burn through that night of time
　In which suns perished; others more sublime,
　Struck by the envious wrath of man or god,
　Have sunk, extinct in their refulgent prime;
　And some yet live, treading the thorny road,
Which leads, through toil and hate, to Fame's serene abode.

### VI

But now, thy youngest, dearest one, has perished—
　The nursling of thy widowhood, who grew,
　Like a pale flower by some sad maiden cherished,
　And fed with true-love tears, instead of dew;
　Most musical of mourners, weep anew!
　Thy extreme hope, the loveliest and the last,
　The bloom, whose petals nipped before they blew
　Died on the promise of the fruit, is waste;
The broken lily lies—the storm is overpast.

## VII

To that high Capital, where kingly Death
Keeps his pale court in beauty and decay,
He came; and bought, with price of purest breath,
A grave among the eternal.—Come away!
Haste, while the vault of blue Italian day
Is yet his fitting charnel-roof! while still
He lies, as if in dewy sleep he lay;
Awake him not! surely he takes his fill
Of deep and liquid rest, forgetful of all ill.

## VIII

He will awake no more, oh, never more !—
Within the twilight chamber spreads apace
The shadow of white Death, and at the door
Invisible Corruption waits to trace
His extreme way to her dim dwelling-place;
The eternal-Hunger sits, but pity and awe
Soothe her pale rage, nor dares she to deface
So fair a prey, till darkness, and the law
Of change, shall o'er his sleep the mortal curtain draw.

## IX

Oh, weep for Adonais!—The quick Dreams,
The passion-wingèd Ministers of thought,
Who were his flocks, whom near the living streams
Of his young spirit he fed, and whom he taught
The love which was its music, wander not,—
Wander no more, from kindling brain to brain,
But droop there, whence they sprung; and mourn their lot
Round the cold heart, where, after their sweet pain,
They ne'er will gather strength, or find a home again.

## X

And one with trembling hands clasps his cold head,
And fans him with her moonlight wings, and cries;
Our love, our hope, our sorrow, is not dead;
See, on the silken fringe of his faint eyes,

Like dew upon a sleeping flower, there lies
A tear some Dream has loosened from his brain.
Last Angel of a ruined Paradise!
She knew not 'twas her own; as with no stain
She faded, like a cloud which had outwept its rain.

### XI

One from a lucid urn of starry dew
Washed his light limbs as if embalming them;
Another clipped her profuse locks, and threw
The wreath upon him, like an anadem,
Which frozen tears instead of pearls begem;
Another in her wilful grief would break
Her bow and wingèd reeds, as if to stem
A greater loss with one which was more weak;
And dull the barbèd fire against his frozen cheek.

### XII

Another Splendour on his mouth alit,
That mouth, whence it was wont to draw the breath
Which gave it strength to pierce the guarded wit,
And pass into the panting heart beneath
With lightning and with music: the damp death
Quenched its caress upon his icy lips;
And, as a dying meteor stains a wreath
Of moonlight vapour, which the cold night clips,
It flushed through his pale limbs, and passed to its eclipse.

### XIII

And others came . . . Desires and Adorations,
Wingèd Persuasions and veiled Destinies,
Splendours, and Glooms, and glimmering Incarnations
Of hopes and fears, and twilight Phantasies;
And Sorrow, with her family of Sighs,
And Pleasure, blind with tears, led by the gleam
Of her own dying smile instead of eyes,
Came in slow pomp;—the moving pomp might seem
Like pageantry of mist on an autumnal stream.

### XIV

All he had loved, and moulded into thought,
From shape, and hue, and odour, and sweet sound,
Lamented Adonais. Morning sought
Her eastern watch-tower, and her hair unbound,
Wet with the tears which should adorn the ground,
Dimmed the aëreal eyes that kindle day;
Afar the melancholy thunder moaned,
Pale Ocean in unquiet slumber lay,
And the wild Winds flew round, sobbing in their dismay.

### XV

Lost Echo sits amid the voiceless mountains,
And feeds her grief with his remembered lay,
And will no more reply to winds or fountains,
Or amorous birds perched on the young green spray,
Or herdsman's horn, or bell at closing day;
Since she can mimic not his lips, more dear
Than those for whose disdain she pined away
Into a shadow of all sounds:—a drear
Murmur, between their songs, is all the woodmen hear.

### XVI

Grief made the young Spring wild, and she threw down
Her kindling buds, as if she Autumn were,
Or they dead leaves; since her delight is flown,
For whom should she have waked the sullen year?
To Phoebus was not Hyacinth so dear
Nor to himself Narcissus, as to both
Thou, Adonais: wan they stand and sere
Amid the faint companions of their youth,
With dew all turned to tears; odour, to sighing ruth.

### XVII

Thy spirit's sister, the lorn nightingale
Mourns not her mate with such melodious pain;
Not so the eagle, who like thee could scale
Heaven, and could nourish in the sun's domain

Her mighty youth with morning, doth complain,
Soaring and screaming round her empty nest,
As Albion wails for thee: the curse of Cain
Light on his head who pierced thy innocent breast,
And scared the angel soul that was its earthly guest!

### XVIII

Ah, woe is me! Winter is come and gone,
But grief returns with the revolving year;
The airs and streams renew their joyous tone;
The ants, the bees, the swallows reappear;
Fresh leaves and flowers deck the dead Seasons' bier;
The amorous birds now pair in every brake,
And build their mossy homes in field and brere;
And the green lizard, and the golden snake,
Like unimprisoned flames, out of their trance awake.

### XIX

Through wood and stream and field and hill and Ocean
A quickening life from the Earth's heart has burst
As it has ever done, with change and motion,
From the great morning of the world when first
God dawned on Chaos; in its stream immersed,
The lamps of Heaven flash with a softer light;
All baser things pant with life's sacred thirst;
Diffuse themselves; and spend in love's delight,
The beauty and the joy of their renewèd might.

### XX

The leprous corpse, touched by this spirit tender,
Exhales itself in flowers of gentle breath;
Like incarnations of the stars, when splendour
Is changed to fragrance, they illumine death
And mock the merry worm that wakes beneath:
Nought we know, dies. Shall that alone which knows
Be as a sword consumed before the sheath
By sightless lightning?—the intense atom glows
A moment, then is quenched in a most cold repose.

### XXI

Alas! that all we loved of him should be,
But for our grief, as if it had not been,
And grief itself be mortal! Woe is me!
Whence are we, and why are we? of what scene
The actors or spectators? Great and mean
Meet massed in death, who lends what life must borrow.
As long as skies are blue, and fields are green,
Evening must usher night, night urge the morrow,
Month follow month with woe, and year wake year to sorrow.

### XXII

*He* will awake no more, oh, never more!
"Wake thou," cried Misery, "childless Mother, rise
Out of thy sleep, and slake, in thy heart's core,
A wound more fierce than his, with tears and sighs."
And all the Dreams that watched Urania's eyes,
And all the Echoes whom their sister's song
Had held in holy silence, cried: "Arise!"
Swift as a Thought by the snake Memory stung.
From her ambrosial rest the fading Splendour sprung.

### XXIII

She rose like an autumnal Night, that springs
Out of the East, and follows wild and drear
The golden Day, which, on eternal wings,
Even as a ghost abandoning a bier,
Had left the Earth a corpse. Sorrow and fear
So struck, so roused, so rapped Urania;
So saddened round her like an atmosphere
Of stormy mist; so swept her on her way
Even to the mournful place where Adonais lay.

### XXIV

Out of her secret Paradise she sped,
Through camps and cities rough with stone, and steel,
And human hearts, which to her aery tread
Yielding not, wounded the invisible

Palms of her tender feet where 'er they fell:

And barbèd tongues, and thoughts more sharp than they.

Rent the soft Form they never could repel,

Whose sacred blood, like the young tears of May,

Paved with eternal flowers that undeserving way.

## XXV

In the death-chamber for a moment Death,

Shamed by the presence of that living Might,

Blushed to annihilation, and the breath

Revisited those lips, and Life's pale light

Flashed through those limbs, so late her dear delight.

"Leave me not wild and drear and comfortless,

As silent lightning leaves the starless night!

Leave me not!" cried Urania: her distress

Roused Death: Death rose and smiled, and met her vain caress.

## XXVI

"Stay yet awhile! speak to me once again;

Kiss me, so long but as a kiss may live;

And in my heartless breast and burning brain

That word, that kiss, shall all thoughts else survive,

With food of saddest memory kept alive,

Now thou art dead, as if it were a part

Of thee, my Adonais! I would give

All that I am to be as thou now art!

But I am chained to Time, and cannot thence depart!

## XXVII

"O gentle child, beautiful as thou wert,

Why didst thou leave the trodden paths of men

Too soon, and with weak hands though mighty heart

Dare the unpastured dragon in his den?

Defenceless as thou wert, oh, where was then

Wisdom the mirrored shield, or scorn the spear?

Or hadst thou waited the full cycle, when

Thy spirit should have filled its crescent sphere,

The monsters of life's waste had fled from thee like deer.

### XXVIII

The herded wolves, bold only to pursue;
The obscene ravens, clamorous o'er the dead;
The vultures to the conqueror's banner true
Who feed where Desolation first has fed,
And whose wings rain contagion;—how they fled,
When, like Apollo, from his golden bow
The Pythian of the age one arrow sped
And smiled!—The spoilers tempt no second blow,
They fawn on the proud feet that spurn them lying low.

### XXIX

"The sun comes forth, and many reptiles spawn;
He sets, and each ephemeral insect then
Is gathered into death without a dawn,
And the immortal stars awake again;
So is it in the world of living men:
A godlike mind soars forth, in its delight
Making earth bare and veiling heaven, and when
It sinks, the swarms that dimmed or shared its light
Leave to its kindred lamps the spirit's awful night."

### XXX

Thus ceased she: and the mountain shepherds came,
Their garlands sere, their magic mantles rent;
The Pilgrim of Eternity, whose fame
Over his living head like Heaven is bent,
An early but enduring monument,
Came, veiling all the lightnings of his song
In sorrow; from her wilds Ierne sent
The sweetest lyrist of her saddest wrong.
And Love taught Grief to fall like music from his tongue.

### XXXI

Midst others of less note, came one frail Form,
A phantom among men; companionless
As the last cloud of an expiring storm
Whose thunder is its knell; he, as I guess,

Had gazed on Nature's naked loveliness,
Actaeon-like, and now he fled astray
With feeble steps o'er the world's wilderness,
And his own thoughts, along that rugged way,
Pursued, like raging hounds, their father and their prey.

### XXXII

A pardlike Spirit beautiful and swift—
A Love in desolation masked;—a Power
Girt round with weakness;—it can scarce uplift
The weight of the superincumbent hour;
It is a dying lamp, a falling shower,
A breaking billow;—even whilst we speak
Is it not broken? On the withering flower
The killing sun smiles brightly: on a cheek
The life can burn in blood, even while the heart may break.

### XXXIII

His head was bound with pansies overblown,
And faded violets, white, and pied, and blue;
And a light spear topped with a cypress cone,
Round whose rude shaft dark ivy-tresses grew
Yet dripping with the forest's noonday dew,
Vibrated, as the ever-beating heart
Shook the weak hand that grasped it; of that crew
He came the last, neglected and apart;
A herd-abandoned deer struck by the hunter's dart.

### XXXIV

All stood aloof, and at his partial moan
Smiled through their tears; well knew that gentle band
Who in another's fate now wept his own,
As in the accents of an unknown land
He sung new sorrow; sad Urania scanned
The Stranger's mien, and murmured: "Who art thou?"
He answered not, but with a sudden hand
Made bare his branded and ensanguined brow,
Which was like Cain's or Christ's—oh! that it should be so!

### XXXV

What softer voice is hushed over the dead?
Athwart what brow is that dark mantle thrown?
What form leans sadly o'er the white death-bed,
In mockery of monumental stone,
The heavy heart heaving without a moan?
If it be He, who, gentlest of the wise,
Taught, soothed, loved, honoured the departed one,
Let me not vex, with inharmonious sighs,
The silence of that heart's accepted sacrifice.

### XXXVI

Our Adonais has drunk poison—oh!
What deaf and viperous murderer could crown
Life's early cup with such a draught of woe?
The nameless worm would now itself disown:
It felt, yet could escape, the magic tone
Whose prelude held all envy, hate, and wrong,
But what was howling in one breast alone,
Silent with expectation of the song,
Whose master's hand is cold, whose silver lyre unstrung.

### XXXVII

Live thou, whose infamy is not thy fame!
Live! fear no heavier chastisement from me,
Thou noteless blot on a remembered name!
But be thyself, and know thyself to be!
And ever at thy season be thou free
To spill the venom when thy fangs o'erflow:
Remorse and Self-contempt shall cling to thee;
Hot Shame shall burn upon thy secret brow,
And like a beaten hound tremble thou shalt—as now.

### XXXVIII

Nor let us weep that our delight is fled
Far from these carrion kites that scream below;
He wakes or sleeps with the enduring dead;
Thou canst not soar where he is sitting now.—

Dust to the dust! but the pure spirit shall flow
Back to the burning fountain whence it came,
A portion of the Eternal, which must glow
Through time and change, unquenchably the same,
Whilst thy cold embers choke the sordid hearth of shame.

### XXXIX

Peace, peace! he is not dead, he doth not sleep—
He hath awakened from the dream of life—
'Tis we, who lost in stormy visions, keep
With phantoms an unprofitable strife,
And in mad trance, strike with our spirit's knife
Invulnerable nothings.—*We* decay
Like corpses in a charnel; fear and grief
Convulse us and consume us day by day,
And cold hopes swarm like worms within our living clay.

### XL

He has outsoared the shadow of our night;
Envy and calumny and hate and pain,
And that unrest which men miscall delight,
Can touch him not and torture not again;
From the contagion of the world's slow stain
He is secure, and now can never mourn
A heart grown cold, a head grown gray in vain;
Nor, when the spirit's self has ceased to burn,
With sparkless ashes load an unlamented urn.

### XLI

He lives, he wakes—'tis Death is dead, not he;
Mourn not for Adonais.—Thou young Dawn,
Turn all thy dew to splendour, for from thee
The spirit thou lamentest is not gone;
Ye caverns and ye forests, cease to moan!
Cease, ye faint flowers and fountains, and thou Air,
Which like a mourning veil thy scarf hadst thrown
O'er the abandoned Earth, now leave it bare
Even to the joyous stars which smile on its despair!

## XLII

He is made one with Nature: there is heard
His voice in all her music, from the moan
Of thunder, to the song of night's sweet bird;
He is a presence to be felt and known
In darkness and in light, from herb and stone,
Spreading itself where'er that Power may move
Which has withdrawn his being to its own;
Which wields the world with never-wearied love,
Sustains it from beneath, and kindles it above.

## XLIII

He is a portion of the loveliness
Which once he made more lovely: he doth bear
His part, while the one Spirit's plastic stress
Sweeps through the dull dense world, compelling there,
All new successions to the forms they wear;
Torturing th' unwilling dross that checks its flight
To its own likeness, as each mass may bear;
And bursting in its beauty and its might
From trees and beasts and men into the Heaven's light.

## XLIV

The splendours of the firmament of time
May be eclipsed, but are extinguished not;
Like stars to their appointed height they climb,
And death is a low mist which cannot blot
The brightness it may veil. When lofty thought
Lifts a young heart above its mortal lair,
And love and life contend in it, for what
Shall be its earthly doom, the dead live there
And move like winds of light on dark and stormy air.

## XLV

The inheritors of unfulfilled renown
Rose from their thrones, built beyond mortal thought,
Far in the Unapparent. Chatterton
Rose pale,—his solemn agony had not

Yet faded from him; Sidney, as he fought
And as he fell and as he lived and loved
Sublimely mild, a Spirit without spot,
Arose; and Lucan by his death approved:
Oblivion as they rose shrank like a thing reproved.

### XLVI

And many more, whose names on Earth are dark,
But whose transmitted effluence cannot die
So long as fire outlives the parent spark,
Rose, robed in dazzling immortality.
"Thou art become as one of us," they cry,
"It was for thee yon kingless sphere has long
Swung blind in unascended majesty,
Silent alone amid an Heaven of Song.
Assume thy wingèd throne, thou Vesper of our throng!"

### XLVII

Who mourns for Adonais? Oh, come forth,
Fond wretch! and know thyself and him aright.
Clasp with thy panting soul the pendulous Earth;
As from a centre, dart thy spirit's light
Beyond all worlds, until its spacious might
Satiate the void circumference: then shrink
Even to a point within our day and night;
And keep thy heart light lest it make thee sink
When hope has kindled hope, and lured thee to the brink.

### XLVIII

Or go to Rome, which is the sepulchre,
Oh, not of him, but of our joy: 'tis nought
That ages, empires, and religions there
Lie buried in the ravage they have wrought;
For such as he can lend,—they borrow not
Glory from those who made the world their prey;
And he is gathered to the kings of thought
Who waged contention with their time's decay.
And of the past are all that cannot pass away.

### XLIX

Go thou to Rome,—at once the Paradise,
The grave, the city, and the wilderness;
And where its wrecks like shattered mountains rise,
And flowering weeds, and fragrant copses dress
The bones of Desolation's nakedness
Pass, till the spirit of the spot shall lead
Thy footsteps to a slope of green access
Where, like an infant's smile, over the dead
A light of laughing flowers along the grass is spread;

### L

And gray walls moulder round, on which dull Time
Feeds, like slow fire upon a hoary brand;
And one keen pyramid with wedge sublime,
Pavilioning the dust of him who planned
This refuge for his memory, doth stand
Like flame transformed to marble; and beneath,
A field is spread, on which a newer band
Have pitched in Heaven's smile their camp of death,
Welcoming him we lose with scarce extinguished breath.

### LI

Here pause: these graves are all too young as yet
To have outgrown the sorrow which consigned
Its charge to each; and if the seal is set,
Here, on one fountain of a mourning mind,
Break it not thou! too surely shalt thou find
Thine own well full, if thou returnest home,
Of tears and gall. From the world's bitter wind
Seek shelter in the shadow of the tomb.
What Adonais is, why fear we to become?

### LII

The One remains, the many change and pass;
Heaven's light forever shines, Earth's shadows fly;
Life, like a dome of many-coloured glass,
Stains the white radiance of Eternity,

Until Death tramples it to fragments.—Die,
  If thou wouldst be with that which thou dost seek!
  Follow where all is fled!—Rome's azure sky,
  Flowers, ruins, statues, music, words, are weak
The glory they transfuse with fitting truth to speak.

### LIII

  Why linger, why turn back, why shrink, my Heart?
  Thy hopes are gone before: from all things here
  They have departed; thou shouldst now depart!
  A light is passed from the revolving year,
  And man, and woman; and what still is dear
  Attracts to crush, repels to make thee wither.
  The soft sky smiles,—the low wind whispers near:
  'Tis Adonais calls! oh, hasten thither,
No more let Life divide what Death can join together.

### LIV

  That Light whose smile kindles the Universe,
  That Beauty in which all things work and move,
  That Benediction which the eclipsing Curse
  Of birth can quench not, that sustaining Love
  Which through the web of being blindly wove
  By man and beast and earth and air and sea,
  Burns bright or dim, as each are mirrors of
  The fire for which all thirst; now beams on me,
Consuming the last clouds of cold mortality.

### LV

  The breath whose might I have invoked in song
  Descends on me; my spirit's bark is driven,
  Far from the shore, far from the trembling throng
  Whose sails were never to the tempest given;
  The massy earth and spherèd skies are riven!
  I am borne darkly, fearfully, afar;
  Whilst, burning through the inmost veil of Heaven,
  The soul of Adonais, like a star,
Beacons from the abode whore the Eternal are.

# JOHN KEATS
## (1795–1821)

## On First Looking into Chapman's Homer

Much have I travell'd in the realms of gold,
    And many goodly states and kingdoms seen;
    Round many western islands have I been
Which bards in fealty to Apollo hold.
Oft of one wide expanse had I been told
    That deep-brow'd Homer ruled as his demesne;
    Yet did I never breathe its pure serene
Till I heard Chapman speak out loud and bold:
Then felt I like some watcher of the skies
    When a new planet swims into his ken;
Or like stout Cortez when with eagle eyes
    He star'd at the Pacific—and all his men
Look'd at each other with a wild surmise
    Silent, upon a peak in Darien.

## The Eve of St. Agnes

### I

St. Agnes' Eve—Ah, bitter chill it was!
The owl, for all his feathers, was a-cold;
The hare limp'd trembling through the frozen grass,
And silent was the flock in woolly fold:
Numb were the Beadsman's fingers, while he told
His rosary, and while his frosted breath,

Like pious incense from a censer old,
  Seem'd taking flight for heaven, without a death,
Past the sweet Virgin's picture, while his prayer he saith.

II

His prayer he saith, this patient, holy man;
  Then takes his lamp, and riseth from his knees,
And back returneth, meagre, barefoot, wan.
  Along the chapel aisle by slow degrees:
The sculptur'd dead, on each side, seem to freeze,
  Emprison'd in black, purgatorial rails:
Knights, ladies, praying in dumb orat'ries,
  He passeth by; and his weak spirit fails
To think how they may ache in icy hoods and mails.

III

Northward he turneth through a little door,
  And scarce three steps, ere Music's golden tongue
Flatter'd to tears this aged man and poor;
  But no—already had his deathbell rung:
The joys of all his life were said and sung:
  His was harsh penance on St. Agnes' Eve:
Another way he went, and soon among
  Rough ashes sat he for his soul's reprieve,
And all night kept awake, for sinners' sake to grieve.

IV

That ancient Beadsman heard the prelude soft;
  And so it chanc'd, for many a door was wide,
From hurry to and fro. Soon, up aloft,
  The silver, snarling trumpets 'gan to chide:
The level chambers, ready with their pride,
  Were glowing to receive a thousand guests:
The carved angels, ever eager-eyed,
  Star'd, where upon their heads the cornice rests,
With hair blown back, and wings put cross-wise on their breasts.

### V

At length burst in the argent revelry,
With plume, tiara, and all rich array,
Numerous as shadows haunting faerily
The brain, new stuff'd, in youth, with triumphs gay
Of old romance. These let us wish away,
And turn, sole-thoughted, to one Lady there,
Whose heart had brooded, all that wintry day,
On love, and wing'd St. Agnes' saintly care,
As she had heard old dames full many times declare.

### VI

They told her how, upon St. Agnes' Eve,
Young virgins might have visions of delight,
And soft adorings from their loves receive
Upon the honey'd middle of the night,
If ceremonies due they did aright;
As, supperless to bed they must retire,
And couch supine their beauties, lilly white;
Nor look behind, nor sideways, but require
Of Heaven with upward eyes for all that they desire.

### VII

Full of this whim was thoughtful Madeline:
The music, yearning like a God in pain,
She scarcely heard: her maiden eyes divine,
Fix'd on the floor, saw many a sweeping train
Pass by—she heeded not at all: in vain
Came many a tiptoe, amorous cavalier,
And back retir'd; not cool'd by high disdain,
But she saw not: her heart was otherwhere:
She sigh'd for Agnes' dreams, the sweetest of the year.

### VIII

She danc'd along with vague, regardless eyes,
Anxious her lips, her breathing quick and short:
The hallow'd hour was near at hand: she sighs
Amid the timbrels, and the throng'd resort

Of whisperers in anger, or in sport;
　'Mid looks of love, defiance, hate, and scorn,
　Hoodwink'd with faery fancy; all amort,
　Save to St. Agnes and her lambs unshorn,
And all the bliss to be before to-morrow morn.

### IX

So, purposing each moment to retire,
　She linger'd still. Meantime, across the moors,
　Had come young Porphyro, with heart on fire
For Madeline. Beside the portal doors,
Buttress'd from moonlight, stands he, and implores
　All saints to give him sight of Madeline,
　But for one moment in the tedious hours,
　That he might gaze and worship all unseen;
Perchance speak, kneel, touch, kiss—in sooth such things have been.

### X

He ventures in: let no buzz'd whisper tell:
　All eyes be muffled, or a hundred swords
　Will storm his heart, Love's fev'rous citadel:
For him, those chambers held barbarian hordes,
Hyena foemen, and hot-blooded lords,
　Whose very dogs would execrations howl
　Against his lineage: not one breast affords
　Him any mercy, in that mansion foul,
Save one old beldame, weak in body and in soul.

### XI

Ah, happy chance! the aged creature came,
　Shuffling along with ivory-headed wand,
　To where he stood, hid from the torch's flame,
Behind a broad hall-pillar, far beyond
The sound of merriment and chorus bland:
　He startled her; but soon she knew his face,
　And grasp'd his fingers in her palsied hand,
　Saying, "Mercy, Porphyro! hie thee from this place!
They are all here to-night, the whole blood-thirsty race:

### XII

"Get hence! get hence! there's dwarfish Hildebrand;
He had a fever late, and in the fit
He cursed thee and thine, both house and land:
Then there's that old Lord Maurice, not a whit
More tame for his gray hairs—Alas me! flit!
Flit like a ghost away."—"Ah, Gossip dear,
We're safe enough; here in this arm-chair sit,
And tell me how"—"Good Saints! not here, not here;
Follow me, child, or else these stones will be thy bier."

### XIII

He follow'd through a lowly arched way,
Brushing the cobwebs with his lofty plume,
And as she mutter'd "Well-a—well-a-day!"
He found him in a little moonlight room,
Pale, lattic'd, chill, and silent as a tomb.
"Now tell me where is Madeline," said he,
"O tell me, Angela, by the holy loom
Which none but secret sisterhood may see,
When they St. Agnes' wool are weaving piously."

### XIV

"St. Agnes! Ah! it is St. Agnes' Eve—
Yet men will murder upon holy days:
Thou must hold water in a witch's sieve,
And be liege-lord of all the Elves and Fays,
To venture so: it fills me with amaze
To see thee, Porphyro!—St. Agnes' Eve!
God's help! my lady fair the conjuror plays
This very night: good angels her deceive!
But let me laugh awhile, I've mickle time to grieve."

### XV

Feebly she laugheth in the languid moon,
While Porphyro upon her face doth look,
Like puzzled urchin on an aged crone
Who keepeth clos'd a wond'rous riddle-book,

As spectacled she sits in chimney nook.
But soon his eyes grew brilliant, when she told
His lady's purpose; and he scarce could brook
  Tears, at the thought of those enchantments cold,
And Madeline asleep in lap of legends old.

### XVI

Sudden a thought came like a full-blown rose,
Flushing his brow, and in his pained heart
Made purple riot: then doth he propose
A stratagem, that makes the beldame start:
"A cruel man and impious thou art:
Sweet lady, let her pray, and sleep, and dream
Alone with her good angels, far apart
  From wicked men like thee. Go, go!—I deem
Thou canst not surely be the same that thou didst seem."

### XVII

"I will not harm her, by all saints I swear,"
Quoth Porphyro: "O may I ne'er find grace
When my weak voice shall whisper its last prayer,
If one of her soft ringlets I displace,
Or look with ruffian passion in her face:
Good Angela, believe me by these tears;
Or I will, even in a moment's space,
  Awake, with horrid shout, my foemen's ears,
And beard them, though they be more fang'd than wolves and bears."

### XVIII

"Ah! why wilt thou affright a feeble soul?
A poor, weak, palsy-stricken, churchyard thing,
Whose passing-bell may ere the midnight toll;
Whose prayers for thee, each morn and evening,
Were never miss'd."—Thus plaining, doth she bring
A gentler speech from burning Porphyro;
So woful, and of such deep sorrowing,
  That Angela gives promise she will do
Whatever he shall wish, betide her weal or woe.

### XIX

Which was, to lead him, in close secrecy,
Even to Madeline's chamber, and there hide
Him in a closet, of such privacy
That he might see her beauty unespied,
And win perhaps that night a peerless bride,
While legion'd faeries pac'd the coverlet,
And pale enchantment held her sleepy-eyed.
Never on such a night have lovers met,
Since Merlin paid his Demon all the monstrous debt.

### XX

"It shall be as thou wishest," said the Dame:
"All cates and dainties shall be stored there
Quickly on this feast-night: by the tambour frame
Her own lute thou wilt see: no time to spare,
For I am slow and feeble, and scarce dare
On such a catering trust my dizzy head.
Wait here, my child, with patience; kneel in prayer
The while: Ah! thou must needs the lady wed,
Or may I never leave my grave among the dead."

### XXI

So saying, she hobbled off with busy fear.
The lover's endless minutes slowly pass'd;
The dame return'd, and whisper'd in his ear
To follow her; with aged eyes aghast
From fright of dim espial. Safe at last,
Through many a dusky gallery, they gain
The maiden's chamber, silken, hush'd, and chaste;
Where Porphyro took covert, pleas'd amain.
His poor guide hurried back with agues in her brain.

### XXII

Her falt'ring hand upon the balustrade,
Old Angela was feeling for the stair,
When Madeline, St. Agnes' charmed maid,
Rose, like a mission'd spirit, unaware:

With silver taper's light, and pious care,
She turn'd, and down the aged gossip led
To a safe level matting. Now prepare,
Young Porphyro, for gazing on that bed;
She comes, she comes again, like ring-dove fray'd and fled.

### XXIII

Out went the taper as she hurried in;
Its little smoke, in pallid moonshine, died:
She clos'd the door, she panted, all akin
To spirits of the air, and visions wide:
No uttered syllable, or, woe betide!
But to her heart, her heart was voluble,
Paining with eloquence her balmy side;
As though a tongueless nightingale should swell
Her throat in vain, and die, heart-stifled, in her dell.

### XXIV

A casement high and triple-arch'd there was,
All garlanded with carven imag'ries
Of fruits, and flowers, and bunches of knot-grass,
And diamonded with panes of quaint device,
Innumerable of stains and splendid dyes,
As are the tiger-moth's deep-damask'd wings;
And in the midst, 'mong thousand heraldries,
And twilight saints, and dim emblazonings,
A shielded scutcheon blush'd with blood of queens and kings.

### XXV

Full on this casement shone the wintry moon,
And threw warm gules on Madeline's fair breast,
As down she knelt for heaven's grace and boon;
Rose-bloom fell on her hands, together prest,
And on her silver cross soft amethyst,
And on her hair a glory, like a saint:
She seem'd a splendid angel, newly drest,
Save wings, for heaven:—Porphyro grew faint:
She knelt, so pure a thing, so free from mortal taint.

### XXVI

Anon his heart revives: her vespers done,
  Of all its wreathed pearls her hair she frees;
  Unclasps her warmed jewels one by one;
  Loosens her fragrant boddice; by degrees
  Her rich attire creeps rustling to her knees:
  Half-hidden, like a mermaid in sea-weed,
  Pensive awhile she dreams awake, and sees,
  In fancy, fair St. Agnes in her bed,
But dares not look behind, or all the charm is fled.

### XXVII

Soon, trembling in her soft and chilly nest,
  In sort of wakeful swoon, perplex'd she lay,
  Until the poppied warmth of sleep oppress'd
  Her soothed limbs, and soul fatigued away;
  Flown, like a thought, until the morrow-day;
  Blissfully haven'd both from joy and pain;
  Clasp'd like a missal where swart Paynims pray;
  Blinded alike from sunshine and from rain,
As though a rose should shut, and be a bud again.

### XXVIII

Stol'n to this paradise, and so entranced,
  Porphyro gazed upon her empty dress,
  And listen'd to her breathing, if it chanced
  To wake into a slumberous tenderness;
  Which when he heard, that minute did he bless,
  And breath'd himself: then from the closet crept,
  Noiseless as fear in a wide wilderness,
  And over the hush'd carpet, silent, stept,
And 'tween the curtains peep'd, where, lo!—how fast she slept.

### XXIX

Then by the bed-side, where the faded moon
  Made a dim, silver twilight, soft he set
  A table, and, half anguish'd, threw thereon
  A cloth of woven crimson, gold, and jet:—

O for some drowsy Morphean amulet!
The boisterous, midnight, festive clarion,
The kettle-drum, and far-heard clarinet,
Affray his ears, though but in dying tone:—
The hall door shuts again, and all the noise is gone.

### XXX

And still she slept an azure-lidded sleep,
In blanched linen, smooth, and lavender'd,
While he from forth the closet brought a heap
Of candied apple, quince, and plum, and gourd;
With jellies soother than the creamy curd,
And lucent syrops, tinct with cinnamon;
Manna and dates, in argosy transferr'd
From Fez; and spiced dainties, every one,
From silken Samarcand to cedar'd Lebanon.

### XXXI

These delicates he heap'd with glowing hand
On golden dishes and in baskets bright
Of wreathed silver: sumptuous they stand
In the retired quiet of the night,
Filling the chilly room with perfume light.—
"And now, my love, my seraph fair, awake!
Thou art my heaven, and I thine eremite:
Open thine eyes, for meek St. Agnes' sake,
Or I shall drowse beside thee, so my soul doth ache."

### XXXII

Thus whispering, his warm, unnerved arm
Sank in her pillow. Shaded was her dream
By the dusk curtains:—'twas a midnight charm
Impossible to melt as iced stream:
The lustrous salvers in the moonlight gleam;
Broad golden fringe upon the carpet lies:
It seem'd he never, never could redeem
From such a stedfast spell his lady's eyes;
So mus'd awhile, entoil'd in woofed phantasies.

### XXXIII

Awakening up, he took her hollow lute,—
Tumultuous,—and, in chords that tenderest be,
He play'd an ancient ditty, long since mute,
In Provence call'd, "La belle dame sans mercy":
Close to her ear touching the melody;—
Wherewith disturb'd, she utter'd a soft moan:
He ceased—she panted quick—and suddenly
Her blue affrayed eyes wide open shone:
Upon his knees he sank, pale as smooth-sculptured stone.

### XXXIV

Her eyes were open, but she still beheld,
Now wide awake, the vision of her sleep:
There was a painful change, that nigh expell'd
The blisses of her dream so pure and deep
At which fair Madeline began to weep,
And moan forth witless words with many a sigh;
While still her gaze on Porphyro would keep;
Who knelt, with joined hands and piteous eye,
Fearing to move or speak, she look'd so dreamingly.

### XXXV

"Ah, Porphyro!" said she, "but even now
Thy voice was at sweet tremble in mine ear,
Made tuneable with every sweetest vow;
And those sad eyes were spiritual and clear:
How chang'd thou art! how pallid, chill, and drear!
Give me that voice again, my Porphyro,
Those looks immortal, those complainings dear!
Oh leave me not in this eternal woe,
For if thou diest, my Love, I know not where to go."

### XXXVI

Beyond a mortal man impassion'd far
At these voluptuous accents, he arose,
Ethereal, flush'd, and like a throbbing star
Seen mid the sapphire heaven's deep repose;

Into her dream he melted, as the rose
Blendeth its odour with the violet,—
Solution sweet: meantime the frost-wind blows
Like Love's alarum pattering the sharp sleet
Against the window-panes; St. Agnes' moon hath set.

### XXXVII

'Tis dark: quick pattereth the flaw-blown sleet:
"This is no dream, my bride, my Madeline!"
'Tis dark: the iced gusts still rave and beat:
"No dream, alas! alas! and woe is mine!
Porphyro will leave me here to fade and pine.—
Cruel! what traitor could thee hither bring?
I curse not, for my heart is lost in thine,
Though thou forsakest a deceived thing;—
A dove forlorn and lost with sick unpruned wing."

### XXXVIII

"My Madeline! sweet dreamer! lovely bride!
Say, may I be for aye thy vassal blest?
Thy beauty's shield, heart-shap'd and vermeil dyed?
Ah, silver shrine, here will I take my rest
After so many hours of toil and quest,
A famish'd pilgrim,—sav'd by miracle.
Though I have found, I will not rob thy nest
Saving of thy sweet self; if thou think'st well
To trust, fair Madeline, to no rude infidel.

### XXXIX

"Hark! 'tis an elfin-storm from faery land,
Of haggard seeming, but a boon indeed:
Arise    arise! the morning is at hand;—
The bloated wassaillers will never heed:
Let us away, my love, with happy speed;
There are no ears to hear, or eyes to see,—
Drown'd all in Rhenish and the sleepy mead:
Awake! arise! my love, and fearless be,
For o'er the southern moors I have a home for thee."

### XL

She hurried at his words, beset with fears,
For there were sleeping dragons all around,
At glaring watch, perhaps, with ready spears—
Down the wide stairs a darkling way they found.—
In all the house was heard no human sound.
A chain-droop'd lamp was flickering by each door;
The arras, rich with horseman, hawk, and hound,
Flutter'd in the besieging wind's uproar;
And the long carpets rose along the gusty floor.

### XLI

They glide, like phantoms, into the wide hall;
Like phantoms, to the iron porch, they glide;
Where lay the Porter, in uneasy sprawl,
With a huge empty flaggon by his side:
The wakeful bloodhound rose, and shook his hide,
But his sagacious eye an inmate owns:
By one, and one, the bolts full easy slide:—
The chains lie silent on the footworn stones;—
The key turns, and the door upon its hinges groans.

### XLII

And they are gone: aye, ages long ago
These lovers fled away into the storm.
That night the Baron dreamt of many a woe,
And all his warrior-guests, with shade and form
Of witch, and demon, and large coffin-worm,
Were long be-nightmar'd. Angela the old
Died palsy-twitch'd, with meagre face deform;
The Beadsman, after thousand aves told,
For aye unsought for slept among his ashes cold.

# Ode to a Nightingale

### I

My heart aches, and a drowsy numbness pains
   My sense, as though of hemlock I had drunk,
Or emptied some dull opiate to the drains
   One minute past, and Lethe-wards had sunk:
'Tis not through envy of thy happy lot,
   But being too happy in thine happiness,—
      That thou, light-winged Dryad of the trees,
        In some melodious plot
Of beechen green, and shadows numberless,
   Singest of summer in full-throated ease.

### II

O, for a draught of vintage! that hath been
   Cool'd a long age in the deep-delved earth,
Tasting of Flora and the country green,
   Dance, and Provençal song, and sunburnt mirth!
O for a beaker full of the warm South,
   Full of the true, the blushful Hippocrene,
      With beaded bubbles winking at the brim,
        And purple-stained mouth;
That I might drink, and leave the world unseen,
   And with thee fade away into the forest dim:

### III

Fade far away, dissolve, and quite forget
   What thou among the leaves hast never known,
The weariness, the fever, and the fret,
   Here, where men sit and hear each other groan;
Where palsy shakes a few, sad, last gray hairs,
   Where youth grows pale, and spectre-thin, and dies;
      Where but to think is to be full of sorrow
        And leaden-eyed despairs,
Where Beauty cannot keep her lustrous eyes,
   Or new Love pine at them beyond to-morrow.

### IV

Away! away! for I will fly to thee,
   Not charioted by Bacchus and his pards,
But on the viewles wings of Poesy,
   Though the dull brain perplexes and retards:
Already with thee! tender is the night,
    And haply the Queen-Moon is on her throne,
      Cluster'd around by all her starry Fays;
        But here there is no light,
Save what from heaven is with the breezes blown
    Through verdurous glooms and winding mossy ways.

### V

I cannot see what flowers are at my feet,
   Nor what soft incense hangs upon the boughs,
But, in embalmed darkness, guess each sweet
   Wherewith the seasonable month endows
The grass, the thicket, and the fruit-tree wild;
   White hawthorn, and the pastoral eglantine;
     Fast fading violets cover'd up in leaves;
      And mid-May's eldest child,
The coming musk-rose, full of dewy wine,
    The murmurous haunt of flies on summer eves.

### VI

Darkling I listen; and, for many a time
   I have been half in love with easeful Death,
Call'd him soft names in many a mused rhyme,
   To take into the air my quiet breath;
Now more than ever seems it rich to die,
   To cease upon the midnight with no pain,
     While thou art pouring forth thy soul abroad
      In such an ecstasy!
Still wouldst thou sing, and I have ears in vain—
    To thy high requiem become a sod.

### VII

Thou wast not born for death, immortal Bird!
  No hungry generations tread thee down;
The voice I hear this passing night was heard
  In ancient days by emperor and clown:
Perhaps the self-same song that found a path
    Through the sad heart of Ruth, when, sick for home.
      She stood in tears amid the alien corn;
        The same that oft-times hath
Charm'd magic casements, opening on the foam
  Of perilous seas, in faery lands forlorn.

### VIII

Forlorn! the very word is like a bell
  To toll me back from thee to my sole self!
Adieu! the fancy cannot cheat so well
  As she is fam'd to do, deceiving elf.
Adieu! adieu! thy plaintive anthem fades
  Past the near meadows, over the still stream,
    Up the hill-side; and now 'tis buried deep
      In the next valley-glades:
Was it a vision, or a waking dream?
  Fled is that music:—Do I wake or sleep?

# Ode on a Grecian Urn

### I

Thou still-unravish'd bride of quietness,
  Thou foster-child of silence and slow time,
Sylvan historian, who canst thus express
  A flowery tale more sweetly than our rhyme:
What leaf-fring'd legend haunts about thy shape
  Of deities or mortals, or of both,
    In Tempe or the dales of Arcady?
  What men or gods are these? What maidens loth?
What mad pursuit? What struggle to escape?
  What pipes and timbrels? What wild ecstasy?

## II

Heard melodies are sweet, but those unheard
  Are sweeter; therefore, ye soft pipes, play on;
Not to the sensual ear, but, more endear'd,
  Pipe to the spirit ditties of no tone:
Fair youth, beneath the trees, thou canst not leave
  Thy song, nor ever can those trees be bare;
    Bold Lover, never, never canst thou kiss,
Though winning near the goal—yet, do not grieve;
  She cannot fade, though thou hast not thy bliss,
    For ever wilt thou love, and she be fair!

## III

Ah, happy, happy boughs! that cannot shed
  Your leaves, nor ever bid the Spring adieu;
And, happy melodist, unwearied,
  For ever piping songs for ever new;
More happy love! more happy, happy love!
  For ever warm and still to be enjoy'd,
    For ever panting, and for ever young;
All breathing human passion far above,
  That leaves a heart high-sorrowful and cloy'd,
    A burning forehead, and a parching tongue.

## IV

Who are these coming to the sacrifice?
  To what green altar, O mysterious priest,
Lead'st thou that heifer lowing at the skies,
  And all her silken flanks with garlands drest?
What little town by river or sea shore,
  Or mountain-built with peaceful citadel,
    Is emptied of this folk, this pious morn?
And, little town, thy streets for evermore
  Will silent be; and not a soul to tell
    Why thou art desolate, can e'er return.

V

O Attic shape! Fair attitude! with brede
　　Of marble men and maidens overwrought,
With forest branches and the trodden weed;
　　Thou, silent form, dost tease us out of thought
As doth eternity: Cold Pastoral!
　　When old age shall this generation waste,
　　　Thou shalt remain, in midst of other woe
Than ours, a friend to man, to whom thou say'st,
　　"Beauty is truth, truth beauty,— that is all
　　　Ye know on earth, and all ye need to know."

## Ode to Psyche

O Goddess! hear these tuneless numbers, wrung
　　By sweet enforcement and remembrance dear,
And pardon that thy secrets should be sung
　　Even into thine own soft-conched-ear:
Surely I dreamt to-day, or did I see
　　The winged Psyche with awaken'd eyes?
I wander'd in a forest thoughtlessly,
　　And, on the sudden, fainting with surprise,
Saw two fair creatures, couched side by side
　　In deepest grass, beneath the whisp'ring roof
　　Of leaves and trembled blossoms, where there ran
　　　A brooklet, scarce espied:

'Mid hush'd, cool-rooted flowers, fragrant-eyed,
　　Blue, silver-white, and budded Tyrian,
They lay calm-breathing on the bedded grass;
　　Their arms embraced, and their pinions too;
　　Their lips touch'd not, but had not bade adieu,
As if disjoined by soft-handed slumber,
And ready still past kisses to outnumber

At tender eye-dawn of aurorean love:
 The winged boy I knew;
But who wast thou, O happy, happy dove?
 His Psyche true!

O latest born and loveliest vision far
 Of all Olympus' faded hierarchy!
Fairer than Phoebe's sapphire-region'd star,
 Or Vesper, amorous glow-worm of the sky;
Fairer than these, though temple thou hast none,
 Nor altar heap'd with flowers;
Nor virgin-choir to make delicious moan
 Upon the midnight hours;
No voice, no lute, no pipe, no incense sweet
 From chain-swung censer teeming;
No shrine, no grove, no oracle, no heat
 Of pale-mouth'd prophet dreaming.

O brightest! though too late for antique vows,
 Too, too late for the fond believing lyre,
When holy were the haunted forest boughs,
 Holy the air, the water, and the fire;
Yet even in these days so far retir'd
 From happy pieties, thy lucent fans,
 Fluttering among the faint Olympians,
I see, and sing, by my own eyes inspir'd.
So let me be thy choir, and make a moan
 Upon the midnight hours;
Thy voice, thy lute, thy pipe, thy incense sweet
 From swinged censer teeming;
Thy shrine, thy grove, thy oracle, thy heat
 Of pale-mouth'd prophet dreaming.

Yes, I will be thy priest, and build a fane
 In some untrodden region of my mind,
Where branched thoughts, new grown with pleasant pain,
 Instead of pines shall murmur in the wind:

Far, far around shall those dark-cluster'd trees
   Fledge the wild-ridged mountains steep by steep;
And there by zephyrs, streams, and birds, and bees,
   The moss-lain Dryads shall be lull'd to sleep;
And in the midst of this wide quietness
A rosy sanctuary will I dress
With the wreath'd trellis of a working brain,
   With buds, and bells, and stars without a name,
With all the gardener Fancy e'er could feign,
   Who breeding flowers, will never breed the same:
And there shall be for thee all soft delight
   That shadowy thought can win,
A bright torch, and a casement ope at night,
   To let the warm Love in!

## To Autumn

### I

Season of mists and mellow fruitfulness,
   Close bosom-friend of the maturing sun;
Conspiring with him how to load and bless
   With fruit the vines that round the thatch-eves run;
To bend with apples the moss'd cottage-trees,
   And fill all fruit with ripeness to the core;
     To swell the gourd, and plump the hazel shells
   With a sweet kernel; to set budding more,
And still more, later flowers for the bees,
Until they think warm days will never cease,
     For Summer has o'er-brimm'd their clammy cells.

### II

Who hath not seen thee oft amid thy store?
   Sometimes whoever seeks abroad may find
Thee sitting careless on a granary floor,
   Thy hair soft-lifted by the winnowing wind;

Or on a half-reap'd furrow sound asleep,
   Drows'd with the fume of poppies, while thy hook
      Spares the next swath and all its twined flowers:
And sometimes like a gleaner thou dost keep
   Steady thy laden head across a brook;
   Or by a cyder-press, with patient look,
      Thou watchest the last oozings hours by hours.

### III

Where are the songs of Spring? Ay, where are they?
   Think not of them, thou hast thy music too,—
While barred clouds bloom the soft-dying day,
   And touch the stubble-plains with rosy hue;
Then in a wailful choir the small gnats mourn
   Among the river sallows, borne aloft
      Or sinking as the light wind lives or dies;
And full-grown lambs loud bleat from hilly bourn;
   Hedge-crickets sing; and now with treble soft
   The red-breast whistles from a garden-croft;
      And gathering swallows twitter in the skies.

# Ode on Melancholy

### I

No, no, go not to Lethe, neither twist
   Wolfs-bane, tight-rooted, for its poisonous wine;
Nor suffer thy pale forehead to be kiss'd
   By nightshade, ruby grape of Proserpine,
Make not your rosary of yew-berries,
   Nor let the beetle, nor the death-moth be
      Your mournful Psyche, nor the downy owl
A partner in your sorrow's mysteries;
   For shade to shade will come too drowsily,
      And drown the wakeful anguish of the soul.

## II

But when the melancholy fit shall fall
    Sudden from heaven like a weeping cloud,
That fosters the droop-headed flowers all,
    And hides the green hill in an April shroud;
Then glut thy sorrow on a morning rose,
    Or on the rainbow of the salt sand-wave,
      Or on the wealth of globed peonies;
Or if thy mistress some rich anger shows,
    Emprison her soft hand, and let her rave,
      And feed deep, deep upon her peerless eyes.

## III

She dwells with Beauty—Beauty that must die;
    And Joy, whose hand is ever at his lips
Bidding adieu; and aching Pleasure nigh,
    Turning to Poison while the bee-mouth sips:
Ay, in the very temple of delight
    Veil'd Melancholy has her sovran shrine,
      Though seen of none save him whose strenuous tongue
Can burst Joy's grape against his palate fine;
His soul shall taste the sadness of her might,
    And be among her cloudy trophies hung.

SONNET

# When I Have Fears That I May Cease to Be

When I have fears that I may cease to be
    Before my pen has glean'd my teeming brain,
Before high-piled books, in charactery,
    Hold like rich garners the full ripen'd grain;
When I behold, upon the night's starr'd face,
    Huge cloudy symbols of a high romance,
And think that I may never live to trace
    Their shadows, with the magic hand of chance;

And when I feel, fair creature of an hour,
   That I shall never look upon thee more,
Never have relish in the faery power
   Of unreflecting love;—then on the shore
Of the wide world I stand alone, and think
Till love and fame to nothingness do sink.

## La Belle Dame Sans Merci

### I

Ah, what can ail thee, wretched wight,
   Alone and palely loitering;
The sedge is wither'd from the lake,
   And no birds sing.

### II

Ah, what can ail thee, wretched wight,
   So haggard and so woe-begone?
The squirrel's granary is full,
   And the harvest's done.

### III

I see a lilly on thy brow,
   With anguish moist and fever dew;
And on thy cheek a fading rose
   Fast withereth too.

### IV

I met a lady in the meads
   Full beautiful, a faery's child;
Her hair was long, her foot was light,
   And her eyes were wild.

### V

I set her on my pacing steed,
    And nothing else saw all day long;
For sideways would she lean, and sing
    A faery's song.

### VI

I made a garland for her head,
    And bracelets too, and fragrant zone;
She look'd at me as she did love,
    And made sweet moan.

### VII

She found me roots of relish sweet,
    And honey wild, and manna dew;
And sure in language strange she said,
    I love thee true.

### VIII

She took me to her elfin grot,
    And there she gaz'd and sighed deep,
And there I shut her wild sad eyes —
    So kiss'd to sleep.

### IX

And there we slumber'd on the moss,
    And there I dream'd, ah woe betide,
The latest dream I ever dream'd
    On the cold hill side.

### X

I saw pale kings, and princes too,
    Pale warriors, death-pale were they all;
Who cry'd—"La belle Dame sans merci
    Hath thee in thrall!

### XI

I saw their starv'd lips in the gloam
  With horrid warning gaped wide,
And I awoke, and found me here
  On the cold hill side.

### XII

And this is why I sojourn here
  Alone and palely loitering,
Though the sedge is wither'd from the lake,
  And no birds sing.

<hr>

SONNET

# To Sleep

O Soft embalmer of the still midnight,
  Shutting, with careful lingers and benign,
Our gloom-pleas'd eyes, embower'd from the light,
  Enshaded in forgetfulness divine:
O soothest Sleep! if so it please thee, close
  In midst of this thine hymn my willing eyes,
Or wait the "Amen," ere thy poppy throws
  Around my bed its lulling charities.
Then save me, or the passed day will shine
Upon my pillow, breeding many woes,—
  Save me from curious Conscience, that still lords
Its strength for darkness, burrowing like a mole;
  Turn the key deftly in the oiled wards,
And seal the hushed Casket of my Soul.

<hr>

# Ode on Indolence

*"They toil not, neither do they spin."*

### I

One morn before me were three figures seen,
  With bowed necks, and joined hands, side-faced;
And one behind the other stepp'd serene,
  In placid sandals, and in white robes graced;
They pass'd, like figures on a marble urn,
  When shifted round to see the other side;
    They came again; as when the urn once more
Is shifted round, the first seen shades return;
  And they were strange to me, as may betide
    With vases, to one deep in Phidian lore.

### II

How is it, Shadows! that I knew ye not?
  How came ye muffled in so hush a mask?
Was it a silent deep-disguised plot
  To steal away, and leave without a task
My idle days? Ripe was the drowsy hour;
  The blissful cloud of summer-indolence
    Benumb'd my eyes; my pulse grew less and less;
Pain had no sting, and pleasure's wreath no flower:
  O, why did ye not melt, and leave my sense
    Unhaunted quite of all but—nothingness?

### III

A third time pass'd they by, and, passing, turn'd
  Each one the face a moment whiles to me;
Then faded, and to follow them I burn'd
  And ach'd for wings because I knew the three;
The first was a fair Maid, and Love her name;
  The second was Ambition, pale of cheek,
    And ever watchful with fatigued eye;
The last, whom I love more, the more of blame
  Is heap'd upon her, maiden most unmeek,—
    I knew to be my demon Poesy.

### IV

They faded, and, forsooth! I wanted wings:
   O folly! What is love! and where is it?
And for that poor Ambition! it springs
   From a man's little heart's short fever-fit;
For Poesy!—no,—she has not a joy,—
   At least for me,—so sweet as drowsy noons,
     And evenings steep'd in honied indolence;
O, for an age so shelter'd from annoy,
   That I may never know how change the moons,
     Or hear the voice of busy common-sense!

### V

And once more came they by;—alas! wherefore?
   My sleep had been embroider'd with dim dreams;
My soul had been a lawn besprinkled o'er
   With flowers, and stirring shades, and baffled beams:
The morn was clouded, but no shower fell,
   Tho' in her lids hung the sweet tears of May;
     The open casement press'd a new-leav'd vine,
   Let in the budding warmth and throstle's lay;
O Shadows! 'twas a time to bid farewell!
   Upon your skirts had fallen no tears of mine.

### VI

So, ye three Ghosts, adieu! Ye cannot raise
   My head cool-bedded in the flowery grass;
For I would not be dieted with praise,
   A pet-lamb in a sentimental farce!
Fade softly from my eyes, and be once more
   In masque-like figures on the dreamy urn;
     Farewell! I yet have visions for the night,
And for the day faint visions there is store;
     Vanish, ye Phantoms! from my idle spright,
   Into the clouds, and never more return!

SONNET

# Bright Star

Bright star, would I were stedfast as thou art—
  Not in lone splendour hung aloft the night
And watching, with eternal lids apart,
  Like nature's patient, sleepless Eremite,
The moving waters at their priestlike task
  Of pure ablution round earth's human shores,
Or gazing on the new soft-fallen mask
  Of snow upon the mountains and the moors—
No—yet still stedfast, still unchangeable,
  Pillow'd upon my fair love's ripening breast,
To feel for ever its soft fall and swell,
  Awake for ever in a sweet unrest,
Still, still to hear her tender-taken breath,
And so live ever—or else swoon to death.

# WILLIAM CULLEN BRYANT

## (1794–1878)

## Thanatopsis

To him who in the love of Nature holds
Communion with her visible forms, she speaks
A various language; for his gayer hours
She has a voice of gladness, and a smile
And eloquence of beauty, and she glides
Into his darker musings, with a mild
And healing sympathy, that steals away
Their sharpness, ere he is aware. When thoughts
Of the last bitter hour come like a blight
Over thy spirit, and sad images
Of the stern agony, and shroud, and pall,
And breathless darkness, and the narrow house,
Make thee to shudder, and grow sick at heart;—
Go forth, under the open sky, and list
To Nature's teachings, while from all around—
Earth and her waters, and the depths of air—
Comes a still voice—Yet a few days, and thee
The all-beholding sun shall see no more
In all his course; nor yet in the cold ground,
Where thy pale form was laid, with many tears,
Nor in the embrace of ocean, shall exist
Thy image. Earth, that nourished thee, shall claim
Thy growth, to be resolved to earth again,
And, lost each human trace, surrendering up
Thine individual being, shalt thou go
To mix for ever with the elements,

To be a brother to the insensible rock
And to the sluggish clod, which the rude swain
Turns with his share, and treads upon. The oak
Shall send his roots abroad, and pierce thy mould.

Yet not to thine eternal resting-place
Shalt thou retire alone, nor couldst thou wish
Couch more magnificent. Thou shalt lie down
With patriarchs of the infant world—with kings,
The powerful of the earth—the wise, the good,
Fair forms, and hoary seers of ages past,
All in one mighty sepulchre. The hills
Rock-ribbed and ancient as the sun,—the vales
Stretching in pensive quietness between;
The venerable woods—rivers that move
In majesty, and the complaining brooks
That make the meadows green; and, poured round all
Old Ocean's gray and melancholy waste,—
Are but the solemn decorations all
Of the great tomb of man. The golden sun,
The planets, all the infinite host of heaven,
Are shining on the sad abodes of death,
Through the still lapse of ages. All that tread
The globe are but a handful to the tribes
That slumber in its bosom.—Take the wings
Of morning, pierce the Barcan wilderness,
Or lose thyself in the continuous woods
Where rolls the Oregon, and hears no sound,
Save his own dashings—yet the dead are there:
And millions in those solitudes, since first
The flight of years began, have laid them down
In their last sleep—the dead reign there alone.
So shalt thou rest, and what if thou withdraw
In silence from the living, and no friend
Take note of thy departure? All that breathe
Will share thy destiny. The gay will laugh
When thou art gone, the solemn brood of care

Plod on, and each one as before will chase
His favorite phantom; yet all these shall leave
Their mirth and their employments, and shall come
And make their bed with thee. As the long train
Of ages glide away, the sons of men,
The youth in life's green spring, and he who goes
In the full strength of years, matron and maid,
The speechless babe, and the gray-headed man—
Shall one by one be gathered to thy side,
By those, who in their turn shall follow them.

So live, that when thy summons comes to join
The innumerable caravan, which moves
To that mysterious realm, where each shall take
His chamber in the silent halls of death,
Thou go not, like the quarry-slave at night,
Scourged to his dungeon, but, sustained and soothed
By an unfaltering trust, approach thy grave,
Like one who wraps the drapery of his couch
About him, and lies down to pleasant dreams.

## To a Waterfowl

Whither, midst falling dew,
While glow the heavens with the last steps of day,
Far, through their rosy depths, dost thou pursue
Thy solitary way?

Vainly the fowler's eye
Might mark thy distant flight to do thee wrong,
As, darkly seen against the crimson sky,
Thy figure floats along.

Seek'st thou the plashy brink
Of weedy lake, or marge of river wide,
Or where the rocking billows rise and sink
On the chafed ocean-side?

There is a Power whose care
Teaches thy way along that pathless coast—
The desert and illimitable air—
    Lone wandering, but not lost.

All day thy wings have fanned,
At that far height, the cold, thin atmosphere,
Yet stoop not, weary, to the welcome land,
    Though the dark night is near.

And soon that toil shall end;
Soon shalt thou find a summer home, and rest,
And scream among thy fellows; reeds shall bend,
    Soon, o'er thy sheltered nest.

Thou'rt gone, the abyss of heaven
Hath swallowed up thy form; yet, on my heart
Deeply has sunk the lesson thou hast given,
    And shall not soon depart.

He who, from zone to zone,
Guides through the boundless sky thy certain flight,
In the long way that I must tread alone,
    Will lead my steps aright.

# RALPH WALDO EMERSON
## (1803–1882)

## Uriel

It fell in the ancient periods
    Which the brooding soul surveys,
Or ever the wild Time coined itself
    Into calendar months and days.

This was the lapse of Uriel,
Which in Paradise befell.
Once, among the Pleiads walking,
Seyd overheard the young gods talking;
And the treason, too long pent,
To his ears was evident.
The young deities discussed
Laws of form, and metre just,
Orb, quintessence, and sunbeams,
What subsisteth, and what seems.
One, with low tones that decide,
And doubt and reverend use defied,
With a look that solved the sphere,
And stirred the devils everywhere,
Gave his sentiment divine
Against the being of a line.
"Line in nature is not found;
Unit and universe are round;
In vain produced, all rays return;—
Evil will bless, and ice will burn."
As Uriel spoke with piercing eye,

A shudder ran around the sky;
The stern old war-gods shook their heads,
The seraphs frowned from myrtle-beds;
Seemed to the holy festival
The rash word boded ill to all;
The balance-beam of Fate was bent;
The bounds of good and ill were rent;
Strong Hades could not keep his own,
But all slid to confusion.

A sad self-knowledge, withering, fell
On the beauty of Uriel;
In heaven once eminent, the god
Withdrew, that hour, into his cloud;
Whether doomed to long gyration
In the sea of generation,
Or by knowledge grown too bright
To hit the nerve of feebler sight.
Straightway, a forgetting wind
Stole over the celestial kind,
And their lips the secret kept,
If in ashes the fire-seed slept.
But now and then, truth-speaking things
Shamed the angels' veiling wings;
And, shrilling from the solar course,
Or from fruit of chemic force,
Procession of a soul in matter,
Or the speeding change of water,
Or out of the good of evil born,
Came Uriel's voice of cherub scorn,
And a blush tinged the upper sky,
And the gods shook, they knew not why.

# Destiny

That you are fair or wise is vain,
Or strong, or rich, or generous;
You must add the untaught strain
That sheds beauty on the rose.
There's a melody born of melody,
Which melts the world into a sea.
Toil could never compass it;
Art its height could never hit;
It came never out of wit;
But a music music-born
Well may Jove and Juno scorn.
Thy beauty, if it lack the fire
Which drives me mad with sweet desire,
What boots it? What the soldier's mail,
Unless he conquer and prevail?
What all the goods thy pride which lift,
If thou pine for another's gift?
Alas! that one is born in blight,
Victim of perpetual slight:
When thou lookest on his face,
Thy heart saith, "Brother, go thy ways!
None shall ask thee what thou doest,
Or care a rush for what thou knowest,
Or listen when thou repliest,
Or remember where thou liest,
Or how thy supper is sodden";
And another is born
To make the sun forgotten.
Surely he carries a talisman
Under his tongue;
Broad his shoulders are and strong;
And his eye is scornful,
Threatening and young.
I hold it of little matter
Whether your jewel be of pure water,

A rose diamond or a white,
But whether it dazzle me with light.
I care not how you are dressed,
In coarsest weeds or in the best;
Nor whether your name is base or brave:
Nor for the fashion of your behavior;
But whether you charm me,
Bid my bread feed and my fire warm me,
And dress up Nature in your favor.
One thing is forever good;
That one thing is Success,—
Dear to the Eumenides,
And to all the heavenly brood.
Who bides at home, nor looks abroad,
Carries the eagles, and masters the sword.

## Ode

### INSCRIBED TO W.H. CHANNING

Though loath to grieve
The evil time's sole patriot,
I cannot leave
My honied thought
For the priest's cant,
Or statesman's rant.
If I refuse
My study for their politique,
Which at the best is trick,
The angry Muse
Puts confusion in my brain.

But who is he that prates
Of the culture of mankind,
Of better arts and life?
Go, blindworm, go,
Behold the famous States

Harrying Mexico
With rifle and with knife!

Or who, with accent bolder,
Dare praise the freedom-loving mountaineer?
I found by thee, O rushing Contoocook!
And in thy valleys, Agiochook!
The jackals of the negro-holder.

The God who made New Hampshire
Taunted the lofty land
With little men;—
Small bat and wren
House in the oak:—
If earth-fire cleave
The upheaved land, and bury the folk,
The southern crocodile would grieve.
Virtue palters; Right is hence;
Freedom praised, but hid;
Funeral eloquence
Rattles the coffin-lid.
What boots thy zeal,
O glowing friend,
That would indignant rend
The northland from the south?
Wherefore? to what good end?
Boston Bay and Bunker Hill
Would serve things still; —
Things are of the snake.

The horseman serves the horse,
The neatherd serves the neat,
The merchant serves the purse,
The eater serves his meat;
'Tis the day of the chattel,
Web to weave, and corn to grind;
Things are in the saddle,
And ride mankind.

There are two laws discrete,
Not reconciled,—
Law for man, and law for thing;
The last builds town and fleet,
But it runs wild,
And doth the man unking.

'Tis fit the forest fall,
The steep be graded,
The mountain tunnelled,
The sand shaded,
The orchard planted,
The glebe tilled,
The prairie granted,
The steamer built.

Let man serve law for man;
Live for friendship, live for love,
For truth's and harmony's behoof;
The state may follow how it can,
As Olympus follows Jove.

　　Yet do not I implore
The wrinkled shopman to my sounding woods,
Nor bid the unwilling senator
Ask votes of thrushes in the solitudes.
Every one to his chosen work;—
Foolish hands may mix and mar;
Wise and sure the issues are.
Round they roll till dark is light,
Sex to sex, and even to odd;—
The over-god
Who marries Right to Might,
Who peoples, unpeoples,—
He who exterminates
Races by stronger races,
Black by white faces,—
Knows to bring honey

Out of the lion;
Grafts gentlest scion
On pirate and Turk.

The Cossack eats Poland,
Like stolen fruit;
Her last noble is ruined,
Her last poet mute:
Straight, into double band
The victors divide;
Half for freedom strike and stand;—
The astonished Muse finds thousands at her side.

# Concord Hymn

### SUNG AT THE COMPLETION OF THE BATTLE MONUMENT
### APRIL 19, 1836

By the rude bridge that arched the flood,
   Their flag to April's breeze unfurled,
Here once the embattled farmers stood,
   And fired the shot heard round the world.

The foe long since in silence slept;
   Alike the conqueror silent sleeps;
And Time the ruined bridge has swept
   Down the dark stream which seaward creeps.

On this green bank, by this soft stream,
   We set to-day a votive stone;
That memory may their deed redeem,
   When, like our sires, our sons are gone.

Spirit, that made those heroes dare
   To die, and leave their children free,
Bid Time and Nature gently spare
   The shaft we raise to them and thee.

# Fate

Deep in the man sits fast his fate
To mould his fortunes mean or great:
Unknown to Cromwell as to me
Was Cromwell's measure or degree;
Unknown to him as to his horse,
If he than his groom be better or worse.
He works, plots, fights, in rude affairs,
With squires, lords, kings, his craft compares,
Till late he learned, through doubt and fear,
Broad England harbored not his peer:
Obeying Time, the last to own
The Genius from its cloudy throne.
For the prevision is allied
Unto the thing so signified;
Or say, the foresight that awaits
Is the same Genius that creates.

# Days

Daughters of Time, the hypocritic Days,
Muffled and dumb like barefoot dervishes,
And marching single in an endless file,
Bring diadems and fagots in their hands.
To each they offer gifts after his will,
Bread, kingdoms, stars, and sky that holds them all.
I, in my pleached garden, watched the pomp,
Forgot my morning wishes, hastily
Took a few herbs and apples, and the Day
Turned and departed silent. I, too late,
Under her solemn fillet saw the scorn.

# HENRY WADSWORTH LONGFELLOW
## (1807–1882)

### Snow-Flakes

Out of the bosom of the Air,
   Out of the cloud-folds of her garments shaken,
Over the woodlands brown and bare,
   Over the harvest-fields forsaken,
     Silent, and soft, and slow
     Descends the snow.

Even as our cloudy fancies take
   Suddenly shape in some divine expression,
Even as the troubled heart doth make
   In the white countenance confession,
     The troubled sky reveals
     The grief it feels.

This is the poem of the air,
   Slowly in silent syllables recorded;
This is the secret of despair,
   Long in its cloudy bosom hoarded,
     Now whispered and revealed
     To wood and field.

# The Cross of Snow

In the long, sleepless watches of the night,
    A gentle face—the face of one long dead—
    Looks at me from the wall, where round its head
    The night-lamp casts a halo of pale light.
Here in this room she died; and soul more white
    Never through martyrdom of fire was led
    To its repose; nor can in books be read
    The legend of a life more benedight.
There is a mountain in the distant West
    That, sun-defying, in its deep ravines
    Displays a cross of snow upon its side.
Such is the cross I wear upon my breast
    These eighteen years, through all the changing scenes
    And seasons, changeless since the day she died.

# The Skeleton in Armor

"Speak! speak! thou fearful guest!
Who, with thy hollow breast
Still in rude armor drest,
    Comest to daunt me!
Wrapt not in Eastern balms,
But with thy fleshless palms
Stretched, as if asking alms,
    Why dost thou haunt me?"

Then, from those cavernous eyes
Pale flashes seemed to rise,
As when the Northern skies
    Gleam in December;
And, like the water's flow
Under December's snow,
Came a dull voice of woe
    From the heart's chamber.

"I was a Viking old!
My deeds, though manifold,
No Skald in song has told,
    No Saga taught thee!
Take heed, that in thy verse
Thou dost the tale rehearse,
Else dread a dead man's curse;
    For this I sought thee.

"Far in the Northern Land,
By the wild Baltic's strand,
I, with my childish hand,
    Tamed the gerfalcon;
And, with my skates fast-bound,
Skimmed the half-frozen Sound,
That the poor whimpering hound
    Trembled to walk on.

"Oft to his frozen lair
Tracked I the grisly bear,
While from my path the hare
    Fled like a shadow;
Oft through the forest dark
Followed the were-wolf's bark,
Until the soaring lark
    Sang from the meadow.

"But when I older grew,
Joining a corsair's crew,
O'er the dark sea I flew
    With the marauders.
Wild was the life we led;
Many the souls that sped,
Many the hearts that bled,
    By our stern orders.

"Many a wassail-bout
Wore the long Winter out;
Often our midnight shout
   Set the cocks crowing,
As we the Berserk's tale
Measured in cups of ale,
Draining the oaken pail,
   Filled to o'erflowing.

"Once as I told in glee
Tales of the stormy sea,
Soft eyes did gaze on me,
   Burning yet tender;
And as the white stars shine
On the dark Norway pine,
On that dark heart of mine
   Fell their soft splendor.

"I wooed the blue-eyed maid,
Yielding, yet half afraid,
And in the forest's shade
   Our vows were plighted.
Under its loosened vest
Fluttered her little breast,
Like birds within their nest
   By the hawk frighted.

"Bright in her father's hall
Shields gleamed upon the wall,
Loud sang the minstrels all,
   Chanting his glory;
When of old Hildebrand
I asked his daughter's hand,
Mute did the minstrels stand
   To hear my story.

"While the brown ale he quaffed,
Loud then the champion laughed,
And as the wind-gusts waft
　　The sea-foam brightly,
So the loud laugh of scorn,
Out of those lips unshorn,
From the deep drinking-horn
　　Blew the foam lightly.

"She was a Prince's child,
I but a Viking wild,
And though she blushed and smiled,
　　I was discarded!
Should not the dove so white
Follow the sea-mew's flight,
Why did they leave that night
　　Her nest unguarded?

"Scarce had I put to sea,
Bearing the maid with me,
Fairest of all was she
　　Among the Norsemen!
When on the white sea-strand,
Waving his armed hand,
Saw we old Hildebrand,
　　With twenty horsemen.

"Then launched they to the blast,
Bent like a reed each mast,
Yet we were gaining fast,
　　When the wind failed us;
And with a sudden flaw
Came round the gusty Skaw,
So that our foe we saw
　　Laugh as he hailed us.

"And as to catch the gale
Round veered the flapping sail,
'Death!' was the helmsman's hail,
   'Death without quarter!'
Mid-ships with iron keel
Struck we her ribs of steel;
Down her black hulk did reel
   Through the black water!

"As with his wings aslant.
Sails the fierce cormorant,
Seeking some rocky haunt,
   With his prey laden,—
So toward the open main,
Beating to sea again,
Through the wild hurricane,
   Bore I the maiden.

"Three weeks we westward bore,
And when the storm was o'er,
Cloud-like we saw the shore
   Stretching to leeward;
There for my lady's bower
Built I the lofty tower,
Which, to this very hour,
   Stands looking seaward.

"There lived we many years;
Time dried the maiden's tears;
She had forgot her fears,
   She was a mother;
Death closed her mild blue eyes,
Under that tower she lies;
Ne'er shall the sun arise
   On such another!

"Still grew my bosom then,
Still as a stagnant fen!
Hateful to me were men,
 The sunlight hateful!
In the vast forest here,
Clad in my warlike gear,
Fell I upon my spear,
 Oh, death was grateful!

"Thus, seamed with many scars,
Bursting these prison bars,
Up to its native stars
 My soul ascended!
There from the flowing bowl
Deep drinks the warrior's soul,
*Skoal!* to the Northland! *skoal!*"
 Thus the tale ended.

## The Wreck of the Hesperus

It was the schooner Hesperus,
 That sailed the wintry sea;
And the skipper had taken his little daughter,
 To bear him company.

Blue were her eyes as the fairy-flax,
 Her cheeks like the dawn of day,
And her bosom white as the hawthorn buds,
 That ope in the month of May.

The skipper he stood beside the helm,
 His pipe was in his mouth,
And he watched how the veering flaw did blow
 The smoke now West, now South.

Then up and spake an old Sailor,
　　Had sailed to the Spanish Main,
"I pray thee, put into yonder port,
　　For I fear a hurricane.

"Last night, the moon had a golden ring,
　　And to-night no moon we see!"
The skipper, he blew a whiff from his pipe,
　　And a scornful laugh laughed he.

Colder and louder blew the wind,
　　A gale from the Northeast,
The snow fell hissing in the brine,
　　And the billows frothed like yeast.

Down came the storm, and smote amain
　　The vessel in its strength;
She shuddered and paused, like a frighted steed,
　　Then leaped her cable's length.

"Come hither! come hither! my little daughter,
　　And do not tremble so;
For I can weather the roughest gale
　　That ever wind did blow."

He wrapped her warm in his seaman's coat
　　Against the stinging blast;
He cut a rope from a broken spar,
　　And bound her to the mast.

"O father! I hear the church-bells ring,
　　Oh say, what may it be?"
"'Tis a fog-bell on a rock-bound coast!"—
　　And he steered for the open sea.

"O father! I hear the sound of guns,
Oh say, what may it be?"
"Some ship in distress that cannot live
In such an angry sea!"

"O father! I see a gleaming light,
Oh say, what may it be?"
But the father answered never a word,
A frozen corpse was he.

Lashed to the helm, all stiff and stark,
With his face turned to the skies,
The lantern gleamed through the gleaming snow
On his fixed and glassy eyes.

Then the maiden clasped her hands and prayed
That-savèd she might be;
And she thought of Christ, who stilled the wave,
On the Lake of Galilee.

And fast through the midnight dark and drear,
Through the whistling sleet and snow,
Like a sheeted ghost, the vessel swept
Tow'rds the reef of Norman's Woe.

And ever the fitful gusts between
A sound came from the land;
It was the sound of the trampling surf
On the rocks and the hard sea-sand.

The breakers were right beneath her bows,
She drifted a dreary wreck,
And a whooping billow swept the crew
Like icicles from her deck.

She struck where the white and fleecy waves
    Looked soft as carded wool,
But the cruel rocks, they gored her side
    Like the horns of an angry bull.

Her rattling shrouds, all sheathed in ice,
    With the masts went by the board;
Like a vessel of glass, she stove and sank.
    Ho! ho! the breakers roared!

At daybreak, on the bleak sea-beach,
    A fisherman stood aghast,
To see the form of a maiden fair,
    Lashed close to a drifting mast.

The salt sea was frozen on her breast,
    The salt tears in her eyes;
And he saw her hair, like the brown sea-weed,
    On the billows fall and rise.

Such was the wreck of the Hesperus,
    In the midnight and the snow!
Christ save us all from a death like this,
    On the reef of Norman's Woe!

# EDGAR ALLAN POE
## (1809–1849)

## The Raven

Once upon a midnight dreary, while I pondered, weak and weary,
Over many a quaint and curious volume of forgotten lore—
While I nodded, nearly napping, suddenly there came a tapping,
As of some one gently rapping, rapping at my chamber door.
"'Tis some visiter," I muttered, "tapping at my chamber door—
                       Only this and nothing more."

Ah, distinctly I remember it was in the bleak December,
And each separate dying ember wrought its ghost upon the floor.
Eagerly I wished the morrow;—vainly I had sought to borrow
From my books surcease of sorrow—sorrow for the lost Lenore—
For the rare and radiant maiden whom the angels name Lenore—
                       Nameless here for evermore.

And the silken sad uncertain rustling of each purple curtain
Thrilled me—filled me with fantastic terrors never felt before;
So that now, to still the beating of my heart, I stood repeating
"'Tis some visiter entreating entrance at my chamber door—
Some late visiter entreating entrance at my chamber door;
                       This it is and nothing more."

Presently my soul grew stronger; hesitating then no longer,
 "Sir," said I, "or Madam, truly your forgiveness I implore;
But the fact is I was napping, and so gently you came rapping,
And so faintly you came tapping, tapping at my chamber door,
That I scarce was sure I heard you"—here I opened wide the door;—
                       Darkness there and nothing more.

Deep into that darkness peering, long I stood there wondering, fearing,
Doubting, dreaming dreams no mortals ever dared to dream before;
But the silence was unbroken, and the stillness gave no token,
And the only word there spoken was the whispered word, "Lenore?"
This I whispered, and an echo murmured back the word, "Lenore!"—
Merely this and nothing more.

Back into the chamber turning, all my soul within me burning,
Soon again I heard a tapping something louder than before.
"Surely," said I, "surely that is something at my window lattice;
Let me see, then, what thereat is and this mystery explore—
Let my heart be still a moment and this mystery explore;—
'Tis the wind and nothing more."

Open here I flung the shutter, when, with many a flirt and flutter,
In there stepped a stately Raven of the saintly days of yore.
Not the least obeisance made he; not a minute stopped or stayed he;
But, with mien of lord or lady, perched above my chamber door—
Perched upon a bust of Pallas just above my chamber door—
Perched, and sat, and nothing more.

Then this ebony bird beguiling my sad fancy into smiling,
By the grave and stern decorum of the countenance it wore,
"Though thy crest be shorn and shaven, thou," I said, "art sure no craven,
Ghastly grim and ancient Raven wandering from the Nightly shore
Tell me what thy lordly name is on the Night's Plutonian shore!"
Quoth the Raven, "Nevermore."

Much I marvelled this ungainly fowl to hear discourse so plainly,
Though its answer little meaning—little relevancy bore;
For we cannot help agreeing that no living human being
Ever yet was blessed with seeing bird above his chamber door—
Bird or beast upon the sculptured bust above his chamber door,
With such name as "Nevermore."

But the Raven, sitting lonely on that placid bust, spoke only
That one word, as if his soul in that one word he did outpour.
Nothing farther then he uttered; not a feather then he fluttered—
Till I scarcely more than muttered "Other friends have flown before—
On the morrow *he* will leave me, as my Hopes have flown before."
                     Then the bird said "Nevermore."

Startled at the stillness broken by reply so aptly spoken,
"Doubtless," said I, "what it utters is its only stock and store
Caught from some unhappy master whom unmerciful Disaster
Followed fast and followed faster till his songs one burden bore—
Till the dirges of his Hope that melancholy burden bore
                     Of 'Never—nevermore.' "

But the Raven still beguiling all my sad soul into smiling,
Straight I wheeled a cushioned seat in front of bird and bust and door;
Then, upon the velvet sinking, I betook myself to linking
Fancy unto fancy, thinking what this ominous bird of yore—
What this grim, ungainly, ghastly, gaunt, and ominous bird of yore
                     Meant in croaking "Nevermore."

This I sat engaged in guessing, but no syllable expressing
To the fowl whose fiery eyes now burned into my bosom's core;
This and more I sat divining, with my head at ease reclining
On the cushion's velvet lining that the lamp-light gloated o'er,
But whose velvet violet lining with the lamp-light gloating o'er
                     *She* shall press, ah, nevermore!

Then, methought, the air grew denser, perfumed from an unseen censer
Swung by Seraphim whose foot-falls tinkled on the tufted floor.
"Wretch," I cried, "thy God hath lent thee—by these angels he hath sent thee
Respite—respite and nepenthe from thy memories of Lenore!
Quaff, oh quaff this kind nepenthe and forget this lost Lenore!"
                     Quoth the Raven, "Nevermore."

"Prophet!" said I, "thing of evil!—prophet still, if bird or devil!—
Whether Tempter sent, or whether tempest tossed thee here ashore,
Desolate yet all undaunted, on this desert land enchanted—
On this home by Horror haunted—tell me truly, I implore—
Is there—*is* there balm in Gilead?—tell me—tell me, I implore!"
                    Quoth the Raven, "Nevermore."

"Prophet!" said I, "thing of evil—prophet still, if bird or devil!
By that Heaven that bends above us—by that God we both adore—
Tell this soul with sorrow laden if, within the distant Aidenn,
It shall clasp a sainted maiden whom the angels name Lenore—
Clasp a rare and radiant maiden whom the angels name Lenore."
                    Quoth the Raven, "Nevermore."

"Be that word our sign of parting, bird or fiend!" I shrieked, upstarting—
"Get thee back into the tempest and the Night's Plutonian shore!
Leave no black plume as a token of that lie thy soul hath spoken!
Leave my loneliness unbroken!—quit the bust above my door!
Take thy beak from out my heart, and take thy form from off my door!"
                    Quoth the Raven, "Nevermore."

And the Raven, never flitting, still is sitting, still is sitting
On the pallid bust of Pallas just above my chamber door;
And his eyes have all the seeming of a demon's that is dreaming,
And the lamp-light o'er him streaming throws his shadow on the floor;
And my soul from out that shadow that lies floating on the floor
                    Shall be lifted—nevermore!

## Ulalume

The skies they were ashen and sober;
    The leaves they were crisped and sere—
    The leaves they were withering and sere;
It was night in the lonesome October
    Of my most immemorial year;

It was hard by the dim lake of Auber,
    In the misty mid region of Weir—
It was down by the dank tarn of Auber,
    In the ghoul-haunted woodland of Weir.

Here once, through an alley Titantic,
    Of cypress, I roamed with my Soul—
    Of cypress, with Psyche, my Soul.
These were days when my heart was volcanic
    As the scoriac rivers that roll—
    As the lavas that restlessly roll
Their sulphurous currents down Yaanek
    In the ultimate climes of the pole—
That groan as they roll down Mount Yaanek
    In the realms of the boreal pole.

Our talk had been serious and sober,
    But our thoughts they were palsied and sere—
    Our memories were treacherous and sere—
For we knew not the month was October,
    And we marked not the night of the year—
    (Ah, night of all nights in the year!)
We noted not the dim lake of Auber—
    (Though once we had journeyed down here)—
Remembered not the dank tarn of Auber,
    Nor the ghoul-haunted woodland of Weir.

And now, as the night was senescent
    And star-dials pointed to morn—
    As the star-dials hinted of morn—
At the end of our path a liquescent
    And nebulous lustre was born,
Out of which a miraculous crescent
    Arose with a duplicate horn—
Astarte's bediamonded crescent
    Distinct with its duplicate horn.

And I said—"She is warmer than Dian:
    She rolls through an ether of sighs—
    She revels in a region of sighs:
She has seen that the tears are not dry on
    These cheeks, where the worm never dies,
And has come past the stars of the Lion
    To point us the path to the skies—
    To the Lethean peace of the skies—
Come up, in despite of the Lion,
    To shine on us with her bright eyes—
Come up through the lair of the Lion,
    With love in her luminous eyes."

But Psyche, uplifting her finger,
    Said—"Sadly this star I mistrust—
    Her pallor I strangely mistrust:—
Oh, hasten!—oh, let us not linger!
    Oh, fly!—let us fly!—for we must."
In terror she spoke, letting sink her
    Wings until they trailed in the dust—
In agony sobbed, letting sink her
    Plumes till they trailed in the dust—
    Till they sorrowfully trailed in the dust.

I replied—"This is nothing but dreaming:
    Let us on by this tremulous light!
    Let us bathe in this crystalline light!
Its Sybilic splendor is beaming
    With Hope and in Beauty to-night:—
    See!—it flickers up the sky through the night!
Ah, we safely may trust to its gleaming,
    And be sure it will lead us aright—
We safely may trust to a gleaming
    That cannot but guide us aright,
    Since it flickers up to Heaven through the night."

Thus I pacified Psyche and kissed her,
　　And tempted her out of her gloom—
　　And conquered her scruples and gloom;
And we passed to the end of the vista,
　　But were stopped by the door of a tomb—
　　By the door of a legended tomb;
And I said—"What is written, sweet sister,
　　On the door of this legended tomb?"
　　She replied—"Ulalume—Ulalume—
　　'Tis the vault of thy lost Ulalume!"

Then my heart it grew ashen and sober
　　As the leaves that were crisped and sere—
　　As the leaves that were withering and sere,
And I cried—"It was surely October
　　On *this* very night of last year
　　That I journeyed—I journeyed down here—
　　That I brought a dread burden down here—
　　On this night of all nights in the year,
　　Ah, what demon has tempted me here?
Well I know, now, this dim lake of Auber—
　　This misty mid region of Weir—
Well I know, now, this dank tarn of Auber,
　　This ghoul-haunted woodland of Weir."

## The Bells

### I

Hear the sledges with the bells—
　　Silver bells!
What a world of merriment their melody foretells!
　　How they tinkle, tinkle, tinkle,
　　　　In the icy air of night!
　　While the stars that oversprinkle
　　All the heavens, seem to twinkle
　　　　With a crystalline delight;

Keeping time, time, time,
In a sort of Runic rhyme,
To the tintinabulation that so musically wells
From the bells, bells, bells, bells,
Bells, bells, bells—
From the jingling and the tinkling of the bells.

II

Hear the mellow wedding bells,
Golden bells!
What a world of happiness their harmony foretells!
Through the balmy air of night
How they ring out their delight!
From the molten-golden notes,
And all in tune,
What a liquid ditty floats
To the turtle-dove that listens, while she gloats
On the moon!
Oh, from out the sounding cells,
What a gush of euphony voluminously wells!
How it swells!
How it dwells
On the Future! how it tells
Of the rapture that impels
To the swinging and the ringing
Of the bells, bells, bells,
Of the bells, bells, bells, bells,
Bells, bells, bells—
To the rhyming and the chiming of the bells!

III

Hear the loud alarum bells—
Brazen bells!
What a tale of terror, now, their turbulency tells!
In the startled ear of night
How they scream out their affright!
Too much horrified to speak,

They can only shriek, shriek,
Out of tune,
In a clamorous appealing to the mercy of the fire,
In a mad expostulation with the deaf and frantic fire
Leaping higher, higher, higher,
With a desperate desire,
And a resolute endeavor
Now—now to sit or never,
By the side of the pale-faced moon.
Oh, the bells, bells, bells!
What a tale their terror tells
Of Despair!
How they clang, and clash, and roar!
What a horror they outpour
On the bosom of the palpitating air!
Yet the ear it fully knows,
By the twanging,
And the clanging,
How the danger ebbs and flows;
Yet the ear distinctly tells,
In the jangling,
And the wrangling,
How the danger sinks and swells,
By the sinking or the swelling in the anger of the bells—
Of the bells—
Of the bells, bells, bells, bells,
Bells, bells, bells—
In the clamor and the clangor of the bells!

IV

Hear the tolling of the bells—
Iron bells!
What a world of solemn thought their monody compels!
In the silence of the night,
How we shiver with affright
At the melancholy menace of their tone!
For every sound that floats

From the rust within their throats
Is a groan.
And the people—ah, the people—
They that dwell up in the steeple,
All alone,
And who tolling, tolling, tolling,
In that muffled monotone,
Feel a glory in so rolling
On the human heart a stone—
They are neither man nor woman—
They are neither brute nor human—
They are Ghouls:
And their king it is who tolls;
And he rolls, rolls, rolls,
Rolls
A pæan from the bells!
And his merry bosom swells
With the pæan of the bells!
And he dances, and he yells;
Keeping time, time, time,
In a sort of Runic rhyme,
To the pæan of the bells—
Of the bells:
Keeping time, time, time,
In a sort of Runic rhyme,
To the throbbing of the bells—
Of the bells, bells, bells—
To the sobbing of the bells;
Keeping time, time, time,
As he knells, knells, knells,
In a happy Runic rhyme,
To the rolling of the bells—
Of the bells, bells, bells—
To the tolling of the bells,
Of the bells, bells, bells, bells—
Bells, bells, bells—
To the moaning and the groaning of the bells.

## Annabel Lee

It was many and many a year ago,
    In a kingdom by the sea,
That a maiden there lived whom you may know
    By the name of ANNABEL LEE;
And this maiden she lived with no other thought
    Than to love and be loved by me.

*I* was a child and *she* was a child,
    In this kingdom by the sea:
But we loved with a love that was more than love—
    I and my ANNABEL LEE;
With a love that the winged seraphs of heaven
    Coveted her and me.

And this was the reason that, long ago,
    In this kingdom by the sea,
A wind blew out of a cloud, chilling
    My beautiful ANNABEL LEE;
So that her highborn kinsman came
    And bore her away from me,
To shut her up in a sepulchre
    In this kingdom by the sea.

The angels, not half so happy in heaven,
    Went envying her and me—
Yes!—that was the reason (as all men know,
    In this kingdom by the sea)
That the wind came out of the cloud by night,
    Chilling and killing my ANNABEL LEE.

But our love it was stronger by far than the love
    Of those who were older than we—
    Of many far wiser than we—
And neither the angels in heaven above,
    Nor the demons down under the sea,

Can ever dissever my soul from the soul
    Of the beautiful ANNABEL LEE:

For the moon never beams, without bringing me dreams
    Of the beautiful ANNABEL LEE;
And the stars never rise, but I feel the bright eyes
    Of the beautiful ANNABEL LEE;
And so, all the night-tide, I lie down by the side
Of my darling—my darling—my life and my bride,
    In the sepulchre there by the sea,
    In her tomb by the sounding sea.

## The Haunted Palace

In the greenest of our valleys
    By good angels tenanted,
Once a fair and stately palace—
    Radiant palace—reared its head.
In the monarch Thought's dominion—
    It stood there!
Never seraph spread a pinion
    Over fabric half so fair!

Banners yellow, glorious, golden,
    On its roof did float and flow,
(This—all this—was in the olden
    Time long ago,)
And every gentle air that dallied,
    In that sweet day,
Along the ramparts plumed and pallid,
    A wingéd odour went away.

Wanderers in that happy valley,
    Through two luminous windows, saw
Spirits moving musically,
    To a lute's well-tunéd law,

Round about a throne where, sitting
  (Porphyrogene!)
In state his glory well befitting,
  The ruler of the realm was seen.

And all with pearl and ruby glowing
  Was the fair palace door,
Through which came flowing, flowing, flowing,
  And sparkling evermore,
A troop of Echoes, whose sweet duty
  Was but to sing,
In voices of surpassing beauty,
  The wit and wisdom of their king.

But evil things, in robes of sorrow,
  Assailed the monarch's high estate.
(Ah, let us mourn!—for never morrow
  Shall dawn upon him desolate!)
And round about his home the glory
  That blushed and bloomed,
Is but a dim-remembered story
  Of the old time entombed.

And travellers, now, within that valley,
  Through the red-litten windows see
Vast forms, that move fantastically
  To a discordant melody,
While, like a ghastly rapid river,
  Through the pale door
A hideous throng rush out forever
  And laugh—but smile no more.

# The Conqueror Worm

Lo! 'tis a gala night
    Within the lonesome latter years!
An angel throng, bewinged, bedight
    In veils, and drowned in tears,
Sit in a theatre, to see
    A play of hopes and fears,
While the orchestra breathes fitfully
    The music of the spheres.

Mimes, in the form of God on high,
    Mutter and mumble low,
And hither and thither fly—
    Mere puppets they, who come and go
At bidding of vast formless things
    That shift the scenery to and fro,
Flapping from out their Condor wings
    Invisible Wo!

That motley drama—oh, be sure
    It shall not be forgot!
With its phantom chased for evermore,
    By a crowd that seize it not,
Through a circle that ever returneth in
    To the self-same spot,
And much of Madness, and more of Sin,
    And Horror the soul of the plot.

But see, amid the mimic rout
    A crawling shape intrude!
A blood-red thing that writhes from out
    The scenic solitude!
It writhes!—it writhes!—with mortal pangs
    The mimes become its food,
And the angels sob at vermin fangs
    In human gore imbued.

Out—out are the lights—out all!
 And, over each quivering form,
The curtain, a funeral pall,
 Comes down with the rush of a storm,
And the angels, all pallid and wan,
 Uprising, unveiling, affirm
That the play is the tragedy, "Man,"
 And its hero the Conqueror Worm.

## The City in the Sea

Lo! Death has reared himself a throne
In a strange city lying alone
Far down within the dim West,
Where the good and the bad and the worst and the best
Have gone to their eternal rest.
There shrines and palaces and towers
(Time-eaten towers that tremble not!)
Resemble nothing that is ours.
Around, by lifting winds forgot,
Resignedly beneath the sky
The melancholy waters lie.

No rays from the holy heaven come down
On the long night-time of that town;
But light from out the lurid sea
Streams up the turrets silently—
Gleams up the pinnacles far and free—
Up domes—up spires—up kingly halls—
Up fanes—up Babylon-like walls—
Up shadowy long-forgotten bowers
Of sculptured ivy and stone flowers—
Up many and many a marvellous shrine
Whose wreathéd friezes interwine
The viol, the violet, and the vine.

Resignedly beneath the sky
The melancholy waters lie.
So blend the turrets and shadows there
That all seem pendulous in air,
While from a proud tower in the town
Death looks gigantically down.

There open fanes and gaping graves
Yawn level with the luminous waves;
But not the riches there that lie
In each idol's diamond eye—
Not the gaily jeweled dead
Tempt the waters from their bed;
For no ripples curl, alas!
Along that wilderness of glass—
No swellings tell that winds may be
Upon some far-off happier sea—
No heavings hint that winds have been
On seas less hideously serene.

But lo, a stir is in the air!
The wave—there is a movement there!
As if the towers had thrust aside,
In slightly sinking the dull tide—
As if their tops had feebly given
A void within the filmy Heaven.
The waves have now a redder glow—
The hours are breathing faint and low—
And when, amid no earthly moans,
Down, down that town shall settle hence,
Hell, rising from a thousand thrones,
Shall do it reverence.

## A Dream Within a Dream

Take this kiss upon the brow!
And, in parting from you now,
Thus much let me avow—
You are not wrong, who deem
That my days have been a dream;
Yet if hope has flown away
In a night, or in a day,
In a vision, or in none,
Is it therefore the less *gone*?
*All* that we see or seem
Is but a dream within a dream.

I stand amid the roar
Of a surf-tormented shore,
And I hold within my hand
Grains of the golden sand—
How few! yet how they creep
Through my fingers to the deep,
While I weep—while I weep!
O God! can I not grasp
Them with a tighter clasp?
O God! can I not save
*One* from the pitiless wave?
Is *all* that we see or seem
But a dream within a dream?

## Eldorado

Gaily bedight,
A gallant knight,
In sunshine and in shadow,
Had journeyed long,
Singing a song,
In search of Eldorado.

But he grew old—
This knight so bold—
And o'er his heart a shadow
Fell as he found
No spot of ground
That looked like Eldorado.

And, as his strength
Failed him at length,
He met a pilgrim shadow—
"Shadow," said he,
"Where can it be—
This land of Eldorado?"

"Over the Mountains
Of the Moon,
Down the Valley of Shadow,
Ride boldly, ride,"
The shade replied, —
"If you seek for Eldorado!"

# WALT WHITMAN
## (1819–1892)

## One's-Self I Sing

One's-self I sing, a simple separate person,
Yet utter the word Democratic, the word En-Masse.

Of physiology from top to toe I sing,
Not physiognomy alone nor brain alone is worthy for the Muse, I say the Form
    complete is worthier far,
The Female equally with the Male I sing.

Of Life immense in passion, pulse, and power,
Cheerful, for freest action form'd under the laws divine,
The Modern Man I sing.

## Starting from Paumanok

### I

Starting from fish-shape Paumanok where I was born,
Well-begotten, and rais'd by a perfect mother,
After roaming many lands, lover of populous pavements,
Dweller in Mannahatta my city, or on southern savannas,
Or a soldier camp'd or carrying my knapsack and gun, or a miner in California,
Or rude in my home in Dakota's woods, my diet meat, my drink from the spring,
Or withdrawn to muse and meditate in some deep recess,
Far from the clank of crowds intervals passing rapt and happy,
Aware of the fresh free giver the flowing Missouri, aware of mighty Niagara,
Aware of the buffalo herds grazing the plains, the hirsute and strong-breasted bull,

Of earth, rocks, Fifth-month flowers experienced, stars, rain, snow, my amaze,
Having studied the mocking-bird's tones and the flight of the mountain-hawk,
And heard at dawn the unrivall'd one, the hermit thrush from the swamp-cedars,
Solitary, singing in the West, I strike up for a New World.

## II

Victory, union, faith, identity, time,
The indissoluble compacts, riches, mystery,
Eternal progress, the kosmos, and the modern reports.

This then is life,
Here is what has come to the surface after so many throes and  convulsions.

How curious! how real!
Underfoot the divine soil, overhead the sun.

See revolving the globe,
The ancestor-continents away group'd together,
The present and future continents north and south, with the isthmus between.

See, vast trackless spaces,
As in a dream they change, they swiftly fill,
Countless masses debouch upon them,
They are now cover'd with the foremost people, arts, institutions, known.

See, projected through time,
For me an audience interminable.

With firm and regular step they wend, they never stop,
Successions of men, Americanos, a hundred millions,
One generation playing its part and passing on,
Another generation playing its part and passing on in its turn,
With faces turn'd sideways or backward towards me to listen,
With eyes retrospective towards me.

## III

Americanos! conquerors! marches humanitarian!
Foremost! century marches! Libertad! masses!
For you a programme of chants.

Chants of the prairies,
Chants of the long-running Mississippi, and down to the Mexican sea,
Chants of Ohio, Indiana, Illinois, Iowa, Wisconsin and Minnesota,
Chants going forth from the centre from Kansas, and thence equidistant,
Shooting in pulses of fire ceaseless to vivify all.


IV

Take my leaves America, take them South and take them North,
Make welcome for them everywhere, for they are your own offspring,
Surround them East and West, for they would surround you,
And you precedents, connect lovingly with them, for they connect  lovingly with
    you.


I conn'd old times,
I sat studying at the feet of the great masters,
Now if eligible O that the great masters might return and study me.


In the name of these States shall I scorn the antique?
Why these are the children of the antique to justify it.


V

Dead poets, philosophs, priests,
Martyrs, artists, inventors, governments long since,
Language-shapers on other shores,
Nations once powerful, now reduced, withdrawn, or desolate,
I dare not proceed till I respectfully credit what you have left wafted hither,
I have perused it, own it is admirable, (moving awhile among it,)
Think nothing can ever be greater, nothing can ever deserve more than it deserves,
Regarding it all intently a long while, then dismissing it,
I stand in my place with my own day here.


Here lands female and male,
Here the heir-ship and heiress-ship of the world, here the flame of  materials,
Here spirituality the translatress, the openly-avow'd,
The ever-tending, the finale of visible forms,
The satisfier, after due long-waiting now advancing,
Yes here comes my mistress the soul.

## VI

The soul,

Forever and forever—longer than soil is brown and solid—longer than water ebbs
　　and flows.


I will make the poems of materials, for I think they are to be the most spiritual
　　poems,

And I will make the poems of my body and of mortality,

For I think I shall then supply myself with the poems of my soul and of immortality.


I will make a song for these States that no one State may under any circumstances
　　be subjected to another State,

And I will make a song that there shall be comity by day and by night between all
　　the States, and between any two of them,

And I will make a song for the ears of the President, full of weapons with menacing
　　points,

And behind the weapons countless dissatisfied faces;

And a song make I of the One form'd out of all,

The fang'd and glittering One whose head is over all,

Resolute warlike One including and over all,

(However high the head of any else that head is over all.)


I will acknowledge contemporary lands,

I will trail the whole geography of the globe and salute courteously every city large
　　and small,

And employments! I will put in my poems that with you is heroism upon land and
　　sea,

And I will report all heroism from an American point of view.


I will sing the song of companionship,

I will show what alone must finally compact these,

I believe these are to found their own ideal of manly love, indicating it in me,

I will therefore let flame from me the burning fires that were threatening to
　　consume me,

I will lift what has too long kept down those smouldering fires,

I will give them complete abandonment,

I will write the evangel-poem of comrades and of love,

For who but I should understand love with all its sorrow and joy?
And who but I should be the poet of comrades?

## VII

I am the credulous man of qualities, ages, races,
I advance from the people in their own spirit,
Here is what sings unrestricted faith.

Omnes! omnes! let others ignore what they may,
I make the poem of evil also, I commemorate that part also,
I am myself just as much evil as good, and my nation is—and I say there is in fact no
    evil,
(Or if there is I say it is just as important to you, to the land or to me, as any thing
    else.)

I too, following many and follow'd by many, inaugurate a religion, I descend into
    the arena,
(It may be I am destin'd to utter the loudest cries there, the winner's pealing shouts,
Who knows? they may rise from me yet, and soar above every thing.)

Each is not for its own sake,
I say the whole earth and all the stars in the sky are for religion's sake.

I say no man has ever yet been half devout enough,
None has ever yet adored or worship'd half enough,
None has begun to think how divine he himself is, and how certain the future is.

I say that the real and permanent grandeur of these States must be their religion,
Otherwise there is no real and permanent grandeur;
(Nor character nor life worthy the name without religion,
Nor land nor man or woman without religion.)

## VIII

What are you doing young man?
Are you so earnest, so given up to literature, science, art, amours?
These ostensible realities, politics, points?
Your ambition or business whatever it may be?

It is well—against such I say not a word, I am their poet also,
But behold! such swiftly subside, burnt up for religion's sake,
For not all matter is fuel to heat, impalpable flame, the essential life of the earth,
Any more than such are to religion.

IX

What do you seek so pensive and silent?
What do you need camerado?
Dear son do you think it is love?

Listen dear son—listen America, daughter or son,
It is a painful thing to love a man or woman to excess, and yet it satisfies, it is great,
But there is something else very great, it makes the whole coincide,
It, magnificent, beyond materials, with continuous hands sweeps and provides for all.

X

Know you, solely to drop in the earth the germs of a greater religion,
The following chants each for its kind I sing.

My comrade!
For you to share with me two greatnesses, and a third one rising inclusive and more
    resplendent,
The greatness of Love and Democracy, and the greatness of Religion.

Melange mine own, the unseen and the seen,
Mysterious ocean where the streams empty,
Prophetic spirit of materials shifting and flickering around me,
Living beings, identities now doubtless near us in the air that we know not of,
Contact daily and hourly that will not release me,
These selecting, these in hints demanded of me.

Not he with a daily kiss onward from childhood kissing me,
Has winded and twisted around me that which holds me to him,
Any more than I am held to the heavens and all the spiritual world,
After what they have done to me, suggesting themes.

O such themes—equalities! O divine average!
Warblings under the sun, usher'd as now, or at noon, or setting,
Strains musical flowing through ages, now reaching hither,
I take to your reckless and composite chords, add to them, and cheerfully pass them
      forward.


XI

As I have walk'd in Alabama my morning walk,
I have seen where the she-bird the mocking-bird sat on her nest in the briers
      hatching her brood.

I have seen the he-bird also,
I have paus'd to hear him near at hand inflating his throat and joyfully singing.

And while I paus'd it came to me that what he really sang for was not there only,
Nor for his mate nor himself only, nor all sent back by the echoes,
But subtle, clandestine, away beyond,
A charge transmitted and gift occult for those being born.


XII

Democracy! near at hand to you a throat is now inflating itself and joyfully singing.

Ma femme! for the brood beyond us and of us,
For those who belong here and those to come,
I exultant to be ready for them will now shake out carols stronger and haughtier
      than have ever yet been heard upon earth.

I will make the songs of passion to give them their way,
And your songs outlaw'd offenders, for I scan you with kindred eyes, and carry you
      with me the same as any.

I will make the true poem of riches,
To earn for the body and the mind whatever adheres and goes forward and is not
      dropt by death;
I will effuse egotism and show it underlying all, and I will be the bard of personality,
And I will show of male and female that either is but the equal of the other,
And sexual organs and acts! do you concentrate in me, for I am determin'd to tell
      you with courageous clear voice to prove you illustrious,

And I will show that there is no imperfection in the present, and can be none in the
     future,
And I will show that whatever happens to anybody it may be turn'd to beautiful
     results,
And I will show that nothing can happen more beautiful than death,
And I will thread a thread through my poems that time and events are compact,
And that all the things of the universe are perfect miracles, each as profound as any.

I will not make poems with reference to parts,
But I will make poems, songs, thoughts, with reference to ensemble,
And I will not sing with reference to a day, but with reference to all days,
And I will not make a poem nor the least part of a poem but has reference to the
     soul,
Because having look'd at the objects of the universe, I find there is no one nor any
     particle of one but has reference to the soul.

### XIII

Was somebody asking to see the soul?
See, your own shape and countenance, persons, substances, beasts,  the trees, the
     running rivers, the rocks and sands.

All hold spiritual joys and afterwards loosen them;
How can the real body ever die and be buried?

Of your real body and any man's or woman's real body,
Item for item it will elude the hands of the corpse-cleaners and pass to fitting
     spheres,
Carrying what has accrued to it from the moment of birth to the moment of death.

Not the types set up by the printer return their impression, the meaning, the main
     concern,
Any more than a man's substance and life or a woman's substance and life return in
     the body and the soul,
Indifferently before death and after death.

Behold, the body includes and is the meaning, the main concern, and includes and is
     the soul;
Whoever you are, how superb and how divine is your body, or any part of it!

XIV

Whoever you are, to you endless announcements!

Daughter of the lands did you wait for your poet?
Did you wait for one with a flowing mouth and indicative hand?
Toward the male of the States, and toward the female of the States,
Exulting words, words to Democracy's lands.

Interlink'd, food-yielding lands!
Land of coal and iron! land of gold! land of cotton, sugar, rice!
Land of wheat, beef, pork! land of wool and hemp! land of the apple and the grape!
Land of the pastoral plains, the grass-fields of the world! land of those sweet-air'd
     interminable plateaus!
Land of the herd, the garden, the healthy house of adobie!
Lands where the north-west Columbia winds, and where the southwest Colorado
     winds!
Land of the eastern Chesapeake! land of the Delaware!
Land of Ontario, Erie, Huron, Michigan!
Land of the Old Thirteen! Massachusetts land! land of Vermont and Connecticut!
Land of the ocean shores! land of sierras and peaks!
Land of boatmen and sailors! fishermen's land!
Inextricable lands! the clutch'd together! the passionate ones!
The side by side! the elder and younger brothers! the bony-limb'd!
The great women's land! the feminine! the experienced sisters and the inexperienced
     sisters!
Far breath'd land! Arctic braced! Mexican breez'd! the diverse! the compact!
The Pennsylvania! the Virginian! the double Carolinian!
O all and each well-loved by me! my intrepid nations! O I at any rate include you all
     with perfect love!
I cannot be discharged from you! not from one any sooner than another!
O death! O for all that, I am yet of you unseen this hour with irrepressible love,
Walking New England, a friend, a traveler,
Splashing my bare feet in the edge of the summer ripples on Paumanok's sands,
Crossing the prairies, dwelling again in Chicago, dwelling in every town,
Observing shows, births, improvements, structures, arts,
Listening to orators and oratresses in public halls,
Of and through the States as during life, each man and woman my neighbor,

The Louisianian, the Georgian, as near to me, and I as near to him and her,
The Mississippian and Arkansian yet with me, and I yet with any of them,
Yet upon the plains west of the spinal river, yet in my house of adobie,
Yet returning eastward, yet in the Seaside State or in Maryland,
Yet Kanadian cheerily braving the winter, the snow and ice welcome to me,
Yet a true son either of Maine or of the Granite State, or the Narragansett Bay State, or the Empire State,
Yet sailing to other shores to annex the same, yet welcoming every new brother,
Hereby applying these leaves to the new ones from the hour they unite with the old ones,
Coming among the new ones myself to be their companion and equal, coming personally to you now,
Enjoining you to acts, characters, spectacles, with me.

## XV

With me with firm holding, yet haste, haste on.

For your life adhere to me,
(I may have to be persuaded many times before I consent to give myself really to you, but what of that?
Must not Nature be persuaded many times?)

No dainty dolce affettuoso I,
Bearded, sun-burnt, gray-neck'd, forbidding, I have arrived,
To be wrestled with as I pass for the solid prizes of the universe,
For such I afford whoever can persevere to win them.

## XVI

On my way a moment I pause,
Here for you! and here for America!
Still the present I raise aloft, still the future of the States I harbinge glad and sublime,
And for the past I pronounce what the air holds of the red aborigines.

The red aborigines,
Leaving natural breaths, sounds of rain and winds, calls as of birds and animals in the woods, syllabled to us for names,
Okonee, Koosa, Ottawa, Monongahela, Sauk, Natchez, Chattahoochee, Kaqueta, Oronoco,

Wabash, Miami, Saginaw, Chippewa, Oshkosh, Walla-Walla,
Leaving such to the States they melt, they depart, charging the water and the land
    with names.

## XVII

Expanding and swift, henceforth,
Elements, breeds, adjustments, turbulent, quick and audacious,
A world primal again, vistas of glory incessant and branching,
A new race dominating previous ones and grander far, with new contests,
New politics, new literatures and religions, new inventions and arts.

These, my voice announcing—I will sleep no more but arise,
You oceans that have been calm within me! how I feel you, fathomless, stirring,
    preparing unprecedented waves and storms.

## XVIII

See, steamers steaming through my poems,
See, in my poems immigrants continually coming and landing,
See, in arriere, the wigwam, the trail, the hunter's hut, the flat-boat, the maize-leaf,
    the claim, the rude fence, and the backwoods village,
See, on the one side the Western Sea and on the other the Eastern Sea, how they
    advance and retreat upon my poems as upon their own shores,
See, pastures and forests in my poems—see, animals wild and tame—see, beyond
    the Kaw, countless herds of buffalo feeding on short curly grass,
See, in my poems, cities, solid, vast, inland, with paved streets, with iron and stone
    edifices, ceaseless vehicles, and commerce,
See, the many-cylinder'd steam printing-press—see, the electric telegraph
    stretching across the continent,
See, through Atlantica's depths pulses American Europe reaching, pulses of Europe
    duly return'd,
See, the strong and quick locomotive as it departs, panting, blowing the steam-
    whistle,
See, ploughmen ploughing farms—see, miners digging mines—see, the numberless
    factories,
See, mechanics busy at their benches with tools—see from among them superior
    judges, philosophs, Presidents, emerge, drest in working dresses,

See, lounging through the shops and fields of the States, me well-belov'd, close-held
    by day and night,
Hear the loud echoes of my songs there—read the hints come at last.

### XIX

O camerado close! O you and me at last, and us two only.
O a word to clear one's path ahead endlessly!
O something ecstatic and undemonstrable! O music wild!
O now I triumph—and you shall also;
O hand in hand—O wholesome pleasure—O one more desirer and lover!
O to haste firm holding—to haste, haste on with me.

# Crossing Brooklyn Ferry

### I

Flood-tide below me! I see you face to face!
Clouds of the west—sun there half an hour high—I see you also face to face.

Crowds of men and women attired in the usual costumes, how curious you are to
    me!
On the ferry-boats the hundreds and hundreds that cross, returning home, are more
    curious to me than you suppose,
And you that shall cross from shore to shore years hence are more to me, and more
    in my meditations, than you might suppose.

### II

The impalpable sustenance of me from all things at all hours of the day,
The simple, compact, well-join'd scheme, myself disintegrated, every one
    disintegrated yet part of the scheme,
The similitudes of the past and those of the future,
The glories strung like beads on my smallest sights and hearings, on the walk in the
    street and the passage over the river,
The current rushing so swiftly and swimming with me far away,
The others that are to follow me, the ties between me and them,
The certainty of others, the life, love, sight, hearing of others.

Others will enter the gates of the ferry and cross from shore to shore,
Others will watch the run of the flood-tide,
Others will see the shipping of Manhattan north and west, and the heights of
      Brooklyn to the south and east,
Others will see the islands large and small;
Fifty years hence, others will see them as they cross, the sun half an hour high,
A hundred years hence, or ever so many hundred years hence, others will see them,
Will enjoy the sunset, the pouring-in of the flood-tide, the falling-back to the sea of
      the ebb-tide.

III

It avails not, time nor place—distance avails not,
I am with you, you men and women of a generation, or ever so many generations
      hence,
Just as you feel when you look on the river and sky, so I felt,
Just as any of you is one of a living crowd, I was one of a crowd,
Just as you are refresh'd by the gladness of the river and the bright flow,
I was refresh'd,
Just as you stand and lean on the rail, yet hurry with the swift current, I stood yet
      was hurried,
Just as you look on the numberless masts of ships and the thick-stemm'd pipes of
      steamboats, I look'd.

I too many and many a time cross'd the river of old,
Watched the Twelfth-month sea-gulls, saw them high in the air floating with
      motionless wings, oscillating their bodies,
Saw how the glistening yellow lit up parts of their bodies and left the rest in strong
      shadow,
Saw the slow-wheeling circles and the gradual edging toward the south,
Saw the reflection of the summer sky in the water,
Had my eyes dazzled by the shimmering track of beams,
Look'd at the fine centrifugal spokes of light round the shape of my head in the
      sunlit water,
Look'd on the haze on the hills southward and south-westward,
Look'd on the vapor as it flew in fleeces tinged with violet,
Look'd toward the lower bay to notice the vessels arriving,
Saw their approach, saw aboard those that were near me,

Saw the white sails of schooners and sloops, saw the ships at anchor,

The sailors at work in the rigging or out astride the spars,

The round masts, the swinging motion of the hulls, the slender serpentine pennants,

The large and small steamers in motion, the pilots in their pilot-houses,

The white wake left by the passage, the quick tremulous whirl of the wheels,

The flags of all nations, the falling of them at sunset,

The scallop-edged waves in the twilight, the ladled cups, the frolicsome crests and
  glistening,

The stretch afar growing dimmer and dimmer, the gray walls of the granite
  storehouses by the docks,

On the river the shadowy group, the big steam-tug closely flank'd on each side by
  the barges, the hay-boat, the belated lighter,

On the neighboring shore the fires from the foundry chimneys burning high and
  glaringly into the night,

Casting their flicker of black contrasted with wild red and yellow light over the tops
  of houses, and down into the clefts of streets.

IV

These and all else were to me the same as they are to you,

I loved well those cities, loved well the stately and rapid river,

The men and women I saw were all near to me,

Others the same—others who look back on me because I look'd forward to them,

(The time will come, though I stop here to-day and to-night.)

V

What is it then between us?

What is the count of the scores or hundreds of years between us?

Whatever it is, it avails not—distance avails not, and place avails not,

I too lived, Brooklyn of ample hills was mine,

I too walk'd the streets of Manhattan island, and bathed in the waters around it,

I too felt the curious abrupt questionings stir within me,

In the day among crowds of people sometimes they came upon me,

In my walks home late at night or as I lay in my bed they came upon me,

I too had been struck from the float forever held in solution,

I too had receiv'd identity by my body,

That I was I knew was of my body, and what I should be I knew I should be of my
  body.

## VI

It is not upon you alone the dark patches fall,
The dark threw its patches down upon me also,
The best I had done seem'd to me blank and suspicious,
My great thoughts as I supposed them, were they not in reality meagre?
Nor is it you alone who know what it is to be evil,
I am he who knew what it was to be evil,
I too knitted the old knot of contrariety,
Blabb'd, blush'd, resented, lied, stole, grudg'd,
Had guile, anger, lust, hot wishes I dared not speak,
Was wayward, vain, greedy, shallow, sly, cowardly, malignant,
The wolf, the snake, the hog, not wanting in me,
The cheating look, the frivolous word, the adulterous wish, not wanting,
Refusals, hates, postponements, meanness, laziness, none of these wanting,
Was one with the rest, the days and haps of the rest,
Was call'd by my nighest name by clear loud voices of young men as they saw me
    approaching or passing,
Felt their arms on my neck as I stood, or the negligent leaning of their flesh against
    me as I sat,
Saw many I loved in the street or ferry-boat or public assembly, yet never told them
    a word,
Lived the same life with the rest, the same old laughing, gnawing, sleeping,
Play'd the part that still looks back on the actor or actress,
The same old role, the role that is what we make it, as great as we like,
Or as small as we like, or both great and small.

## VII

Closer yet I approach you,
What thought you have of me now, I had as much of you—I laid in my stores in
    advance,
I consider'd long and seriously of you before you were born.

Who was to know what should come home to me?
Who knows but I am enjoying this?
Who knows, for all the distance, but I am as good as looking at you now, for all you
    cannot see me?

## VIII

Ah, what can ever be more stately and admirable to me than mast-hemm'd
    Manhattan?

River and sunset and scallop-edg'd waves of flood-tide?

The sea-gulls oscillating their bodies, the hay-boat in the twilight, and the belated
    lighter?

What gods can exceed these that clasp me by the hand, and with voices I love call me
    promptly and loudly by my nighest name as I approach?

What is more subtle than this which ties me to the woman or man that looks in my
    face?

Which fuses me into you now, and pours my meaning into you?

We understand then do we not?

What I promis'd without mentioning it, have you not accepted?

What the study could not teach—what the preaching could not accomplish is
    accomplish'd, is it not?

## IX

Flow on, river! flow with the flood-tide, and ebb with the ebb-tide!

Frolic on, crested and scallop-edg'd waves!

Gorgeous clouds of the sunset! drench with your splendor me, or the men and
    women generations after me!

Cross from shore to shore, countless crowds of passengers!

Stand up, tall masts of Mannahatta! stand up, beautiful hills of Brooklyn!

Throb, baffled and curious brain! throw out questions and answers!

Suspend here and everywhere, eternal float of solution!

Gaze, loving and thirsting eyes, in the house or street or public assembly!

Sound out, voices of young men! loudly and musically call me by my nighest name!

Live, old life! play the part that looks back on the actor or actress!

Play the old role, the role that is great or small according as one makes it!

Consider, you who peruse me, whether I may not in unknown ways be looking upon
    you;

Be firm, rail over the river, to support those who lean idly, yet haste with the hasting
    current;

Fly on, sea-birds! fly sideways, or wheel in large circles high in the air;

Receive the summer sky, you water, and faithfully hold it till all downcast eyes have
　　time to take it from you!
Diverge, fine spokes of light, from the shape of my head, or any one's head, in the
　　sunlit water!
Come on, ships from the lower bay! pass up or down, white-sail'd schooners, sloops,
　　lighters!
Flaunt away, flags of all nations! be duly lower'd at sunset!
Burn high your fires, foundry chimneys! cast black shadows at nightfall! cast red and
　　yellow light over the tops of the houses!
Appearances, now or henceforth, indicate what you are,
You necessary film, continue to envelop the soul,
About my body for me, and your body for you, be hung our divinest aromas,
Thrive, cities—bring your freight, bring your shows, ample and sufficient rivers,
Expand, being than which none else is perhaps more spiritual,
Keep your places, objects than which none else is more lasting.

You have waited, you always wait, you dumb, beautiful ministers,
We receive you with free sense at last, and are insatiate hence-forward,
Not you any more shall be able to foil us, or withhold yourselves from us,
We use you, and do not cast you aside—we plant you permanently within us,
We fathom you not—we love you—there is perfection in you also,
You furnish your parts toward eternity,
Great or small, you furnish your parts toward the soul.

## When Lilacs Last in the Dooryard Bloom'd

### I

When lilacs last in the dooryard bloom'd,
And the great star early droop'd in the western sky in the night,
I mourn'd, and yet shall mourn with ever-returning spring.

Ever-returning spring, trinity sure to me you bring,
Lilac blooming perennial and drooping star in the west,
And thought of him I love.

## II

O powerful western fallen star!
O shades of night—O moody, tearful night!
O great star disappear'd—O the black murk that hides the star!
O cruel hands that hold me powerless—O helpless soul of me!
O harsh surrounding cloud that will not free my soul.

## III

In the dooryard fronting an old farm-house near the white-wash'd palings,
Stands the lilac-bush tall-growing with heart-shaped leaves of rich green,
With many a pointed blossom rising delicate, with the perfume strong I love,
With every leaf a miracle—and from this bush in the dooryard,
With delicate-color'd blossoms and heart-shaped leaves of rich green,
A sprig with its flower I break.

## IV ·

In the swamp in secluded recesses,
A shy and hidden bird is warbling a song.

Solitary the thrush,
The hermit withdrawn to himself, avoiding the settlements,
Sings by himself a song.

Song of the bleeding throat,
Death's outlet song of life, (for well dear brother I know,
It thou wast not granted to sing thou would'st surely die.)

## V

Over the breast of the spring, the land, amid cities,
Amid lanes and through old woods, where lately the violets peep'd from the ground,
        spotting the gray debris,
Amid the grass in the fields each side of the lanes, passing the endless grass,
Passing the yellow-spear'd wheat, every grain from its shroud in the dark-brown
        fields uprisen,
Passing the apple-tree blows of white and pink in the orchards,
Carrying a corpse to where it shall rest in the grave,
Night and day journeys a coffin.

### VI

Coffin that passes through lanes and streets,
Through day and night with the great cloud darkening the land,
With the pomp of the inloop'd flags with the cities draped in black,
With the show of the States themselves as of crape-veil'd women standing,
With processions long and winding and the flambeaus of the night,
With the countless torches lit, with the silent sea of faces and the unbared heads,
With the waiting depot, the arriving coffin, and the sombre faces,
With dirges through the night, with the thousand voices rising strong and solemn,
With all the mournful voices of the dirges pour'd around the coffin,
The dim-lit churches and the shuddering organs—where amid these you journey,
With the tolling tolling bells' perpetual clang,
Here, coffin that slowly passes,
I give you my sprig of lilac.

### VII

(Nor for you, for one alone,
Blossoms and branches green to coffins all I bring,
For fresh as the morning, thus would I chant a song for you O sane and sacred
    death.

All over bouquets of roses,
O death, I cover you over with roses and early lilies,
But mostly and now the lilac that blooms the first,
Copious I break, I break the sprigs from the bushes,
With loaded arms I come, pouring for you,
For you and the coffins all of you O death.)

### VIII

O western orb sailing the heaven,
Now I know what you must have meant as a month since I walk'd,
As I walk'd in silence the transparent shadowy night,
As I saw you had something to tell as you bent to me night after night,
As you droop'd from the sky low down as if to my side, (while the other stars all
    look'd on,)
As we wander'd together the solemn night, (for something I know not what kept me
    from sleep,)

As the night advanced, and I saw on the rim of the west how full you were of woe,
As I stood on the rising ground in the breeze in the cool transparent night,
As I watch'd where you pass'd and was lost in the netherward black of the night,
As my soul in its trouble dissatisfied sank, as where you sad orb,
Concluded, dropt in the night, and was gone.

IX

Sing on there in the swamp,
O singer bashful and tender, I hear your notes, I hear your call,
I hear, I come presently, I understand you,
But a moment I linger, for the lustrous star has detain'd me,
The star my departing comrade holds and detains me.

X

O how shall I warble myself for the dead one there I loved?
And how shall I deck my song for the large sweet soul that has gone?
And what shall my perfume be for the grave of him I love?

Sea-winds blown from east and west,
Blown from the Eastern sea and blown from the Western sea, till there on the
        prairies meeting,
These and with these and the breath of my chant,
I'll perfume the grave of him I love.

XI

O what shall I hang on the chamber walls?
And what shall the pictures be that I hang on the walls,
To adorn the burial-house of him I love?

Pictures of growing spring and farms and homes,
With the Fourth-month eve at sundown, and the gray smoke lucid and bright,
With floods of the yellow gold of the gorgeous, indolent, sinking sun, burning,
        expanding the air,
With the fresh sweet herbage under foot, and the pale green leaves of the trees
        prolific,
In the distance the flowing glaze, the breast of the river, with a wind-dapple here and
        there,

With ranging hills on the banks, with many a line against the sky, and shadows,
And the city at hand with dwellings so dense, and stacks of chimneys,
And all the scenes of life and the workshops, and the workmen homeward returning.

XII

Lo, body and soul—this land,
My own Manhattan with spires, and the sparkling and hurrying tides, and the ships,
The varied and ample land, the South and the North in the light, Ohio's shores and
    flashing Missouri,
And ever the far-spreading prairies cover'd with grass and corn.

Lo, the most excellent sun so calm and haughty,
The violet and purple morn with just-felt breezes,
The gentle soft-born measureless light,
The miracle spreading bathing all, the fulfill'd noon,
The coming eve delicious, the welcome night and the stars,
Over my cities shining all, enveloping man and land.

XIII

Sing on, sing on you gray-brown bird,
Sing from the swamps, the recesses, pour your chant from the bushes,
Limitless out of the dusk, out of the cedars and pines.

Sing on dearest brother, warble your reedy song,
Loud human song, with voice of uttermost woe.

O liquid and free and tender!
O wild and loose to my soul—O wondrous singer!
You only I hear—yet the star holds me, (but will soon depart,)
Yet the lilac with mastering odor holds me.

XIV

Now while I sat in the day and look'd forth,
In the close of the day with its light and the fields of spring, and the farmers
    preparing their crops,
In the large unconscious scenery of my land with its lakes and forests,
In the heavenly aerial beauty, (after the perturb'd winds and the storms,)
Under the arching heavens of the afternoon swift passing, and the voices of children
    and women,

The many-moving sea-tides, and I saw the ships how they sail'd,
And the summer approaching with richness, and the fields all busy with labor,
And the infinite separate houses, how they all went on, each with its meals and
    minutia of daily usages,
And the streets how their throbbings throbb'd, and the cities pent—lo, then and
    there,
Falling upon them all and among them all, enveloping me with the rest,
Appear'd the cloud, appear'd the long black trail,
And I knew death, its thought, and the sacred knowledge of death.

Then with the knowledge of death as walking one side of me,
And the thought of death close-walking the other side of me,
And I in the middle as with companions, and as holding the hands of companions,
I fled forth to the hiding receiving night that talks not,
Down to the shores of the water, the path by the swamp in the dimness,
To the solemn shadowy cedars and ghostly pines so still.

And the singer so shy to the rest receiv'd me,
The gray-brown bird I know receiv'd us comrades three,
And he sang the carol of death, and a verse for him I love.

From deep secluded recesses,
From the fragrant cedars and the ghostly pines so still,
Came the carol of the bird.

And the charm of the carol rapt me,
As I held as if by their hands my comrades in the night,
And the voice of my spirit tallied the song of the bird.

*Come lovely and soothing death,*
*Undulate round the world, serenely arriving, arriving,*
*In the day, in the night, to all, to each,*
*Sooner or later delicate death.*

*Praised be the fathomless universe,*
*For life and joy, and for objects and knowledge curious,*
*And for love, sweet love—but praise! praise! praise!*
*For the sure-enwinding arms of cool-enfolding death.*

*Dark mother always gliding near with soft feet,*
*Have none chanted for thee a chant of fullest welcome?*
*Then I chant it for thee, I glorify thee above all,*
*I bring thee a song that when thou must indeed come, come unfalteringly.*

*Approach strong deliveress,*
*When it is so, when thou hast taken them I joyously sing the dead,*
*Lost in the loving floating ocean of thee,*
*Laved in the flood of thy bliss O death.*

*From me to thee glad serenades,*
*Dances for thee I propose saluting thee, adornments and feastings for thee,*
*And the sights of the open landscape and the high-spread sky are fitting,*
*And life and the fields, and the huge and thoughtful night.*

*The night in silence under many a star,*
*The ocean shore and the husky whispering wave whose voice I know,*
*And the soul turning to thee O vast and well-veil'd death,*
*And the body gratefully nestling close to thee.*

*Over the tree-tops I float thee a song,*
*Over the rising and sinking waves, over the myriad fields and the prairies wide,*
*Over the dense-pack'd cities all and the teeming wharves and ways,*
*I float this carol with joy, with joy to thee O death.*

## XV

To the tally of my soul,
Loud and strong kept up the gray-brown bird,
With pure deliberate notes spreading filling the night.

Loud in the pines and cedars dim,
Clear in the freshness moist and the swamp-perfume,
And I with my comrades there in the night.

While my sight that was bound in my eyes unclosed,
As to long panoramas of visions.

And I saw askant the armies,
I saw as in noiseless dreams hundreds of battle-flags,
Borne through the smoke of the battles and pierc'd with missiles I saw them,
And carried hither and yon through the smoke, and torn and bloody,
And at last but a few shreds left on the staffs, (and all in silence,)
And the staffs all splinter'd and broken.

I saw battle-corpses, myriads of them,
And the white skeletons of young men, I saw them,
I saw the debris and debris of all the slain soldiers of the war,
But I saw they were not as was thought,
They themselves were fully at rest, they suffer'd not,
The living remain'd and suffer'd, the mother suffer'd,
And the wife and the child and the musing comrade suffer'd,
And the armies that remain'd suffer'd.

## XVI

Passing the visions, passing the night,
Passing, unloosing the hold of my comrades' hands,
Passing the song of the hermit bird and the tallying song of my soul,
Victorious song, death's outlet song, yet varying ever-altering song,
As low and wailing, yet clear the notes, rising and falling, flooding the night,
Sadly sinking and fainting, as warning and warning, and yet again bursting with joy,
Covering the earth and filling the spread of the heaven,
As that powerful psalm in the night I heard from recesses,
Passing, I leave thee lilac with heart-shaped leaves,
I leave thee there in the door-yard, blooming, returning with spring.

I cease from my song for thee,
From my gaze on thee in the west, fronting the west, communing with thee,
O comrade lustrous with silver face in the night.

Yet each to keep and all, retrievements out of the night,
The song, the wondrous chant of the gray-brown bird,
And the tallying chant, the echo arous'd in my soul,
With the lustrous and drooping star with the countenance full of woe,

With the holders holding my hand nearing the call of the bird,
Comrades mine and I in the midst, and their memory ever to keep, for the dead I
    loved so well,
For the sweetest, wisest soul of all my days and lands—and this for his dear sake,
Lilac and star and bird twined with the chant of my soul,
There in the fragrant pines and the cedars dusk and dim.

## O Captain! My Captain!

O Captain! my Captain! our fearful trip is done,
The ship has weather'd every rack, the prize we sought is won,
The port is near, the bells I hear, the people all exulting,
While follow eyes the steady keel, the vessel grim and daring;
        But O heart! heart! heart!
          O the bleeding drops of red,
            Where on the deck my Captain lies,
            Fallen cold and dead.

O Captain! my Captain! rise up and hear the bells;
Rise up—for you the flag is flung—for you the bugle trills,
For you bouquets and ribbon'd wreaths—for you the shores a-crowding,
For you they call, the swaying mass, their eager faces turning;
        Here Captain! dear father!
          This arm beneath your head!
            It is some dream that on the deck,
            You've fallen cold and dead.

My Captain does not answer, his lips are pale and still,
My father does not feel my arm, he has no pulse nor will,
The ship is anchor'd safe and sound, its voyage closed and done,
From fearful trip the victor ship comes in with object won;
        Exult O shores, and ring O bells!
          But I with mournful tread,
            Walk the deck my Captain lies,
            Fallen cold and dead.

# EMILY DICKINSON
## (1830–1886)

## "The heart asks pleasure first"

The heart asks pleasure first,
And then, excuse from pain;
And then, those little anodynes
That deaden suffering;

And then, to go to sleep;
And then, if it should be
The will of its Inquisitor,
The liberty to die.

## "Hope is the thing with feathers"

Hope is the thing with feathers
That perches in the soul,
And sings the tune without the words,
And never stops at all,

And sweetest in the gale is heard;
And sore must be the storm
That could abash the little bird
That kept so many warm.

I've heard it in the chillest land,
And on the strangest sea;
Yet, never, in extremity,
It asked a crumb of me.

## "When I hoped I feared"

When I hoped I feared,
Since I hoped I dared;
Everywhere alone
As a church remain;
Spectre cannot harm,
Serpent cannot charm;
He deposes doom,
Who hath suffered him.

## "A route of evanescence"

A route of evanescence
With a revolving wheel;
A resonance of emerald,
A rush of cochineal;
And every blossom on the bush
Adjusts its tumbled head,—
The mail from Tunis, probably,
An easy morning's ride.

## "I started early, took my dog"

I started early, took my dog,
And visited the sea;
The mermaids in the basement
Came out to look at me,

And frigates in the upper floor
Extended hempen hands.
Presuming me to be a mouse
Aground, upon the sands.

But no man moved me till the tide
Went past my simple shoe,
And past my apron and my belt,
And past my bodice too,

And made as he would eat me up
As wholly as a dew
Upon a dandelion's sleeve—
And then I started too.

And he—he followed close behind;
I felt his silver heel
Upon my ankle,—then my shoes
Would overflow with pearl.

Until we met the solid town,
No man he seemed to know;
And bowing with a mighty look
At me, the sea withdrew.

## "As imperceptibly as grief"

As imperceptibly as grief
The summer lapsed away,—
Too imperceptible, at last,
To seem like perfidy.

A quietness distilled,
As twilight long begun,
Or Nature, spending with herself
Sequestered afternoon.

The dusk drew earlier in,
The morning foreign shone,—
A courteous, yet harrowing grace,
As guest who would be gone.

And thus, without a wing,
Or service of a keel,
Our summer made her light escape
Into the beautiful.

## "There's a certain slant of light"

There's a certain slant of light,
On winter afternoons,
That oppresses, like the weight
Of cathedral tunes.

Heavenly hurt it gives us;
We can find no scar,
But internal difference
Where the meanings are.

None may teach it anything,
'Tis the seal, despair,—
An imperial affliction
Sent us of the air.

When it comes, the landscape listens,
Shadows hold their breath;
When it goes, 'tis like the distance
On the look of death.

## "Tell all the Truth but tell it slant—"

Tell all the Truth but tell it slant—
Success in Circuit lies
Too bright for our infirm Delight
The Truth's superb surprise
As Lightning to the Children eased
With explanation kind
The Truth must dazzle gradually
Or every man be blind—

## "Wild nights! Wild nights!"

Wild nights! Wild nights!
Were I with thee,
Wild nights should be
Our luxury!

Futile the winds
To a heart in port,—
Done with the compass,
Done with the chart.

Rowing in Eden!
Ah! the sea!
Might I but moor
To-night in thee!

———

## "A light exists in spring"

A light exists in spring
    Not present on the year
At any other period.
    When March is scarcely here

A color stands abroad
    On solitary hills
That science cannot overtake,
    But human nature *feels*.

It waits upon the lawn;
    It shows the furthest tree
Upon the furthest slope we know;
    It almost speaks to me.

Then, as horizons step,
    Or noons report away,
Without the formula of sound,
    It passes, and we stay:

A quality of loss
　　Affecting our content,
As trade had suddenly encroached
　　Upon a sacrament.

———

## "Mine by the right of white election!"

Mine by the right of the white election!
Mine by the royal seal!
Mine by the sign in the scarlet prison
Bars cannot conceal!

Mine, here in vision and in veto!
Mine, by the grave's repeal
Titled, confirmed,—delirious charter!
Mine, while the ages steal!

———

## "I cannot live with you"

I cannot live with you,
It would be life,
And life is over there
Behind the shelf

The sexton keeps the key to,
Putting up
Our life, his porcelain,
Like a cup

Discarded of the housewife,
Quaint or broken;
A newer Sèvres pleases,
Old ones crack.

I could not die with you,
For one must wait
To shut the other's gaze down,—
You could not.

And I, could I stand by
And see you freeze,
Without my right of frost,
Death's privilege?

Nor could I rise with you,
Because your face
Would put out Jesus',
That new grace

Glow plain and foreign
On my homesick eye,
Except that you, than he
Shone closer by.

They'd judge us—how?
For you served Heaven, you know,
Or sought to;
I could not,

Because you saturated sight,
And I had no more eyes
For sordid excellence
As Paradise.

And were you lost, I would be,
Though my name
Rang loudest
On the heavenly fame.

And were you saved,
And I condemned to be
Where you were not,
That self were hell to me.

So we must keep apart,
You there, I here,
With just the door ajar
That oceans are,
And prayer,
And that pale sustenance,
Despair!

———

## "Split the lark and you'll find the music"

Split the lark and you'll find the music,
  Bulb after bulb, in silver rolled,
Scantily dealt to the summer morning,
  Saved for your ear when lutes be old.

Loose the flood, you shall find it patent,
  Gush after gush, reserved for you;
Scarlet experiment! sceptic Thomas,
  Now, do you doubt that your bird was true?

———

## "Safe in their alabaster chambers"

Safe in their alabaster chambers,
Untouched by morning and untouched by noon,
Sleep the meek members of the resurrection,
Rafter of satin, and roof of stone.

Light laughs the breeze in her castle of sunshine;
Babbles the bee in a stolid ear;
Pipe the sweet birds in ignorant cadence,—
Ah, what sagacity perished here!

Grand go the years in the crescent above them;
Worlds scoop their arcs, and firmaments row,
Diadems drop and Doges surrender,
Soundless as dots on a disk of snow.

## "I like a look of agony"

I like a look of agony,
Because I know it's true;
Men do not sham convulsion,
Nor simulate a throe.

The eyes glaze once, and that is death.
Impossible to feign
The beads upon the forehead
By homely anguish strung.

## "Because I could not stop for Death"

Because I could not stop for Death,
He kindly stopped for me;
The carriage held but just ourselves
And Immortality.

We slowly drove, he knew no haste,
And I had put away
My labor, and my leisure too,
For his civility.

We passed the school where children played
At wrestling in a ring;
We passed the fields of gazing grain,
We passed the setting sun.

We paused before a house that seemed
A swelling of the ground;
The roof was scarcely visible,
The cornice but a mound.

Since then 'tis centuries; but each
Feels shorter than the day
I first surmised the horses' heads
Were toward eternity.

## "Our journey had advanced"

Our journey had advanced;
Our feet were almost come
To that odd fork in Being's road,
Eternity by term.

Our pace took sudden awe,
Our feet reluctant led.
Before were cities, but between,
The forest of the dead.

Retreat was out of hope,—
Behind, a sealéd route,
Eternity's white flag before,
And God at every gate.

## "I never lost as much but twice"

I never lost as much but twice,
And that was in the sod;
Twice have I stood a beggar
Before the door of God!

Angels, twice descending,
Reimbursed my store.
Burglar, banker, father,
I am poor once more!

## "I felt a funeral in my brain"

I felt a funeral in my brain,
    And mourners, to and fro,
Kept treading, treading, till it seemed
    That sense was breaking through.

And when they all were seated,
   A service like a drum
Kept beating, beating, till I thought
   My mind was going numb.

And then I heard them lift a box,
   And creak across my soul
With those same boots of lead, again.
   Then space began to toll

As all the heavens were a bell,
   And Being but an ear,
And I and silence some strange race,
   Wrecked, solitary, here.

## "In winter, in my room"

In winter, in my room,
I came upon a worm,
Pink, lank, and warm.
But as he was a worm
And worms presume,
Not quite with him at home—
Secured him by a string
To something neighboring,
And went along.

A trifle afterward
A thing occurred,
I'd not believe it if I heard—
But state with creeping blood;
A snake, with mottles rare,
Surveyed my chamber floor,
In feature as the worm before,
But ringed with power.
The very string
With which I tied him, too,

When he was mean and new,
That string was there.

I shrank—"How fair you are!"
Propitiation's claw—
"Afraid," he hissed,
"Of me?"
"No cordiality?"
He fathomed me.
Then, to a rhythm slim
Secreted in his form,
As patterns swim,
Projected him.

That time I flew,
Both eyes his way,
Lest he pursue—
Nor ever ceased to run,
Till, in a distant town,
Towns on from mine—
I sat me down;
This was a dream.

## "The Bible is an antique volume"

The Bible is an antique volume
Written by faded men,
At the suggestion of Holy Spectres—
Subjects—Bethlehem
Eden—the ancient Homestead—
Satan—the Brigadier,
Judas—the great Defaulter,
David—the Troubadour.
Sin—a distinguished Precipice
Others must resist,
Boys that "believe"
Are very lonesome

Other boys are "lost."
Had but the tale a warbling Teller
All the boys would come—
Orpheus' sermon captivated,
It did not condemn.

## "I reckon, when I count at all"

I reckon, when I count at all,
First Poets—then the Sun—
Then Summer—then the Heaven of God—
And then the list is done.
But looking back—the first so seems
To comprehend the whole—
The others look a needless show,
So I write Poets—All.
This summer lasts a solid year,
They can afford a sun
The East would deem extravagant,
And if the final Heaven
Be beautiful as they disclose
To those who trust in them,
It is too difficult a grace
To justify the dream.

## "I dwell in Possibility"

I dwell in Possibility,
A fairer house than Prose,
More numerous of windows,
Superior of doors.

Of chambers, as the cedars—
Impregnable of eye;
And for an everlasting roof
The gables of the sky.

Of visitors—the fairest—
For occupation—this—
The spreading wide my narrow hands
To gather Paradise.

---

## "My life had stood a loaded gun"

My life had stood a loaded gun
In corners, till a day
The owner passed—identified,
And carried me away.

And now we roam the sov'reign woods,
And now we hunt the doe—
And every time I speak for him
The mountains straight reply.

And do I smile, such cordial light
Upon the valley glow—
It is as a Vesuvian face
Had let its pleasure through.

And when at night, our good day done,
I guard my master's head,
'Tis better than the eider duck's
Deep pillow to have shared.

To foe of his I'm deadly foe,
None stir the second time
On whom I lay a yellow eye
Or an emphatic thumb.

Though I than he may longer live,
He longer must than I,
For I have but the art to kill—
Without the power to die.

# "After great pains a formal feeling comes—"

After great pain a formal feeling comes—
The nerves sit ceremonious like tombs;
The stiff Heart questions—was it He that bore?
And yesterday—or centuries before?

The feet mechanical
Go round a wooden way
Of ground or air or Ought, regardless grown,
A quartz contentment like a stone.

This is the hour of lead
Remembered if outlived,
As freezing persons recollect the snow—
First chill, then stupor, then the letting go.

# ALFRED, LORD TENNYSON
## (1809–1892)

## The Kraken

Below the thunders of the upper deep,
Far, far beneath in the abysmal sea,
His ancient, dreamless, uninvaded sleep
The Kraken sleepeth: faintest sunlights flee
About his shadowy sides; above him swell
Huge sponges of millennial growth and height;
And far away into the sickly light,
From many a wondrous grot and secret cell
Unnumber'd and enormous polypi
Winnow with giant arms the slumbering green.
There hath he lain for ages, and will lie
Battening upon huge sea-worms in his sleep,
Until the latter fire shall heat the deep;
Then once by man and angels to be seen,
In roaring he shall rise and on the surface die.

## Mariana

> Mariana in the moated grange.
> *Measure for Measure*

With blackest moss the flower-plots
    Were thickly crusted, one and all;
The rusted nails fell from the knots
    That held the pear to the gable-wall.

The broken sheds look'd sad and strange:
   Unlifted was the clinking latch;
   Weeded and worn the ancient thatch
Upon the lonely moated grange.
      She only said, "My life is dreary,
        He cometh not," she said;
      She said, "I am aweary, aweary,
        I would that I were dead!"

Her tears fell with the dews at even;
   Her tears fell ere the dews were dried;
She could not look on the sweet heaven,
   Either at morn or eventide.
After the flitting of the bats,
   When thickest dark did trance the sky,
   She drew her casement-curtain by,
And glanced athwart the glooming flats.
      She only said, "The night is dreary,
        He cometh not," she said;
      She said, "I am aweary, aweary,
        I would that I were dead!"

Upon the middle of the night,
   Waking she heard the night-fowl crow;
The cock sung out an hour ere light;
   From the dark fen the oxen's low
Came to her; without hope of change,
   In sleep she seem'd to walk forlorn,
   Till cold winds woke the gray-eyed morn
About the lonely moated grange.
      She only said, "The night is dreary,
        He cometh not," she said;
      She said, "I am aweary, aweary,
        I would that I were dead!"

About a stone-cast from the wall
   A sluice with blacken'd waters slept,

And o'er it many, round and small,
   The cluster'd marish-mosses crept.
Hard by a poplar shook alway,
   All silver-green with gnarled bark:
   For leagues no other tree did mark
The level waste, the rounding gray.
      She only said, "The night is dreary,
        He cometh not," she said;
      She said, "I am aweary, aweary,
        I would that I were dead!"

And ever when the moon was low,
   And the shrill winds were up and away,
In the white curtain, to and fro,
   She saw the gusty shadow sway.
But when the moon was very low,
   And wild winds bound within their cell,
   The shadow of the poplar fell
Upon her bed, across her brow.
      She only said, "The night is dreary,
        He cometh not," she said;
      She said, "I am aweary, aweary,
        I would that I were dead!"

All day within the dreamy house,
   The doors upon their hinges creak'd;
The blue fly sung in the pane; the mouse
   Behind the mouldering wainscot shriek'd,
Or from the crevice peer'd about.
   Old faces glimmer'd thro' the doors,
   Old footsteps trod the upper floors,
Old voices called her from without.
      She only said, "The night is dreary,
        He cometh not," she said;
      She said, "I am aweary, aweary,
        I would that I were dead!"

The sparrow's chirrup on the roof,
   The slow clock ticking, and the sound
Which to the wooing wind aloof
   The poplar made, did all confound
Her sense; but most she loathed the hour
   When the thick-moted sunbeam lay
   Athwart the chambers, and the day
Was sloping toward his western bower.
     Then said she, "I am very dreary,
      He will not come," she said;
     She wept, "I am aweary, aweary,
      O God, that I were dead!"

# The Lady of Shalott

## PART I

On either side the river lie
Long fields of barley and of rye,
That clothe the wold and meet the sky;
Aud thro' the field the road runs by
     To many-tower'd Camelot;
And up and down the people go,
Gazing where the lilies blow
Round an island there below,
     The island of Shalott.

Willows whiten, aspens quiver,
Little breezes dusk and shiver
Thro' the wave that runs for ever
By the island in the river
     Flowing down to Camelot.
Four gray walls, and four gray towers,
Overlook a space of flowers,
And the silent isle imbowers
     The Lady of Shalott.

By the margin, willow-veil'd,
Slide the heavy barges trail'd
By slow horses; and unhail'd
The shallop flitteth silken-sail'd
        Skimming down to Camelot:
But who hath seen her wave her hand?
Or at the casement seen her stand?
Or is she known in all the land,
        The Lady of Shalott?

Only reapers, reaping early
In among the bearded barley,
Hear a song that echoes cheerly
From the river winding clearly,
        Down to tower'd Camelot;
And by the moon the reaper weary,
Piling sheaves in uplands airy,
Listening, whispers " 'Tis the fairy
        Lady of Shalott."

## PART II

There she weaves by night and day
A magic web with colors gay.
She has heard a whisper say,
A curse is on her if she stay
        To look down to Camelot.
She knows not what the curse may be,
And so she weaveth steadily,
And little other care hath she,
        The Lady of Shalott.

And moving thro' a mirror clear
That hangs before her all the year,
Shadows of the world appear.
There she sees the highway near
        Winding down to Camelot;
There the river eddy whirls,

And there the surly village-churls,
And the red cloaks of market girls,
     Pass onward from Shalott.

Sometimes a troop of damsels glad,
An abbot on an ambling pad,
Sometimes a curly shepherd-lad,
Or long-hair'd page in crimson clad,
     Goes by to tower'd Camelot;
And sometimes thro' the mirror blue
The knights come riding two and two:
She hath no loyal knight and true,
     The Lady of Shalott.

But in her web she still delights
To weave the mirror's magic sights,
For often thro' the silent nights
A funeral, with plumes and lights
     And music, went to Camelot;
Or when the moon was overhead,
Came two young lovers lately wed:
"I am half sick of shadows," said
     The Lady of Shalott.

### PART III

A bow-shot from her bower-eaves,
He rode between the barley-sheaves.
The sun came dazzling thro' the leaves,
And flamed upon the brazen greaves
     Of bold Sir Lancelot.
A red-cross knight for ever kneel'd
To a lady in his shield,
That sparkled on the yellow field,
     Beside remote Shalott.

The gemmy bridle glitter'd free,
Like to some branch of stars we see

Hung in the golden Galaxy.
The bridle bells rang merrily
　　　　As he rode down to Camelot;
And from his blazon'd baldric slung
A mighty silver bugle hung,
And as he rode his armor rung,
　　　　Beside remote Shalott.

All in the blue unclouded weather
Thick-jewell'd shone the saddle-leather,
The helmet and the helmet-feather
Burn'd like one burning flame together,
　　　　As he rode down to Camelot;
As often thro' the purple night,
Below the starry clusters bright,
Some bearded meteor, trailing light,
　　　　Moves over still Shalott.

His broad clear brow in sunlight glow'd;
On burnish'd hooves his war-horse trode;
From underneath his helmet flow'd
His coal-black curls as on he rode,
　　　　As he rode down to Camelot.
From the bank and from the river
He flash'd into the crystal mirror,
"Tirra lirra," by the river
　　　　Sang Sir Lancelot.

She left the web, she left the loom,
She made three paces thro' the room,
She saw the water-lily bloom,
She saw the helmet and the plume,
　　　　She look'd down to Camelot.
Out flew the web and floated wide;
The mirror crack'd from side to side;
"The curse is come upon me," cried
　　　　The Lady of Shalott.

## PART IV

In the stormy east-wind straining,
The pale yellow woods were waning,
The broad stream in his banks complaining,
Heavily the low sky raining
      Over tower'd Camelot;
Down she came and found a boat
Beneath a willow left afloat,
And round about the prow she wrote
      *The Lady of Shalott.*

And down the river's dim expanse
Like some bold seër in a trance,
Seeing all his own mischance—
With a glassy countenance
      Did she look to Camelot.
And at the closing of the day
She loosed the chain, and down she lay
The broad stream bore her far away,
      The Lady of Shalott.

Lying, robed in snowy white
That loosely flew to left and right—
The leaves upon her falling light—
Thro' the noises of the night
      She floated down to Camelot;
And as the boat-head wound along
The willowy hills and fields among,
They heard her singing her last song,
      The Lady of Shalott.

Heard a carol, mournful, holy,
Chanted loudly, chanted lowly,
Till her blood was frozen slowly,
And her eyes were darken'd wholly,
      Turn'd to tower'd Camelot.
For ere she reach'd upon the tide

The first house by the water-side,
Singing in her song she died,
    The Lady of Shalott.

Under tower and balcony,
By garden-wall and gallery,
A gleaming shape she floated by,
Dead-pale between the houses high,
    Silent into Camelot.
Out upon the wharfs they came,
Knight and burgher, lord and dame,
And round the prow they read her name,
    *The Lady of Shalott.*

Who is this? and what is here?
And in the lighted palace near
Died the sound of royal cheer;
And they cross'd themselves for fear,
    All the knights at Camelot:
But Lancelot mused a little space;
He said, "She has a lovely face;
God in his mercy lend her grace,
    The Lady of Shalott."

## Morte d'Arthur

So all day long the noise of battle roll'd
Among the mountains by the winter sea,
Until King Arthur's table, man by man,
Had fallen in Lyonness about their lord,
King Arthur; then, because his wound was deep,
The bold Sir Bedivere uplifted him,
Sir Bedivere, the last of all his knights,
And bore him to a chapel nigh the field,
A broken chancel with a broken cross,
That stood on a dark strait of barren land.

On one side lay the ocean, and on one
Lay a great water, and the moon was full.
   Then spake King Arthur to Sir Bedivere:
"The sequel of to-day unsolders all
The goodliest fellowship of famous knights
Whereof this world holds record. Such a sleep
They sleep—the men I loved. I think that we
Shall never more, at any future time,
Delight our souls with talk of knightly deeds,
Walking about the gardens and the halls
Of Camelot, as in the days that were.
I perish by this people which I made,—
Tho' Merlin sware that I should come again
To rule once more—but let what will be be,
I am so deeply smitten thro' the helm
That without help I cannot last till morn.
Thou therefore take my brand Excalibur,
Which was my pride; for thou rememberest how
In those old days, one summer noon, an arm
Rose up from out the bosom of the lake,
Clothed in white samite, mystic, wonderful,
Holding the sword—and how I row'd across
And took it, and have worn it, like a king;
And, wheresoever I am sung or told
In aftertime, this also shall be known.
But now delay not; take Excalibur,
And fling him far into the middle mere;
Watch what thou seest, and lightly bring me word."
   To him replied the bold Sir Bedivere:
"It is not meet, Sir King, to leave thee thus,
Aidless, alone, and smitten thro' the helm.
A little thing may harm a wounded man.
Yet I thy best will all perform at full,
Watch what I see, and lightly bring thee word."
   So saying, from the ruin'd shrine he stept
And in the moon athwart the place of tombs,
Where lay the mighty bones of ancient men,

Old knights, and over them the sea-wind sang
Shrill, chill, with flakes of foam. He, stepping down
By zigzag paths and juts of pointed rock,
Came on the shining levels of the lake.

There drew he forth the brand Excalibur,
And o'er him, drawing it, the winter moon,
Brightening the skirts of a long cloud, ran forth
And sparkled keen with frost against the hilt;
For all the haft twinkled with diamond sparks,
Myriads of topaz-lights, and jacinth-work
Of subtlest jewellery. He gazed so long
That both his eyes were dazzled, as he stood,
This way and that dividing the swift mind,
In act to throw; but at the last it seem'd
Better to leave Excalibur conceal'd
There in the many-knotted water-flags,
That whistled stiff and dry about marge.
So strode he back slow to the wounded king.

Then spake King Arthur to Sir Bedivere:
"Hast thou perform'd my mission which I gave?
What is it thou hast seen, or what hast heard?"

And answer made the bold Sir Bedivere:
"I heard the ripple washing in the reeds,
And the wild water lapping on the crag."

To whom replied King Arthur, faint and pale:
"Thou hast betray'd thy nature and thy name,
Not rendering true answer, as beseem'd
Thy fealty, nor like a noble knight;
For surer sign had followed, either hand,
Or voice, or else a motion of the mere.
This is a shameful thing for men to lie.
Yet now. I charge thee, quickly go again
As thou art lief and dear, and do the thing
I bade thee, watch, and lightly bring me word."

Then went Sir Bedivere the second time
Across the ridge, and paced beside the mere,
Counting the dewy pebbles, fix'd in thought;

But when he saw the wonder of the hilt,
How curiously and strangely chased, he smote
His palms together, and lie cried aloud:

   "And if indeed I cast the brand away,
Surely a precious thing, one worthy note,
Should thus be lost forever from the earth,
Which might have pleased the eyes of many men.
What good should follow this, if this were done?
What harm, undone? deep harm to disobey,
Seeing obedience is the bond of rule.
Were it well to obey then, if a king demand
An act unprofitable, against himself?
The king is sick, and knows not what he does.
What record, or what relic of my lord
Should be to aftertime, but empty breath
And rumors of a doubt? but were this kept,
Stored in some treasure-house of mighty kings,
Some one might show it at a joust of arms,
Saying, "King Arthur's sword, Excalibur.
Wrought by the lonely maiden of the lake;
Nine years she wrought it, sitting in the deeps
Upon the hidden bases of the hills."
So might some old man speak in the aftertime
To all the people, winning reverence;
But now much honor and much fame were lost."

   So spake he, clouded with his own conceit,
And hid Excalibur the second time,
And so strode back slow to the wounded king.

   Then spoke King Arthur, breathing heavily:
"What is it thou hast seen, or what hast heard?"

   And answer made the bold Sir Bedivere:
"I heard the water lapping on the crag,
And the long ripple washing in the reeds."

   To whom replied King Arthur, much in wrath:
"Ah, miserable and unkind, untrue,
Unknightly, traitor-hearted! Woe is me!
Authority forgets a dying king,

Laid widow'd of the power in his eye
That bow'd the will. I see thee what thou art,
For thou, the latest-left of all my knights,
In whom should meet the offices of all,
Thou wouldst betray me for the precious hilt;
Either from lust of gold, or like a girl
Valuing the giddy pleasure of the eyes.
Yet, for a man may fail in duty twice,
And the third time may prosper, get thee hence;
But, if thou spare to fling Excalibur,
I will arise and slay thee with my hands."
    Then quickly rose Sir Bedivere, and ran,
And, leaping down the ridges lightly, plunged
Among the bulrush-beds, and clutch'd the sword,
And strongly wheel'd and threw it. The great brand
Made lightnings in the splendor of the moon,
And flashing round and round, and whirl'd in an arch,
Shot like a streamer of the northern morn,
Seen where the moving isles of winter shock
By night, with noises of the northern sea.
So flash'd and fell the brand Excalibur;
But ere be dipt the surface, rose an arm
Cloth'd in white samite, mystic, wonderful,
And caught him by the hilt, and brandish'd him
Three times, and drew him under in the mere.
And lightly went the other to the king.
    Then spoke King Arthur, drawing thicker breath:
"Now see I by thine eyes that this is done.
Speak out; what is it thou hast heard, or seen?"
    And answer made the bold Sir Bedivere:
"Sir King, I closed mine eyelids, lest the gems
Should blind my purpose, for I never saw,
Nor shall see, here or elsewhere, till I die,
Not tho' I live three lives of mortal men,
So great a miracle as yonder hilt.
Then with both hands I flung him, wheeling him;
But when I look'd again, behold an arm,

Clothed in white samite, mystic, wonderful,
That caught him by the hilt, and brandish'd him
Three times, and drew him under in the mere."

And answer made King Arthur, breathing hard:
"My end draws nigh; 'tis time that I were gone.
Make broad thy shoulders to receive my weight,
And bear me to the margin; yet I fear
My wound hath taken cold, and I shall die."

So saying, from the pavement he half rose,
Slowly, with pain, reclining on his arm,
And looking wistfully with wide blue eyes
As in a picture. Him Sir Bedivere
Remorsefully regarded thro' his tears,
And would have spoken, but he found not words,
Then took with care, and kneeling on one knee,
O'er both his shoulders drew the languid hands,
And rising bore him thro' the place of tombs.

But, as he walk'd, King Arthur panted hard,
Like one that feels a nightmare on his bed
When all the house is mute. So sigh'd the king,
Muttering and murmuring at his ear, "Quick, quick!
I fear it is too late, and I shall die."
But the other swiftly strode from ridge to ridge,
Clothed with his breath, and looking, as he walk'd,
Larger than human on the frozen hills.
He heard the deep behind him, and a cry
Before. His own thought drove him like a goad.
Dry clash'd his harness in the icy caves
And barren chasms, and all to left and right
The bare black cliff clang'd round him, as he based
His feet on juts of slippery crag that rang
Sharp-smitten with the dint of armed heels—
And on a sudden, lo! the level lake,
And the long glories of the winter moon.

Then saw they how there hove a dusky barge,
Dark as a funeral scarf from stem to stern,
Beneath them; and descending they were ware

That all the decks were dense with stately forms
Black-stoled, black-hooded, like a dream—by these
Three queens with crowns of gold—and from them rose
A cry that shiver'd to the tingling stars,
And, as it were one voice, an agony
Of lamentation, like a wind that shrills
All night in a waste land, where no one comes,
Or hath come, since the making of the world.
    Then murmur'd Arthur, "Place me in the barge,"
And to the barge they came. There those three queens
Put forth their hands, and took the king, and wept.
But she that rose the tallest of them all
And fairest laid his head upon her lap,
And loosed the shatter'd casque, and chafed his hands,
And call'd him by his name, complaining loud,
And dropping bitter tears against his brow
Striped with dark blood; for all his face was white
And colorless, and like the wither'd moon
Smote by the fresh beam of the springing east;
And all his greaves and cuisses dash'd with drops
Of onset; and the light and lustrous curls—
That made his forehead like a rising sun
High from the dais-throne—were parch'd with dust;
Or, clotted into points and hanging loose,
Mix'd with the knightly growth that fringed his lips.
So like a shatter'd column lay the king;
Not like that Arthur who, with lance in rest,
From spur to plume a star of tournament,
Shot thro' the lists at Camelot, and charged
Before the eyes of ladies and of kings.
    Then loudly cried the bold Sir Bedivere:
"Ah! my Lord Arthur, whither shall I go?
Where shall I hide my forehead and my eyes?
For now I see the true old times are dead,
When every morning brought a noble chance,
And every chance brought out a noble knight.
Such times have been not since the light that led

The holy Elders with the gift of myrrh.
But now the whole ROUND TABLE is dissolved
Which was an image of the mighty world;
And I, the last, go forth companionless,
And the days darken round me, and the years,
Among new men, strange faces, other minds."
    And slowly answer'd Arthur from the barge:
"The old order changeth, yielding place to new,
And God fulfils himself in many ways,
Lest one good custom should corrupt the world.
Comfort thyself: what comfort is in me?
I have lived my life, and that which I have done
May He within himself make pure! but thou,
If thou shouldst never see my face again,
Pray for my soul. More things are wrought by prayer
Than this world dreams of. Wherefore, let thy voice
Rise like a fountain for me night and day.
For what are men better than sheep or goats
That nourish a blind life within the brain,
If, knowing God, they lift not hands of prayer
Both for themselves and those who call them friend?
For so the whole round earth is every way
Bound by gold chains about the feet of God.
But now farewell. I am going a long way
With these thou seest—if indeed I go—
For all my mind is clouded with a doubt—
To the island-valley of Avilion;
Where falls not hail, or rain, or any snow,
Nor ever wind blows loudly, but it lies
Deep-meadow'd, happy, fair with orchard lawns
And bowery hollows crown'd with summer sea,
Where I will heal me of my grievous wound."
    So said he, and the barge with oar and sail
Moved from the brink, like some full-breasted swan
That, fluting a wild carol ere her death,
Ruffles her pure cold plume, and takes the flood
With swarthy webs. Long stood Sir Bedivere

Revolving many memories, till the hull
Look'd one black dot against the verge of dawn,
And on the mere the wailing died away.

    Here ended Hall, and our last light, that long
Had wink'd and threaten'd darkness, flare and fell;
At which the parson, sent to sleep with sound,
And waked with silence, grunted "Good!" but we
Sat rapt: it was the tone with which he read—
Perhaps some modern touches here and there
Redeem'd it from the charge of nothingness—
Or else we loved the man, and prized his work;
I know not; but we sitting, as I said,
The cock crew loud, as at that time of year
The lusty bird takes every hour for dawn.
Then Francis, muttering, like a man ill-used,
"There now—that's nothing!" drew a little back,
And drove his heel into the smoulder'd log,
That sent a blast of sparkles up the flue.
And so to bed, where yet in sleep I seem'd
To sail with Arthur under looming shores,
Point after point; till on to dawn, when dreams
Begin to feel the truth and stir of day,
To me, methought, who waited with the crowd,
There came a bark that, blowing forward, bore
King Arthur, like a modern gentleman
Of stateliest port; and all the people cried,
"Arthur is come again: he cannot die."
Then those that stood upon the hills behind
Repeated—"Come again, and thrice as fair";
And, further inland, voices echoed—"Come
With all good things, and war shall be no more."
At this a hundred bells began to peal,
That with the sound I woke, and heard indeed
The clear church-bells ring in the Christmas morn.

# Locksley Hall

Comrades, leave me here a little, while as yet 'tis early morn;
Leave me here, and when you want me, sound upon the bugle-horn.

'Tis the place, and all around it, as of old, the curlews call,
Dreary gleams about the moorland flying over Locksley Hall;

Locksley Hall, that in the distance overlooks the sandy tracts,
And the hollow ocean-ridges roaring into cataracts.

Many a night from yonder ivied casement, ere I went to rest,
Did I look on great Orion sloping slowly to the west.

Many a night I saw the Pleiads, rising thro' the mellow shade,
Glitter like a swarm of fireflies tangled in a silver braid.

Here about the beach I wander'd, nourishing a youth sublime
With the fairy tales of science, and the long result of time;

When the centuries behind me like a fruitful land reposed;
When I clung to all the present for the promise that it closed;

When I dipt into the future far as human eye could see,
Saw the vision of the world and all the wonder that would be.—

In the spring a fuller crimson comes upon the robin's breast;
In the spring the wanton lapwing gets himself another crest;

In the spring a livelier iris changes on the burnish'd dove;
In the spring a young man's fancy lightly turns to thoughts of love.

Then her cheek was pale and thinner than should be for one so young,
And her eyes on all my motions with a mute observance hung.

And I said, "My cousin Amy, speak, and speak the truth to me,
Trust me, cousin, all the current of my being sets to thee."

On her pallid cheek and forehead came a color and a light,
As I have seen the rosy red flushing in the northern night.

And she turn'd—her bosom shaken with a sudden storm of sighs—
All the spirit deeply dawning in the dark of hazel eyes—

Saying, "I have hid my feelings, fearing they should do me wrong";
Saying, "Dost thou love me, cousin?" weeping, "I have loved thee long."

Love took up the glass of Time, and turn'd it in his glowing hands;
Every moment, lightly shaken, ran itself in golden sands.

Love took up the harp of Life, and smote on all the chords with might;
Smote the chord of Self, that, trembling, past in music out of sight.

Many a morning on the moorland did we hear the copses ring,
And her whisper throng'd my pulses with the fulness of the spring.

Many an evening by the waters did we watch the stately ships,
And our spirits rush'd together at the touching of the lips.

O my cousin, shallow-hearted! O my Amy, mine no more!
O the dreary, dreary moorland! O the barren, barren shore!

Falser than all fancy fathoms, falser than all songs have sung,
Puppet to a father's threat, and servile to a shrewish tongue!

Is it well to wish thee happy?—having known me—to decline
On a range of lower feelings and a narrower heart than mine!

Yet it shall be; thou shalt lower to his level day by day,
What is fine within thee growing coarse to sympathize with clay.

As the husband is, the wife is; thou art mated with a clown,
And the grossness of his nature will have weight to drag thee down.

He will hold thee, when his passion shall have spent its novel force,
Something better than his dog, a little dearer than his horse.

What is this? his eyes are heavy; think not they are glazed with wine.
Go to him, it is thy duty; kiss him, take his hand in thine.

It may be my lord is weary, that his brain is overwrought;
Soothe him with thy finer fancies, touch him with thy lighter thought.

He will answer to the purpose, easy things to understand—
Better thou wert dead before me, tho' I slew thee with my hand!

Better thou and I were lying, hidden from the heart's disgrace,
Roll'd in one another's arms, and silent in a last embrace.

Cursed be the social wants that sin against the strength of youth!
Cursed be the social lies that warp us from the living truth!

Cursed be the sickly forms that err from honest Nature's rule!
Cursed be the gold that gilds the straiten'd forehead of the fool!

Well—'tis well that I should bluster!—Hadst thou less unworthy proved—
Would to God—for I had loved thee more than ever wife was loved.

Am I mad, that I should cherish that which bears but bitter fruit?
I will pluck it from my bosom, tho' my heart be at the root.

Never, tho' my mortal summers to such length of years should come
As the many-winter'd crow that leads the clanging rookery home.

Where is comfort? in division of the records of the mind?
Can I part her from herself, and love her, as I knew her, kind?

I remember one that perish'd; sweetly did she speak and move;
Such a one do I remember, whom to look at was to love.

Can I think of her as dead, and love her for the love she bore?
No—she never loved me truly; love is love for evermore.

Comfort? comfort scorn'd of devils! this is truth the poet sings,
That a sorrow's crown of sorrow is remembering happier things.

Drug thy memories, lest thou learn it, lest thy heart be put to proof,
In the dead unhappy night, and when the rain is on the roof.

Like a dog, he hunts in dreams, and thou art staring at the wall,
Where the dying night-lamp flickers, and the shadows rise and fall.

Then a hand shall pass before thee, pointing to his drunken sleep,
To thy widow'd marriage-pillows, to the tears that thou wilt weep.

Thou shalt bear the "Never, never," whisper'd by the phantom years,
And a song from out the distance in the ringing of thine ears;

And an eye shall vex thee, looking ancient kindness on thy pain.
Turn thee, turn thee on thy pillow; get thee to thy rest again.

Nay, but Nature brings thee solace; for a tender voice will cry.
'Tis a purer life than thine, a lip to drain thy trouble dry.

Baby lips will laugh me down; my latest rival brings thee rest.
Baby fingers, waxen touches, press me from the mother's breast.

O, the child too clothes the father with a dearness not his due.
Half is thine and half is his; it will be worthy of the two.

O, I see thee old and formal, fitted to thy petty part,
With a little hoard of maxims preaching down a daughter's heart.

"They were dangerous guides the feelings—she herself was not exempt—
Truly, she herself had suffer'd"—Perish in thy self-contempt!

Overlive it—lower yet—be happy! wherefore should I care?
I myself must mix with action, lest I wither by despair.

What is that which I should turn to, lighting upon days like these?
Every door is barr'd with gold, and opens but to golden keys.

Every gate is throng'd with suitors, all the markets overflow.
I have but an angry fancy; what is that which I should do?

I had been content to perish, falling on the foeman's ground,
When the ranks are roll'd in vapor, and the winds are laid with sound.

But the jingling of the guinea helps the hurt that Honor feels,
And the nations do but murmur, snarling at each other's heels.

Can I but relive in sadness? I will turn that earlier page.
Hide me from my deep emotion, O thou Wondrous Mother-Age!

Make me feel the wild pulsation that I felt before the strife,
When I heard my days before me, and the tumult of my life;

Yearning for the large excitement that the coming years would yield,
Eager-hearted as a boy when first he leaves his father's field,

And at night along the dusky highway near and nearer drawn,
Sees in heaven the light of London flaring like a dreary dawn;

And his spirit leaps within him to be gone before him then,
Underneath the light he looks at, in among the throngs of men;

Men, my brothers, men the workers, ever reaping something new;
That which they have done but earnest of the things that they shall do.

For I dipt into the future, far as human eye could see,
Saw the Vision of the world, and all the wonder that would be;

Saw the heavens fill with commerce, argosies of magic sails,
Pilots of the purple twilight, dropping down with costly bales;

Heard the heavens fill with shouting, and there rain'd a ghastly dew
From the nations' airy navies grappling in the central blue;

Far along the world-wide whisper of the south-wind rushing warm,
With the standards of the peoples plunging thro' the thunder storm;

Till the war-drum throbb'd no longer, and the battle-flags were furl'd
In the Parliament of man, the Federation of the world.

There the common sense of most shall hold a fretful realm in awe.
And the kindly earth shall slumber, lapt in universal law.

So I triumph'd ere my passion sweeping thro' me left me dry,
Left me with the palsied heart, and left me with the jaundiced eye;

Eye, to which all order festers, all things here are out of joint.
Science moves, but slowly, slowly, creeping on from point to point;

Slowly comes a hungry people, as a lion, creeping nigher,
Glares at one that nods and winks behind a slowly-dying fire.

Yet I doubt not thro' the ages one increasing purpose runs,
And the thoughts of men are widen'd with the process of the suns.

What is that to him that reaps not harvest of his youthful joys,
Tho' the deep heart of existence beat for ever like a boy's?

Knowledge comes, but wisdom lingers, and I linger on the shore,
And the individual withers, and the world is more and more.

Knowledge comes, but wisdom lingers, and he bears a laden breast,
Full of sad experience, moving toward the stillness of his rest.

Hark, my merry comrades call me, sounding on the bugle-horn,
They to whom my foolish passion were a target for their scorn.

Shall it not be scorn to me to harp on such a moulder'd string?
I am shamed thro' all my nature to have loved so slight a thing.

Weakness to be wroth with weakness! woman's pleasure, woman's pain—
Nature made them blinder motions bounded in a shallower brain.

Woman is the lesser man, and all thy passions, match'd with mine,
Are as moonlight unto sunlight, and as water unto wine —

Here at least, where nature sickens, nothing. Ah, for some retreat
Deep in yonder shining Orient, where my life began to beat,

Where in wild Mahratta-battle fell my father evil-starr'd;—
I was left a trampled orphan, and a selfish uncle's ward.

Or to burst all links of habit—there to wander far away,
On from island unto island at the gateways of the day.

Larger constellations burning, mellow moons and happy skies,
Breadths of tropic shade and palms in cluster, knots of Paradise.

Never come? the trader, never floats an European flag,
Slides the bird o'er lustrous woodland, swings the trailer from the crag;

Droops the heavy-blossom'd bower, hangs the heavy-fruited tree—
Summer isles of Eden lying in dark-purple spheres of sea.

There methinks would be enjoyment more than in this march of mind,
In the steamship, in the railway, in the thoughts that shake mankind.

There the passions cramp'd no longer shall have scope and breathing space;
I will take some savage woman, she shall rear my dusky race.

Iron-jointed, supple-sinew'd, they shall dive, and they shall run,
Catch the wild goat by the hair, and hurl their lances in the sun;

Whistle back the parrot's call, and leap the rainbows of the brooks,
Not with blinded eyesight poring over miserable books—

Fool, again the dream, the fancy! but I *know* my words are wild,
But I count the gray barbarian lower than the Christian child.

I, to herd with narrow foreheads, vacant of our glorious gains,
Like a beast with lower pleasures, like a beast with lower pains!

Mated with a squalid savage—what to me were sun or clime?
I the heir of all the ages, in the foremost files of time—

I that rather held it better men should perish one by one,
Than that earth should stand at gaze like Joshua's moon in Ajalon!

Not in vain the distance beacons. Forward, forward let us range,
Let the great world spin for ever down the ringing grooves of change.

Thro' the shadow of the globe we sweep into the younger day;
Better fifty years of Europe than a cycle of Cathay.

Mother-Age,—for mine I knew not,—help me as when life begun;
Rift the hills, and roll the waters, flash the lightnings, weigh the sun.

O, I see the crescent promise of my spirit hath not set.
Ancient founts of inspiration well thro' all my fancy yet.

Howsoever these things be, a long farewell to Locksley Hall!
Now for me the woods may wither, now for me the roof-tree fall.

Comes a vapor from the margin, blackening over heath and holt,
Cramming all the blast before it, in its breast a thunderbolt.

Let it fall on Locksley Hall, with rain or hail, or fire or snow;
For the mighty wind arises, roaring seaward, and I go.

# The Charge of the Light Brigade

### I

Half a league, half a league,
Half a league onward,
All in the valley of Death
   Rode the six hundred.
"Forward the Light Brigade!
Charge for the guns!" he said.
Into the valley of Death
   Rode the six hundred.

### II

"Forward, the Light Brigade!"
Was there a man dismay'd?
Not tho' the soldier knew
   Some one had blunder'd.
Theirs not to make reply,
Theirs not to reason why,
Theirs but to do and die.
Into the valley of Death
   Rode the six hundred.

### III

Cannon to right of them,
Cannon to left of them,
Cannon in front of them
   Volley'd and thunder'd;
Storm'd at with shot and shell,
Boldly they rode and well,
Into the jaws of Death,
Into the mouth of hell
   Rode the six hundred.

### IV

Flash'd all their sabers bare,
Flash'd as they turn'd in air
Sabring the gunners there,
Charging an army, while
    All the world wonder'd.
Plung'd in the battery-smoke
Right thro' the line they broke;
Cossack and Russian
Reel'd from the sabre-stroke
    Shatter'd and sunder'd.
Then they rode back, but not,
    Not the six hundred.

### V

Cannon to the right of them,
Cannon to the left of them,
Cannon behind them
    Volley'd and thunder'd;
Storm'd at with shot and shell,
While horse and hero fell,
They that had fought so well
Came thro' the jaws of Death,
Back from the mouth of hell,
All that was left of them,
    Left of six hundred.

### VI

When can their glory fade?
O the wild charge they made!
    All the world wonder'd.
Honor the charge they made!
Honor the Light Brigade,
    Noble six hundred!

## "Frater Ave Atque Vale"

Row us out from Desenzano, to your Sirmione row!
So they row'd, and there we landed—"O venusta Sirmio!"
There to me thro' all the groves of olive in the summer glow,
There beneath the Roman ruin where the purple flowers grow,
Came that "Ave atque Vale" of the Poet's hopeless woe,
Tenderest of Roman poets nineteen hundred years ago,
"Frater Ave atque Vale"— as we wander'd to and fro
Gazing at the Lydian laughter of the Garda Lake below
Sweet Catullus's all-but-island, olive-silvery Sirmio!

## Crossing the Bar

Sunset and evening star,
    And one clear call for me!
And may there be no moaning of the bar,
    When I put out to sea,

But such a tide as moving seems asleep,
    Too full for sound and foam.
When that which drew from out the boundless deep
    Turns again home.

Twilight and evening bell,
    And after that the dark!
And may there be no sadness of farewell,
    When I embark;

For tho' from out our bourne of Time and Place
    The flood may bear me far,
I hope to see my Pilot face to face
    When I have crost the bar.

# EDWARD FITZGERALD
## (1809–1883)

## The Rubáiyát of Omar Khayyám

### I

Wake! For the Sun, who scatter'd into flight
The Stars before him from the Field of Night,
   Drives Night along with them from Heav'n, and strikes
The Sultán's Turret with a Shaft of Light.

### II

Before the phantom of False morning died,
Methought a Voice within the Tavern cried,
   "When all the Temple is prepared within,
Why nods the drowsy Worshiper outside?"

### III

And, as the Cock crew, those who stood before
The Tavern shouted—"Open then the Door!
   You know how little while we have to stay,
And, once departed, may return no more."

### IV

Now the New Year reviving old Desires,
The thoughtful Soul to Solitude retires,
   Where the WHITE HAND OF MOSES on the Bough
Puts out, and Jesus from the Ground suspires.

### V

Iram indeed is gone with all his Rose,
And Jamshyd's Sev'n-ring'd Cup where no one knows;
　　But still a Ruby kindles in the Vine,
And many a Garden by the Water blows.

### VI

And David's Lips are lockt; but in divine
High-piping Pehleví, with "Wine! Wine! Wine!
　　Red Wine!"—the Nightingale cries to the Rose
That sallow cheek of hers to' incarnadine.

### VII

Come, fill the Cup, and in the fire of Spring
Your Winter-garment of Repentance fling:
　　The Bird of Time has but a little way
To flutter—and the Bird is on the Wing.

### VIII

Whether at Naishápúr or Babylon,
Whether the Cup with sweet or bitter run,
　　The Wine of Life keeps oozing drop by drop,
The Leaves of Life keep falling one by one.

### IX

Each Morn a thousand Roses brings, you say:
Yes, but where leaves the Rose of Yesterday?
　　And this first Summer month that brings the Rose
Shall take Jamshyd and Kaikobád away.

### X

Well, let it take them! What have we to do
With Kaikobád the Great, or Kaikhosrú?
　　Let Zál and Rustum bluster as they will,
Or Hátim call to Supper—heed not you.

### XI

With me along the strip of Herbage strown
That just divides the desert from the sown,
  Where name of Slave and Sultán is forgot—
And Peace to Mahmúd on his golden Throne!

### XII

A Book of Verses underneath the Bough,
A Jug of Wine, a Loaf of Bread—and Thou
  Beside me singing in the Wilderness—
Oh, Wilderness were Paradise enow!

### XIII

Some for the Glories of This World; and some
Sigh for the Prophet's Paradise to come;
  Ah, take the Cash, and let the Credit go,
Nor heed the rumble of a distant Drum!

### XIV

Look to the blowing Rose about us—"Lo,
Laughing," she says, "into the world I blow,
  At once the silken tassel of my Purse
Tear, and its Treasure on the Garden throw."

### XV

And those who husbanded the Golden grain,
And those who flung it to the winds like Rain,
  Alike to no such aureate Earth are turn'd
As, buried once, Men want dug up again.

### XVI

The Worldly Hope men set their Hearts upon
Turns Ashes—or it prospers; and anon,
  Like Snow upon the Desert's dusty Face,
Lighting a little hour or two—is gone.

### XVII

Think, in this batter'd Caravanserai
Whose Portals are alternate Night and Day,
   How Sultán after Sultán with his Pomp
Abode his destined Hour, and went his way.

### XVIII

They say the Lion and the Lizard keep
The courts where Jamshyd gloried and drank deep:
   And Bahrám, that great Hunter—the Wild Ass
Stamps o'er his Head, but cannot break his Sleep.

### XIX

I sometimes think that never blows so red
The Rose as where some buried Caesar bled;
   That every Hyacinth the Garden wears
Dropt in her Lap from some once lovely Head.

### XX

And this reviving Herb whose tender Green
Fledges the River-Lip on which we lean—
   Ah, lean upon it lightly! for who knows
From what once lovely Lip it springs unseen!

### XXI

Ah, my Belovéd, fill the Cup that clears
To-DAY of past Regrets and future Fears:
   *To-morrow!*—Why, To-morrow I may be
Myself with Yesterday's Sev'n thousand Years.

### XXII

For some we loved, the loveliest and the best
That from his Vintage rolling Time hath prest,
   Have drunk their Cup a Round or two before,
And one by one crept silently to rest.

## XXIII

And we, that now make merry in the Room
They left, and Summer dresses in new bloom,
  Ourselves must we beneath the Couch of Earth
Descend—ourselves to make a Couch—for whom?

## XXIV

Ah, make the most of what we yet may spend,
Before we too into the Dust descend;
  Dust into Dust, and under Dust to lie,
Sans Wine, sans Song, sans Singer, and—sans End!

## XXV

Alike for those who for To-DAY prepare,
And those that after some To-MORROW stare,
  A Muezzín from the Tower of Darkness cries,
"Fools! your Reward is neither Here nor There."

## XXVI

Why, all the Saints and Sages who discuss'd
Of the Two Worlds so wisely—they are thrust
  Like foolish Prophets forth; their Words to Scorn
Are scatter'd, and their Mouths are stopt with Dust.

## XXVII

Myself when young did eagerly frequent
Doctor and Saint, and heard great argument
  About it and about: but evermore
Came out by the same door where in I went.

## XXVIII

With them the seed of Wisdom did I sow,
And with mine own hand wrought to make it grow;
  And this was all the Harvest that I reap'd—
"I came like Water, and like Wind I go."

## XXIX

Into this Universe, and *Why* not knowing
Nor *Whence*, like Water willy-nilly flowing;
   And out of it, as Wind along the Waste,
I know not *Whither*, willy-nilly blowing.

## XXX

What, without asking, hither hurried *Whence?*
And, without asking, *Whither* hurried hence!
   Oh, many a Cup of this forbidden Wine
Must drown the memory of that insolence!

## XXXI

Up from Earth's Centre through the Seventh Gate
I rose, and on the Throne of Saturn sate,
   And many a Knot unravel'd by the Road;
But not the Master-knot of Human Fate.

## XXXII

There was the Door to which I found no Key;
There was the Veil through which I might not see:
   Some little talk awhile of ME and THEE
There was—and then no more of THEE and ME.

## XXXIII

Earth could not answer; nor the Seas that mourn
In flowing Purple, of their Lord forlorn;
   Nor rolling Heaven, with all his Signs reveal'd
And hidden by the sleeve of Night and Morn.

## XXXIV

Then of the THEE IN ME who works behind
The Veil, I lifted up my hands to find
   A lamp amid the Darkness; and I heard,
As from Without—"THE ME WITHIN THEE BLIND!"

## XXXV

Then to the Lip of this poor earthen Urn
I lean'd, the Secret of my Life to learn:
   And Lip to Lip it murmur'd—"While you live,
Drink!—for, once dead, you never shall return."

## XXXVI

I think the Vessel, that with fugitive
Articulation answer'd, once did live,
   And drink; and Ah! the passive Lip I kiss'd,
How many Kisses might it take—and give!

## XXXVII

For I remember stopping by the way
To watch a Potter thumping his wet Clay:
   And with its all-obliterated Tongue
It murmur'd—"Gently, Brother, gently, pray!"

## XXXVIII

And has not such a Story from of Old
Down Man's successive generations roll'd
   Of such a clod of saturated Earth
Cast by the Maker into Human mould?

## XXXIX

And not a drop that from our Cups we throw
For Earth to drink of, but may steal below
   To quench the fire of Anguish in some Eye
There hidden—far beneath, and long ago.

## XL

As then the Tulip for her morning sup
Of Heav'nly Vintage from the soil looks up,
   Do you devoutly do the like, till Heav'n
To Earth invert you—like an empty Cup.

### XLI

Perplext no more with Human or Divine,
To-morrow's tangle to the winds resign,
    And lose your fingers in the tresses of
The Cypress-slender Minister of Wine.

### XLII

And if the Wine you drink, the Lip you press,
End in what All begins and ends in—Yes;
    Think then you are TO-DAY what YESTERDAY
You were—TO-MORROW you shall not be less.

### XLIII

So when that Angel of the darker Drink
At last shall find you by the river-brink,
    And, offering his Cup, invite your Soul
Forth to your Lips to quaff—you shall not shrink.

### XLIV

Why, if the Soul can fling the Dust aside,
And naked on the Air of Heaven ride,
    Were't not a Shame—were't not a Shame for him
In this clay carcase crippled to abide?

### XLV

'Tis but a Tent where takes his one day's rest
A Sultán to the realm of Death addrest;
    The Sultán rises, and the dark Ferrásh
Strikes, and prepares it for another Guest.

### XLVI

And fear not lest Existence closing your
Account, and mine, should know the like no more;
    The Eternal Sáki from that Bowl has pour'd
Millions of Bubbles like us, and will pour.

### XLVII

When You and I behind the Veil are past,
Oh, but the long, long while the World shall last,
   Which of our Coming and Departure heeds
As the Sea's self should heed a pebble-cast.

### XLVIII

A Moment's Halt—a momentary taste
Of Being from the Well amid the Waste—
   And Lo!—the phantom Caravan has reach'd
The Nothing it set out from—Oh, make haste!

### XLIX

Would you that spangle of Existence spend
About The secret—quick about it, Friend!
   A Hair perhaps divides the False from True—
And upon what, prithee, may life depend?

### L

A Hair perhaps divides the False and True;
Yes; and a single Alif were the clue—
   Could you but find it—to the Treasure-house,
And peradventure to The Master too;

### LI

Whose secret Presence through Creation's veins
Running Quicksilver-like eludes your pains;
   Taking all shapes from Máh to Máhi; and
They change and perish all—but He remains;

### LII

A moment guess'd—then back behind the Fold
Immerst of Darkness round the Drama roll'd
   Which, for the Pastime of Eternity,
He doth Himself contrive, enact, behold.

### LIII

But if in vain, down on the stubborn floor
Of Earth, and up to Heav'n's unopening Door,
   You gaze TO-DAY, while You are You—how then
TO-MORROW, when You shall be You no more?

### LIV

Waste not your Hour, nor in the vain pursuit
Of This and That endeavor and dispute;
   Better be jocund with the fruitful Grape
Than sadden after none, or bitter, Fruit.

### LV

You know, my Friends, with what a brave Carouse
I made a Second Marriage in my house;
   Divorced old barren Reason from my Bed,
And took the Daughter of the Vine to Spouse.

### LVI

For "Is" and "Is-NOT" though with Rule and Line
And "UP-AND-DOWN" by Logic I define,
   Of all that one should care to fathom, I
Was never deep in anything but—Wine.

### LVII

Ah, by my Computations, People say,
Reduce the Year to better reckoning?—Nay,
   'Twas only striking from the Calendar
Unborn To-morrow and dead Yesterday.

### LVIII

And lately, by the Tavern Door agape,
Came shining through the Dusk an Angel Shape
   Bearing a Vessel on his Shoulder; and
He bid me taste of it; and 'twas—the Grape!

## LIX

The Grape that can with Logic absolute
The Two-and-Seventy jarring Sects confute:
    The sovereign Alchemist that in a trice
Life's leaden metal into Gold transmute;

## LX

The mighty Mahmúd, Allah-breathing Lord,
That all the misbelieving and black Horde
    Of Fears and Sorrows that infest the Soul
Scatters before him with his whirlwind Sword.

## LXI

Why, be this Juice the growth of God, who dare
Blaspheme the twisted tendril as a Snare?
    A Blessing, we should use it, should we not?
And if a Curse—why, then, who set it there?

## LXII

I must abjure the Balm of Life, I must,
Scared by some After-reckoning ta'en on trust,
    Or lured with Hope of some Diviner Drink,
To fill the Cup—when crumbled into Dust!

## LXIII

Of threats of Hell and Hopes of Paradise!
One thing at least is certain—*This* Life flies;
    One thing is certain and the rest is Lies;
The Flower that once has blown for ever dies.

## LXIV

Strange, is it not? that of the myriads who
Before us pass'd the door of Darkness through,
    Not one returns to tell us of the Road,
Which to discover we must travel too.

### LXV

The Revelations of Devout and Learn'd
Who rose before us, and as Prophets burn'd,
   Are all but Stories, which, awoke from Sleep
They told their comrades, and to Sleep return'd.

### LXVI

I sent my Soul through the Invisible,
Some letter of that After-life to spell:
   And by and by my Soul return'd to me,
And answer'd "I Myself am Heav'n and Hell":

### LXVII

Heav'n but the Vision of fulfill'd Desire,
And Hell the Shadow from a Soul on fire,
   Cast on the Darkness into which Ourselves,
So late emerged from, shall so soon expire.

### LXVIII

We are no other than a moving row
Of Magic Shadow-shapes that come and go
   Round with the Sun-illumined Lantern held
In Midnight by the Master of the Show;

### LXIX

But helpless Pieces of the Game He plays
Upon this Chequer-board of Nights and Days;
   Hither and thither moves, and checks, and slays,
And one by one back in the Closet lays.

### LXX

The Ball no question makes of Ayes and Noes,
But Here or There as strikes the Player goes;
   And He that toss'd you down into the Field,
*He* knows about it all— HE knows—HE knows!

### LXXI

The Moving Finger writes; and, having writ,
Moves on: nor all your Piety nor Wit
   Shall lure it back to cancel half a Line,
Nor all your Tears wash out a Word of it.

### LXXII

And that inverted Bowl they call the Sky,
Whereunder crawling coop'd we live and die,
   Lift not your hands to *It* for help—for It
As impotently moves as you or I.

### LXXIII

With Earth's first Clay They did the Last Man knead,
And there of the Last Harvest sow'd the Seed:
   And the first Morning of Creation wrote
What the Last Dawn of Reckoning shall read.

### LXXIV

YESTERDAY *This* Day's Madness did prepare;
To-morrow's Silence, Triumph, or Despair:
   Drink! for you not know whence you came, nor why:
Drink! for you know not why you go, nor where.

### LXXV

I tell you this—When, started from the Goal,
Over the flaming shoulders of the Foal
   Of Heav'n Parwín and Mushtarí they flung,
In my predestined Plot of Dust and Soul.

### LXXVI

The Vine had struck a fiber: which about
It clings my Being—let the Dervish flout;
   Of my Base metal may be filed a Key
That shall unlock the Door he howls without.

## LXXVII

And this I know: whether the one True Light
Kindle to Love, or Wrath consume me quite,
    One Flash of It within the Tavern caught
Better than in the Temple lost outright.

## LXXVIII

What! out of senseless Nothing to provoke
A conscious Something to resent the yoke
    Of unpermitted Pleasure, under pain
Of Everlasting Penalties, if broke!

## LXXIX

What! from his helpless Creature be repaid
Pure Gold for what he lent him dross-allay'd—
    Sue for a Debt he never did contract,
And cannot answer—Oh the sorry trade!

## LXXX

Oh Thou, who didst with pitfall and with gin
Beset the Road I was to wander in,
    Thou wilt not with Predestined Evil round
Enmesh, and then impute my Fall to Sin!

## LXXXI

Oh Thou, who Man of baser Earth didst make,
And ev'n with Paradise devise the Snake:
    For all the Sin wherewith the Face of Man
Is blacken'd—Man's forgiveness give—and take!

## LXXXII

As under cover of departing Day
Slunk hunger-stricken Ramazán away,
    Once more within the Potter's house alone
I stood, surrounded by the Shapes of Clay.

### LXXXIII

Shapes of all Sorts and Sizes, great and small,
That stood along the floor and by the wall;
    And some loquacious Vessels were; and some
Listen'd perhaps, but never talk'd at all.

### LXXXIV

Said one among them—"Surely not in vain
My substance of the common Earth was ta'en
    And to this Figure molded, to be broke,
Or trampled back to shapeless Earth again."

### LXXXV

Then said a Second—"Ne'er a peevish Boy
Would break the Bowl from which he drank in joy;
    And He that with his hand the Vessel made
Will surely not in after Wrath destroy."

### LXXXVI

After a momentary silence spake
Some Vessel of a more ungainly Make;
    "They sneer at me for leaning all awry:
What! did the Hand then of the Potter shake?"

### LXXXVII

Whereat some one of the loquacious Lot—
I think a Súfi pipkin—waxing hot—
    "All this of Pot and Potter—Tell me then,
Who is the Potter, pray, and who the Pot?"

### LXXXVIII

"Why," said another, "Some there are who tell
Of one who threatens he will toss to Hell
    The luckless Pots he marr'd in making—Pish!
He's a Good Fellow, and 'twill all be well."

## LXXXIX

"Well," murmured one, "Let whoso make or buy,
My Clay with long Oblivion is gone dry:
    But fill me with the old familiar Juice,
Methinks I might recover by and by."

## XC

So while the Vessels one by one were speaking,
The little Moon look'd in that all were seeking:
    And then they jogg'd each other, "Brother! Brother!
Now for the Porter's shoulders' knot a-creaking!"

## XCI

Ah, with the Grape my fading life provide,
And wash the Body whence the Life has died,
    And lay me, shrouded in the living Leaf,
By some not unfrequented Garden-side.

## XCII

That ev'n buried Ashes such a snare
Of Vintage shall fling up into the Air
    As not a True-believer passing by
But shall be overtaken unaware.

## XCIII

Indeed the Idols I have loved so long
Have done my credit in this World much wrong:
    Have drown'd my Glory in a shallow Cup,
And sold my Reputation for a Song.

## XCIV

Indeed, indeed, Repentance oft before
I swore—but was I sober when I swore?
    And then and then came Spring, and Rose-in-hand
My thread-bare Penitence apieces tore.

### XCV

And much as Wine has play'd the Infidel,
And robb'd me of my Robe of Honour—Well,
    I wonder often what the Vintners buy
One half so precious as the stuff they sell.

### XCVI

Yet Ah, that Spring should vanish with the Rose!
That Youth's sweet-scented manuscript should close!
    The Nightingale that in the branches sang,
Ah whence, and whither flown again, who knows!

### XCVII

Would but the Desert of the Fountain yield
One glimpse—if dimly, yet indeed, reveal'd,
    To which the fainting Traveller might spring,
As springs the trampled herbage of the field!

### XCVIII

Would but some wingéd Angel ere too late
Arrest the yet unfolded Roll of Fate,
    And make the stern Recorder otherwise
Enregister, or quite obliterate!

### XCIX

Ah Love! could you and I with Him conspire
To grasp this sorry Scheme of Things entire,
    Would not we shatter it to bits—and then
Re-mould it nearer to the Heart's Desire!

### C

Yon rising Moon that looks for us again—
How oft hereafter will she wax and wane;
    How oft hereafter rising look for us
Through this same Garden—and for *one* in vain!

## CI

And when like her, oh Sákí, you shall pass
Among the Guests Star-scatter'd on the Grass,
 And in your joyous errand reach the spot
Where I made One—turn down an empty Glass!

TAMAM.

# ROBERT BROWNING

## (1812–1889)

## Andrea Del Sarto

### (CALLED "THE FAULTLESS PAINTER")

But do not let us quarrel any more,
No, my Lucrezia; bear with me for once:
Sit down and all shall happen as you wish.
You turn your face, but does it bring your heart?
I'll work then for your friend's friend, never fear,
Treat his own subject after his own way,
Fix his own time, accept too his own price,
And shut the money into this small hand
When next it takes mine. Will it? tenderly?
Oh, I'll content him,—but to-morrow, Love!
I often am much wearier than you think,
This evening more than usual, and it seems
As if—forgive now—should you let me sit
Here by the window with your hand in mine
And look a half-hour forth on Fiesole,
Both of one mind, as married people use,
Quietly, quietly the evening through,
I might get up to-morrow to my work
Cheerful and fresh as ever. Let us try.
To-morrow, how you shall be glad for this!
Your soft hand is a woman of itself,
And mine the man's bared breast she curls inside.
Don't count the time lost, neither; you must serve
For each of the five pictures we require:

It saves a model. So! keep looking so—
My serpentining beauty, rounds on rounds!
—How could you ever prick those perfect ears,
Even to put the pearl there! oh, so sweet—
My face, my moon, my everybody's moon,
Which everybody looks on and calls his,
And, I suppose, is looked on by in turn,
While she looks—no one's: very dear, no less.
You smile? why, there's my picture ready made,
There's what we painters call our harmony!
A common greyness silvers everything,—
All in a twilight, you and I alike
—You, at the point of your first pride in me
(That's gone you know),—but I, at every point;
My youth, my hope, my art, being all toned down
To yonder sober pleasant Fiesole.
There's the bell clinking from the chapel-top;
That length of convent-wall across the way
Holds the trees safer, huddled more inside;
The last monk leaves the garden; days decrease,
And autumn grows, autumn in everything.
Eh? the whole seems to fall into a shape
As if I saw alike my work and self
And all that I was born to be and do,
A twilight-piece. Love, we are in God's hand.
How strange now, looks the life he makes us lead;
So free we seem, so fettered fast we are!
I feel he laid the fetter: let it lie!
This chamber for example—turn your head—
All that's behind us! You don't understand
Nor care to understand about my art,
But you can hear at least when people speak:
And that cartoon, the second from the door
—It is the thing, Love! so such things should be—
Behold Madonna!—I am bold to say.
I can do with my pencil what I know,
What I see, what at bottom of my heart

I wish for, if I ever wish so deep—
Do easily, too—what I say, perfectly,
I do not boast, perhaps: yourself are judge,
Who listened to the Legate's talk last week,
And just as much they used to say in France.
At any rate 'tis easy, all of it!
No sketches first, no studies, that's long past:
I do what many dream of, all their lives,
—Dream? strive to do, and agonize to do,
And fail in doing. I could count twenty such
On twice your fingers, and not leave this town,
Who strive—you don't know how the others strive
To paint a little thing like that you smeared
Carelessly passing with your robes afloat,—
Yet do much less, so much less, Someone says,
(I know his name, no matter)—so much less!
Well, less is more, Lucrezia: I am judged.
There burns a truer light of God in them,
In their vexed beating stuffed and stopped-up brain,
Heart, or whate'er else, than goes on to prompt
This low-pulsed forthright craftsman's hand of mine.
Their works drop groundward, but themselves, I know,
Reach many a time a heaven that's shut to me,
Enter and take their place there sure enough,
Though they come back and cannot tell the world.
My works are nearer heaven, but I sit here.
The sudden blood of these men! at a word—
Praise them, it boils, or blame them, it boils too.
I, painting from myself and to myself,
Know what I do, am unmoved by men's blame
Or their praise either. Somebody remarks
Morello's outline there is wrongly traced,
His hue mistaken; what of that? or else,
Rightly traced and well ordered; what of that?
Speak as they please, what does the mountain care?
Ah, but a man's reach should exceed his grasp,
Or what's a heaven for? All is silver-grey

Placid and perfect with my art: the worse!
I know both what I want and what might gain,
And yet how profitless to know, to sigh
"Had I been two, another and myself,
Our head would have o'erlooked the world!" No doubt.
Yonder's a work now, of that famous youth
The Urbinate who died five years ago.
('Tis copied, George Vasari sent it me.)
Well, I can fancy how he did it all,
Pouring his soul, with kings and popes to see,
Reaching, that heaven might so replenish him,
Above and through his art—for it gives way;
That arm is wrongly put—and there again—
A fault to pardon in the drawing's lines,
Its body, so to speak: its soul is right,
He means right—that, a child may understand.
Still, what an arm! and I could alter it:
But all the play, the insight and the stretch—
Out of me, out of me! And wherefore out?
Had you enjoined them on me, given me soul,
We might have risen to Rafael, I and you!
Nay, Love, you did give all I asked, I think—
More than I merit, yes, by many times.
But had you—oh, with the same perfect brow,
And perfect eyes, and more than perfect mouth,
And the low voice my soul hears, as a bird
The fowler's pipe, and follows to the snare—
Had you, with these the same, but brought a mind!
Some women do so. Had the mouth there urged
"God and the glory! never care for gain.
The present by the future, what is that?
Live for fame, side by side with Agnolo!
Rafael is waiting: up to God, all three!"
I might have done it for you. So it seems:
Perhaps not. All is as God over-rules.
Beside, incentives come from the soul's self;
The rest avail not. Why do I need you?

What wife had Rafael, or has Agnolo?
In this world, who can do a thing, will not;
And who would do it, cannot, I perceive:
Yet the will's somewhat—somewhat, too, the power—
And thus we half-men struggle. At the end,
God, I conclude, compensates, punishes.
'Tis safer for me, if the award be strict,
That I am something underrated here,
Poor this long while, despised, to speak the truth.
I dared not, do you know, leave home all day,
For fear of chancing on the Paris lords.
The best is when they pass and look aside;
But they speak sometimes; I must bear it all.
Well may they speak! That Francis, that first time,
And that long festal year at Fontainebleau!
I surely then could sometimes leave the ground,
Put on the glory, Rafael's daily wear,
In that humane great monarch's golden look,—
One finger in his beard or twisted curl
Over his mouth's good mark that made the smile,
One arm about my shoulder, round my neck,
The jingle of his gold chain in my ear,
I painting proudly with his breath on me,
All his court round him, seeing with his eyes,
Such frank French eyes, and such a fire of souls
Profuse, my hand kept plying by those hearts,—
And, best of all, this, this, this face beyond,
This in the background, waiting on my work,
To crown the issue with a last reward!
A good time, was it not, my kingly days?
And had you not grown restless . . . but I know—
'Tis done and past; 'twas right, my instinct said;
Too live the life grew, golden and not grey,
And I'm the weak-eyed bat no sun should tempt
Out of the grange whose four walls make his world.
How could it end in any other way?
You called me, and I came home to your heart.

The triumph was—to reach and stay there; since
I reached it ere the triumph, what is lost?
Let my hands frame your face in your hair's gold,
You beautiful Lucrezia that are mine!
"Rafael did this, Andrea painted that;
The Roman's is the better when you pray,
But still the other's Virgin was his wife—"
Men will excuse me. I am glad to judge
Both pictures in your presence; clearer grows
My better fortune, I resolve to think.
For, do you know, Lucrezia, as God lives,
Said one day Agnolo, his very self,
To Rafael . . . I have known it all these years . . .
(When the young man was flaming out his thoughts
Upon a palace-wall for Rome to see,
Too lifted up in heart because of it)
"Friend, there's a certain sorry little scrub
Goes up and down our Florence, none cares how,
Who, were he set to plan and execute
As you are, pricked on by your popes and kings,
Would bring the sweat into that brow of yours!"
To Rafael's!—And indeed the arm is wrong.
I hardly dare . . . yet, only you to see,
Give the chalk here—quick, thus the line should go!
Ay, but the soul! he's Rafael! rub it out!
Still, all I care for, if he spoke the truth,
(What he? why, who but Michel Agnolo?
Do you forget already words like those?)
If really there was such a chance, so lost,—
Is, whether you're—not grateful—but more pleased.
Well, let me think so. And you smile indeed!
This hour has been an hour! Another smile?
If you would sit thus by me every night
I should work better, do you comprehend?
I mean that I should earn more, give you more.
See, it is settled dusk now; there's a star;
Morello's gone, the watch-lights show the wall,

The cue-owls speak the name we call them by,
Come from the window, love,—come in, at last,
Inside the melancholy little house
We built to be so gay with. God is just.
King Francis may forgive me: oft at nights
When I look up from painting, eyes tired out,
The walls become illumined, brick from brick
Distinct, instead of mortar, fierce bright gold,
That gold of his I did cement them with!
Let us but love each other. Must you go?
That Cousin here again? he waits outside?
Must see you—you, and not with me? Those loans?
More gaming debts to pay? you smiled for that?
Well, let smiles buy me! have you more to spend?
While hand and eye and something of a heart
Are left me, work's my ware, and what's it worth?
I'll pay my fancy. Only let me sit
The grey remainder of the evening out,
Idle, you call it, and muse perfectly
How I could paint, were I but back in France,
One picture, just one more—the Virgin's face,
Not yours this time! I want you at my side
To hear them—that is, Michel Agnolo—
Judge all I do and tell you of its worth.
Will you? To-morrow, satisfy your friend.
I take the subjects for his corridor,
Finish the portrait out of hand—there, there,
And throw him in another thing or two
If he demurs; the whole should prove enough
To pay for this same Cousin's freak. Beside,
What's better and what's all I care about,
Get you the thirteen scudi for the ruff!
Love, does that please you? Ah, but what does he,
The Cousin! what does he to please you more?

  I am grown peaceful as old age to-night.
I regret little, I would change still less.

Since there my past life lies, why alter it?
The very wrong to Francis!—it is true
I took his coin, was tempted and complied,
And built this house and sinned, and all is said.
My father and my mother died of want.
Well, had I riches of my own? you see
How one gets rich! Let each one bear his lot.
They were born poor, lived poor, and poor they died:
And I have laboured somewhat in my time
And not been paid profusely. Some good son
Paint my two hundred pictures—let him try!
No doubt, there's something strikes a balance. Yes,
You loved me quite enough, it seems to-night.
This must suffice me here. What would one have?
In heaven, perhaps, new chances, one more chance—
Four great walls in the New Jerusalem,
Meted on each side by the angel's reed,
For Leonard, Rafael, Agnolo and me
To cover—the three first without a wife,
While I have mine! So—still they overcome
Because there's still Lucrezia,—as I choose.

Again the Cousin's whistle! Go, my Love.

## Fra Lippo Lippi

I am poor brother Lippo, by your leave!
You need not clap your torches to my face.
Zooks, what's to blame? you think you see a monk!
What, 'tis past midnight, and you go the rounds,
And here you catch me at an alley's end
Where sportive ladies leave their doors ajar?
The Carmine's my cloister: hunt it up,
Do,—harry out, if you must show your zeal,
Whatever rat, there, haps on his wrong hole,
And nip each softling of a wee white mouse,

*Weke, weke,* that's crept to keep him company!
Aha, you know your betters! Then, you'll take
Your hand away that's fiddling on my throat,
And please to know me likewise. Who am I?
Why, one, sir, who is lodging with a friend
Three streets off—he's a certain . . . how d'ye call?
Master—a . . . Cosimo of the Medici,
I' the house that caps the corner. Boh! you were best!
Remember and tell me, the day you're hanged,
How you affected such a gullet's-gripe!
But you, sir, it concerns you that your knaves
Pick up a manner nor discredit you:
Zooks, are we pilchards, that they sweep the streets
And count fair prize what comes into their net?
He's Judas to a tittle, that man is!
Just such a face! Why, sir, you make amends.
Lord, I'm not angry! Bid your hangdogs go
Drink out this quarter-florin to the health
Of the munificent House that harbours me
(And many more beside, lads! more beside!)
And all's come square again. I'd like his face—
His, elbowing on his comrade in the door
With the pike and lantern,—for the slave that holds
John Baptist's head a-dangle by the hair
With one hand ("Look you, now," as who should say)
And his weapon in the other, yet unwiped!
It's not your chance to have a bit of chalk,
A wood-coal or the like? or you should see!
Yes, I'm the painter, since you style me so.
What, brother Lippo's doings, up and down,
You know them and they take you? like enough!
I saw the proper twinkle in your eye—
'Tell you, I liked your looks at very first.
Let's sit and set things straight now, hip to haunch.
Here's spring come, and the nights one makes up bands
To roam the town and sing out carnival,
And I've been three weeks shut within my mew,

A-painting for the great man, saints and saints
And saints again. I could not paint all night—
Ouf! I leaned out of window for fresh air.
There came a hurry of feet and little feet,
A sweep of lute-strings, laughs, and whiffs of song,—
*Flower o' the broom,*
*Take away love, and our earth is a tomb!*
*Flower o' the quince,*
*I let Lisa go, and what good in life since?*
*Flower o' the thyme*—and so on. Round they went.
Scarce had they turned the corner when a titter
Like the skipping of rabbits by moonlight,—three slim shapes,
And a face that looked up . . . zooks, sir, flesh and blood,
That's all I'm made of! Into shreds it went,
Curtain and counterpane and coverlet,
All the bed-furniture—a dozen knots,
There was a ladder! Down I let myself,
Hands and feet, scrambling somehow, and so dropped,
And after them. I came up with the fun
Hard by Saint Laurence, hail fellow, well met,—
*Flower o' the rose,*
*If I've been merry, what matter who knows?*
And so as I was stealing back again
To get to bed and have a bit of sleep
Ere I rise up to-morrow and go work
On Jerome knocking at his poor old breast
With his great round stone to subdue the flesh,
You snap me of the sudden. Ah, I see!
Though your eye twinkles still, you shake your head—
Mine's shaved—a monk, you say—the sting's in that!
If Master Cosimo announced himself,
Mum's the word naturally; but a monk!
Come, what am I a beast for? tell us, now!
I was a baby when my mother died
And father died and left me in the street.
I starved there, God knows how, a year or two
On fig-skins, melon-parings, rinds and shucks,

Refuse and rubbish. One fine frosty day,
My stomach being empty as your hat,
The wind doubled me up and down I went.
Old Aunt Lapaccia trussed me with one hand,
(Its fellow was a stinger as I knew)
And so along the wall, over the bridge;
By the straight cut to the convent. Six words there,
While I stood munching my first bread that month:
"So, boy, you're minded," quoth the good fat father
Wiping his own mouth, 'twas refection-time,—
"To quit this very miserable world?
Will you renounce" . . . "the mouthful of bread?" thought I;
By no means! Brief, they made a monk of me;
I did renounce the world, its pride and greed,
Palace, farm, villa, shop and banking-house,
Trash, such as these poor devils of Medici
Have given their hearts to—all at eight years old.
Well, sir, I found in time, you may be sure,
'Twas not for nothing—the good bellyful,
The warm serge and the rope that goes all round,
And day-long blessed idleness beside!
"Let's see what the urchin's fit for"—that came next.
Not overmuch their way, I must confess.
Such a to-do! They tried me with their books:
Lord, they'd have taught me Latin in pure waste!
*Flower o' the clove,*
*All the Latin I construe is, "amo" I love!*
But, mind you, when a boy starves in the streets
Eight years together, as my fortune was,
Watching folk's faces to know who will fling
The bit of half-stripped grape-bunch he desires,
And who will curse or kick him for his pains,—
Which gentleman processional and fine,
Holding a candle to the Sacrament,
Will wink and let him lift a plate and catch
The droppings of the wax to sell again,
Or holla for the Eight and have him whipped,—

How say I?—nay, which dog bites, which lets drop
His bone from the heap of offal in the street,—
Why, soul and sense of him grow sharp alike,
He learns the look of things, and none the less
For admonition from the hunger-pinch.
I had a store of such remarks, be sure,
Which, after I found leisure, turned to use.
I drew men's faces on my copy-books,
Scrawled them within the antiphonary's marge,
Joined legs and arms to the long music-notes,
Found eyes and nose and chin for A's and B's,
And made a string of pictures of the world
Betwixt the ins and outs of verb and noun,
On the wall, the bench, the door. The monks looked black.
"Nay," quoth the Prior, "turn him out, d' ye say?
In no wise. Lose a crow and catch a lark.
What if at last we get our man of parts,
We Carmelites, like those Camaldolese
And Preaching Friars, to do our church up fine
And put the front on it that ought to be!"
And hereupon he bade me daub away.
Thank you! my head being crammed, the walls a blank,
Never was such prompt disemburdening.
First, every sort of monk, the black and white,
I drew them, fat and lean: then, folk at church,
From good old gossips waiting to confess
Their cribs of barrel-droppings, candle-ends,—
To the breathless fellow at the altar-foot,
Fresh from his murder, safe and sitting there
With the little children round him in a row
Of admiration, half for his beard and half
For that white anger of his victim's son
Shaking a fist at him with one fierce arm,
Signing himself with the other because of Christ
(Whose sad face on the cross sees only this
After the passion of a thousand years)
Till some poor girl, her apron o'er her head,

(Which the intense eyes looked through) came at eve
On tiptoe, said a word, dropped in a loaf,
Her pair of earrings and a bunch of flowers
(The brute took growling), prayed, and so was gone.
I painted all, then cried " 'Tis ask and have;
Choose, for more's ready!"—laid the ladder flat,
And showed my covered bit of cloister-wall
The monks closed in a circle and praised loud
Till checked, taught what to see and not to see,
Being simple bodies,—"That's the very man!
Look at the boy who stoops to pat the dog!
That woman's like the Prior's niece who comes
To care about his asthma: it's the life!"
But there my triumph's straw-fire flared and funked;
Their betters took their turn to see and say:
The Prior and the learned pulled a face
And stopped all that in no time. "How? what's here?
Quite from the mark of painting, bless us all!
Faces, arms, legs and bodies like the true
As much as pea and pea! it's devil's-game!
Your business is not to catch men with show,
With homage to the perishable clay,
But lift them over it, ignore it all,
Make them forget there's such a thing as flesh.
Your business is to paint the souls of men—
Man's soul, and it's a fire, smoke . . . no, it's not . . .
It's vapour done up like a new-born babe—
(In that shape when you die it leaves your mouth)
It's . . . well, what matters talking, it's the soul!
Give us no more of body than shows soul!
Here's Giotto, with his Saint a-praising God,
That sets us praising,—why not stop with him?
Why put all thoughts of praise out of our head
With wonder at lines, colours, and what not?
Paint the soul, never mind the legs and arms!
Rub all out, try at it a second time.
Oh, that white smallish female with the breasts,

She's just my niece . . . Herodias, I would say,—
Who went and danced and got men's heads cut off!
Have it all out!" Now, is this sense, I ask?
A fine way to paint soul, by painting body
So ill, the eye can't stop there, must go further
And can't fare worse! Thus, yellow does for white
When what you put for yellow's simply black,
And any sort of meaning looks intense
When all beside itself means and looks nought.
Why can't a painter lift each foot in turn,
Left foot and right foot, go a double step,
Make his flesh liker and his soul more like,
Both in their order? Take the prettiest face,
The Prior's niece . . . patron-saint—is it so pretty
You can't discover if it means hope, fear,
Sorrow or joy? won't beauty go with these?
Suppose I've made her eyes all right and blue,
Can't I take breath and try to add life's flash,
And then add soul and heighten them threefold?
Or say there's beauty with no soul at all—
(I never saw it—put the case the same—)
If you get simple beauty and nought else,
You get about the best thing God invents:
That's somewhat: and you'll find the soul you have missed,
Within yourself, when you return him thanks.
"Rub all out!" Well, well, there's my life, in short,
And so the thing has gone on ever since.
I'm grown a man no doubt, I've broken bounds:
You should not take a fellow eight years old
And make him swear to never kiss the girls.
I'm my own master, paint now as I please—
Having a friend, you see, in the Corner-house!
Lord, it's fast holding by the rings in front—
Those great rings serve more purposes than just
To plant a flag in, or tie up a horse!
And yet the old schooling sticks, the old grave eyes
Are peeping o'er my shoulder as I work,

The heads shake still—"It's art's decline, my son!
You're not of the true painters, great and old;
Brother Angelico's the man, you'll find;
Brother Lorenzo stands his single peer:
Fag on at flesh, you'll never make the third!"
*Flower o' the pine,*
*You keep your mistr . . . manners, and I'll stick to mine!*
I'm not the third, then: bless us, they must know!
Don't you think they're the likeliest to know,
They with their Latin? So, I swallow my rage,
Clench my teeth, suck my lips in tight, and paint
To please them—sometimes do and sometimes don't;
For, doing most, there's pretty sure to come
A turn, some warm eve finds me at my saints—
A laugh, a cry, the business of the world—
*(Flower o' the peach,*
*Death for us all, and his own life for each!)*
And my whole soul revolves, the cup runs over,
The world and life's too big to pass for a dream,
And I do these wild things in sheer despite,
And play the fooleries you catch me at,
In pure rage! The old mill-horse, out at grass
After hard years, throws up his stiff heels so,
Although the miller does not preach to him
The only good of grass is to make chaff.
What would men have? Do they like grass or no—
May they or mayn't they? all I want's the thing
Settled for ever one way. As it is,
You tell too many lies and hurt yourself:
You don't like what you only like too much,
You do like what, if given you at your word,
You find abundantly detestable.
For me, I think I speak as I was taught;
I always see the garden and God there
A-making man's wife: and, my lesson learned,
The value and significance of flesh,
I can't unlearn ten minutes afterwards,

You understand me: I'm a beast, I know.
But see, now—why, I see as certainly
As that the morning-star's about to shine,
What will hap some day. We've a youngster here
Comes to our convent, studies what I do,
Slouches and stares and lets no atom drop:
His name is Guidi—he'll not mind the monks—
They call him Hulking Tom, he lets them talk—
He picks my practice up—he'll paint apace,
I hope so—though I never live so long,
I know what's sure to follow. You be judge!
You speak no Latin more than I, belike;
However, you're my man, you've seen the world
—The beauty and the wonder and the power,
The shapes of things, their colours, lights and shades,
Changes, surprises,—and God made it all!
—For what? Do you feel thankful, ay or no,
For this fair town's face, yonder river's line,
The mountain round it and the sky above,
Much more the figures of man, woman, child,
These are the frame to? What's it all about?
To be passed over, despised? or dwelt upon,
Wondered at? oh, this last of course!—you say.
But why not do as well as say,—paint these
Just as they are, careless what comes of it?
God's works—paint anyone, and count it crime
To let a truth slip. Don't object, "His works
Are here already; nature is complete:
Suppose you reproduce her—(which you can't)
There's no advantage! you must beat her, then."
For, don't you mark? we're made so that we love
First when we see them painted, things we have passed
Perhaps a hundred times nor cared to see;
And so they are better, painted—better to us,
Which is the same thing. Art was given for that;
God uses us to help each other so,
Lending our minds out. Have you noticed, now,

Your cullion's hanging face? A bit of chalk,
And trust me but you should, though! How much more,
If I drew higher things with the same truth!
That were to take the Prior's pulpit-place,
Interpret God to all of you! Oh, oh,
It makes me mad to see what men shall do
And we in our graves! This world's no blot for us,
Nor blank; it means intensely, and means good:
To find its meaning is my meat and drink.
"Ay, but you don't so instigate to prayer!"
Strikes in the Prior: "when your meaning's plain
It does not say to folk—remember matins,
Or, mind you fast next Friday!" Why, for this
What need of art at all? A skull and bones,
Two bits of stick nailed crosswise, or, what's best,
A bell to chime the hour with, does as well.
I painted a Saint Laurence six months since
At Prato, splashed the fresco in fine style:
"How looks my painting, now the scaffold's down?"
I ask a brother: "Hugely," he returns—
"Already not one phiz of your three slaves
Who turn the Deacon off his toasted side,
But's scratched and prodded to our heart's content,
The pious people have so eased their own
With coming to say prayers there in a rage:
We get on fast to see the bricks beneath.
Expect another job this time next year,
For pity and religion grow i' the crowd—
Your painting serves its purpose!" Hang the fools!

   —That is—you'll not mistake an idle word
Spoke in a huff by a poor monk, Got wot,
Tasting the air this spicy night which turns
The unaccustomed head like Chianti wine!
Oh, the church knows! don't misreport me, now!
It's natural a poor monk out of bounds
Should have his apt word to excuse himself:

And hearken how I plot to make amends.
I have bethought me: I shall paint a piece
. . . There's for you! Give me six months, then go, see
Something in Sant' Ambrogio's! Bless the nuns!
They want a cast o' my office. I shall paint
God in the midst, Madonna and her babe,
Ringed by a bowery flowery angel-brood,
Lilies and vestments and white faces, sweet
As puff on puff of grated orris-root
When ladies crowd to Church at midsummer.
And then i' the front, of course a saint or two—
Saint John, because he saves the Florentines,
Saint Ambrose, who puts down in black and white
The convent's friends and gives them a long day,
And Job, I must have him there past mistake,
The man of Uz (and Us without the z,
Painters who need his patience). Well, all these
Secured at their devotion, up shall come
Out of a corner when you least expect,
As one by a dark stair into a great light,
Music and talking, who but Lippo! I!—
Mazed, motionless and moonstruck—I'm the man!
Back I shrink—what is this I see and hear?
I, caught up with my monk's-things by mistake,
My old serge gown and rope that goes all round,
I, in this presence, this pure company!
Where's a hole, where's a corner for escape?
Then steps a sweet angelic slip of a thing
Forward, puts out a soft palm—"Not so fast!"
—Addresses the celestial presence, "nay—
He made you and devised you, after all,
Though he's none of you! Could Saint John there draw—
His camel-hair make up a painting-brush?
We come to brother Lippo for all that,
*Iste perfecit opus!*" So, all smile—
I shuffle sideways with my blushing face
Under the cover of a hundred wings

Thrown like a spread of kirtles when you're gay
And play hot cockles, all the doors being shut,
Till, wholly unexpected, in there pops
The hothead husband! Thus I scuttle off
To some safe bench behind, not letting go
The palm of her, the little lily thing
That spoke the good word for me in the nick,
Like the Prior's niece . . . Saint Lucy, I would say.
And so all's saved for me, and for the church
A pretty picture gained. Go, six months hence!
Your hand, sir, and good-bye: no lights, no lights!
The street's hushed, and I know my own way back,
Don't fear me! There's the grey beginning. Zooks!

---

## The Bishop Orders His Tomb at Saint Praxed's Church

### ROME, 15—

Vanity, saith the preacher, vanity!
Draw round my bed: is Anselm keeping back?
Nephews—sons mine . . . ah God, I know not! Well—
She, men would have to be your mother once,
Old Gandolf envied me, so fair she was!
What's done is done, and she is dead beside,
Dead long ago, and I am Bishop since,
And as she died so must we die ourselves,
And thence ye may perceive the world's a dream.
Life, how and what is it? As here I lie
In this state-chamber, dying by degrees,
Hours and long hours in the dead night, I ask
"Do I live, am I dead?" Peace, peace seems all.
Saint Praxed's ever was the church for peace;
And so, about this tomb of mine. I fought
With tooth and nail to save my niche, ye know:
—Old Gandolf cozened me, despite my care;
Shrewd was that snatch from out the corner South

He graced his carrion with, God curse the same!
Yet still my niche is not so cramped but thence
One sees the pulpit o' the epistle-side,
And somewhat of the choir, those silent seats,
And up into the aery dome where live
The angels, and a sunbeam's sure to lurk:
And I shall fill my slab of basalt there,
And 'neath my tabernacle take my rest,
With those nine columns round me, two and two,
The odd one at my feet where Anselm stands:
Peach-blossom marble all, the rare, the ripe
As fresh-poured red wine of a mighty pulse.
—Old Gandolf with his paltry onion-stone,
Put me where I may look at him! True peach,
Rosy and flawless: how I earned the prize!
Draw close: that conflagration of my church
—What then? So much was saved if aught were missed!
My sons, ye would not be my death? Go dig
The white-grape vineyard where the oil-press stood,
Drop water gently till the surface sink,
And if ye find . . . Ah God, I know not, I! . . .
Bedded in store of rotten fig-leaves soft,
And corded up in a tight olive-frail,
Some lump, ah God, of *lapis lazuli,*
Big as a Jew's head cut off at the nape,
Blue as a vein o'er the Madonna's breast . . .
Sons, all have I bequeathed you, villas, all,
That brave Frascati villa with its bath,
So, let the blue lump poise between my knees,
Like God the Father's globe on both his hands
Ye worship in the Jesu Church so gay,
For Gandolf shall not choose but see and burst!
Swift as a weaver's shuttle fleet our years:
Man goeth to the grave, and where is he?
Did I say basalt for my slab, sons? Black—
'Twas ever antique-black I meant! How else
Shall ye contrast my frieze to come beneath?

The bas-relief in bronze ye promised me,
Those Pans and Nymphs ye wot of, and perchance
Some tripod, thyrsus, with a vase or so,
The Saviour at his sermon on the mount,
Saint Praxed in a glory, and one Pan
Ready to twitch the Nymph's last garment off,
And Moses with the tables . . . but I know
Ye mark me not! What do they whisper thee,
Child of my bowels, Anselm? Ah, ye hope
To revel down my villas while I gasp
Bricked o'er with beggar's mouldy travertine
Which Gandolf from his tomb-top chuckles at!
Nay, boys, ye love me—all of jasper, then!
'Tis jasper ye stand pledged to, lest I grieve.
My bath must needs be left behind, alas!
One block, pure green as a pistachio-nut,
There's plenty jasper somewhere in the world—
And have I not Saint Praxed's ear to pray
Horses for ye, and brown Greek manuscripts,
And mistresses with great smooth marbly limbs?
    That's if ye carve my epitaph aright,
Choice Latin, picked phrase, Tully's every word,
No gaudy ware like Gandolf s second line—
Tully, my masters? Ulpian serves his need!
And then how I shall lie through centuries,
And hear the blessed mutter of the mass,
And see God made and eaten all day long,
And feel the steady candle-flame, and taste
Good strong thick stupefying incense-smoke!
For as I lie here, hours of the dead night,
Dying in state and by such slow degrees,
I fold my arms as if they clasped a crook,
And stretch my feet forth straight as stone can point,
And let the bedclothes, for a mortcloth, drop
Into great laps and folds of sculptor's-work:
And as yon tapers dwindle, and strange thoughts
Grow, with a certain humming in my ears,

About the life before I lived this life,
And this life too, popes, cardinals and priests,
Saint Praxed at his sermon on the mount,
Your tall pale mother with her talking eyes,
And new-found agate urns as fresh as day,
And marble's language, Latin pure, discreet,
—Aha, ELUCESCEBAT quoth our friend?
No Tully, said I, Ulpian at the best!
Evil and brief hath been my pilgrimage.
All *lapis*, all, sons! Else I give the Pope
My villas! Will ye ever eat my heart?
Ever your eyes were as a lizard's quick,
They glitter like your mother's for my soul,
Or ye would heighten my impoverished frieze,
Piece out its starved design, and fill my vase
With grapes, and add a vizor and a Term,
And to the tripod ye would tie a lynx
That in his struggle throws the thyrsus down,
To comfort me on my entablature
Whereon I am to lie till I must ask
"Do I live, am I dead?" There, leave me, there!
For ye have stabbed me with ingratitude
To death—ye wish it—God, ye wish it! Stone—
Gritstone, a-crumble! Clammy squares which sweat
As if the corpse they keep were oozing through—
And no more *lapis* to delight the world!
Well go! I bless ye. Fewer tapers there,
But in a row: and, going, turn your backs
—Ay, like departing altar-ministrants,
And leave me in my church, the church for peace,
That I may watch at leisure if he leers—
Old Gandolf, at me, from his onion-stone,
As still he envied me, so fair she was!

# My Last Duchess

### FERARRA

That's my last Duchess painted on the wall,
Looking as if she were alive. I call
That piece a wonder, now: Frà Pandolf's hands
Worked busily a day, and there she stands.
Will't please you sit and look at her? I said
"Frà Pandolf" by design, for never read
Strangers like you that pictured countenance,
The depth and passion of its earnest glance,
But to myself they turned (since none puts by
The curtain I have drawn for you, but I)
And seemed as they would ask me, if they durst,
How such a glance came there; so, not the first
Are you to turn and ask thus. Sir, 'twas not
Her husband's presence only, called that spot
Of joy into the Duchess' cheek: perhaps
Frà Pandolf chanced to say "Her mantle laps
Over my lady's wrist too much," or "Paint
Must never hope to reproduce the faint
Half-flush that dies along her throat": such stuff
Was courtesy, she thought, and cause enough
For calling up that spot of joy. She had
A heart—how shall I say?—too soon made glad,
Too easily impressed! she liked whate'er
She looked on, and her looks went everywhere.
Sir, 'twas all one! My favour at her breast,
The dropping of the daylight in the West,
The bough of cherries some officious fool
Broke in the orchard for her, the white mule
She rode with round the terrace—all and each
Would draw from her alike the approving speech,
Or blush, at least. She thanked men,—good! but thanked
Somehow—I know not how—as if she ranked
My gift of a nine-hundred-years-old name
With anybody's gift. Who'd stoop to blame

This sort of trifling? Even had you skill
In speech—(which I have not)—to make your will
Quite clear to such an one, and say, "Just this
Or that in you disgusts me; here you miss,
Or there exceed the mark"—and if she let
Herself be lessoned so, nor plainly set
Her wits to yours, forsooth, and made excuse,
—E'en then would be some stooping; and I choose
Never to stoop. Oh sir, she smiled, no doubt,
Whene'er I passed her; but who passed without
Much the same smile? This grew; I gave commands;
Then all smiles stopped together. There she stands
As if alive. Will't please you rise? We'll meet
The company below, then. I repeat,
The Count your master's known munificence
Is ample warrant that no just pretence
Of mine for dowry will be disallowed;
Though his fair daughter's self, as I avowed
At starting, is my object. Nay, we'll go
Together down, sir. Notice Neptune, though,
Taming a sea-horse, thought a rarity,
Which Claus of Innsbruck cast in bronze for me!

---

## Soliloquy of the Spanish Cloister

### I

Gr-r-r—there go, my heart's abhorrence!
　　Water your damned flower-pots, do!
If hate killed men, Brother Lawrence,
　　God's blood, would not mine kill you!
What? your myrtle-bush wants trimming?
　　Oh, that rose has prior claims—
Needs its leaden vase filled brimming?
　　Hell dry you up with its flames!

## II

At the meal we sit together:
    *Salve tibi!* I must hear
Wise talk of the kind of weather,
    Sort of season, time of year:
*Not a plenteous cork-crop: scarcely*
    *Dare we hope oak-galls, I doubt:*
*What's the Latin name for "parsley"?*
    What's the Greek name for Swine's Snout?

## III

Whew! We'll have our platter burnished,
    Laid with care on our own shelf!
With a fire-new spoon we're furnished,
    And a goblet for ourself,
Rinsed like something sacrificial
    Ere 'tis fit to touch our chaps—
Marked with L. for our initial!
    (He-he! There his lily snaps!)

## IV

*Saint,* forsooth! While brown Dolores
    Squats outside the Convent bank
With Sanchicha, telling stories,
    Steeping tresses in the tank,
Blue-black, lustrous, thick like horsehairs,
    —Can't I see his dead eye glow,
Bright as 'twere a Barbary corsair's?
    (That is, if he'd let it show!)

## V

When he finishes refection,
    Knife and fork he never lays
Cross-wise, to my recollection,
    As do I, in Jesu's praise.

I the Trinity illustrate,
  Drinking watered orange-pulp—
In three sips the Arian frustrate;
  While he drains his at one gulp.

### VI

Oh, those melons? If he's able
  We're to have a feast! so nice!
One goes to the Abbot's table,
  All of us get each a slice.
How go on your flowers? None double?
  Not one fruit-sort can you spy?
Strange!—And I, too, at such trouble,
  Keep them close-nipped on the sly!

### VII

There's a great text in Galatians,
  Once you trip on it, entails
Twenty-nine distinct damnations,
  One sure, if another fails:
If I trip him just a-dying,
  Sure of heaven as sure can be,
Spin him round and send him flying
  Off to hell, a Manichee?

### VIII

Or, my scrofulous French novel
  On grey paper with blunt type!
Simply glance at it, you grovel
  Hand and foot in Belial's gripe:
If I double down its pages
  At the woeful sixteenth print,
When he gathers his greengages,
  Ope a sieve and slip it in't?

## IX

Or, there's Satan!—one might venture
    Pledge one's soul to him, yet leave
Such a flaw in the indenture
    As he'd miss till, past retrieve,
Blasted lay that rose-acacia
    We're so proud of! *Hy, Zy, Hine* . . .
'St, there's Vespers! *Plena gratiâ*
    *Ave, Virgo!* Gr-r-r—you swine!

# "Childe Roland to the Dark Tower Came"

(See Edgar's song in "LEAR.")

## I

My first thought was, he lied in every word,
    That hoary cripple, with malicious eye
    Askance to watch the working of his lie
On mine, and mouth scarce able to afford
Suppression of the glee, that pursed and scored
    Its edge, at one more victim gained thereby.

## II

What else should he be set for, with his staff?
    What, save to waylay with his lies, ensnare
    All travellers who might find him posted there,
And ask the road? I guessed what skull-like laugh
Would break, what crutch 'gin write my epitaph
    For pastime in the dusty thoroughfare,

## III

If at his counsel I should turn aside
    Into that ominous tract which, all agree,
    Hides the Dark Tower. Yet acquiescingly
I did turn as he pointed: neither pride
Nor hope rekindling at the end descried,
    So much as gladness that some end might be

### IV

For, what with my whole world-wide wandering,
    What with my search drawn out thro' years, my hope
    Dwindled into a ghost not fit to cope
With that obstreperous joy success would bring,—
I hardly tried now to rebuke the spring
    My heart made, finding failure in its scope.

### V

As when a sick man very near to death
    Seems dead indeed, and feels begin and end
    The tears and takes the farewell of each friend,
And hears one bid the other go, draw breath
Freelier outside, ("since all is o'er," he saith,
    "And the blow fallen no grieving can amend");

### VI

While some discuss if near the other graves
    Be room enough for this, and when a day
    Suits best for carrying the corpse away,
With care about the banners, scarves and staves:
And still the man hears all, and only craves
    He may not shame such tender love and stay.

### VII

Thus, I had so long suffered in this quest,
    Heard failure prophesied so oft, been writ
    So many times among "The Band"—to wit,
The knights who to the Dark Tower's search addressed
Their steps—that just to fail as they, seemed best,
    And all the doubt was now—should I be fit?

### VIII

So, quiet as despair, I turned from him,
    That hateful cripple, out of his highway
    Into the path he pointed. All the day

Had been a dreary one at best, and dim
Was settling to its close, yet shot one grim
   Red leer to see the plain catch its estray.


IX

For mark! no sooner was I fairly found
   Pledged to the plain, after a pace or two,
   Than, pausing to throw backward a last view
O'er the safe road, 'twas gone; grey plain all round:
Nothing but plain to the horizon's bound.
   I might go on; nought else remained to do.


X

So, on I went. I think I never saw
   Such starved ignoble nature; nothing throve:
   For flowers—as well expect a cedar grove!
But cockle, spurge, according to their law
Might propagate their kind, with none to awe,
   You'd think; a burr had been a treasure-trove.


XI

No! penury, inertness and grimace,
   In some strange sort, were the land's portion. "See
   Or shut your eyes," said Nature peevishly,
"It nothing skills: I cannot help my case:
'Tis the Last Judgment's fire must cure this place,
   Calcine its clods and set my prisoners free."


XII

If there pushed any ragged thistle-stalk
   Above its mates, the head was chopped; the bents
   Were jealous else. What made those holes and rents
In the dock's harsh swarth leaves, bruised as to baulk
All hope of greenness? 'tis a brute must walk
   Pashing their life out, with a brute's intents.

### XIII

As for the grass, it grew as scant as hair
 In leprosy; thin dry blades pricked the mud
 Which underneath looked kneaded up with blood.
One stiff blind horse, his every bone a-stare,
Stood stupefied, however he came there:
 Thrust out past service from the devil's stud!

### XIV

Alive? he might be dead for aught I know,
 With that red gaunt and colloped neck a-strain,
 And shut eyes underneath the rusty mane;
Seldom went such grotesqueness with such woe;
I never saw a brute I hated so;
 He must be wicked to deserve such pain.

### XV

I shut my eyes and turned them on my heart.
 As a man calls for wine before he fights,
 I asked one draught of earlier, happier sights,
Ere fitly I could hope to play my part.
Think first, fight afterwards—the soldier's art:
 One taste of the old time sets all to rights.

### XVI

Not it! I fancied Cuthbert's reddening face
 Beneath its garniture of curly gold,
 Dear fellow, till I almost felt him fold
An arm in mine to fix me to the place,
That way he used. Alas, one night's disgrace!
 Out went my heart's new fire and left it cold.

### XVII

Giles then, the soul of honour—there he stands
 Frank as ten years ago when knighted first.
 What honest man should dare (he said) he durst.

Good—but the scene shifts—faugh! what hangman-hands
Pin to his breast a parchment? His own bands
   Read it. Poor traitor, spit upon and curst!

### XVIII

Better this present than a past like that;
   Back therefore to my darkening path again!
   No sound, no sight as far as eye could strain.
Will the night send a howlet or a bat?
I asked: when something on the dismal flat
   Came to arrest my thoughts and change their train.

### XIX

A sudden little river crossed my path
   As unexpected as a serpent comes.
   No sluggish tide congenial to the glooms;
This, as it frothed by, might have been a bath
For the fiend's glowing hoof—to see the wrath
   Of its black eddy bespate with flakes and spumes.

### XX

So petty yet so spiteful! All along,
   Low scrubby alders kneeled down over it;
   Drenched willows flung them headlong in a fit
Of mute despair, a suicidal throng:
The river which had done them all the wrong,
   Whate'er that was, rolled by, deterred no whit.

### XXI

Which, while I forded,—good saints, how I feared
   To set my foot upon a dead man's cheek,
   Each step, or feel the spear I thrust to seek
For hollows, tangled in his hair or beard!
—It may have been a water-rat I speared,
   But, ugh! it sounded like a baby's shriek.

### XXII

Glad was I when I reached the other bank.
    Now for a better country. Vain presage!
    Who were the strugglers, what war did they wage,
Whose savage trample thus could pad the dank
Soil to a plash? Toads in a poisoned tank,
    Or wild cats in a red-hot iron cage—

### XXIII

The fight must so have seemed in that fell cirque.
    What penned them there, with all the plain to choose?
    No foot-print leading to that horrid mews,
None out of it. Mad brewage set to work
Their brains, no doubt, like galley-slaves the Turk
    Pits for his pastime, Christians against Jews.

### XXIV

And more than that—a furlong on—why, there!
    What bad use was that engine for, that wheel,
    Or brake, not wheel—that harrow fit to reel
Men's bodies out like silk? with all the air
Of Tophet's tool, on earth left unaware,
    Or brought to sharpen its rusty teeth of steel.

### XXV

Then came a bit of stubbed ground, once a wood,
    Next a marsh, it would seem, and now mere earth
    Desperate and done with; (so a fool finds mirth,
Makes a thing and then mars it, till his mood
Changes and off he goes!) within a rood—
    Bog, clay and rubble, sand and stark black dearth.

### XXVI

Now blotches rankling, coloured gay and grim,
    Now patches where some leanness of the soil's
    Broke into moss or substances like boils;

Then came some palsied oak, a cleft in him
Like a distorted mouth that splits its rim
   Gaping at death, and dies while it recoils.

## XXVII

And just as far as ever from the end!
   Nought in the distance but the evening, nought
   To point my footstep further! At the thought,
A great black bird, Apollyon's bosom-friend,
Sailed past, nor beat his wide wing dragon-penned
   That brushed my cap—perchance the guide I sought.

## XXVIII

For, looking up, aware I somehow grew,
   'Spite of the dusk, the plain had given place
   All round to mountains—with such name to grace
Mere ugly heights and heaps now stolen in view.
How thus they had surprised me,—solve it, you!
   How to get from them was no clearer case.

## XXIX

Yet half I seemed to recognize some trick
   Of mischief happened to me, God knows when—
   In a bad dream perhaps. Here ended, then,
Progress this way. When, in the very nick
Of giving up, one time more, came a click
   As when a trap shuts—you're inside the den!

## XXX

Burningly it came on me all at once,
   This was the place! those two hills on the right,
   Crouched like two bulls locked horn in horn in fight;
While to the left, a tall scalped mountain . . . Dunce,
Dotard, a-dozing at the very nonce,
   After a life spent training for the sight!

## XXXI

What in the midst lay but the Tower itself?
  The round squat turret, blind as the fool's heart,
  Built of brown stone, without a counterpart
In the whole world. The tempest's mocking elf
Points to the shipman thus the unseen shelf
  He strikes on, only when the timbers start.

## XXXII

Not see? because of night perhaps?—why, day
  Came back again for that! before it left,
  The dying sunset kindled through a cleft:
The hills, like giants at a hunting, lay,
Chin upon hand, to see the game at bay,—
  "Now stab and end the creature—to the heft!"

## XXXIII

Not hear? when noise was everywhere! it tolled
  Increasing like a bell. Names in my ears
  Of all the lost adventurers my peers,—
How such a one was strong, and such was bold,
And such was fortunate, yet each of old
  Lost, lost! one moment knelled the woe of years.

## XXXIV

There they stood, ranged along the hill-sides, met
  To view the last of me, a living frame
  For one more picture! in a sheet of flame
I saw them and I knew them all. And yet
Dauntless the slug-horn to my lips I set,
  And blew. *"Childe Roland to the Dark Tower came."*

# ELIZABETH BARRETT BROWNING
## (1806–1861)

## The Deserted Garden

I mind me in the days departed,
How often underneath the sun
With childish bounds I used to run
    To a garden long deserted.

The beds and walks were vanished quite;
And wheresoe'er had struck the spade,
The greenest grasses Nature laid
    To sanctify her right.

I called the place my wilderness,
For no one entered there but I;
The sheep looked in, the grass to espy,
    And passed it ne'ertheless.

The trees were interwoven wild,
And spread their boughs enough about
To keep both sheep and shepherd out,
    But not a happy child.

Adventurous joy it was for me!
I crept beneath the boughs, and found
A circle smooth of mossy ground
    Beneath a poplar tree.

Old garden rose-trees hedged it in,
Bedropt with roses waxen-white
Well satisfied with dew and light
   And careless to be seen.

Long years ago it might befall,
When all the garden flowers were trim,
The grave old gardener prided him
   On these the most of all.

Some lady, stately overmuch,
Here moving with a silken noise,
Has blushed beside them at the voice
   That likened her to such.

And these, to make a diadem,
She often may have plucked and twined,
Half-smiling as it came to mind
   That few would look at *them*.

Oh, little thought that lady proud,
A child would watch her fair white rose,
When buried lay her whiter brows,
   And silk was changed for shroud!

Nor thought that gardener, (full of scorns
For men unlearned and simple phrase,)
A child would bring it all its praise
   By creeping through the thorns!

To me upon my low moss seat,
Though never a dream the roses sent
Of science or love's compliment,
   I ween they smelt as sweet.

It did not move my grief to see
The trace of human step departed:
Because the garden was deserted,
   The blither place for me!

Friends, blame me not! a narrow ken
Has childhood 'twixt the sun and sward;
We draw the moral afterward,
   We feel the gladness then.

And gladdest hours for me did glide
In silence at the rose-tree wall:
A thrush made gladness musical
   Upon the other side.

Nor be nor I did e'er incline
To peck or pluck the blossoms white;
How should I know but roses might
   Lead lives as glad as mine?

To make my hermit-home complete,
I brought clear water from the spring
Praised in its own low murmuring,
   And cresses glossy wet.

And so, I thought, my likeness grew
(Without the melancholy tale)
To "gentle hermit of the dale,"
   And Angelina too.

For oft I read within my nook
Such minstrel stories; till the breeze
Made sounds poetic in the trees,
   And then I shut the book.

If I shut this wherein I write
I hear no more the wind athwart
Those trees, nor feel that childish heart
   Delighting in delight.

My childhood from my life is parted,
My footstep from the moss which drew
Its fairy circle round: anew
   The garden is deserted.

Another thrush may there rehearse
The madrigals which sweetest are;
No more for me! myself afar
    Do sing a sadder verse.

Ah me, ah me! when erst I lay
In that child's-nest so greenly wrought,
I laughed unto myself and thought
    "The time will pass away."

And still I laughed, and did not fear
But that, whene'er was past away
The childish time, some happier play
    My womanhood would cheer.

I knew the time would pass away,
And yet, beside the rose-tree wall,
Dear God, how seldom, if at all,
    Did I look up to pray!

The time is past; and now that grows
The cypress high among the trees,
And I behold white sepulchres
    As well as the white rose,—

When graver, meeker thoughts are given,
And I have learnt to lift my face,
Reminded how earth's greenest place
    The color draws from heaven,—

It something saith for earthly pain,
But more for Heavenly promise free,
That I who was, would shrink to be
    That happy child again.

# A Musical Instrument

### I

What was he doing, the great god Pan,
   Down in the reeds by the river?
Spreading ruin and scattering ban,
Splashing and paddling with hoofs of goat,
And breaking the golden lilies afloat
   With the dragon-fly on the river.

### II

He tore out a reed, the great god Pan,
   From the deep cool bed of the river:
The limpid water turbidly ran,
And the broken lilies a-dying lay,
And the dragon-fly had fled away,
   Ere he brought it out of the river.

### III

High on the shore sat the great god Pan
   While turbidly flowed the river;
And backed and hewed as a great god can,
With his hard bleak steel at the patient reed,
Till there was not a sign of the leaf indeed
   To prove it fresh from the river.

### IV

He cut it short, did the great god Pan,
   (How tall it stood in the river!)
Then drew the pith, like the heart of a man,
Steadily from the outside ring,
And notched the poor dry empty thing
   In holes, as he sat by the river.

### V

"This is the way," laughed the great god Pan
   (Laughed while he sat by the river),
"The only way, since gods began

To make sweet music, they could succeed."
Then, dropping his mouth to a hole in the reed,
   He blew in power by the river.

## VI

Sweet, sweet, sweet, O Pan!
   Piercing sweet by the river!
Blinding sweet, O great god Pan!
The sun on the hill forgot to die,
And the lilies revived, and the dragon-fly
   Came back to dream on the river.

## VII

Yet half a beast is the great god Pan,
   To laugh as he sits by the river,
Making a poet out of a man:
The true gods sigh for the cost and pain,—
For the reed which grows nevermore again
   As a reed with the reeds in the river.

# MATTHEW ARNOLD
## (1822–1888)

## Dover Beach

The sea is calm to-night.
The tide is full, the moon lies fair
Upon the straits;—on the French coast the light
Gleams and is gone; the cliffs of England stand,
Glimmering and vast, out in the tranquil bay.
Come to the window, sweet is the night-air!
Only, from the long line of spray
Where the sea meets the moon-blanch'd land,
Listen! you hear the grating roar
Of pebbles which the waves draw back, and fling,
At their return, up the high strand,
Begin, and cease, and then again begin,
With tremulous cadence slow, and bring
The eternal note of sadness in.

Sophocles long ago
Heard it on the Ægæan, and it brought
Into his mind the turbid ebb and flow
Of human misery; we
Find also in the sound a thought,
Hearing it by this distant northern sea.

The Sea of Faith
Was once, too, at the full, and round earth's shore
Lay like the folds of a bright girdle furl'd.
But now I only hear

Its melancholy, long, withdrawing roar,
Retreating, to the breath
Of the night-wind, down the vast edges drear
And naked shingles of the world.

Ah, love, let us be true
To one another! for the world, which seems
To lie before us like a land of dreams,
So various, so beautiful, so new,
Hath really neither joy, nor love, nor light,
Nor certitude, nor peace, nor help for pain;
And we are here as on a darkling plain
Swept with confused alarms of struggle and flight,
Where ignorant armies clash by night.

## Stanzas from the Grande Chartreuse

Through Alpine meadows soft-suffused
With rain, where thick the crocus blows,
Past the dark forges long disused,
The mule-track from Saint Laurent goes.
The bridge is cross'd, and slow we ride,
Through forest, up the mountain-side.

The autumnal evening darkens round,
The wind is up, and drives the rain;
While, hark! far down, with strangled sound
Doth the Dead Guier's stream complain,
Where that wet smoke, among the woods,
Over his boiling cauldron broods.

Swift rush the spectral vapours white
Past limestone scars with ragged pines,
Showing—then blotting from our sight!—
Halt—through the cloud-drift something shines!
High in the valley, wet and drear,
The huts of Courrerie appear.

*Strike leftward!* cries our guide; and higher
Mounts up the stony forest-way.
At last the encircling trees retire;
Look! through the showery twilight grey
What pointed roofs are these advance?—
A palace of the Kings of France?

Approach, for what we seek is here!
Alight, and sparely sup, and wait
For rest in this outbuilding near;
Then cross the sward and reach that gate.
Knock; pass the wicket! Thou art come
To the Carthusians' world-famed home.

The silent courts, where night and day
Into their stone-carved basins cold
The splashing icy fountains play—
The humid corridors behold!
Where, ghostlike in the deepening night,
Cowl'd forms brush by in gleaming white.

The chapel, where no organ's peal
Invests the stern and naked prayer—
With penitential cries they kneel
And wrestle; rising then, with bare
And white uplifted faces stand,
Passing the Host from hand to hand;

Each takes, and then his visage wan
Is buried in his cowl once more.
The cells!—the suffering Son of Man
Upon the wall—the knee-worn floor—
And where they sleep, that wooden bed,
Which shall their coffin be, when dead!

The library, where tract and tome
Not to feed priestly pride are there,

To hymn the conquering march of Rome,
Nor yet to amuse, as ours are!
They paint of souls the inner strife,
Their drops of blood, their death in life.

The garden, overgrown—yet mild,
See, fragrant herbs are flowering there!
Strong children of the Alpine wild
Whose culture is the brethren's care;
Of human tasks their only one,
And cheerful works beneath the sun.

Those halls, too, destined to contain
Each its own pilgrim-host of old,
From England, Germany, or Spain—
All are before me! I behold
The House, the Brotherhood austere!
—And what am I, that I am here?

For rigorous teachers seized my youth,
And purged its faith, and trimm'd its fire,
Show'd me the high, white star of Truth,
There bade me gaze, and there aspire.
Even now their whispers pierce the gloom:
*What dost thou in this living tomb?*

Forgive me, masters of the mind!
At whose behest I long ago
So much unlearnt, so much resign'd—
I come not here to be your foe!
I seek these anchorites, not in ruth,
To curse and to deny your truth;

Not as their friend, or child, I speak!
But as, on some far northern strand,
Thinking of his own Gods, a Greek
In pity and mournful awe might stand

Before some fallen Runic stone—
For both were faiths, and both are gone.

Wandering between two worlds, one dead,
The other powerless to be born,
With nowhere yet to rest my head,
Like these, on earth I wait forlorn.
Their faith, my tears, the world deride—
I come to shed them at their side.

Oh, hide me in your gloom profound,
Ye solemn seats of holy pain!
Take me, cowl'd forms, and fence me round
Till I possess my soul again;
Till free my thoughts before me roll,
Not chafed by hourly false control!

For the world cries your faith is now
But a dead time's exploded dream;
My melancholy, sciolists say,
Is a pass'd mode, an outworn theme—
As if the world had ever had
A faith, or sciolists been sad!

Ah, if it *be* pass'd, take away,
At least, the restlessness, the pain;
Be man henceforth no more a prey
To these out-dated stings again!
The nobleness of grief is gone—
Ah, leave us not the fret alone!

But—if you cannot give us ease—
Last of the race of them who grieve
Here leave us to die out with these
Last of the people who believe!
Silent, while years engrave the brow;
Silent—the best are silent now.

Achilles ponders in his tent,
The kings of modern thought are dumb;
Silent they are, though not content,
And wait to see the future come.
They have the grief men had of yore,
But they contend and cry no more.

Our fathers water'd with their tears
This sea of time whereon we sail,
Their voices were in all men's ears
Who pass'd within their puissant hail.
Still the same ocean round us raves,
But we stand mute, and watch the waves.

For what avail'd it, all the noise
And outcry of the former men?—
Say, have their sons achieved more joys,
Say, is life lighter now than then?
The sufferers died, they left their pain—
The pangs which tortured them remain.

What helps it now, that Byron bore,
With haughty scorn which mock'd the smart,
Through Europe to the Ætolian shore
The pageant of his bleeding heart?
That thousands counted every groan,
And Europe made his woe her own?

What boots it, Shelley! that the breeze
Carried thy lovely wail away,
Musical through Italian trees
Which fringe thy soft blue Spezzian bay?
Inheritors of thy distress
Have restless hearts one throb the less?

Or are we easier, to have read,
O Obermann! the sad, stern page,
Which tells us how thou hidd'st thy head

From the fierce tempest of thine age
In the lone brakes of Fontainebleau,
Or chalets near the Alpine snow?

Ye slumber in your silent grave!—
The world, which for an idle day
Grace to your mood of sadness gave,
Long since hath flung her weeds away.
The eternal trifler breaks your spell;
But we—we learnt your lore too well!

Years hence, perhaps, may dawn an age,
More fortunate, alas! than we,
Which without hardness will be sage,
And gay without frivolity.
Sons of the world, oh, speed those years;
But, while we wait, allow our tears!

Allow them! We admire with awe
The exulting thunder of your race;
You give the universe your law,
You triumph over time and space!
Your pride of life, your tireless powers,
We laud them, but they are not ours.

We are like children rear'd in shade
Beneath some old-world abbey wall,
Forgotten in a forest-glade,
And secret from the eyes of all.
Deep, deep the greenwood round them waves,
Their abbey, and its close of graves!

But, where the road runs near the stream,
Oft through the trees they catch a glance
Of passing troops in the sun's beam—
Pennon, and plume, and flashing lance!
Forth to the world those soldiers fare,
To life, to cities, and to war!

And through the wood, another way,
Faint bugle-notes from far are borne,
Where hunters gather, staghounds bay,
Round some fair forest-lodge at morn.
Gay dames are there, in sylvan green;
Laughter and cries—those notes between!

The banners flashing through the trees
Make their blood dance and chain their eyes
That bugle-music on the breeze
Arrests them with a charm'd surprise.
Banner by turns and bugle woo:
*Ye shy recluses, follow too!*

O children, what do ye reply?—
"Action and pleasure, will ye roam
Through these secluded dells to cry
And call us?—but too late ye come!
Too late for us your call ye blow,
Whose bent was taken long ago.

"Long since we pace this shadow'd nave;
We watch those yellow tapers shine,
Emblems of hope over the grave,
In the high altar's depth divine;
The organ carries to our ear
Its accents of another sphere.

"Fenced early in this cloistral round
Of reverie, of shade, of prayer,
How should we grow in other ground?
How can we flower in foreign air?
—Pass, banners, pass, and bugles, cease;
And leave our desert to its peace!"

# GERARD MANLEY HOPKINS
## (1844–1889)

## God's Grandeur

The world is charged with the grandeur of God.
  It will flame out, like shining from shook foil;
  It gathers to a greatness, like the ooze of oil
Crushed. Why do men then now not reck his rod?
Generations have trod, have trod, have trod;
  And all is seared with trade; bleared, smeared with toil;
  And wears man's smudge and shares man's smell: the soil
Is bare now, nor can foot feel, being shod.

And for all this, nature is never spent;
  There lives the dearest freshness deep down things;
And though the last lights off the black West went
  Oh, morning, at the brown brink eastward, springs—
Because the Holy Ghost over the bent
  World broods with warm breast and with ah! bright wings.

## The Windhover

### To Christ our Lord

I caught this morning morning's minion, king-
  dom of daylight's dauphin, dapple-dawn-drawn Falcon, in his riding
  Of the rolling level underneath him steady air, and striding
High there, how he rung upon the rein of a wimpling wing
In his ecstacy! then off, off forth on swing,
  As a skate's heel sweeps smooth on a bow-bend: the hurl and gliding

Rebuffed the big wind. My heart in hiding
Stirred for a bird,—the achieve of, the mastery of the thing!

Brute beauty and valour and act, oh, air, pride, plume, here
Buckle! AND the fire that breaks from thee then, a billion
Times told lovelier, more dangerous, O my chevalier!

No wonder of it: shéer plód makes plough down sillion
Shine, and blue-bleak embers, ah my dear,
Fall, gall themselves, and gash gold-vermillion.

## Pied Beauty

Glory be to God for dappled things—
For skies of couple-colour as a brinded cow;
For rose-moles all in stipple upon trout that swim:
Fresh-firecoal chestnut-falls; finches' wings;
Landscape plotted and pieced—fold, fallow, and plough;
And áll trádes, their gear and tackle and trim.

All things counter, original, spare, strange;
Whatever is fickle, freckled (who knows how?)
With swift, slow; sweet, sour; adazzle, dim;
He fathers-forth whose beauty is past change:
Praise him.

## Carrion Comfort

Not, I'll not, carrion comfort, Despair, not feast on thee;
Not untwist—slack they may be—these last strands of man
In me ór, most weary, cry *I can no more*. I can;
Can something, hope, wish day come, not choose not to be.
But ah, but O thou terrible, why wouldst thou rude on me
Thy wring-world right foot rock? lay a lionlimb against me? scan
With darksome devouring eyes my bruisèd bones? and fan,
O in turns of tempest, me heaped there; me frantic to avoid thee and flee?

Why? That my chaff might fly; my grain lie, sheer and clear.
Nay in all that toil, that coil, since (seems) I kissed the rod,
Hand rather, my heart lo! lapped strength, stole joy, would laugh, chéer.
Cheer whom though? the hero whose heaven-handling flung me, fóot tród
Me? or me that fought him? O which one? is it each one? That night, that year
Of now done darkness I wretch lay wrestling with (my God!) my God.

## No Worst, There Is None

No worst, there is none. Pitched past pitch of grief,
More pangs will, schooled at forepangs, wilder wring.
Comforter, where, where is your comforting?
Mary, mother of us, where is your relief?
My cries heave, herds-long; huddle in a main, a chief
Woe, world-sorrow; on an age-old anvil wince and sing—
Then lull, then leave off. Fury had shrieked "No ling-
ering! Let me be fell: force I must be brief."

   O the mind, mind has mountains; cliffs of fall
Frightful, sheer, no-man-fathomed. Hold them cheap
May who ne'er hung there. Nor does long our small
Durance deal with that steep or deep. Here! creep,
Wretch, under a comfort serves in a whirlwind: all
Life death does end and each day dies with sleep.

## I Wake and Feel the Fell of Dark

I wake and feel the fell of dark, not day.
What hours, O what black hoürs we have spent
This night! what sights you, heart, saw; ways you went!
And more must, in yet longer light's delay.
   With witness I speak this. But where I say
Hours I mean years, mean life. And my lament
Is cries countless, cries like dead letters sent
To dearest him that lives alas! away.

I am gall, I am heartburn. God's most deep decree
Bitter would have me taste: my taste was me;
Bones built in me, flesh filled, blood brimmed the curse.
    Selfyeast of spirit a dull dough sours. I see
The lost are like this, and their scourge to be
As I am mine, their sweating selves; but worse.

# DANTE GABRIEL ROSSETTI
## (1828–1882)

## The Blessed Damozel

The blessed damozel leaned out
    From the gold bar of Heaven;
Her eyes were deeper than the depth
    Of waters stilled at even;
She had three lilies in her hand,
    And the stars in her hair were seven.

Her robe, ungirt from clasp to hem,
    No wrought flowers did adorn,
But a white rose of Mary's gift,
    For service meetly worn;
Her hair that lay along her back
    Was yellow like ripe corn.

Herseemed she scarce had been a day
    One of God's choristers;
The wonder was not yet quite gone
    From that still look of hers;
Albeit, to them she left, her day
    Had counted as ten years.

(To one, it is ten years of years.
    . . . Yet now, and in this place,
Surely she leaned o'er me—her hair
    Fell all about my face. . . .
Nothing: the autumn fall of leaves.
    The whole year sets apace.)

It was the rampart of God's house
    That she was standing on;
By God built over the sheer depth
    The which is Space begun;
So high, that looking downward thence
    She scarce could see the sun.

It lies in Heaven, across the flood
    Of ether, as a bridge.
Beneath, the tides of day and night
    With flame and darkness ridge
The void, as low as where this earth
    Spins like a fretful midge.

Around her, lovers, newly met
    'Mid deathless love's acclaims,
Spoke evermore among themselves
    Their heart-remembered names;
And the souls mounting up to God
    Went by her like thin flames.

And still she bowed herself and stooped
    Out of the circling charm;
Until her bosom must have made
    The bar she leaned on warm,
And the lilies lay as if asleep
    Along her bended arm.

From the fixed place of Heaven she saw
    Time like a pulse shake fierce
Through all the worlds. Her gaze still strove
    Within the gulf to pierce
Its path; and now she spoke as when
    The stars sang in their spheres.

The sun was gone now; the curled moon
    Was like a little feather
Fluttering far down the gulf; and now
    She spoke through the still weather.
Her voice was like the voice the stars
    Had when they sang together.

(Ah sweet! Even now, in that bird's song,
    Strove not her accents there,
Fain to be hearkened? When those bells
    Possessed the mid-day air,
Strove not her steps to reach my side
    Down all the echoing stair?)

"I wish that he were come to me,
    For he will come," she said.
"Have I not prayed in Heaven?—on earth,
    Lord, Lord, has he not pray'd?
Are not two prayers a perfect strength?
    And shall I feel afraid?

"When round his head the aureole clings,
    And he is clothed in white,
I'll take his hand and go with him
    To the deep wells of light;
As unto a stream we will step down,
    And bathe there in God's sight.

"We two will stand beside that shrine.
    Occult, withheld, untrod,
Whose lamps are stirred continually
    With prayer sent up to God;
And see our old prayers, granted, melt
    Each like a little cloud.

We two will lie i' the shadow of
   That living mystic tree
Within whose secret growth the Dove
   Is sometimes felt to be,
While every leaf that His plumes touch
   Saith His Name audibly.

"And I myself will teach to him,
   I myself, lying so,
The songs I sing here; which his voice
   Shall pause in, hushed and slow,
And find some knowledge at each pause,
   Or some new thing to know."

(Alas! We two, we two, thou say'st!
   Yea, one wast thou with me
That once of old. But shall God lift
   To endless unity
The soul whose likeness with thy soul
   Was but its love for thee ?)

"We two," she said, "will seek the groves
   Where the lady Mary is,
With her five handmaidens, whose names
   Are five sweet symphonies,
Cecily, Gertrude, Magdalen,
   Margaret and Rosalys.

"Circlewise sit they, with bound locks
   And foreheads garlanded;
Into the fine cloth white like flame
   Weaving the golden thread,
To fashion the birth-robes for them
   Who are just born, being dead.

"He shall fear, haply, and be dumb:
　　Then will I lay my cheek
To his, and tell about our love,
　　Not once abashed or weak:
And the dear Mother will approve
　　My pride, and let me speak.

"Herself shall bring us, hand in hand,
　　To Him round whom all souls
Kneel, the clear-ranged unnumbered heads
　　Bowed with their aureoles:
And angels meeting us shall sing
　　To their citherns and citoles.

"There will I ask of Christ the Lord
　　Thus much for him and me:—
Only to live as once on earth
　　With Love, only to be,
As then awhile, for ever now
　　Together, I and he."

She gazed and listened and then said,
　　Less sad of speech than mild,—
"All this is when he comes." She ceased.
　　The light thrilled towards her, fill'd
With angels in strong level flight.
　　Her eyes prayed, and she smil'd.

(I saw her smile.) But soon their path
　　Was vague in distant spheres:
And then she cast her arms along
　　The golden barriers,
And laid her face between her hands,
　　And wept. (I heard her tears.)

## Sudden Light

I have been here before,
But when or how I cannot tell:
I know the grass beyond the door,
The sweet keen smell,
The sighing sound, the lights around the shore.

You have been mine before,—
How long ago I may not know:
But just when at that swallow's soar
Your neck turned so,
Some veil did fall,—I knew it all of yore.

Has this been thus before?
And shall not thus time's eddying flight
Still with our lives our loves restore
In death's despite,
And day and night yield one delight once more?

## The Woodspurge

The wind flapped loose, the wind was still,
Shaken out dead from tree and hill:
I had walked on at the wind's will,—
I sat now, for the wind was still.

Between my knees my forehead was,—
My lips, drawn in, said not Alas!
My hair was over in the grass,
My naked ears heard the day pass.

My eyes, wide open, had the run
Of some ten weeds to fix upon;
Among those few, out of the sun,
The woodspurge flowered, three cups in one.

From perfect grief there need not be
Wisdom or even memory:
One thing then learnt remains to me,—
The woodspurge has a cup of three.

## The Honeysuckle

I plucked a honeysuckle where
    The hedge on high is quick with thorn,
    And climbing for the prize, was torn,
And fouled my feet in quag-water;
    And by the thorns and by the wind
    The blossom that I took was thinn'd,
And yet I found it sweet and fair.

Thence to a richer growth I came,
    Where, nursed in mellow intercourse,
    The honeysuckles sprang by scores,
Not harried like my single stem,
    All virgin lamps of scent and dew.
    So from my hand that first I threw,
Yet plucked not any more of them.

# CHRISTINA ROSSETTI
## (1830–1894)

### Goblin Market

Morning and evening
Maids heard the goblins cry:
"Come buy our orchard fruits,
Come buy, come buy:
Apples and quinces,
Lemons and oranges,
Plump unpecked cherries,
Melons and raspberries,
Bloom-down-cheeked peaches,
Swart-headed mulberries,
Wild free-born cranberries,
Crab-apples, dewberries,
Pine-apples, blackberries,
Apricots, strawberries;—
All ripe together
In summer weather,—
Morns that pass by,
Fair eves that fly;
Come buy, come buy:
Our grapes fresh from the vine,
Pomegranates full and fine,
Dates and sharp bullaces,
Rare pears and greengages,
Damsons and bilberries,
Taste them and try:
Currants and gooseberries,

Bright-fire-like barberries,
Figs to fill your mouth,
Citrons from the South,
Sweet to tongue and sound to eye;
Come buy, come buy."

Evening by evening
Among the brookside rushes,
Laura bowed her head to hear,
Lizzie veiled her blushes:
Crouching close together
In the cooling weather,
With clasping arms and cautioning lips,
With tingling cheeks and finger tips.
"Lie close," Laura said,
Pricking up her golden head:
"We must not look at goblin men,
We must not buy their fruits:
Who knows upon what soil they fed
Their hungry thirsty roots?"
"Come buy," call the goblins
Hobbling down the glen.
"Oh," cried Lizzie, " Laura, Laura,
You should not peep at goblin men."
Lizzie covered up her eyes,
Covered close lest they should look;
Laura reared her glossy head,
And whispered like the restless brook:
"Look, Lizzie, look, Lizzie,
Down the glen tramp little men.
One hauls a basket,
One bears a plate,
One lugs a golden dish
Of many pounds weight.
How fair the vine must grow
Whose grapes are so luscious;
How warm the wind must blow

Through those fruit bushes."
"No," said Lizzie: "No, no, no;
Their offers should not charm us,
Their evil gifts would harm us."
She thrust a dimpled finger
In each ear, shut eyes and ran:
Curious Laura chose to linger
Wondering at each merchant man.
One had a cat's face,
One whisked a tail,
One tramped at a rat's pace,
One crawled like a snail,
One like a wombat prowled obtuse and furry,
One like a ratel tumbled hurry skurry.
She heard a voice like voice of doves
Cooing all together:
They sounded kind and full of loves
In the pleasant weather.

    Laura stretched her gleaming neck
Like a rush-imbedded swan,
Like a lily from the beck,
Like a moonlit poplar branch,
Like a vessel at the launch
When its last restraint is gone.

    Backwards up the mossy glen
Turned and trooped the goblin men,
With their shrill repeated cry,
"Come buy, come buy."
When they reached where Laura was
They stood stock still upon the moss,
Leering at each other,
Brother with queer brother;
Signalling each other,
Brother with sly brother.
One set his basket down,

One reared his plate;
One began to weave a crown
Of tendrils, leaves and rough nuts brown
(Men sell not such in any town);
One heaved the golden weight
Of dish and fruit to offer her:
"Come buy, come buy," was still their cry.
Laura stared but did not stir,
Longed but had no money:
The whisk-tailed merchant bade her taste
In tones as smooth as honey,
The cat-faced purr'd,
The rat-paced spoke a word
Of welcome, and the snail-paced even was heard;
One parrot-voiced and jolly
Cried "Pretty Goblin" still for "Pretty Polly";—
One whistled like a bird.

But sweet-tooth Laura spoke in haste:
"Good folk, I have no coin;
To take were to purloin:
I have no copper in my purse,
I have no silver either,
And all my gold is on the furze
That shakes in windy weather
Above the rusty heather."
"You have much gold upon your head,"
They answered all together:
"Buy from us with a golden curl."
She clipped a precious golden lock,
She dropped a tear more rare than pearl,
Then sucked their fruit globes fair or red:
Sweeter than honey from the rock,
Stronger than man-rejoicing wine,
Clearer than water flowed that juice;
She never tasted such before,
How should it cloy with length of use?

She sucked and sucked and sucked the more
Fruits which that unknown orchard bore;
She sucked until her lips were sore;
Then flung the emptied rinds away
But gathered up one kernel stone,
And knew not was it night or day
As she turned home alone.

    Lizzie met her at the gate
Full of wise upbraidings:
"Dear, you should not stay so late,
Twilight is not good for maidens;
Should not loiter in the glen
In the haunts of goblin men.
Do you not remember Jeanie,
How she met them in the moonlight,
Took their gifts both choice and many,
Ate their fruits and wore their flowers
Plucked from bowers
Where summer ripens at all hours?
But ever in the moonlight
She pined and pined away;
Sought them by night and day,
Found them no more but dwindled and grew grey;
Then fell with the first snow,
While to this day no grass will grow
Where she lies low:
I planted daisies there a year ago
That never blow.
You should not loiter so."
"Nay, hush," said Laura:
"Nay, hush, my sister:
I ate and ate my fill,
Yet my mouth waters still;
To-morrow night I will
Buy more": and kissed her:
"Have done with sorrow;

I'll bring you plums to-morrow
Fresh on their mother twigs,
Cherries worth getting;
You cannot think what figs
My teeth have met in,
What melons icy-cold
Piled on a dish of gold
Too huge for me to hold,
What peaches with a velvet nap,
Pellucid grapes without one seed:
Odorous indeed must be the mead
Whereon they grow, and pure the wave they drink
With lilies at the brink,
And sugar-sweet their sap."

Golden head by golden head,
Like two pigeons in one nest
Folded in each other's wings,
They lay down in their curtained bed:
Like two blossoms on one stem,
Like two flakes of new-fall'n snow,
Like two wands of ivory
Tipped with gold for awful kings.
Moon and stars gazed in at them,
Wind sang to them lullaby,
Lumbering owls forbore to fly,
Not a bat flapped to and fro
Round their rest:
Cheek to cheek and breast to breast
Locked together in one nest.

Early in the morning
When the first cock crowed his warning,
Neat like bees, as sweet and busy,
Laura rose with Lizzie:
Fetched in honey, milked the cows,
Aired and set to rights the house,

Kneaded cakes of whitest wheat,
Cakes for dainty mouths to eat,
Next churned butter, whipped up cream,
Fed their poultry, sat and sewed;
Talked as modest maidens should:
Lizzie with an open heart,
Laura in an absent dream,
One content, one sick in part;
One warbling for the mere bright day's delight,
One longing for the night.

 At length slow evening came:
They went with pitchers to the reedy brook;
Lizzie most placid in her look,
Laura most like a leaping flame.
They drew the gurgling water from its deep;
Lizzie plucked purple and rich golden flags,
Then turning homewards said: "The sunset flushes
Those furthest loftiest crags;
Come, Laura, not another maiden lags,
No wilful squirrel wags,
The beasts and birds are fast asleep."
But Laura loitered still among the rushes
And said the bank was steep.

 And said the hour was early still,
The dew not fall'n, the wind not chill:
Listening ever, but not catching
The customary cry,
"Come buy, come buy,"
With its iterated jingle
Of sugar-baited words:
Not for all her watching
Once discerning even one goblin
Racing, whisking, tumbling, hobbling;
Let alone the herds
That used to tramp along the glen,

In groups or single,
Of brisk fruit-merchant men.

    Till Lizzie urged, "O Laura, come;
I hear the fruit-call but I dare not look:
You should not loiter longer at this brook:
Come with me home.
The stars rise, the moon bends her arc,
Each glowworm winks her spark,
Let us get home before the night grows dark:
For clouds may gather
Though this is summer weather,
Put out the lights and drench us through;
Then if we lost our way what should we do?"

    Laura turned cold as stone
To find her sister heard that cry alone,
That goblin cry,
"Come buy our fruits, come buy."
Must she then buy no more such dainty fruits?
Must she no more such success pasture find,
Gone deaf and blind?
Her tree of life drooped from the root:
She said not one word in her heart's sore ache;
But peering thro' the dimness, nought discerning,
Trudged home, her pitcher dripping all the way;
So crept to bed, and lay
Silent till Lizzie slept;
Then sat up in a passionate yearning,
And gnashed her teeth for baulked desire, and wept
As if her heart would break.

    Day after day, night after night,
Laura kept watch in vain
In sullen silence of exceeding pain.
She never caught again the goblin cry:
"Come buy, come buy";—

She never spied the goblin men
Hawking their fruits along the glen:
But when the noon waxed bright
Her hair grew thin and grey;
She dwindled, as the fair full moon doth turn
To swift decay and burn
Her fire away.

One day remembering her kernel-stone
She set it by a wall that faced the south;
Dewed it with tears, hoped for a root,
Watched for a waxing shoot,
But there came none;
It never saw the sun,
It never felt the trickling moisture run:
While with sunk eyes and faded mouth
She dreamed of melons, as a traveller sees
False waves in desert drouth
With shade of leaf-crowned trees,
And burns the thirstier in the sandful breeze.

She no more swept the house,
Tended the fowls or cows,
Fetched honey, kneaded cakes of wheat,
Brought water from the brook:
But sat down listless in the chimney-nook
And would not eat.

Tender Lizzie could not bear
To watch her sister's cankerous care
Yet not to share.
She night and morning
Caught the goblins' cry:
"Come buy our orchard fruits,
Come buy, come buy":—
Beside the brook, along the glen,
She heard the tramp of goblin men,

The voice and stir
Poor Laura could not hear;
Longed to buy fruit to comfort her,
But feared to pay too dear.
She thought of Jeanie in her grave,
Who should have been a bride;
But who for joys brides hope to have
Fell sick and died
In her gay prime,
In earliest Winter time,
With the first glazing rime,
With the first snow-fall of crisp Winter time.

Till Laura dwindling
Seemed knocking at Death's door:
Then Lizzie weighed no more
Better and worse;
But put a silver penny in her purse,
Kissed Laura, crossed the heath with clumps of furze
At twilight, halted by the brook:
And for the first time in her life
Began to listen and look.

Laughed every goblin
When they spied her peeping:
Came towards her hobbling,
Flying, running, leaping,
Puffing and blowing,
Chuckling, clapping, crowing,
Clucking and gobbling,
Mopping and mowing,
Full of airs and graces,
Pulling wry faces,
Demure grimaces,
Cat-like and rat-like,
Ratel- and wombat-like,
Snail-paced in a hurry,

Parrot-voiced and whistler,
Helter skelter, hurry skurry,
Chattering like magpies,
Fluttering like pigeons,
Gliding like fishes,—
Hugged her and kissed her:
Squeezed and caressed her:
Stretched up their dishes,
Panniers, and plates:
"Look at our apples
Russet and dun,
Bob at our cherries,
Bite at our peaches,
Citrons and dates,
Grapes for the asking,
Pears red with basking
Out in the sun,
Plums on their twigs;
Pluck them and suck them,
Pomegranates, figs."—

   "Good folk," said Lizzie,
Mindful of Jeanie:
"Give me much and many"—
Held out her apron,
Tossed them her penny.
"Nay, take a seat with us,
Honour and eat with us,"
They answered grinning:
"Our feast is but beginning.
Night yet is early,
Warm and dew-pearly,
Wakeful and starry:
Such fruits as these
No man can carry;
Half their bloom would fly,
Half their dew would dry,

Half their flavour would pass by.
Sit down and feast with us,
Be welcome guest with us,
Cheer you and rest with us."—
"Thank you," said Lizzie: "But one waits
At home alone for me:
So without further parleying,
If you will not sell me any
Of your fruits though much and many,
Give me back my silver penny
I tossed you for a fee."—
They began to scratch their pates,
No longer wagging, purring,
But visibly demurring,
Grunting and snarling.
One called her proud,
Cross-grained, uncivil;
Their tones waxed loud,
Their looks were evil.
Lashing their tails
They trod and hustled her,
Elbowed and jostled her,
Clawed with their nails,
Barking, mewing, hissing, mocking,
Tore her gown and soiled her stocking,
Twitched her hair out by the roots,
Stamped upon her tender feet,
Held her hands and squeezed their fruits
Against her mouth to make her eat.

White and golden Lizzie stood,
Like a lily in a flood,—
Like a rock of blue-veined stone
Lashed by tides obstreperously,—
Like a beacon left alone
In a hoary roaring sea,
Sending up a golden fire,—

Like a fruit-crowned orange-tree
White with blossoms honey-sweet
Sore beset by wasp and bee,—
Like a royal virgin town
Topped with gilded dome and spire
Close beleaguered by a fleet
Mad to tug her standard down.

One may lead a horse to water,
Twenty cannot make him drink.
Though the goblins cuffed and caught her,
Coaxed and fought her,
Bullied and besought her,
Scratched her, pinched her black as ink,
Kicked and knocked her,
Mauled and mocked her,
Lizzie uttered not a word;
Would not open lip from lip
Lest they should cram a mouthful in:
But laughed in heart to feel the drip
Of juice that syrupped all her face,
And lodged in dimples of her chin,
And streaked her neck which quaked like curd.
At last the evil people
Worn out by her resistance
Flung back her penny, kicked their fruit
Along whichever road they took,
Not leaving root or stone or shoot;
Some writhed into the ground,
Some dived into the brook
With ring and ripple,
Some scudded on the gale without a sound,
Some vanished in the distance.

In a smart, ache, tingle,
Lizzie went her way;
Knew not was it night or day;

Sprang up the bank, tore thro' the furze,
Threaded copse and dingle,
And heard her penny jingle
Bouncing in her purse,—
Its bounce was music to her ear.
She ran and ran
As if she feared some goblin man
Dogged her with gibe or curse
Or something worse:
But not one goblin skurried after,
Nor was she pricked by fear;
The kind heart made her windy-paced
That urged her home quite out of breath with haste
And inward laughter.

She cried "Laura," up the garden,
"Did you miss me?
Come and kiss me.
Never mind my bruises,
Hug me, kiss me, suck my juices
Squeezed from goblin fruits for you,
Goblin pulp and goblin dew.
Eat me, drink me, love me;
Laura, make much of me:
For your sake I have braved the glen
And had to do with goblin merchant men."

Laura started from her chair,
Flung her arms up in the air,
Clutched her hair:
"Lizzie, Lizzie, have you tasted
For my sake the fruit forbidden?
Must your light like mine be hidden,
Your young life like mine be wasted,
Undone in mine undoing
And ruined in my ruin,
Thirsty, cankered, goblin-ridden?"—

She clung about her sister,
Kissed and kissed and kissed her:
Tears once again
Refreshed her shrunken eyes,
Dropping like rain
After long sultry drouth;
Shaking with aguish fear, and pain,
She kissed and kissed her with a hungry mouth.

    Her lips began to scorch,
That juice was wormwood to her tongue,
She loathed the feast:
Writhing as one possessed she leaped and sung,
Rent all her robe, and wrung
Her hands in lamentable haste,
And beat her breast.
Her locks streamed like the torch
Borne by a racer at full speed,
Or like the mane of horses in their flight,
Or like an eagle when she stems the light
Straight toward the sun,
Or like a caged thing freed,
Or like a flying flag when armies run.

    Swift fire spread through her veins, knocked at her heart,
Met the fire smouldering there
And overbore its lesser flame;
She gorged on bitterness without a name:
Ah! fool, to choose such part
Of soul-consuming care!
Sense failed in the mortal strife:
Like the watch-tower of a town
Which an earthquake shatters down,
Like a lightning-stricken mast,
Like a wind-uprooted tree
Spun about,
Like a foam-topped waterspout

Cast down headlong in the sea,
She fell at last;
Pleasure past and anguish past,
Is it death or is it life?

   Life out of death.
That night long Lizzie watched by her,
Counted her pulse's flagging stir,
Felt for her breath,
Held water to her lips, and cooled her face
With tears and fanning leaves:
But when the first birds chirped about their eaves,
And early reapers plodded to the place
Of golden sheaves,
And dew-wet grass
Bowed in the morning winds so brisk to pass,
And new buds with new day
Opened of cup-like lilies on the stream,
Laura awoke as from a dream,
Laughed in the innocent old way,
Hugged Lizzie but not twice or thrice;
Her gleaming locks showed not one thread of grey,
Her breath was sweet as May
And light danced in her eyes.

   Days, weeks, months, years
Afterwards, when both were wives
With children of their own;
Their mother-hearts beset with fears,
Their lives bound up in tender lives;
Laura would call the little ones
And tell them of her early prime,
Those pleasant days long gone
Of not-returning time:
Would talk about the haunted glen,
The wicked, quaint fruit-merchant men,
Their fruits like honey to the throat

But poison in the blood;
(Men sell not such in any town):
Would tell them how her sister stood
In deadly peril to do her good,
And win the fiery antidote:
Then joining hands to little hands
Would bid them cling together,
"For there is no friend like a sister
In calm or stormy weather;
To cheer one on the tedious way,
To fetch one if one goes astray,
To lift one if one totters down,
To strengthen whilst one stands."

# ALGERNON CHARLES SWINBURNE
## (1837–1909)

### The Garden of Proserpine

Here, where the world is quiet,
   Here, where all trouble seems
Dead winds' and spent waves' riot
   In doubtful dreams of dreams;
I watch the green field growing
For reaping folk and sowing,
For harvest time and mowing,
   A sleepy world of streams.

I am tired of tears and laughter,
   And men that laugh and weep
Of what may come hereafter
   For men that sow to reap:
I am weary of days and hours,
Blown buds of barren flowers,
Desires and dreams and powers
   And everything but sleep.

Here life has death for neighbour
   And far from eye or ear
Wan waves and wet winds labour,
   Weak ships and spirits steer;
They drive adrift, and whither
They wot not who make thither;
But no such winds blow hither,
   And no such things grow here.

No growth of moor or coppice,
   No heather-flower or vine,
But bloomless buds of poppies,
   Green grapes of Proserpine,
Pale beds of blowing rushes
Where no leaf blooms or blushes
Save this whereout she crushes
   For dead men deadly wine.

Pale, without name or number,
   In fruitless fields of corn,
They bow themselves and slumber
   All night till light is born;
And like a soul belated,
In hell and heaven unmated,
By cloud and mist abated
   Comes out of darkness morn.

Though one were strong as seven,
   He too with death shall dwell,
Nor wake with wings in heaven,
   Nor weep for pains in hell;
Though one were fair as roses,
His beauty clouds and closes;
And well though love reposes,
   In the end it is not well.

Pale, beyond porch and portal,
   Crowned with calm leaves, she stands
Who gathers all things mortal
   With cold immortal hands;
Her languid lips are sweeter
Than love's who fears to greet her
To men that mix and meet her
   From many times and lands.

She waits for each and other,
   She waits for all men born;

Forgets the earth her mother,
   The life of fruits and corn;
And spring and seed and swallow
Take wing for her and follow
Where summer song rings hollow
   And flowers are put to scorn.

There go the loves that wither,
   The old loves with wearier wings;
And all dead years draw thither,
   And all disastrous things;
Dead dreams of days forsaken
Blind buds that snows have shaken,
Wild leaves that winds have taken,
   Red strays of ruined springs.

We are not sure of sorrow,
   And joy was never sure;
To-day will die to-morrow;
   Time stoops to no man's lure;
And love, grown faint and fretful,
With lips but half regretful
Sighs, and with eyes forgetful
   Weeps that no loves endure.

From too much love of living,
   From hope and fear set free,
We thank with brief thanksgiving
   Whatever gods may be
That no life lives for ever;
That dead men rise up never;
That even the weariest river
   Winds somewhere safe to sea.

Then star nor sun shall waken,
   Nor any change of light:
Nor sound of waters shaken,
   Nor any sound or sight:

Nor wintry leaves nor vernal,
Nor days nor things diurnal;
Only the sleep eternal
In an eternal night.

## Ave Atque Vale

### IN MEMORY OF CHARLES BAUDELAIRE

#### I

Shall I strew on thee rose or rue or laurel,
   Brother, on this that was the veil of thee?
   Or quiet sea-flower moulded by the sea,
Or simplest growth of meadow-sweet or sorrel,
   Such as the summer-sleepy Dryads weave,
   Waked up by snow-soft sudden rains at eve?
Or wilt thou rather, as on earth before,
   Half-faded fiery blossoms, pale with heat
   And full of bitter summer, but more sweet
To thee than gleanings of a northern shore
   Trod by no tropic feet?

#### II

For always thee the fervid languid glories
   Allured of heavier suns in mightier skies;
   Thine ears knew all the wandering watery sighs
Where the sea sobs round Lesbian promontories,
   The barren kiss of piteous wave to wave
   That knows not where is that Leucadian grave
Which hides too deep the supreme head of song.
   Ah, salt and sterile as her kisses were,
   The wild sea winds her and the green gulfs bear
Hither and thither, and vex and work her wrong,
   Blind gods that cannot spare.

### III

Thou sawest, in thine old singing season, brother,
    Secrets and sorrows unbeheld of us:
    Fierce loves, and lovely leaf-buds poisonous,
Bare to thy subtler eye, but for none other
    Blowing by night in some unbreathed-in clime;
    The hidden harvest of luxurious time,
Sin without shape, and pleasure without speech;
    And where strange dreams in a tumultuous sleep
    Make the shut eyes of stricken spirits weep;
And with each face thou sawest the shadow on each,
    Seeing as men sow men reap.

### IV

Oh sleepless heart and sombre soul unsleeping.
    That were athirst for sleep and no more life
    And no more love, for peace and no more strife!
Now the dim gods of death have in their keeping
    Spirit and body and all the springs of song,
    Is it well now where love can do no wrong,
Where stingless pleasure has no foam or fang
    Behind the unopening closure of her lips?
    Is it not well where soul from body slips
And flesh from bone divides without a pang
    As dew from flower-bell drips?

### V

It is enough; the end and the beginning
    Are one thing to thee, who art past the end.
    Oh hand unclasped of unbeholden friend,
For thee no fruits to pluck, no palms for winning,
    No triumph and no labour and no lust,
    Only dead yew-leaves and a little dust.
Oh quiet eyes wherein the light saith nought,
    Whereto the day is dumb, nor any night
    With obscure finger silences your sight,
Nor in your speech the sudden soul speaks thought,
    Sleep, and have sleep for light.

## VI

Now all strange hours and all strange loves are over,
   Dreams and desires and sombre songs and sweet,
   Hast thou found place at the great knees and feet
Of some pale Titan-woman like a lover,
   Such as thy vision here solicited,
   Under the shadow of her fair vast head,
The deep division of prodigious breasts,
   The solemn slope of mighty limbs asleep,
   The weight of awful tresses that still keep
The savour and shade of old-world pine-forests
   Where the wet hill-winds weep?

## VII

Hast thou found any likeness for thy vision?
   Oh gardener of strange flowers, what bud, what bloom,
   Hast thou found sown, what gathered in the gloom?
What of despair, of rapture, of derision,
   What of life is there, what of ill or good?
   Are the fruits grey like dust or bright like blood?
Does the dim ground grow any seed of ours,
   The faint fields quicken any terrene root,
   In low lands where the sun and moon are mute
And all the stars keep silence? Are there flowers
   At all, or any fruit?

## VIII

Alas, but though my flying song flies after,
   Oh sweet strange elder singer, thy more fleet
   Singing, and footprints of thy fleeter feet,
Some dim derision of mysterious laughter
   From the blind tongueless warders of the dead,
   Some gainless glimpse of Proserpine's veiled head,
Some little sound of unregarded tears
   Wept by effaced unprofitable eyes,
   And from pale mouths some cadence of dead sighs—
These only, these the hearkening spirit hears,
   Sees only such things rise.

## IX

Thou art far too far for wings of words to follow,
  Far too far off for thought or any prayer.
  What ails us with thee, who art wind and air?
What ails us gazing where all seen is hollow?
  Yet with some fancy, yet with some desire,
  Dreams pursue death as winds a flying fire,
Our dreams pursue our dead, and do not find.
  Still, and more swift than they, the thin flame flies,
  The low light fails us in elusive skies,
Still the foiled earnest ear is deaf, and blind
  Are still the eluded eyes.

## X

Not thee, oh never thee, in all time's changes,
  Not thee, but this the sound of thy sad soul,
  The shadow of thy swift spirit, this shut scroll
I lay my hand on, and not death estranges
  My spirit from communion of thy song—
  These memories and these melodies that throng
Veiled porches of a Muse funereal—
  These I salute, these touch, these clasp and fold
  As though a hand were in my hand to hold,
Or through mine ears a mourning musical
  Of many mourners rolled.

## XI

I among these, I also, in such station
  As when the pyre was charred, and piled the sods,
  And offering to the dead made, and their gods,
The old mourners had, standing to make libation,
  I stand, and to the gods and to the dead
  Do reverence without prayer or praise, and shed
Offering to these unknown, the gods of gloom,
  And what of honey and spice my seedlands bear,
  And what I may of fruits in this chilled air,
And lay, Orestes-like, across the tomb
  A curl of severed hair.

### XII

But by no hand nor any treason stricken,
　　Not like the low-lying head of Him, the King,
　　The flame that made of Troy a ruinous thing,
Thou liest and on this dust no tears could quicken
　　There fall no tears like theirs that all men hear
　　Fall tear by sweet imperishable tear
Down the opening leaves of holy poets' pages.
　　Thee not Orestes, not Electra mourns;
　　But bending us-ward with memorial urns
The most high Muses that fulfil all ages
　　Weep, and our God's heart yearns.

### XIII

For, sparing of his sacred strength, not often
　　Among us darkling here the lord of light
　　Makes manifest his music and his might
In hearts that open and in lips that soften
　　With the soft flame and heat of songs that shine.
　　Thy lips indeed he touched with bitter wine,
And nourished them indeed with bitter bread;
　　Yet surely from his hand thy soul's food came,
　　The fire that scarred thy spirit at his flame
Was lighted, and thine hungering heart he fed
　　Who feeds our hearts with fame.

### XIV

Therefore he too now at thy soul's sun-setting,
　　God of all suns and songs, he too bends down
　　To mix his laurel with thy cypress crown,
And save thy dust from blame and from forgetting.
　　Therefore he too, seeing all thou wert and art,
　　Compassionate, with sad and sacred heart,
Mourns thee of many his children the last dead,
　　And hallows with strange tears and alien sighs
　　Thine unmelodious mouth and sunless eyes,
And over thine irrevocable head
　　Sheds light from the under skies.

## XV

And one weeps with him in the ways Lethean,
 And stains with tears her changing bosom chill:
 That obscure Venus of the hollow hill,
That thing transformed which was the Cytherean,
 With lips that lost their Grecian laugh divine
 Long since, and face no more called Erycine;
A ghost, a bitter and luxurious god.
 Thee also with fair flesh and singing spell
 Did she, a sad and second prey, compel
Into the footless places once more trod,
 And shadows hot from hell.

## XVI

And now no sacred staff shall break in blossom,
 No choral salutation lure to light
 A spirit sick with perfume and sweet night
And love's tired eyes and hands and barren bosom.
 There is no help for these things; none to mend,
 And none to mar; not all our songs, O friend,
Will make death clear, or make life durable.
 Howbeit with rose and ivy and wild vine
 And with wild notes about this dust of thine
At least I fill the place where white dreams dwell,
 And wreathe an unseen shrine.

## XVII

Sleep; and if life was bitter to thee, pardon,
 If sweet, give thanks; thou hast no more to live;
 And to give thanks is good, and to forgive.
Out of the mystic and the mournful garden
 Where all day through thine hands in barren braid
 Wove the sick flowers of secrecy and shade,
Green buds of sorrow and sin, and remnants gray,
 Sweet-smelling, pale with poison, sanguine-hearted,
 Passions that sprang from sleep and thoughts that started,
Shall death not bring us all as thee one day
 Among the days departed?

## XVIII

For thee, O now a silent soul, my brother,
   Take at my hands this garland, and farewell.
   Thin is the leaf, and chill the wintry smell,
And chill the solemn earth, a fatal mother,
   With sadder than the Niobean womb,
   And in the hollow of her breasts a tomb.
Content thee, howsoe'er, whose days are done;
   There lies not any troublous thing before,
   Nor sight nor sound to war against thee more,
For whom all winds are quiet as the sun,
   All waters as the shore.

# EDWARD LEAR

## (1812–1888)

## The Owl and the Pussy-Cat

### I

The Owl and the Pussy-Cat went to sea
   In a beautiful pea-green boat:
They took some honey, and plenty of money
   Wrapped up in a five-pound note.
The Owl looked up to the stars above,
   And sang to a small guitar,
   "O lovely Pussy, O Pussy, my love,
   What a beautiful Pussy you are,
      You are,
      You are!
   What a beautiful Pussy you are!"

### II

Pussy said to the Owl, "You elegant fowl,
   How charmingly sweet you sing!
Oh! let us be married; too long we have tarried:
   But what shall we do for a ring?"
They sailed away, for a year and a day,
   To the land where the bong-tree grows;
And there in a wood a Piggy-wig stood,
   With a ring at the end of his nose,
      His nose,
      His nose,
   With a ring at the end of his nose.

### III

"Dear Pig, are you willing to sell for one shilling
   Your ring?" Said the Piggy, "I will."
So they took it away, and were married next day
   By the Turkey who lives on the hill.
They dined on mince and slices of quince,
   Which they ate with a runcible spoon;
And hand in hand, on the edge of the sand
   They danced by the light of the moon,
        The moon,
        The moon,
   They danced by the light of the moon.

## The Jumblies

### I

They went to sea in a sieve, they did;
   In a sieve they went to sea:
In spite of all their friends could say,
On a winter's morn, on a stormy day,
   In a sieve they went to sea.
And when the sieve turned round and round,
And every one cried, "You'll all be drowned!"
They called aloud, "Our sieve ain't big;
But we don't care a button, we don't care a fig:
   In a sieve we'll go to sea!"
     Far and few, far and few,
       Are the lands where the Jumblies live:
       Their heads are green, and their hands are blue;
       And they went to sea in a sieve.

### II

They sailed away in a sieve, they did,
   In a sieve they sailed so fast,
With only a beautiful pea-green veil
Tied with a ribbon, by way of a sail,

To a small tobacco-pipe mast.
And every one said who saw them go,
    "Oh! won't they be soon upset, you know?
For the sky is dark, and the voyage is long;
And, happen what may, it's extremely wrong
        In a sieve to sail so fast."
        Far and few, far and few,
            Are the lands where the Jumblies live:
            Their heads are green, and their hands are blue;
            And they went to sea in a sieve.

### III

The water it soon came in, it did;
    The water it soon came in:
So, to keep them dry, they wrapped their feet
In a pinky paper all folded neat;
    And they fastened it down with a pin.
And they passed the night in a crockery-jar;
And each of them said, "How wise we are!
Though the sky be dark, and the voyage be long,
Yet we never can think we were rash or wrong,
    While round in our sieve we spin."
        Far and few, far and few,
            Are the lands where the Jumblies live:
            Their heads are green, and their hands are blue;
            And they went to sea in a sieve.

### IV

And all night long they sailed away;
    And when the sun went down,
They whistled and warbled a moony song
To the echoing sound of a coppery gong,
    In the shade of the mountains brown.
"O Timballoo! How happy we are
When we live in a sieve and a crockery-jar!
And all night long, in the moonlight pale,
We sail away with a pea-green sail

In the shade of the mountains brown."
    Far and few, far and few,
      Are the lands where the Jumblies live:
      Their heads are green, and their hands are blue;
      And they went to sea in a sieve.

### V

They sailed to the Western Sea, they did,—
    To a land all covered with trees:
And they bought an owl, and a useful cart,
And a pound of rice, and a cranberry-tart,
    And a hive of silvery bees;
And they bought a pig, and some green jackdaws,
And a lovely monkey with lollipop paws,
And forty bottles of ring-bo-ree,
    And no end of Stilton cheese.
    Far and few, far and few,
      Are the lands where the Jumblies live:
      Their heads are green, and their hands are blue;
      And they went to sea in a sieve.

### VI

And in twenty years they all came back,—
    In twenty years or more;
And every one said, "How tall they've grown!
For they've been to the Lakes, and the Torrible Zone,
    And the hills of the Chankly Bore."
And they drank their health, and gave them a feast
Of dumplings made of beautiful yeast;
And every one said, "If we only live,
We, too, will go to sea in a sieve,
    To the hills of the Chankly Bore."
    Far and few, far and few,
      Are the lands where the Jumblies live:
      Their heads are green, and their hands are blue;
      And they went to sea in a sieve.

# LEWIS CARROLL

## (1832–1898)

## The Hunting of the Snark

### *An Agony in Eight Fits*

#### FIT THE FIRST
##### THE LANDING

"Just the place for a Snark!" the Bellman cried,
  As he landed his crew with care;
Supporting each man on the top of the tide
  By a finger entwined in his hair.

"Just the place for a Snark! I have said it twice:
  That alone should encourage the crew.
Just the place for a Snark! I have said it thrice:
  What I tell you three times is true."

The crew was complete: it included a Boots—
  A maker of Bonnets and Hoods—
A Barrister, brought to arrange their disputes—
  And a Broker, to value their goods.

A Billiard-marker, whose skill was immense,
  Might perhaps have won more than his share—
But a Banker, engaged at enormous expense,
  Had the whole of their cash in his care.

There was also a Beaver, that paced on the deck,
 Or would sit making lace in the bow:
And had often (the Bellman said) saved them from wreck,
 Though none of the sailors knew how.

There was one who was famed for the number of things
 He forgot when he entered the ship:
His umbrella, his watch, all his jewels and rings,
 And the clothes he had bought for the trip.

He had forty-two boxes, all carefully packed,
 With his name painted clearly on each:
But, since he omitted to mention the fact,
 They were all left behind on the beach.

The loss of his clothes hardly mattered, because
 He had seven coats on when he came,
With three pair of boots—but the worst of it was,
 He had wholly forgotten his name.

He would answer to "Hi!" or to any loud cry,
 Such as "Fry me!" or "Fritter my wig!"
To "What-you-may-call-um!" or "What-was-his-name!"
 But especially "Thing-um-a-jig!"

While, for those who preferred a more forcible word,
 He had different names from these:
His intimate friends called him "Candle-ends,"
 And his enemies "Toasted-cheese."

"His form is ungainly—his intellect small—"
 (So the Bellman would often remark)
"But his courage is perfect! And that, after all,
 Is the thing that one needs with a Snark."

He would joke with hyænas, returning their stare
 With an impudent wag of the head:

And he once went a walk, paw-in-paw, with a bear,
   "Just to keep up its spirits," he said.

He came as a Baker: but owned, when too late—
   And it drove the poor Bellman half-mad—
He could only bake Bridecake—for which, I may state,
   No materials were to be had.

The last of the crew needs especial remark,
   Though he looked an incredible dunce:
He had just one idea—but that one being "Snark,"
   The good Bellman engaged him at once.

He came as a Butcher: but gravely declared,
   When the ship had been sailing a week,
He could only kill Beavers. The Bellman looked scared,
   And was almost too frightened to speak:

But at length he explained, in a tremulous tone,
   There was only one Beaver on board;
And that was a tame one he had of his own,
   Whose death would be deeply deplored.

The Beaver, who happened to hear the remark,
   Protested, with tears in its eyes,
That not even the rapture of hunting the Snark
   Could atone for that dismal surprise!

It strongly advised that the Butcher should be
   Conveyed in a separate ship:
But the Bellman declared that would never agree
   With the plans he had made for the trip:

Navigation was always a difficult art,
   Though with only one ship and one bell:
And he feared he must really decline, for his part,
   Undertaking another as well.

The Beaver's best course was, no doubt, to procure
    A second-hand dagger-proof coat—
So the Baker advised it—and next, to insure
    Its life in some Office of note:

This the Banker suggested, and offered for hire
    (On moderate terms), or for sale,
Two excellent Policies, one Against Fire,
    And one Against Damage From Hail.

Yet still, ever after that sorrowful day,
    Whenever the Butcher was by,
The Beaver kept looking the opposite way,
    And appeared unaccountably shy.

### FIT THE SECOND

#### THE BELLMAN'S SPEECH

The Bellman himself they all praised to the skies—
    Such a carriage, such ease and such grace!
Such solemnity, too! One could see he was wise,
    The moment one looked in his face!

He had bought a large map representing the sea,
    Without the least vestige of land:
And the crew were much pleased when they found it to be
    A map they could all understand.

"What's the good of Mercator's North Poles and Equators,
    Tropics, Zones, and Meridian Lines?"
So the Bellman would cry: and the crew would reply
    "They are merely conventional signs!

"Other maps are such shapes, with their islands and capes!
    But we've got our brave Captain to thank"
(So the crew would protest) "that he's bought us the best—
    A perfect and absolute blank!"

This was charming, no doubt: but they shortly found out
    That the Captain they trusted so well
Had only one notion for crossing the ocean,
    And that was to tingle his bell.

He was thoughtful and grave—but the orders he gave
    Were enough to bewilder a crew.
When he cried "Steer to starboard, but keep her head larboard!"
    What on earth was the helmsman to do?

Then the bowsprit got mixed with the rudder sometimes:
    A thing, as the Bellman remarked,
That frequently happens in tropical climes,
    When a vessel is, so to speak, "snarked."

But the principal failing occurred in the sailing,
    And the Bellman, perplexed and distressed,
Said he *had* hoped, at least, when the wind blew due East,
    That the ship would *not* travel due West!

But the danger was past—they had landed at last,
    With their boxes, portmanteaus, and bags:
Yet at first sight the crew were not pleased with the view,
    Which consisted of chasms and crags.

The Bellman perceived that their spirits were low,
    And repeated in musical tone
Some jokes he had kept for a season of woe—
    But the crew would do nothing but groan.

He served out some grog with a liberal hand,
    And bade them sit down on the beach:
And they could not but own that their Captain looked grand,
    As he stood and delivered his speech.

"Friends, Romans, and countrymen, lend me your ears!"
    (They were all of them fond of quotations:

So they drank to his health, and they gave him three cheers,
  While he served out additional rations).

"We have sailed many months, we have sailed many weeks,
  (Four weeks to the month you may mark),
But never as yet ('tis your Captain who speaks)
  Have we caught the least glimpse of a Snark!

"We have sailed many weeks, we have sailed many days,
  (Seven days to the week I allow),
But a Snark, on the which we might lovingly gaze,
  We have never beheld till now!

"Come, listen, my men, while I tell you again
  The five unmistakable marks.
By which you may know, wheresoever you go,
  The warranted genuine Snarks.

"Let us take them in order. The first is the taste,
  Which is meagre and hollow, but crisp:
Like a coat that is rather too tight in the waist,
  With a flavour of Will-o-the-wisp.

"Its habit of getting up late you'll agree
  That it carries too far, when I say
That it frequently breakfasts at five-o'clock tea,
  And dines on the following day.

"The third is its slowness in taking a jest.
  Should you happen to venture on one,
It will sigh like a thing that is deeply distressed:
  And it always looks grave at a pun.

"The fourth is its fondness for bathing-machines,
  Which it constantly carries about,
And believes that they add to the beauty of scenes—
  A sentiment open to doubt.

"The fifth is ambition. It next will be right
  To describe each particular batch:
Distinguishing those that have feathers, and bite,
  From those that have whiskers, and scratch.

"For, although common Snarks do no manner of harm,
  Yet, I feel it my duty to say,
Some are Boojums—" The Bellman broke off in alarm,
  For the Baker had fainted away.

## FIT THE THIRD

### THE BAKER'S TALE

They roused him with muffins—they roused him with ice—
  They roused him with mustard and cress—
They roused him with jam and judicious advice—
  They set him conundrums to guess.

When at length he sat up and was able to speak,
  His sad story he offered to tell:
And the Bellman cried "Silence! Not even a shriek!"
  And excitedly tingled his bell.

There was silence supreme! Not a shriek, not a scream,
  Scarcely even a howl or a groan,
As the man they called "Ho!" told his story of woe
  In an antediluvian tone.

"My father and mother were honest, though poor—"
  "Skip all that!" cried the Bellman in haste.
"If it once becomes dark, there's no chance of a Snark—
  We have hardly a minute to waste!"

"I skip forty years," said the Baker, in tears,
  "And proceed without further remark
To the day when you took me aboard of your ship
  To help you in hunting the Snark.

"A dear uncle of mine (after whom I was named)
    Remarked, when I bade him farewell—"
"Oh, skip your dear uncle!" the Bellman exclaimed,
    As he angrily tingled his bell.

"He remarked to me then," said that mildest of men,
    " 'If your Snark be a Snark, that is right:
Fetch it home by all means—you may serve it with greens,
    And it's handy for striking a light.

" 'You may seek it with thimbles—and seek it with care;
    You may hunt it with forks and hope;
You may threaten its life with a railway-share;
    You may charm it with smiles and soap—' "

("That's exactly the method," the Bellman bold
    In a hasty parenthesis cried,
"That's exactly the way I have always been told
    That the capture of Snarks should be tried!")

" 'But oh, beamish nephew, beware of the day,
    If your Snark be a Boojum! For then
You will softly and suddenly vanish away,
    And never be met with again!'

"It is this, it is this that oppresses my soul,
    When I think of my uncle's last words:
And my heart is like nothing so much as a bowl
    Brimming over with quivering curds!

"It is this, it is this—" "We have had that before!"
    The Bellman indignantly said.
And the Baker replied "Let me say it once more.
    It is this, it is this that I dread!

"I engage with the Snark—every night after dark—
    In a dreamy delirious fight:

I serve it with greens in those shadowy scenes,
    And I use it for striking a light:

"But if ever I meet with a Boojum, that day,
    In a moment (of this I am sure),
I shall softly and suddenly vanish away—
    And the notion I cannot endure!"

## FIT THE FOURTH
### THE HUNTING

The Bellman looked uffish, and wrinkled his brow.
    "If only you'd spoken before!
It's excessively awkward to mention it now,
    With the Snark, so to speak, at the door!

"We should all of us grieve, as you well may believe,
    If you never were met with again—
But surely, my man, when the voyage began,
    You might have suggested it then?

"It's excessively awkward to mention it now—
    As I think I've already remarked."
And the man they called "Hi!" replied, with a sigh,
    "I informed you the day we embarked.

"You may charge me with murder—or want of sense—
    (We are all of us weak at times):
But the slightest approach to a false pretence
    Was never among my crimes!

"I said it in Hebrew—I said it in Dutch—
    I said it in German and Greek:
But I wholly forgot (and it vexes me much)
    That English is what you speak!"

"'Tis a pitiful tale," said the Bellman, whose face
    Had grown longer at every word:

"But, now that you've stated the whole of your case,
    More debate would be simply absurd.

"The rest of my speech" (he explained to his men)
    "You shall hear when I've leisure to speak it.
But the Snark is at hand, let me tell you again!
    'Tis your glorious duty to seek it!

"To seek it with thimbles, to seek it with care;
    To pursue it with forks and hope;
To threaten its life with a railway-share;
    To charm it with smiles and soap!

"For the Snark's a peculiar creature, that won't
    Be caught in a commonplace way.
Do all that you know, and try all that you don't:
    Not a chance must be wasted to-day!

"For England expects—I forbear to proceed:
    'Tis a maxim tremendous, but trite:
And you'd best be unpacking the things that you need
    To rig yourselves out for the fight."

Then the Banker endorsed a blank cheque (which he crossed),
    And changed his loose silver for notes.
The Baker with care combed his whiskers and hair,
    And shook the dust out of his coats.

The Boots and the Broker were sharpening a spade—
    Each working the grindstone in turn:
But the Beaver went on making lace, and displayed
    No interest in the concern:

Though the Barrister tried to appeal to its pride,
    And vainly proceeded to cite
A number of cases, in which making laces
    Had proved an infringement of right.

The maker of Bonnets ferociously planned
    A novel arrangement of bows:
While the Billiard-marker with quivering hand
    Was chalking the tip of his nose.

But the Butcher turned nervous, and dressed himself fine,
    With yellow kid gloves and a ruff—
Said he felt it exactly like going to dine,
    Which the Bellman declared was all "stuff."

"Introduce me, now there's a good fellow," he said,
    "If we happen to meet it together!"
And the Bellman sagaciously nodding his head,
    Said "That must depend on the weather."

The Beaver went simply galumphing about,
    And seeing the Butcher so shy:
And even the Baker, though stupid and stout,
    Made an effort to wink with one eye.

"Be a man!" said the Bellman in wrath, as he heard
    The Butcher beginning to sob.
"Should we meet with a Jubjub, that desperate bird,
    We shall need all our strength for the job!"

### FIT THE FIFTH

#### THE BEAVER'S LESSON

They sought it with thimbles, they sought it with care;
    They pursued it with forks and hope;
They threatened its life with a railway-share;
    They charmed it with smiles and soap.

Then the Butcher contrived an ingenious plan
    For making a separate sally;
And had fixed on a spot unfrequented by man,
    A dismal and desolate valley.

But the very same plan to the Beaver occurred:
　　It had chosen the very same place:
Yet neither betrayed, by a sign or a word,
　　The disgust that appeared in his face.

Each thought he was thinking of nothing but "Snark"
　　And the glorious work of the day;
And each tried to pretend that he did not remark
　　That the other was going that way.

But the valley grew narrow and narrower still,
　　And the evening got darker and colder,
Till (merely from nervousness, not from goodwill)
　　They marched along shoulder to shoulder.

Then a scream, shrill and high, rent the shuddering sky,
　　And they knew that some danger was near:
The Beaver turned pale to the tip of its tail,
　　And even the Butcher felt queer.

He thought of his childhood, left far far behind—
　　That blissful and innocent state—
The sound so exactly recalled to his mind
　　A pencil that squeaks on a slate!

"'Tis the voice of the Jubjub !" he suddenly cried.
　　(This man, that they used to call "Dunce.")
"As the Bellman would tell you," he added with pride,
　　"I have uttered that sentiment once.

"'Tis the note of the Jubjub! Keep count, I entreat;
　　You will find I have told it you twice.
'Tis the song of the Jubjub! The proof is complete,
　　If only I've stated it thrice."

The Beaver had counted with scrupulous care,
　　Attending to every word:

But it fairly lost heart, and outgrabe in despair,
    When the third repetition occurred.

It felt that, in spite of all possible pains,
    It had somehow contrived to lose count,
And the only thing now was to rack its poor brains
    By reckoning up the amount.

"Two added to one—if that could but be done,"
    It said, "with one's fingers and thumbs!"
Recollecting with tears how, in earlier years,
    It had taken no pains with its sums.

"The thing can be done," said the Butcher, "I think.
    The thing must be done, I am sure.
The thing shall be done! Bring me paper and ink,
    The best there is time to procure."

The Beaver brought paper, portfolio, pens,
    And ink in unfailing supplies:
While strange creepy creatures came out of their dens,
    And watched them with wondering eyes.

So engrossed was the Butcher, he heeded them not,
    As he wrote with a pen in each hand,
And explained all the while in a popular style
    Which the Beaver could well understand.

"Taking Three as the subject to reason about—
    A convenient number to state—
We add Seven, and Ten, and then multiply out
    By One Thousand diminished by Eight.

"The result we proceed to divide, as you see,
    By Nine Hundred and Ninety and Two:
Then subtract Seventeen, and the answer must be
    Exactly and perfectly true.

"The method employed I would gladly explain,
 While I have it so clear in my head,
If I had but the time and you had but the brain—
 But much yet remains to be said.

"In one moment I've seen what has hitherto been
 Enveloped in absolute mystery,
And without extra charge I will give you at large
 A Lesson in Natural History."

In his genial way he proceeded to say
 (Forgetting all laws of propriety,
And that giving instruction, without introduction,
 Would have caused quite a thrill in Society),

"As to temper the Jubjub's a desperate bird,
 Since it lives in perpetual passion:
Its taste in costume is entirely absurd—
 It is ages ahead of the fashion:

"But it knows any friend it has met once before:
 It never will look at a bribe:
And in charity-meetings it stands at the door,
 And collects—though it does not subscribe.

"Its flavour when cooked is more exquisite far
 Than mutton, or oysters, or eggs:
(Some think it keeps best in an ivory jar,
 And some, in mahogany kegs:)

"You boil it in sawdust: you salt it in glue:
 You condense it with locusts and tape:
Still keeping one principal object in view—
 To preserve its symmetrical shape."

The Butcher would gladly have talked till next day,
 But he felt that the Lesson must end,

And he wept with delight in attempting to say
    He considered the Beaver his friend.

While the Beaver confessed, with affectionate looks
    More eloquent even than tears,
It had learned in ten minutes far more than all books
    Would have taught it in seventy years.

They returned hand-in-hand, and the Bellman, unmanned
    (For a moment) with noble emotion,
Said "This amply repays all the wearisome days
    We have spent on the billowy ocean!"

Such friends, as the Beaver and Butcher became,
    Have seldom if ever been known;
In winter or summer, 'twas always the same—
    You could never meet either alone.

And when quarrels arose—as one frequently finds
    Quarrels will, spite of every endeavour—
The song of the Jubjub recurred to their minds,
    And cemented their friendship for ever!

### FIT THE SIXTH

#### THE BARRISTER'S DREAM

They sought it with thimbles, they sought it with care;
    They pursued it with forks and hope;
They threatened its life with a railway-share;
    They charmed it with smiles and soap.

But the Barrister, weary of proving in vain
    That the Beaver's lace-making was wrong,
Fell asleep, and in dreams saw the creature quite plain
    That his fancy had dwelt on so long.

He dreamed that he stood in a shadowy Court,
    Where the Snark, with a glass in its eye,

Dressed in gown, bands, and wig, was defending a pig
  On the charge of deserting its sty.

The Witnesses proved, without error or flaw,
  That the sty was deserted when found:
And the Judge kept explaining the state of the law
  In a soft under-current of sound.

The indictment had never been clearly expressed,
  And it seemed that the Snark had begun,
And had spoken three hours, before any one guessed
  What the pig was supposed to have done.

The Jury had each formed a different view
  (Long before the indictment was read),
And they all spoke at once, so that none of them knew
  One word that the others had said.

"You must know—" said the Judge: but the Snark exclaimed "Fudge!"
  That statute is obsolete quite!
Let me tell you, my friends, the whole question depends
  On an ancient manorial right.

"In the matter of Treason the pig would appear
  To have aided, but scarcely abetted:
While the charge of Insolvency fails, it is clear,
  If you grant the plea 'never indebted.'

"The fact of Desertion I will not dispute:
  But its guilt, as I trust, is removed
(So far as relates to the costs of this suit)
  By the Alibi which has been proved.

"My poor client's fate now depends on your votes."
  Here the speaker sat down in his place,
And directed the Judge to refer to his notes
  And briefly to sum up the case.

But the Judge said he never had summed up before;
    So the Snark undertook it instead,
And summed it so well that it came to far more
    Than the Witnesses ever had said!

When the verdict was called for, the Jury declined,
    As the word was so puzzling to spell;
But they ventured to hope that the Snark wouldn't mind
    Undertaking that duty as well.

So the Snark found the verdict, although, as it owned,
    It was spent with the toils of the day:
When it said the word "GUILTY!" the Jury all groaned,
    And some of them fainted away.

Then the Snark pronounced sentence, the Judge being quite
    Too nervous to utter a word:
When it rose to its feet, there was silence like night,
    And the fall of a pin might be heard.

"Transportation for life" was the sentence it gave,
    "And *then* to be fined forty pound."
The Jury all cheered, though the Judge said he feared
    That the phrase was not legally sound.

But their wild exultation was suddenly checked
    When the jailer informed them, with tears,
Such a sentence would have not the slightest effect,
    As the pig had been dead for some years.

The Judge left the Court, looking deeply disgusted:
    But the Snark, though a little aghast,
As the lawyer to whom the defence was intrusted,
    Went bellowing on to the last.

Thus the Barrister dreamed, while the bellowing seemed
    To grow every moment more clear:

Till he woke to the knell of a furious bell,
   Which the Bellman rang close at his ear.

## FIT THE SEVENTH

### THE BANKER'S FATE

They sought it with thimbles, they sought it with care;
   They pursued it with forks and hope;
They threatened its life with a railway-share;
   They charmed it with smiles and soap.

And the Banker, inspired with a courage so new
   It was matter for general remark,
Rushed madly ahead and was lost to their view
   In his zeal to discover the Snark.

But while he was seeking with thimbles and care,
   A Bandersnatch swiftly drew nigh
And grabbed at the Banker, who shrieked in despair,
   For he knew it was useless to fly.

He offered large discount—he offered a cheque
   (Drawn "to bearer") for seven-pounds-ten:
But the Bandersnatch merely extended its neck
   And grabbed at the Banker again.

Without rest or pause—while those frumious jaws
   Went savagely snapping around—
He skipped and he hopped, and he floundered and flopped,
   Till fainting he fell to the ground.

The Bandersnatch fled as the others appeared
   Led on by that fear-stricken yell:
And the Bellman remarked "It is just as I feared!"
   And solemnly tolled on his bell.

He was black in the face, and they scarcely could trace
    The least likeness to what he had been:
While so great was his fright that his waistcoat turned white—
    A wonderful thing to be seen!

To the horror of all who were present that day.
    He uprose in full evening dress,
And with senseless grimaces endeavoured to say
    What his tongue could no longer express.

Down he sank in a chair—ran his hands through his hair—
    And chanted in mimsiest tones
Words whose utter inanity proved his insanity,
    While he rattled a couple of bones.

"Leave him here to his fate—it is getting so late!"
    The Bellman exclaimed in a fright.
"We have lost half the day. Any further delay,
    And we sha'n't catch a Snark before night!"

### FIT THE EIGHTH
#### THE VANISHING

They sought it with thimbles, they sought it with care;
    They pursued it with forks and hope;
They threatened its life with a railway-share;
    They charmed it with smiles and soap.

They shuddered to think that the chase might fail,
    And the Beaver, excited at last,
Went bounding along on the tip of its tail,
    For the daylight was nearly past.

"There is Thingumbob shouting!" the Bellman said.
    "He is shouting like mad, only hark!
He is waving his hands, he is wagging his head,
    He has certainly found a Snark!"

They gazed in delight, while the Butcher exclaimed
   "He was always a desperate wag!"
They beheld him—their Baker—their hero unnamed—
   On the top of a neighbouring crag,

Erect and sublime, for one moment of time.
   In the next, that wild figure they saw
(As if stung by a spasm) plunge into a chasm,
   While they waited and listened in awe.

"It's a Snark!" was the sound that first came to their ears,
   And seemed almost too good to be true.
Then followed a torrent of laughter and cheers:
   Then the ominous words "It's a Boo—"

Then, silence. Some fancied they heard in the air
   A weary and wandering sigh
That sounded like "—jum!" but the others declare
   It was only a breeze that went by.

They hunted till darkness came on, but they found
   Not a button, or feather, or mark,
By which they could tell that they stood on the ground
   Where the Baker had met with the Snark.

In the midst of the word he was trying to say,
   In the midst of his laughter and glee,
He had softly and suddenly vanished away—
   For the Snark *was* a Boojum, you see.

# The Walrus and the Carpenter

The sun was shining on the sea,
   Shining with all his might:
He did his very best to make
   The billows smooth and bright—
And this was odd, because it was
   The middle of the night.

The moon was shining sulkily,
   Because she thought the sun
Had got no business to be there
   After the day was done—
"It's very rude of him," she said,
   "To come and spoil the fun!"

The sea was wet as wet could be,
   The sands were dry as dry.
You could not see a cloud, because
   No cloud was in the sky:
No birds were flying over head—
   There were no birds to fly.

The Walrus and the Carpenter
   Were walking close at hand;
They wept like anything to see
   Such quantities of sand:
"If this were only cleared away,"
   They said, "it would be grand!"

"If seven maids with seven mops
   Swept it for half a year,
Do you suppose," the Walrus said,
   "That they could get it clear?"
"I doubt it," said the Carpenter,
   And shed a bitter tear.

"O Oysters, come and walk with us!"
    The Walrus did beseech.
"A pleasant walk, a pleasant talk,
    Along the briny beach:
We cannot do with more than four,
    To give a hand to each."

The eldest Oyster looked at him.
    But never a word he said:
The eldest Oyster winked his eye,
    And shook his heavy head—
Meaning to say he did not choose
    To leave the oyster-bed.

But four young oysters hurried up,
    All eager for the treat:
Their coats were brushed, their faces washed,
    Their shoes were clean and neat—
And this was odd, because, you know,
    They hadn't any feet.

Four other Oysters followed them,
    And yet another four;
And thick and fast they came at last,
    And more, and more, and more—
All hopping through the frothy waves,
    And scrambling to the shore.

The Walrus and the Carpenter
    Walked on a mile or so,
And then they rested on a rock
    Conveniently low:
And all the little Oysters stood
    And waited in a row.

"The time has come," the Walrus said,
   "To talk of many things:
Of shoes—and ships—and sealing-wax—
   Of cabbages—and kings—
And why the sea is boiling hot—
   And whether pigs have wings."

"But wait a bit," the Oysters cried,
   "Before we have our chat;
For some of us are out of breath,
   And all of us are fat!"
"No hurry!" said the Carpenter.
   They thanked him much for that.

"A loaf of bread," the Walrus said,
   "Is what we chiefly need:
Pepper and vinegar besides
   Are very good indeed—
Now if you're ready Oysters dear,
   We can begin to feed."

"But not on us!" the Oysters cried,
   Turning a little blue,
"After such kindness, that would be
   A dismal thing to do!"
"The night is fine," the Walrus said
   "Do you admire the view?"

"It was so kind of you to come!
   And you are very nice!"
The Carpenter said nothing but
   "Cut us another slice:
I wish you were not quite so deaf—
   I've had to ask you twice!"

"It seems a shame," the Walrus said,
  "To play them such a trick,
After we've brought them out so far,
  And made them trot so quick!"
The Carpenter said nothing but
  "The butter's spread too thick!"

"I weep for you," the Walrus said.
  "I deeply sympathize."
With sobs and tears he sorted out
  Those of the largest size.
Holding his pocket-handkerchief
  Before his streaming eyes.

"O Oysters," said the Carpenter.
  "You've had a pleasant run!
Shall we be trotting home again?"
  But answer came there none—
And that was scarcely odd, because
  They'd eaten every one.

# FRANCIS THOMPSON
## (1859–1907)

## The Hound of Heaven

### I

I fled Him, down the nights and down the days;
  I fled Him, down the arches of the years;
I fled Him, down the labyrinthine ways
    Of my own mind; and in the mist of tears
I hid from Him, and under running laughter.
        Up vistaed hopes I sped;
        And shot, precipitated
Adown Titanic glooms of chasmed fears,
  From those strong Feet that followed, followed after.
        But with unhurrying chase,
        And unperturbèd pace,
  Deliberate speed, majestic instancy,
        They beat—and a Voice beat
        More instant than the Feet—
"All things betray thee, who betrayest Me."

### II

        I pleaded, outlaw-wise,
By many a hearted casement, curtained red,
  Trellised with intertwining charities;
(For, though I knew His love Who followèd,
        Yet was I sore adread
Lest, having Him, I must have naught beside)
But, if one little casement parted wide,
  The gust of His approach would clash it to.

Fear wist not to evade, as Love wist to pursue.
Across the margent of the world I fled,
   And troubled the gold gateways of the stars,
   Smiting for shelter on their changèd bars;
        Fretted to dulcet jars
And silvern chatter the pale ports o' the moon.
I said to dawn: Be sudden—to eve: Be soon;
   With thy young skiey blossom heap me over
        From this tremendous Lover!
Float thy vague veil about me, lest He see!
   I tempted all His servitors, but to find
My own betrayal in their constancy,
In faith to Him their fickleness to me,
   Their traitorous trueness, and their loyal deceit.
To all swift things for swiftness did I sue;
   Clung to the whistling mane of every wind.
      But whether they swept, smoothly fleet,
      The long savannahs of the blue;
       Or whether, Thunder-driven,
      They clanged his chariot 'thwart a heaven,
Plashy with flying lightnings round the spurn o' their feet:—
   Fear wist not to evade as Love wist to pursue.
       Still with unhurrying chase,
       And unperturbèd pace,
Deliberate speed, majestic instancy,
       Came on the following Feet,
       And a Voice above their beat—
"Naught shelters thee, who wilt not shelter Me."

### III

I sought no more that, after which I strayed,
      In face of man or maid;
But still within the little children's eyes
      Seems something, something that replies,
*They* at least are for me, surely for me!
I turned me to them very wistfully;
But just as their young eyes grew sudden fair

With dawning answers there,
Their angel plucked them from me by the hair.
"Come then, ye other children, Nature's—share
With me" (said I) "your delicate fellowship;
Let me greet you lip to lip,
Let me twine with you caresses,
Wantoning
With our Lady-Mother's vagrant tresses,
Banqueting
With her in her wind-walled palace,
Underneath her azured daïs,
Quaffing, as your taintless way is,
From a chalice
Lucent-weeping out of the dayspring."
So it was done:
*I* in their delicate fellowship was one—
Drew the bolt of Nature's secrecies.
*I* knew all the swift importings
On the wilful face of skies;
I knew how the clouds arise
Spumed of the wild sea-snortings;
All that's born or dies
Rose and drooped with—made them shapers
Of mine own moods, or wailful or divine—
With them joyed and was bereaven.
I was heavy with the even,
When she lit her glimmering tapers
Round the day's dead sanctities.
I laughed in the morning's eyes.
I triumphed and I saddened with all weather,
Heaven and I wept together,
And its sweet tears were salt with mortal mine;
Against the red throb of its sunset-heart
I laid my own to beat,
And share commingling heat;
But not by that, by that, was eased my human smart.
In vain my tears were wet on Heaven's grey cheek.

For ah! we know not what each other says,
  These things and I; in sound *I* speak—
*Their* sound is but their stir, they speak by silences.
Nature, poor stepdame, cannot slake my drouth;
  Let her, if she would owe me,
Drop yon blue bosom-veil of sky, and show me
  The breasts o' her tenderness:
Never did any milk of hers once bless
   My thirsting mouth.
   Nigh arid nigh draws the chase,
   With unperturbèd pace,
  Deliberate speed, majestic instancy
   And past those noisèd feet
   A voice comes yet more fleet—
"Lo! naught contents thee, who content'st not Me."


IV

Naked I wait Thy love's uplifted stroke!
My harness piece by piece Thou hast hewn from me,
  And smitten me to my knee;
 I am defenceless utterly.
 I slept, methinks, and woke,
And, slowly gazing, find me stripped in sleep.
In the rash lustihead of my young powers,
 I shook the pillaring hours
And pulled my life upon me; grimed with smears,
I stand amid the dust o' the mounded years—
My mangled youth lies dead beneath the heap.
My days have crackled and gone up in smoke,
Have puffed and burst as sun-starts on a stream.
 Yea, faileth now even dream
The dreamer, and the lute the lutanist;
Even the linked fantasies, in whose blossomy twist
I swung the earth a trinket at my wrist,
Are yielding; cords of all too weak account
For earth with heavy griefs so overplussed.
 Ah! is Thy love indeed

A weed, albeit an amaranthine weed,
Suffering no flowers except its own to mount?
      Ah must—
      Designer infinite!—
Ah! must Thou char the wood ere Thou canst limn with it?
My freshness spent its wavering shower i' the dust;
And now my heart is as a broken fount,
Wherein tear-drippings stagnate, spilt down ever
      From the dank thoughts that shiver
Upon the sighful branches of my mind.
      Such is; what is to be?
The pulp so bitter, how shall taste the rind?
I dimly guess what Time in mists confounds;
Yet ever and anon a trumpet sounds
From the hid battlements of Eternity,
Those shaken mists a space unsettle, then
Round the half-glimpsèd turrets slowly wash again;
      But not ere him who summoneth
      I first have seen, enwound
With glooming robes purpureal, cypress-crowned;
His name I know, and what his trumpet saith.
Whether man's heart or life it be which yields
      Thee harvest, must Thy harvest fields
      Be dunged with rotten death?
        Now of that long pursuit
        Comes on at hand the bruit;
That Voice is round me like a bursting sea:
      "And is thy earth so marred,
      Shattered in shard on shard?
Lo, all things fly thee, for thou fliest Me!

V

      "Strange, piteous, futile thing!
Wherefore should any set thee love apart?
Seeing none but I makes much of naught" (He said),
"And human love needs human meriting:
      How hast thou merited—

Of all man's clotted clay the dingiest clot?
    Alack, thou knowest not
How little worthy of any love thou art!
Whom wilt thou find to love ignoble thee,
    Save Me, save only Me?
All which I took from thee I did but take,
    Not for thy harms,
But just that thou might'st seek it in My arms.
    All which thy child's mistake
Fancies as lost, I have stored for thee at home:
    Rise, clasp My hand, and come."

### VI

    Halts by me that footfall:
    Is my gloom, after all,
Shade of His hand, outstretched caressingly?
    "Ah, fondest, blindest, weakest,
    I am He Whom thou seekest!
Thou dravest love from thee, who dravest Me."

# RUDYARD KIPLING

## (1865–1936)

## The Ballad of East and West

*Oh, East is East, and West is West, and never the twain shall meet,*
*Till Earth and Sky stand presently at God's great Judgment Seat;*
*But there is neither East nor West, Border, nor Breed, nor Birth,*
*When two strong men stand face to face, tho' they come from the ends of the earth!*

Kamal is out with twenty men to raise the Border side,
And he has lifted the Colonel's mare that is the Colonel's pride:
He has lifted her out of the stable-door between the dawn and the day,
And turned the calkins upon her feet, and ridden her far away.
Then up and spoke the Colonel's son that led a troop of the Guides:
"Is there never a man of all my men can say where Kamal hides?"
Then up and spoke Mahommed Khan, the son of the Ressaldar,
"If ye know the track of the morning-mist, ye know where his pickets are.
At dusk he harries the Abazai—at dawn he is into Bonair,
But he must go by Fort Bukloh to his own place to fare,
So if ye gallop to Fort Bukloh as fast as a bird can fly,
By the favor of God ye may cut him off ere he win to the Tongue of Jagai,
But if he be passed the Tongue of Jagai, right swiftly turn ye then,
For the length and the breadth of that grisly plain is sown with Kamal's men.
There is rock to the left, and rock to the right, and low lean thorn between,
And ye may hear a breech-bolt snick where never a man is seen."
The Colonel's son has taken a horse, and a raw rough dun was he,
With the mouth of a bell and the heart of Hell, and the head of the gallows-tree.
The Colonel's son to the Fort has won, they bid him stay to eat—
Who rides at the tail of a Border thief, he sits not long at his meat.
He's up and away from Fort Bukloh as fast as he can fly,

Till he was aware of his father's mare in the gut of the Tongue of Jagai,
Till he was aware of his father's mare with Kamal upon her back,
And when he could spy the white of her eye, he made the pistol crack.
He has fired once, he has fired twice, but the whistling ball went wide.
"Ye shoot like a soldier," Kamal said. "Show now if ye can ride."
It's up and over the Tongue of Jagai, as blown dust-devils go,
The dun he fled like a stag of ten, but the mare like a barren doe.
The dun he leaned against the bit and slugged his head above,
But the red mare played with the snaffle-bars, as a maiden plays with a glove.
There was rock to the left and rock to the right, and low lean thorn between,
And thrice he heard a breech-bolt snick tho' never a man was seen.
They have ridden the low moon out of the sky, their hoofs drum up the dawn,
The dun he went like a wounded bull, but the mare like a new-roused fawn.
The dun he fell at a water-course—in a woful heap fell he,
And Kamal has turned the red mare back, and pulled the rider free.
He has knocked the pistol out of his hand—small room was there to strive,
"'Twas only by favor of mine," quoth he, "ye rode so long alive:
There was not a rock for twenty mile, there was not a clump of tree,
But covered a man of my own men with his rifle cocked on his knee.
If I had raised my bridle-hand, as I have held it low,
The little jackals that flee so fast, were feasting all in a row:
If I had bowed my head on my breast, as I have held it high,
The kite that whistles above us now were gorged till she could not fly."
Lightly answered the Colonel's son: "Do good to bird and beast,
But count who come for the broken meats before thou makest a feast.
If there should follow a thousand swords to carry my bones away,
Belike the price of a jackal's meal were more than a thief could pay.
They will feed their horse on the standing crop, their men on the garnered grain,
The thatch of the byres will serve their fires when all the cattle are slain.
But if thou thinkest the price be fair,—thy brethren wait to sup,
The hound is kin to the jackal-spawn,—howl, dog, and call them up!
And if thou thinkest the price be high, in steer and gear and stack,
Give me my father's mare again, and I'll fight my own way back!"
Kamal has gripped him by the hand and set him upon his feet.
"No talk shall be of dogs," said he, "when wolf and grey wolf meet.
May I eat dirt if thou hast hurt of me in deed or breath;
What dam of lances brought thee forth to jest at the dawn with Death?"

Lightly answered the Colonel's son: "I hold by the blood of my clan:
Take up the mare for my father's gift—by God, she has carried a man!"
The red mare ran to the Colonel's son, and nuzzled against his breast,
"We be two strong men," said Kamal then, "but she loveth the younger best.
So she shall go with a lifter's dower, my turquoise-studded rein,
My broidered saddle and saddle-cloth, and silver stirrups twain."
The Colonel's son a pistol drew and held it muzzle-end,
"Ye have taken the one from a foe," said he; "will ye take the mate from a friend?"
"A gift for a gift," said Kamal straight; "a limb for the risk of a limb.
"Thy father has sent his son to me, I'll send my son to him!"
With that he whistled his only son, that dropped from a mountain-crest—
He trod the ling like a buck in spring, and he looked like a lance in rest.
"Now here is thy master," Kamal said, "who leads a troop of the Guides,
And thou must ride at his leftside as shield on shoulder rides.
Till Death or I cut loose the tie, at camp and board and bed,
Thy life is his—thy fate it is to guard him with thy head.
So thou must eat the White Queen's meat, and all her foes are thine,
And thou must harry thy father's hold for the peace of the Border-line,
And thou must make a trooper tough and hack thy way to power—
Belike they will raise thee to Ressaldar when I am hanged in Peshawur."
They have looked each other between the eyes, and there they found no fault,
They have taken the Oath of the Brother-in-Blood on leavened bread and salt:
They have taken the Oath of the Brother-in-Blood on fire and fresh-cut sod,
On the hilt and the haft of the Khyber knife, and the Wondrous Names of God.
The Colonel's son he rides the mare and Kamal's boy the dun,
And two have come back to Fort Bukloh where there went forth but one.
And when they drew to the Quarter-Guard, full twenty swords flew clear—
There was not a man but carried his feud with the blood of the mountaineer.
"Ha' done! ha' done!" said the Colonel's son. "Put up the steel at your sides!
Last night ye had struck at a Border thief—tonight 'tis a man of the Guides!"

*Oh, East is East, and West is West, and never the two shall meet,*
*Till Earth and Sky stand presently at God's great Judgment Seat;*
*But there is neither East nor West, Border, nor Breed, nor Birth,*
*When two strong men stand face to face, tho' they come from the ends of the earth.*

# If

If you can keep your head when all about you
   Are losing theirs and blaming it on you,
If you can trust yourself when all men doubt you,
   But make allowance for their doubting too;
If you can wait and not be tired by waiting,
   Or being lied about, don't deal in lies,
Or being hated don't give way to hating,
   And yet don't look too good, nor talk too wise:

If you can dream—and not make dreams your master;
   If you can think—and not make thoughts your aim,
If you can meet with Triumph and Disaster
   And treat those two impostors just the same;
If you can bear to hear the truth you've spoken
   Twisted by knaves to make a trap for fools,
Or watch the things you gave your life to, broken,
   And stoop and build 'em up with worn-out tools:

If you can make one heap of all your winnings
   And risk it on one turn of pitch-and-toss,
And lose, and start again at your beginnings
   And never breathe a word about your loss;
If you can force your heart and nerve and sinew
   To serve your turn long after they are gone,
And so hold on when there is nothing in you
   Except the Will which says to them: "Hold on!"

If you can talk with crowds and keep your virtue,
   Or walk with Kings—nor lose the common touch,
If neither foes nor loving friends can hurt you,
   If all men count with you, but none too much;
If you can fill the unforgiving minute
   With sixty seconds' worth of distance run,
Yours is the Earth and everything that's in it,
   And—which is more—you'll be a Man, my son!

# WILLIAM BUTLER YEATS
## (1865–1939)

## The Lake Isle of Innisfree

I will arise and go now, and go to Innisfree,
And a small cabin built there, of clay and wattles made;
Nine bean rows will I have there, a hive for the honey bee,
And live alone in the bee-loud glade.

And I shall have some peace there, for peace comes dropping slow,
Dropping from the veils of the morning to where the cricket sings;
There midnight's all a glimmer, and noon a purple glow,
And evening full of the linnet's wings.

I will arise and go now, for always night and day
I hear lake water lapping with low sounds by the shore;
While I stand on the roadway, or on the pavement grey,
I hear it in the deep heart's core.

## The Double Vision of Michael Robartes

### I

On the grey rock of Cashel the mind's eye
Has called up the cold spirits that are born
When the old moon is vanished from the sky
And the new still hides her horn.

Under blank eyes and fingers never still
The particular is pounded till it is man,
When had I my own will?
Oh, not since life began.

Constrained, arraigned, baffled, bent and unbent
By these wire-jointed jaws and limbs of wood,
Themselves obedient,
Knowing not evil and good;

Obedient to some hidden magical breath.
They do not even feel, so abstract are they,
So dead beyond our death,
Triumph that we obey.

## II

On the grey rock of Cashel I suddenly saw
A Sphinx with woman breast and lion paw,
A Buddha, hand at rest,
Hand lifted up that blest;

And right between these two a girl at play
That it may be had danced her life away,
For now being dead it seemed
That she of dancing dreamed.

Although I saw it all in the mind's eye
There can be nothing solider till I die;
I saw by the moon's light
Now at its fifteenth night.

One lashed her tail; her eyes lit by the moon
Gazed upon all things known, all things unknown,
In triumph of intellect
With motionless head erect.

That other's moonlit eyeballs never moved,
Being fixed on all things loved, all things unloved,
Yet little peace he had
For those that love are sad.

Oh, little did they care who danced between,
And little she by whom her dance was seen

So that she danced. No thought,
Body perfection brought,

For what but eye and ear silence the mind
With the minute particulars of mankind?
Mind moved yet seemed to stop
As 'twere a spinning-top.

In contemplation had those three so wrought
Upon a moment, and so stretched it out
That they, time overthrown,
Were dead yet flesh and bone.

### III

I knew that I had seen, had seen at last
That girl my unremembering nights hold fast
Or else my dreams that fly,
If I should rub an eye,

And yet in flying fling into my meat
A crazy juice that makes the pulses beat
As though I had been undone
By Homer's Paragon

Who never gave the burning town a thought;
To such a pitch of folly I am brought,
Being caught between the pull
Of the dark moon and the full,

The commonness of thought and images
That have the frenzy of our western seas.
Thereon I made my moan,
And after kissed a stone,

And after that arranged in a song
Seeing that I, ignorant for so long,
Had been rewarded thus
In Cormac's ruined house.

## Easter, 1916

I have met them at close of day
Coming with vivid faces
From counter or desk among grey
Eighteenth-century houses.
I have passed with a nod of the head
Or polite meaningless words,
Or have lingered awhile and said
Polite meaningless words,
And thought before I had done
Of a mocking tale or a gibe
To please a companion
Around the fire at the club,
Being certain that they and I
But lived where motley is worn:
All changed, changed utterly:
A terrible beauty is born.

That woman's days were spent
In ignorant good-will,
Her nights in argument
Until her voice grew shrill.
What voice more sweet than hers
When, young and beautiful,
She rode to harriers?
This man had kept a school
And rode our wingèd horse;
This other his helper and friend
Was coming into his force;
He might have won fame in the end,
So sensitive his nature seemed,
So daring and sweet his thought.
This other man I had dreamed
A drunken, vainglorious lout.
He had done most bitter wrong
To some who are near my heart,

Yet I number him in the song;
He, too, has resigned his part
In the casual comedy;
He, too, has been changed in his turn,
Transformed utterly:
A terrible beauty is born.

Hearts with one purpose alone
Through summer and winter seem
Enchanted to a stone
To trouble the living stream.
The horse that comes from the road,
The rider, the birds that range
From cloud to tumbling cloud,
Minute by minute they change;
A shadow of cloud on the stream
Changes minute by minute;
A horse-hoof slides on the brim,
And a horse plashes within it;
The long-legged moor-hens dive,
And hens to moor-cocks call;
Minute by minute they live:
The stone's in the midst of all.

Too long a sacrifice
Can make a stone of the heart.
O when may it suffice?
That is Heaven's part, our part
To murmur name upon name,
As a mother names her child
When sleep at last has come
On limbs that had run wild.
What is it but nightfall?
No, no, not night but death;
Was it needless death after all?
For England may keep faith
For all that is done and said.

We know their dream; enough
To know they dreamed and are dead;
And what if excess of love
Bewildered them till they died?
I write it out in a verse—
MacDonagh and MacBride
And Connolly and Pearse
Now and in time to be,
Wherever green is worn,
Are changed, changed utterly:
A terrible beauty is born.

## The Second Coming

Turning and turning in the widening gyre
The falcon cannot hear the falconer;
Things fall apart; the centre cannot hold;
Mere anarchy is loosed upon the world,
The blood-dimmed tide is loosed, and everywhere
The ceremony of innocence is drowned;
The best lack all conviction, while the worst
Are full of passionate intensity.

Surely some revelation is at hand;
Surely the Second Coming is at hand.
The Second Coming! Hardly are those words out
When a vast image out of *Spiritus Mundi*
Troubles my sight: somewhere in sands of the desert
A shape with lion body and the head of a man,
A gaze blank and pitiless as the sun,
Is moving its slow thighs, while all about it
Reel shadows of the indignant desert birds.
The darkness drops again; but now I know
That twenty centuries of stony sleep
Were vexed to nightmare by a rocking cradle,
And what rough beast, its hour come round at last,
Slouches towards Bethlehem to be born?

# THOMAS HARDY

## (1840–1928)

## Afterwards

When the Present has latched its postern behind my tremulous stay,
   And the May month flaps its glad green leaves like wings,
Delicate-filmed as new-spun silk, will the people say,
    "He was a man who used to notice such things"?

If it be in the dusk when, like an eyelid's soundless blink,
   The dewfall-hawk comes crossing the shades to alight
Upon the wind-warped upland thorn, will a gazer think,
    "To him this must have been a familiar sight"?

If I pass during some nocturnal blackness, mothy and warm,
   When the hedgehog travels furtively over the lawn,
Will they say, "He strove that such innocent creatures should come to no harm,
    But he could do little for them; and now he is gone"?

If, when hearing that I have been stilled at last, they stand at the door,
   Watching the full-starred heavens that winter sees,
Will this thought rise on those who will meet my face no more,
    "He was one who had an eye for such mysteries"?

And will any say when my bell of quittance is heard in the gloom,
   And a crossing breeze cuts a pause in its outrollings,
Till they rise again, as they were a new bell's boom,
    "He hears it not now, but used to notice such things"?

## Neutral Tones

We stood by a pond that winter day,
And the sun was white, as though chidden of God,
And a few leaves lay on the starving sod,
    —They had fallen from an ash, and were gray.

Your eyes on me were as eyes that rove
Over tedious riddles solved years ago;
And words played between us to and fro—
    On which lost the more by our love.

The smile on your mouth was the deadest thing
Alive enough to have strength to die;
And a grin of bitterness swept thereby
    Like an ominous bird a-wing. . . .

Since then, keen lessons that love deceives,
And wrings with wrong, have shaped to me
Your face, and the God-curst sun, and a tree,
    And a pond edged with grayish leaves.

## The Darkling Thrush

I leant upon a coppice gate
    When Frost was spectre-gray,
And Winter's dregs made desolate
    The weakening eye of day.
The tangle bine-stems scored the sky
    Like strings of broken lyres,
And all mankind that haunted nigh
    Had sought their household fires.

The land's sharp features seemed to be
    The Century's corpse outleant,
His crypt the cloudy canopy,
    The wind his death-lament.

The ancient pulse of germ and birth
   Was shrunken hard and dry,
And every spirit upon earth
   Seemed fervourless as I.

At once a voice arose among
   The bleak twigs overhead
In a full-hearted evensong
   Of joy illimited;
An aged thrush, frail, gaunt, and small,
   In blast-beruffled plume,
Had chosen thus to fling his soul
   Upon the growing gloom.

So little cause for carollings
   Of such estatic sound
Was written on terrestrial things
   Afar or nigh around,
That I could think there trembled through
   His happy good-night air
Some blessed Hope, whereof he knew
   And I was unaware.

# Hap

If but some vengeful god would call to me
From up the sky, and laugh: "Thou suffering thing,
Know that thy sorrow is my ecstasy,
That thy love's loss is my hate's profiting!"

Then would I bear, and clench myself, and die,
Steeled by the sense of ire unmerited;
Half-eased in that a Powerfuller than I
Had willed and meted me the tears I shed.

But not so. How arrives it joy lies slain,
And why unblooms the best hope ever sown?

—Crass Casualty obstructs the sun and rain,
And dicing Time for gladness casts a moan. . . .
These purblind Doomsters had as readily strown
Blisses about my pilgrimage as pain.

———

# Channel Firing

That night your great guns, unawares,
Shook all our coffins as we lay,
And broke the chancel window-squares,
We thought it was the Judgment-day

And sat upright. While drearisome
Arose the howl of wakened hounds:
The mouse let fall the altar-crumb,
The worms drew back into the mounds,

The glebe cow drooled. Till God called, "No;
It's gunnery practice out at sea
Just as before you went below;
The world is as it used to be:

"All nations striving strong to make
Red war yet redder. Mad as hatters
They do no more for Christés sake
Than you who are helpless in such matters.

"That this is not the judgment-hour
For some of them's a blessed thing,
For if it were they'd have to scour
Hell's floor for so much threatening. . . .

"Ha, ha. It will be warmer when
I blow the trumpet (if indeed
I ever do; for you are men,
And rest eternal sorely need)."

So down we lay again. "I wonder,
Will the world ever saner be,"
Said one, "than when He sent us under
In our indifferent century!"

And many a skeleton shook, his head.
"Instead of preaching forty year,"
My neighbour Parson Thirdly said,
"I wish I had stuck to pipes and beer."

Again the guns disturbed the hour,
Roaring their readiness to avenge,
As far inland as Stourton Tower,
And Camelot, and starlit Stonehenge.

## The Convergence of the Twain

### Lines on the loss of the Titanic

I

In a solitude of the sea
Deep from human vanity,
And the Pride of Life that planned her, stilly couches she.

II

Steel chambers, late the pyres
Of her salamandrine fires,
Cold currents thrid, and turn to rhythmic tidal lyres.

III

Over the mirrors meant
To glass the opulent
The sea-worm crawls—grotesque, slimed, dumb, indifferent.

IV

Jewels in joy designed
To ravish the sensuous mind
Lie lightless, all their sparkles bleared and black and blind.

### V

Dim moon-eyed fishes near
Gaze at the gilded gear
And query: "What does this vaingloriousness down here?" . . .

### VI

Well: while was fashioning
This creature of cleaving wing,
The Immanent Will that stirs and urges everything

### VII

Prepared a sinister mate
For her—so gaily great—
A Shape of Ice, for the time far and dissociate.

### VIII

And as the smart ship grew
In stature, grace, and hue,
In shadowy silent distance grew the Iceberg too.

### IX

Alien they seemed to be:
No mortal eye could see
The intimate welding of their later history,

### X

Or sign that they were bent
By paths coincident
On being anon twin halves of one august event,

### XI

Till the Spinner of the Years
Said "Now!" And each one hears,
And consummation comes, and jars two hemispheres.

# OSCAR WILDE
## (1854–1900)

## The Ballad of Reading Gaol

### I

He did not wear his scarlet coat,
  For blood and wine are red,
And blood and wine were on his hands
  When they found him with the dead.
The poor dead woman whom he loved,
  And murdered in her bed.

He walked amongst the Trial Men
  In a suit of shabby gray;
A cricket cap was on his head,
  And his step seemed light and gay;
But I never saw a man who looked
  So wistfully at the day.

I never saw a man who looked
  With such a wistful eye
Upon that little tent of blue
  Which prisoners call the sky,
And at every drifting cloud that went
  With sails of silver by.

I walked, with other souls in pain,
  Within another ring,
And was wondering if the man had done
  A great or little thing,

When a voice behind me whispered low,
  "*That fellow's got to swing.*"

Dear Christ! the very prison walls
  Suddenly seemed to reel,
And the sky above my head became
  Like a casque of scorching steel;
And, though I was a soul in pain,
  My pain I could not feel.

I only knew what hunted thought
  Quickened his step, and why
He looked upon the garish day
  With such a wistful eye;
The man had killed the thing he loved,
  And so he had to die.

Yet each man kills the thing he loves,
  By each let this be heard,
Some do it with a bitter look,
  Some with a flattering word,
The coward does it with a kiss,
  The brave man with a sword!

Some kill their love when they are young,
  And some when they are old;
Some strangle with the hands of Lust,
  Some with the hands of Gold:
The kindest use a knife, because
  The dead so soon grow cold.

Some love too little, some too long,
  Some sell, and others buy;
Some do the deed with many tears,
  And some without a sigh:
For each man kills the thing he loves,
  Yet each man does not die.

He does not die a death of shame
    On a day of dark disgrace,
Nor have a noose about his neck,
    Nor a cloth upon his face,
Nor drop feet foremost through the floor
    Into an empty space.

He does not sit with silent men
    Who watch him night and day;
Who watch him when he tries to weep,
    And when he tries to pray;
Who watch him lest himself should rob
    The prison of its prey.

He does not wake at dawn to see
    Dread figures throng his room,
The shivering Chaplain robed in white,
    The Sheriff stern with gloom,
And the Governor all in shiny black,
    With the yellow face of Doom.

He does not rise in piteous haste
    To put on convict-clothes,
While some coarse-mouthed Doctor gloats, and notes
    Each new and nerve-twitched pose,
Fingering a watch whose little ticks
    Are like horrible hammer-blows.

He does not know that sickening thirst
    That sands one's throat, before
The hangman with his gardener's gloves
    Slips through the padded door,
And binds one with three leathern thongs,
    That the throat may thirst no more.

He does not bend his head to hear
    The Burial Office read,

Nor, while the terror of his soul
    Tells him he is not dead,
Cross his own coffin, as he moves
    Into the hideous shed.

He does not stare upon the air
    Through a little roof of glass:
He does not pray with lips of clay
    For his agony to pass;
Nor feel upon his shuddering cheek
    The kiss of Caiaphas.

## II

Six weeks our guardsman walked the yard,
    In the suit of shabby gray:
His cricket cap was on his head,
    And his step seemed light and gay,
But I never saw a man who looked
    So wistfully at the day.

I never saw a man who looked
    With such a wistful eye
Upon that little tent of blue
    Which prisoners call the sky,
And at every wandering cloud that trailed
    Its ravelled fleeces by.

He did not wring his hands, as do
    Those witless men who dare
To try to rear the changeling Hope
    In the cave of black Despair:
He only looked upon the sun,
    And drank the morning air.

He did not wring his hands nor weep,
    Nor did he peek or pine,
But he drank the air as though it held
    Some healthful anodyne;

With open mouth he drank the sun
 As though it had been wine!

And I and all the souls in pain,
 Who tramped the other ring,
Forgot if we ourselves had done
 A great or little thing,
And watched with gaze of dull amaze
 The man who had to swing.

And strange it was to see him pass
 With a step so light and gay,
And strange it was to see him look
 So wistfully at the day,
And strange it was to think that he
 Had such a debt to pay.

For oak and elm have pleasant leaves
 That in the spring-time shoot:
But grim to see is the gallows-tree,
 With its adder-bitten root,
And, green or dry, a man must die
 Before it bears its fruit!

The loftiest place is that seat of grace
 For which all worldlings try:
But who would stand in hempen band
 Upon a scaffold high,
And through a murderer's collar take
 His last look at the sky?

It is sweet to dance to violins
 When Love and Life are fair:
To dance to flutes, to dance to lutes
 Is delicate and rare:
But it is not sweet with nimble feet
 To dance upon the air!

So with curious eyes and sick surmise
   We watched him day by day,
And wondered if each one of us
   Would end the self-same way,
For none can tell to what red Hell
   His sightless soul may stray.

At last the dead man walked no more
   Amongst the Trial Men,
And I knew that he was standing up
   In the black dock's dreadful pen,
And that never would I see his face
   In God's sweet world again.

Like two doomed ships that pass in storm
   We had crossed each other's way:
But we made no sign, we said no word,
   We had no word to say;
For we did not meet in the holy night,
   But in the shameful day.

A prison wall was round us both,
   Two outcast men we were:
The world had thrust us from its heart.
   And God from out His care:
And the iron gin that waits for Sin
   Had caught us in its snare.

### III

In Debtors' Yard the stones are hard,
   And the dripping wall is high,
So it was there he took the air
   Beneath the leaden sky,
And by each side a Warder walked,
   For fear the man might die.

Or else he sat with those who watched
   His anguish night and day;

Who watched him when he rose to weep,
    And when he crouched to pray;
Who watched him lest himself should rob
    Their scaffold of its prey.

The Governor was strong upon
    The Regulations Act:
The Doctor said that Death was but
    A scientific fact:
And twice a day the Chaplain called,
    And left a little tract.

And twice a day he smoked his pipe,
    And drank his quart of beer:
His soul was resolute, and held
    No hiding-place for fear;
He often said that he was glad
    The hangman's hands were near.

But why he said so strange a thing
    No Warder dared to ask:
For he to whom a watcher's doom
    Is given as his task,
Must set a lock upon his lips,
    And make his face a mask.

Or else he might be moved, and try
    To comfort or console:
And what should Human Pity do
    Pent up in Murderers' Hole?
What word of grace in such a place
    Could help a brother's soul?

With slouch and swing around the ring
    We trod the Fools' Parade!
We did not care: we knew we were
    The Devil's Own Brigade:

And shaven head and feet of lead
   Make a merry masquerade.

We tore the tarry rope to shreds
   With blunt and bleeding nails;
We rubbed the doors, and scrubbed the floors,
   And cleaned the shining rails:
And, rank by rank, we soaped the plank,
   And clattered with the pails.

We sewed the sacks, we broke the stones,
   We turned the dusty drill:
We banged the tins, and bawled the hymns,
   And sweated on the mill:
But in the heart of every man
   Terror was lying still.

So still it lay that every day
   Crawled like a weed-clogged wave:
And we forgot the bitter lot
   That waits for fool and knave,
Till once, as we tramped in from work,
   We passed an open grave.

With yawning mouth the yellow hole
   Gaped for a living thing;
The very mud cried out for blood
   To the thirsty asphalte ring:
And we knew that ere one dawn grew fair
   Some prisoner had to swing.

Right in we went, with soul intent
   On Death and Dread and Doom:
The hangman, with his little bag,
   Went shuffling through the gloom:
And each man trembled as he crept
   Into his numbered tomb.

That night the empty corridors
    Were full of forms of Fear,
And up and down the iron town
    Stole feet we could not hear,
And through the bars that hide the stars
    White faces seemed to peer.

He lay as one who lies and dreams
    In a pleasant meadow-land,
The watchers watched him as he slept,
    And could not understand
How one could sleep so sweet a sleep
    With a hangman close at hand.

But there is no sleep when men must weep
    Who never yet have wept:
So we—the fool, the fraud, the knave—
    That endless vigil kept,
And through each brain on hands of pain
    Another's terror crept.

Alas! it is a fearful thing
    To feel another's guilt!
For, right within, the sword of Sin
    Pierced to its poisoned hilt,
And as molten lead were the tears we shed
    For the blood we had not spilt.

The Warders with their shoes of felt
    Crept by each padlocked door,
And peeped and saw, with eyes of awe,
    Grey figures on the floor,
And wondered why men knelt to pray
    Who never prayed before.

All through the night we knelt and prayed,
    Mad mourners of a corse!

The troubled plumes of midnight were
    The plumes upon a hearse:
And bitter wine upon a sponge
    Was the savour of Remorse.

The grey cock crew, the red cock crew,
    But never came the day:
And crooked shapes of Terror crouched,
    In the corners where we lay:
And each evil sprite that walks by night
    Before us seemed to play.

They glided past, they glided fast,
    Like travellers through a mist:
They mocked the moon in a rigadoon
    Of delicate turn and twist,
And with formal pace and loathsome grace
    The phantoms kept their tryst.

With mop and mow, we saw them go,
    Slim shadows hand in hand:
About, about, in ghostly rout
    They trod a saraband:
And the damned grotesques made arabesques,
    Like the wind upon the sand!

With the pirouettes of marionettes,
    They tripped on pointed tread:
But with flutes of Fear they filled the ear,
    As their grisly masque they led,
And loud they sang, and long they sang,
    For they sang to wake the dead.

*"Oho!"* they cried, *"The world is wide,*
    *But fettered limbs go lame!*
*And once, or twice, to throw the dice*
    *Is a gentlemanly game,*

*But he does not win who plays with Sin*
*In the secret House of Shame."*

No things of air these antics were,
   That frolicked with such glee:
To men whose lives were held in gyves,
   And whose feet might not go free,
Ah! wounds of Christ! they were living things,
   Most terrible to see.

Around, around, they waltzed and wound;
   Some wheeled in smirking pairs;
With the mincing step of a demirep
   Some sidled up the stairs:
And with subtle sneer, and fawning leer,
   Each helped us at our prayers.

The morning wind began to moan,
   But still the night went on:
Through its giant loom the web of gloom
   Crept till each thread was spun:
And, as we prayed, we grew afraid
   Of the Justice of the Sun.

The moaning wind went wandering round
   The weeping prison-wail:
Till like a wheel of turning steel
   We felt the minutes crawl:
O moaning wind! what had we done
   To have such a seneschal?

At last I saw the shadowed bars,
   Like a lattice wrought in lead,
Move right across the whitewashed wall
   That faced my three-plank bed,
And I knew that somewhere in the world
   God's dreadful dawn was red.

At six o'clock we cleaned our cells,
 At seven all was still,
But the sough and swing of a mighty wing
 The prison seemed to fill,
For the Lord of Death with icy breath
 Had entered in to kill.

He did not pass in purple pomp,
 Nor ride a moon-white steed.
Three yards of cord and a sliding board
 Are all the gallows' need:
So with rope of shame the Herald came
 To do the secret deed.

We were as men who through a fen
 Of filthy darkness grope:
We did not dare to breathe a prayer,
 Or to give our anguish scope:
Something was dead in each of us,
 And what was dead was Hope.

For Man's grim Justice goes its way,
 And will not swerve aside:
It slays the weak, it slays the strong,
 It has a deadly stride:
With iron heel it slays the strong,
 The monstrous parricide!

We waited for the stroke of eight:
 Each tongue was thick with thirst:
For the stroke of eight is the stroke of Fate
 That makes a man accursed,
And Fate will use a running noose
 For the best man and the worst.

We had no other thing to do,
 Save to wait for the sign to come:

So, like things of stone in a valley lone,
    Quiet we sat and dumb:
But each man's heart beat thick and quick
    Like a madman on a drum!

With sudden shock the prison-clock
    Smote on the shivering air,
And from all the gaol rose up a wail
    Of impotent despair,
Like the sound that frightened marshes hear
    From some leper in his lair.

And as one sees most fearful things
    In the crystal of a dream,
We saw the greasy hempen rope
    Hooked to the blackened beam,
And heard the prayer the hangman's snare
    Strangled into a scream.

And all the woe that moved him so
    That he gave that bitter cry,
And the wild regrets, and the bloody sweats,
    None knew so well as I:
For he who lives more lives than one
    More deaths than one must die.

## IV

There is no chapel on the day
    On which they hang a man:
The Chaplain's heart is far too sick,
    Or his face is far too wan,
Or there is that written in his eyes
    Which none should look upon.

So they kept us close till nigh on noon,
    And then they rang the bell,
And the Warders with their jingling keys
    Opened each listening cell,

And down the iron stair we tramped,
   Each from his separate Hell.

Out into God's sweet air we went,
   But not in wonted way,
For this man's face was white with fear,
   And that man's face was grey,
And I never saw sad men who looked
   So wistfully at the day.

I never saw sad men who looked
   With such a wistful eye
Upon that little tent of blue
   We prisoners called the sky,
And at every careless cloud that passed
   In happy freedom by.

But there were those amongst us all
   Who walked with downcast head,
And knew that, had each got his due,
   They should have died instead:
He had but killed a thing that lived,
   Whilst they had killed the dead.

For he who sins a second time
   Wakes a dead soul to pain,
And draws it from its spotted shroud,
   And makes it bleed again,
And makes it bleed great gouts of blood,
   And makes it bleed in vain!

Like ape or clown, in monstrous garb
   With crooked arrows starred,
Silently we went round and round
   The slippery asphalte yard;
Silently we went round and round,
   And no man spoke a word.

Silently we went round and round,
   And through each hollow mind
The Memory of dreadful things
   Rushed like a dreadful wind,
And Horror stalked before each man,
   And Terror crept behind.

The Warders strutted up and down,
   And kept their herd of brutes,
Their uniforms were spick and span,
   And they wore their Sunday suits,
But we knew the work they had been at,
   By the quicklime on their boots.

For where a grave had opened wide,
   There was no grave at all:
Only a stretch of mud and sand
   By the hideous prison-wall,
And a little heap of burning lime,
   That the man should have his pall.

For he has a pall, this wretched man,
   Such as few men can claim:
Deep down below a prison-yard,
   Naked for greater shame,
He lies, with fetters on each foot,
   Wrapt in a sheet of flame!

And all the while the burning lime
   Eats flesh and bone away,
It eats the brittle bone by night,
   And the soft flesh by day,
It eats the flesh and bone by turns,
   But it eats the heart alway.

For three long years they will not sow
   Or root or seedling there:

For three long years the unblessed spot
   Will sterile be and bare,
And look upon the wondering sky
   With unreproachful stare.

They think a murderer's heart would taint
   Each simple seed they sow.
It is not true! God's kindly earth
   Is kindlier than men know,
And the red rose would but blow more red,
   The white rose whiter blow.

Out of his mouth a red, red rose!
   Out of his heart a white!
For who can say by what strange way,
   Christ brings His will to light,
Since the barren staff the pilgrim bore
   Bloomed in the great Pope's sight?

But neither milk-white rose nor red
   May bloom in prison air;
The shard, the pebble, and the flint,
   Are what they give us there:
For flowers have been known to heal
   A common man's despair.

So never will wine-red rose or white,
   Petal by petal, fall
On that stretch of mud and sand that lies
   By the hideous prison-wall,
To tell the men who tramp the yard
   That God's Son died for all.

Yet though the hideous prison-wall
   Still hems him round and round,
And a spirit may not walk by night
   That is with fetters bound,

And a spirit may but weep that lies
   In such unholy ground,

He is at peace—this wretched man—
   At peace, or will be soon:
There is no thing to make him mad,
   Nor does Terror walk at noon,
For the lampless Earth in which he lies
   Has neither Sun nor Moon.

They hanged him as a beast is hanged:
   They did not even toll
A requiem that might have brought
   Rest to his startled soul,
But hurriedly they took him out,
   And hid him in a hole.

They stripped him of his canvas clothes,
   And gave him to the flies:
They mocked the swollen purple throat,
   And the stark and staring eyes:
And with laughter loud they heaped the shroud
   In which their convict lies.

The Chaplain would not kneel to pray
   By his dishonoured grave:
Nor mark it with that blessed Cross
   That Christ for sinners gave,
Because the man was one of those
   Whom Christ came down to save

Yet all is well; he has but passed
   To Life's appointed bourne:
And alien tears will fill for him
   Pity's long-broken urn,
For his mourners will be outcast men
   And outcasts always mourn.

V

I know not whether Laws be right
    Or whether Laws be wrong;
All that we know who lie in gaol
    Is that the wall is strong;
And that each day is like a year,
    A year whose days are long.

But this I know, that every Law
    That men have made for Man,
Since first Man took his brother's life,
    And the sad world began,
But straws the wheat and saves the chaff
    With a most evil fan.

This too I know—and wise it were
    If each could know the same—
That every prison that men build
    Is built with bricks of shame,
And bound with bars lest Christ should see
    How men their brothers maim.

With bars they blur the gracious moon,
    And blind the goodly sun:
And they do well to hide their Hell,
    For in it things are done
That Son of God nor son of Man
    Ever should look upon!

The vilest deeds like poison weeds
    Bloom well in prison-air:
It is only what is good in Man
    That wastes and withers there:
Pale Anguish keeps the heavy gate,
    And the Warder is Despair.

For they starve the little frightened child
    Till it weeps both night and day:

And they scourge the weak, and flog the fool,
    And gibe the old and gray,
And some grow mad, and all grow bad,
    And none a word may say.

Each narrow cell in which we dwell
    Is a foul and dark latrine,
And the fetid breath of living Death
    Chokes up each grated screen,
And all, but Lust, is turned to dust
    In Humanity's machine.

The brackish water that we drink
    Creeps with a loathsome slime,
And the bitter bread they weigh in scales
    Is full of chalk and lime,
And Sleep will not lie down, but walks
    Wild-eyed, and cries to Time.

But though lean Hunger and green Thirst
    Like asp with adder fight,
We have little care of prison fare,
    For what chills and kills outright
Is that every stone one lifts by day
    Becomes one's heart by night.

With midnight always in one's heart,
    And twilight in one's cell.
We turn the crank, or tear the rope,
    Each in his separate Hell,
And the silence is more awful far
    Than the sound of a brazen bell.

And never a human voice comes near
    To speak a gentle word:
And the eye that watches through the door
    Is pitiless and hard:

And by all forgot we rot and rot,
    With soul and body marred.

And thus we rust Life's iron chain
    Degraded and alone:
And some men curse, and some men weep,
    And some men make no moan:
But God's eternal Laws are kind
    And break the heart of stone.

And every human heart that breaks,
    In prison-cell or yard,
Is as that broken box that gave
    Its treasure to the Lord,
And filled the unclean leper's house
    With the scent of costliest nard.

Ah! happy they whose hearts can break
    And peace of pardon win!
How else may man make straight his plan
    And cleanse his soul from Sin?
How else but through a broken heart
    May Lord Christ enter in?

And he of the swollen purple throat,
    And the stark and staring eyes,
Waits for the holy hands that took
    The Thief to Paradise;
And a broken and a contrite heart
    The Lord will not despise.

The man in red who reads the Law
    Gave him three weeks of life,
Three little weeks in which to heal
    His soul of his soul's strife,
And cleanse from every blot of blood
    The hand that held the knife.

And with tears of blood he cleansed the hand,
   The hand that held the steel:
For only blood can wipe out blood,
   And only tears can heal:
And the crimson stain that was of Cain
   Became Christ's snow-white seal.

## VI

In Reading gaol by Reading town
   There is a pit of shame,
And in it lies a wretched man
   Eaten by teeth of flame,
In a burning winding-sheet he lies,
   And his grave has got no name.

And there, till Christ call forth the dead
   In silence let him lie:
No need to waste the foolish tear,
   Or heave the windy sigh:
The man had killed the thing he loved,
   And so he had to die.

And all men kill the thing they love,
   By all let this be heard,
Some do it with a bitter look,
   Some with a flattering word,
The coward does it with a kiss,
   The brave man with a sword!

# WALTER DE LA MARE
## (1873–1956)

## The Listeners

"Is there anybody there?" said the Traveller,
    Knocking on the moonlit door;
And his horse in the silence champed the grasses
    Of the forest's ferny floor:
And a bird flew up out of the turret,
    Above the Traveller's head:
And he smote upon the door again a second time;
    "Is there anybody there?" he said.
But no one descended to the Traveller;
    No head from the leaf-fringed sill
Leaned over and looked into his grey eyes,
    Where he stood perplexed and still.
But only a host of phantom listeners
    That dwelt in the lone house then
Stood listening in the quiet of the moonlight
    To that voice from the world of men:
Stood thronging the faint moonbeams on the dark stair,
    That goes down to the empty hall,
Hearkening in an air stirred and shaken
    By the lonely Traveller's call.
And he felt in his heart their strangeness,
    Their stillness answering his cry,
While his horse moved, cropping the dark turf,
    'Neath the starred and leafy sky;
For he suddenly smote on the door, even
    Louder, and lifted his head:—

"Tell them I came, and no one answered,
   That I kept my word," he said.
Never the least stir made the listeners,
   Though every word he spake
Fell echoing through the shadowiness of the still house
   From the one man left awake:
Ay, they heard his foot upon the stirrup,
   And the sound of iron on stone,
And how the silence surged softly backward,
   When the plunging hoofs were gone.

# WILFRED OWEN
## (1893–1918)

## Strange Meeting

It seemed that out of the battle I escaped
Down some profound dull tunnel, long since scooped
Through granites which titanic wars had groined.
Yet also there encumbered sleepers groaned,
Too fast in thought or death to be bestirred.
Then, as I probed them, one sprang up, and stared
With piteous recognition in fixed eyes,
Lifting distressful hands as if to bless.
And by his smile, I knew that sullen hall,
By his dead smile I knew we stood in Hell.
With a thousand pains that vision's face was grained;
Yet no blood reached there from the upper ground,
And no guns thumped, or down the flues made moan.
"Strange friend," I said, "here is no cause to mourn."
"None," said the other, "Save the undone years,
The hopelessness. Whatever hope is yours,
Was my life also; I went hunting wild
After the wildest beauty in the world,
Which lies not calm in eyes, or braided hair,
But mocks the steady running of the hour,
And if it grieves, grieves richlier than here.
For by my glee might many men have laughed,
And of my weeping something has been left,
Which must die now. I mean the truth untold,
The pity of war, the pity war distilled.
Now men will go content with what we spoiled.

Or, discontent, boil bloody, and be spilled.
They will be swift with swiftness of the tigress,
None will break ranks, though nations trek from progress.
Courage was mine, and I had mystery,
Wisdom was mine, and I had mastery:
To miss the march of this retreating world
Into vain citadels that are not walled.
Then, when much blood had clogged their chariot-wheels,
I would go up and wash them from sweet wells,
Even with truths that lie too deep for taint.
I would have poured my spirit without stint
But not through wounds; not on the cess of war.
Foreheads of men have bled where no wounds were.
I am the enemy you killed, my friend.
I knew you in this dark; for so you frowned
Yesterday through me as you jabbed and killed.
I parried; but my hands were loath and cold.
Let us sleep now. . . ."

## Anthem for Doomed Youth

What passing-bells for these who die as cattle?
    Only the monstrous anger of the guns.
    Only the stuttering rifles' rapid rattle
Can patter out their hasty orisons.
No mockeries for them; no prayers nor bells,
Nor any voice of mourning save the choirs,—
The shrill, demented choirs of wailing shells;
And bugles calling for them from sad shires.

What candles may be held to speed them all?
    Not in the hands of boys, but in their eyes
Shall shine the holy glimmers of goodbyes.
    The pallor of girls' brows shall be their pall;
Their flowers the tenderness of patient minds,
And each slow dusk a drawing-down of blinds.

# Insensibility

### I

Happy are men who yet before they are killed
Can let their veins run cold.
Whom no compassion fleers
Or makes their feet
Sore on the alleys cobbled with their brothers.
The front line withers,
But they are troops who fade, not flowers
For poets' tearful fooling:
Men, gaps for filling
Losses who might have fought
Longer; but no one bothers.

### II

And some cease feeling
Even themselves or for themselves.
Dullness best solves
The tease and doubt of shelling,
And Chance's strange arithmetic
Comes simpler than the reckoning of their shilling.
They keep no check on Armies' decimation.

### III

Happy are these who lose imagination:
They have enough to carry with ammunition.
Their spirit drags no pack.
Their old wounds save with cold can not more ache.
Having seen all things red,
Their eyes are rid
Of the hurt of the colour of blood for ever.
And terror's first constriction over,
Their hearts remain small drawn.
Their senses in some scorching cautery of battle
Now long since ironed,
Can laugh among the dying, unconcerned.

## IV

Happy the soldier home, with not a notion
How somewhere, every dawn, some men attack,
And many sighs are drained.
Happy the lad whose mind was never trained:
His days are worth forgetting more than not.
He sings along the march
Which we march taciturn, because of dusk,
The long, forlorn, relentless trend
From larger day to huger night.

## V

We wise, who with a thought besmirch
Blood over all our soul,
How should we see our task
But through his blunt and lashless eyes?
Alive, he is not vital overmuch;
Dying, not mortal overmuch;
Nor sad, nor proud,
Nor curious at all.
He cannot tell
Old men's placidity from his.

## VI

But cursed are dullards whom no cannon stuns,
That they should be as stones.
Wretched are they, and mean
With paucity that never was simplicity.
By choice they made themselves immune
To pity and whatever mourns in man
Before the last sea and the hapless stars;
Whatever mourns when many leave these shores;
Whatever shares
The eternal reciprocity of tears.

# Dulce et Decorum Est

Bent double, like old beggars under sacks,
Knock-kneed, coughing like hags, we cursed through sludge,
Till on the haunting flares we turned our backs,
And towards our distant rest began to trudge.
Men marched asleep. Many had lost their boots,
But limped on, blood-shod. All went lame, all blind;
Drunk with fatigue; deaf even to the hoots
Of gas-shells dropping softly behind.

Gas! GAS! Quick, boys!—An ecstasy of fumbling
Fitting the clumsy helmets just in time,
But someone still was yelling out and stumbling
And flound'ring like a man in fire or lime.—
Dim through the misty panes and thick green light,
As under a green sea, I saw him drowning.

In all my dreams before my helpless sight
He plunges at me, guttering, choking, drowning.

If in some smothering dreams, you too could pace
Behind the wagon that we flung him in,
And watch the white eyes writhing in his face,
His hanging face, like a devil's sick of sin,
If you could hear, at every jolt, the blood
Come gargling from the froth-corrupted lungs
Bitten as the cud
Of vile, incurable sores on innocent tongues,—
My friend, you would not tell with such high zest
To children ardent for some desperate glory,
The old Lie: *Dulce et decorum est*
*Pro Patria mori.*

# Futility

Move him into the sun—
Gently its touch awoke him once,
At home, whispering of fields unsown.
Always it woke him, even in France,
Until this morning and this snow.
If anything might rouse him now
The kind old sun will know.

Think how it wakes the seeds—
Woke, once, the clays of a cold star.
Are limbs so dear-achieved, are sides
Full-nerved,—still warm,—too hard to stir?
Was it for this the clay grew tall?
—O what made fatuous sunbeams toil
To break earth's sleep at all?

# RUPERT BROOKE
## (1887–1915)

WAR SONNET I

## Peace

Now, God be thanked Who has matched us with His hour,
    And caught our youth, and wakened us from sleeping,
With hand made sure, clear eye, and sharpened power,
    To turn, as swimmers into cleanness leaping,
Glad from a world grown old and cold and weary,
    Leave the sick hearts that honour could not move,
And half-men, and their dirty songs and dreary,
    And all the little emptiness of love!

Oh! we, who have known shame, we have found release there,
    Where there's no ill, no grief, but sleep has mending,
      Naught broken save this body, lost but breath;
Nothing to shake the laughing heart's long peace there
    But only agony, and that has ending;
      And the worst friend and enemy is but Death.

WAR SONNET II

## Safety

Dear! of all happy in the hour, most blest
    He who has found our hid security,
Assured in the dark tides of the world that rest,
    And heard our word, "Who is so safe as we?"
We have found safety with all things undying,
    The winds, and morning, tears of men and mirth,

The deep night, and birds singing, and clouds flying,
    And sleep, and freedom, and the autumnal earth.
We have built a house that is not for Time's throwing.
    We have gained a peace unshaken by pain for ever.
War knows no power. Safe shall be my going,
    Secretly armed against all death's endeavour;
Safe though all safety's lost; safe where men fall;
And if these poor limbs die, safest of all.

### WAR SONNET III

## The Dead

Blow out, you bugles, over the rich Dead!
    There's none of these so lonely and poor of old,
    But, dying, has made us rarer gifts than gold.
These laid the world away; poured out the red
Sweet wine of youth; gave up the years to be
    Of work and joy, and that unhoped serene,
    That men call age; and those who would have been,
Their sons, they gave, their immortality.

Blow, bugles, blow! They brought us, for our dearth,
    Holiness, lacked so long, and Love, and Pain.
Honour has come back, as a king, to earth,
    And paid his subjects with a royal wage;
And Nobleness walks in our ways again;
    And we have come into our heritage.

### WAR SONNET IV

## The Dead

These hearts were woven of human joys and cares,
    Washed marvellously with sorrow, swift to mirth.
The years had given them kindness. Dawn was theirs,
    And sunset, and the colours of the earth.
These had seen movement, and heard music; known
    Slumber and waking; loved; gone proudly friended;
Felt the quick stir of wonder; sat alone;
    Touched flowers and furs and cheeks. All this is ended.

There are waters blown by changing winds to laughter
    And lit by the rich skies, all day. And after,
Frost, with a gesture, stays the waves that dance
    And wandering loveliness. He leaves a white
Unbroken glory, a gathered radiance,
    A width, a shining peace, under the night.

WAR SONNET V

## The Soldier

If I should die, think only this of me:
    That there's some corner of a foreign field
That is for ever England. There shall be
    In that rich earth a richer dust concealed;
A dust whom England bore, shaped, made aware,
    Gave, once, her flowers to love, her ways to roam,
A body of England's, breathing English air,
    Washed by the rivers, blest by suns of home.

And think, this heart, all evil shed away,
    A pulse in the eternal mind, no less
        Gives somewhere back the thoughts by England given;
Her sights and sounds; dreams happy as her day;
    And laughter, learnt of friends; and gentleness,
        In hearts at peace, under an English heaven.

# EDWARD ARLINGTON ROBINSON
## (1869–1935)

## Luke Havergal

Go to the western gate, Luke Havergal,—
There where the vines cling crimson on the wall,—
And in the twilight wait for what will come.
The wind will moan, the leaves will whisper some—
Whisper of her, and strike you as they fall;
But go, and if you trust her she will call.
Go to the western gate, Luke Havergal —
Luke Havergal.

No, there is not a dawn in eastern skies
To rift the fiery night that's in your eyes;
But there, where western glooms are gathering,
The dark will end the dark, if anything:
God slays Himself with every leaf that flies,
And hell is more than half of paradise.
No, there is not a dawn in eastern skies—
In eastern skies.

Out of a grave I come to tell you this,—
Out of a grave I come to quench the kiss
That flames upon your forehead with a glow
That blinds you to the way that you must go.
Yes, there is yet one way to where she is,—
Bitter, but one that faith can never miss.
Out of a grave I come to tell you this—
To tell you this.

There is the western gate, Luke Havergal,
There are the crimson leaves upon the wall.
Go,—for the winds are tearing them away,—
Nor think to riddle the dead words they say,
Nor any more to feel them as they fall;
But go! and if you trust her she will call.
There is the western gate, Luke Havergal—
Luke Havergal.

## Richard Cory

Whenever Richard Cory went down town,
We people on the pavement looked at him:
He was a gentleman from sole to crown,
Clean favored, and imperially slim.

And he was always quietly arrayed,
And he was always human when he talked;
But still he fluttered pulses when he said,
"Good-morning," and he glittered when he walked.

And he was rich,—yes, richer than a king,—
And admirably schooled in every grace:
In fine, we thought that he was everything
To make us wish that we were in his place.

So on we worked, and waited for the light,
And went without the meat, and cursed the bread;
And Richard Cory, one calm summer night,
Went home and put a bullet through his head.

## Shadrach O'Leary

O'Leary was a poet—for a while:
He sang of many ladies frail and fair,
The rolling glory of their golden hair,
And emperors extinguished with a smile.
They foiled his years with many an ancient wile,
And if they limped, O'Leary didn't care:
He turned them loose and had them everywhere,
Undoing saints and senates with their guile.
But this was not the end. A year ago
I met him—and to meet was to admire:
Forgotten were the ladies and the lyre,
And the small, ink-fed Eros of his dream.
By questioning I found a man to know—
A failure spared, a Shadrach of the Gleam.

## Miniver Cheevy

Miniver Cheevy, child of scorn,
    Grew lean while he assailed the seasons;
He wept that he was ever born,
    And he had reasons.

Miniver loved the days of old
    When swords were bright and steeds were prancing;
The vision of a warrior bold
    Would set him dancing.

Miniver sighed for what was not,
    And dreamed, and rested from his labors;
He dreamed of Thebes and Camelot,
    And Priam's neighbors.

Miniver mourned the ripe renown
　　That made so many a name so fragrant;
He mourned Romance, now on the town,
　　And Art, a vagrant.

Miniver loved the Medici,
　　Albeit he had never seen one;
He would have sinned incessantly
　　Could he have been one.

Miniver cursed the commonplace
　　And eyed a khaki suit with loathing;
He missed the mediæval grace
　　Of iron clothing.

Miniver scorned the gold he sought,
　　But sore annoyed was he without it;
Miniver thought, and thought, and thought,
　　And thought about it.

Miniver Cheevy, born too late,
　　Scratched his head and kept on thinking;
Miniver coughed, and called it fate,
　　And kept on drinking.

# EDGAR LEE MASTERS
## (1868–1950)

## Serepta Mason

My life's blossom might have bloomed on all sides
Save for a bitter wind which stunted my petals
On the side of me which you in the village could see.
From the dust I lift a voice of protest:
My flowering side you never saw!
Ye living ones, ye are fools indeed
Who do not know the ways of the wind
And the unseen forces
That govern the processes of life.

## Amanda Barker

Henry got me with child,
Knowing that I could not bring forth life
Without losing my own.
In my youth therefore I entered the portals of dust.
Traveler, it is believed in the village where I lived
That Henry loved me with a husband's love,
But I proclaim from the dust
That he slew me to gratify his hatred.

## Constance Hately

You praise my self-sacrifice, Spoon River,
In rearing Irene and Mary,
Orphans of my older sister!
And you censure Irene and Mary
For their contempt for me!
But praise not my self-sacrifice,
And censure not their contempt;
I reared them, I cared for them, true enough!—
But I poisoned my benefactions
With constant reminders of their dependence.

## Benjamin Pantier

Together in this grave lie Benjamin Pantier, attorney at law,
And Nig, his dog, constant companion, solace and friend.
Down the gray road, friends, children, men and women,
Passing one by one out of life, left me till I was alone
With Nig for partner, bed-fellow, comrade in drink.
In the morning of life I knew aspiration and saw glory.
Then she, who survives me, snared my soul
With a snare which bled me to death,
Till I, once strong of will, lay broken, indifferent,
Living with Nig in a room back of a dingy office.
Under my jaw-bone is snuggled the bony nose of Nig—
Our story is lost in silence. Go by, mad world!

## Mrs. Benjamin Pantier

I know that he told that I snared his soul
With a snare which bled him to death.
And all the men loved him,
And most of the women pitied him.
But suppose you are really a lady, and have delicate tastes,

And loathe the smell of whiskey and onions.
And the rhythm of Wordsworth's "Ode" runs in your ears,
While he goes about from morning till night
Repeating bits of that common thing;
"Oh, why should the spirit of mortal be proud?"
And then, suppose:
You are a woman well endowed,
And the only man with whom the law and morality
Permit you to have the marital relation
Is the very man that fills you with disgust
Every time you think of it—while you think of it
Every time you see him?
That's why I drove him away from home
To live with his dog in a dingy room
Back of his office.

## Reuben Pantier

Well, Emily Sparks, your prayers were not wasted,
Your love was not all in vain.
I owe whatever I was in life
To your hope that would not give me up,
To your love that saw me still as good.
Dear Emily Sparks, let me tell you the story.
I pass the effect of my father and mother;
The milliner's daughter made me trouble
And out I went in the world,
Where I passed through every peril known
Of wine and women and joy of life.
One night, in a room in the Rue de Rivoli,
I was drinking wine with a black-eyed cocotte,
And the tears swam into my eyes.
She thought they were amorous tears and smiled
For thought of her conquest over me.
But my soul was three thousand miles away,
In the days when you taught me in Spoon River.

And just because you no more could love me,
Nor pray for me, nor write me letters,
The eternal silence of you spoke instead.
And the black-eyed cocotte took the tears for hers,
As well as the deceiving kisses I gave her.
Somehow, from that hour, I had a new vision—
Dear Emily Sparks!

## Trainor, The Druggist

Only the chemist can tell, and not always the chemist,
What will result from compounding
Fluids or solids.
And who can tell
How men and women will interact
On each other, or what children will result?
There were Benjamin Pantier and his wife,
Good in themselves, but evil toward each other:
He oxygen, she hydrogen,
Their son, a devastating fire.
I Trainor, the druggist, a mixer of chemicals,
Killed while making an experiment,
Lived unwedded.

## Minerva Jones

I am Minerva, the village poetess,
Hooted at, jeered at by the Yahoos of the street
For my heavy body, cock-eye, and rolling walk,
And all the more when "Butch" Weldy
Captured me after a brutal hunt.
He left me to my fate with Doctor Meyers;
And I sank into death, growing numb from the feet up,
Like one stepping deeper and deeper into a stream of ice.

Will some one go to the village newspaper,
And gather into a book the verses I wrote?—
I thirsted so for love!
I hungered so for life!

## "Indignation" Jones

You would not believe, would you,
That I came from good Welsh stock?
That I was purer blooded than the white trash here?
And of more direct lineage than the New Englanders
And Virginians of Spoon River?
You would not believe that I had been to school
And read some books.
You saw me only as a run-down man,
With matted hair and beard
And ragged clothes.
Sometimes a man's life turns into a cancer
From being bruised and continually bruised,
And swells into a purplish mass,
Like growths on stalks of corn.
Here was I, a carpenter, mired in a bog of life
Into which I walked, thinking it was a meadow,
With a slattern for a wife, and poor Minerva, my daughter,
Whom you tormented and drove to death.
So I crept, crept, like a snail through the days
Of my life.
No more you hear my footsteps in the morning,
Resounding on the hollow sidewalk,
Going to the grocery store for a little corn meal
And a nickel's worth of bacon.

## Doctor Meyers

No other man, unless it was Doc Hill,
Did more for people in this town than I.
And all the weak, the halt, the improvident
And those who could not pay flocked to me.
I was good-hearted, easy Doctor Meyers.
I was healthy, happy, in comfortable fortune,
Blessed with a congenial mate, my children raised,
All wedded, doing well in the world.
And then one night, Minerva, the poetess,
Came to me in her trouble, crying.
I tried to help her out—she died—
They indicted me, the newspapers disgraced me,
My wife perished of a broken heart.
And pneumonia finished me.

## Mrs. Meyers

He protested all his life long
The newspapers lied about him villainously;
That he was not at fault for Minerva's fall,
But only tried to help her.
Poor soul so sunk in sin he could not see
That even trying to help her, as he called it,
He had broken the law human and divine.
Passers by, an ancient admonition to you:
If your ways would be ways of pleasantness,
And all your pathways peace,
Love God and keep his commandments.

## "Butch" Weldy

After I got religion and steadied down
They gave me a job in the canning works,
And every morning I had to fill
The tank in the yard with gasoline,
That fed the blow-fires in the sheds
To heat the soldering irons.
And I mounted a rickety ladder to do it,
Carrying buckets full of the stuff.
One morning, as I stood there pouring,
The air grew still and seemed to heave,
And I shot up as the tank exploded,
And down I came with both legs broken,
And my eyes burned crisp as a couple of eggs.
For someone left a blow-fire going,
And something sucked the flame in the tank.
The Circuit Judge said whoever did it
Was a fellow-servant of mine, and so
Old Rhodes' son didn't have to pay me.
And I sat on the witness stand as blind
As Jack the Fiddler, saying over and over,
"I didn't know him at all."

## A.D. Blood

If you in the village think that my work was a good one,
Who closed the saloons and stopped all playing at cards,
And haled old Daisy Fraser before Justice Arnett,
In many a crusade to purge the people of sin;
Why do you let the milliner's daughter Dora,
And the worthless son of Benjamin Pantier,
Nightly make my grave their unholy pillow?

## Editor Whedon

To be able to see every side of every question;
To be on every side, to be everything, to be nothing long;
To pervert truth, to ride it for a purpose,
To use great feelings and passions of the human family
For base designs, for cunning ends,
To wear a mask like the Greek actors—
Your eight-page paper—behind which you huddle,
Bawling through the megaphone of big type:
"This is I, the giant."
Thereby also living the life of a sneak-thief,
Poisoned with the anonymous words
Of your clandestine soul.
To scratch dirt over scandal for money,
And exhume it to the winds for revenge,
Or to sell papers,
Crushing reputations, or bodies, if need be,
To win at any cost, save your own life.
To glory in demoniac power, ditching civilization,
As a paranoiac boy puts a log on the track
And derails the express train.
To be an editor, as I was.
Then to lie here close by the river over the place
Where the sewage flows from the village,
And the empty cans and garbage are dumped,
And abortions are hidden.

## Ralph Rhodes

All they said was true:
I wrecked my father's bank with my loans
To dabble in wheat; but this was true—
I was buying wheat for him as well,
Who couldn't margin the deal in his name
Because of his church relationship.

And while George Reece was serving his term
I chased the will-o'-the-wisp of women,
And the mockery of wine in New York.
It's deathly to sicken of wine and women
When nothing else is left in life.
But suppose your head is gray, and bowed
On a table covered with acrid stubs
Of cigarettes and empty glasses,
And a knock is heard, and you know it's the knock
So long drowned out by popping corks
And the pea-cock screams of demireps—
And you look up, and there's your Theft,
Who waited until your head was gray,
And your heart skipped beats to say to you:
The game is ended. I've called for you.
Go out on Broadway and be run over,
They'll ship you back to Spoon River.

———

## Archibald Higbie

I loathed you, Spoon River. I tried to rise above you,
I was ashamed of you. I despised you
As the place of my nativity.
And there in Rome, among the artists,
Speaking Italian, speaking French,
I seemed to myself at times to be free
Of every trace of my origin.
I seemed to be reaching the heights of art
And to breathe the air that the masters breathed,
And to see the world with their eyes.
But still they'd pass my work and say:
"What are you driving at, my friend?
Sometimes the face looks like Apollo's,
At others it has a trace of Lincoln's."
There was no culture, you know, in Spoon River,

And I burned with shame and held my peace.
And what could I do, all covered over
And weighted down with western soil,
Except aspire, and pray for another
Birth in the world, with all of Spoon River
Rooted out of my soul?

# ROBERT FROST

## (1874–1963)

## Mending Wall

Something there is that doesn't love a wall,
That sends the frozen-ground-swell under it,
And spills the upper boulders in the sun;
And makes gaps even two can pass abreast.
The work of hunters is another thing:
I have come after them and made repair
Where they have left not one stone on a stone,
But they would have the rabbit out of hiding,
To please the yelping dogs. The gaps I mean,
No one has seen them made or heard them made,
But at spring mending-time we find them there.
I let my neighbour know beyond the hill;
And on a day we meet to walk the line
And set the wall between us once again.
We keep the wall between us as we go.
To each the boulders that have fallen to each.
And some are loaves and some so nearly balls
We have to use a spell to make them balance:
"Stay where you are until our backs are turned!"
We wear our fingers rough with handling them.
Oh, just another kind of out-door game,
One on a side. It comes to little more:
There where it is we do not need the wall:
He is all pine and I am apple orchard.
My apple trees will never get across
And eat the cones under his pines, I tell him.

He only says, "Good fences make good neighbours."
Spring is the mischief in me, and I wonder
If I could put a notion in his head:
"*Why* do they make good neighbours? Isn't it
Where there are cows? But here there are no cows.
Before I built a wall I'd ask to know
What I was walling in or walling out,
And to whom I was like to give offence.
Something there is that doesn't love a wall,
That wants it down." I could say "Elves" to him,
But it's not elves exactly, and I'd rather
He said it for himself. I see him there
Bringing a stone grasped firmly by the top
In each hand, like an old-stone savage armed.
He moves in darkness as it seems to me,
Not of woods only and the shade of trees.
He will not go behind his father's saying,
And he likes having thought of it so well
He says again, "Good fences make good neighbours."

## The Death of the Hired Man

Mary sat musing on the lamp-flame at the table
Waiting for Warren. When she heard his step,
She ran on tip-toe down the darkened passage
To meet him in the doorway with the news
And put him on his guard. "Silas is back."
She pushed him outward with her through the door
And shut it after her. "Be kind," she said.
She took the market things from Warren's arms
And set them on the porch, then drew him down
To sit beside her on the wooden steps.

"When was I ever anything but kind to him?
But I'll not have the fellow back," he said.
"I told him so last haying, didn't I?

'If he left then,' I said, 'that ended it.'
What good is he? Who else will harbour him
At his age for the little he can do?
What help he is there's no depending on.
Off he goes always when I need him most.
'He thinks he ought to earn a little pay,
Enough at least to buy tobacco with,
So he won't have to beg and be beholden.'
'All right,' I say, 'I can't afford to pay
Any fixed wages, though I wish I could.'
'Someone else can.' 'Then someone else will have to.'
I shouldn't mind his bettering himself
If that was what it was. You can be certain,
When he begins like that, there's someone at him
Trying to coax him off with pocket-money,—
In haying time, when any help is scarce.
In winter he comes back to us. I'm done."

"Sh! not so loud: he'll hear you," Mary said.

"I want him to: he'll have to soon or late."

"He's worn out. He's asleep beside the stove.
When I came up from Rowe's I found him here,
Huddled against the barn-door fast asleep,
A miserable sight, and frightening, too—
You needn't smile—I didn't recognise him—
I wasn't looking for him—and he's changed.
Wait till you see."

       "Where did you say he'd been?"

"He didn't say. I dragged him to the house,
And gave him tea and tried to make him smoke.
I tried to make him talk about his travels.
Nothing would do: he just kept nodding off."

"What did he say? Did he say anything?"

"But little."

           "Anything? Mary, confess
He said he'd come to ditch the meadow for me

"Warren!"

           "But did he? I just want to know."

"Of course he did. What would you have him say?
Surely you wouldn't grudge the poor old man
Some humble way to save his self-respect.
He added, if you really care to know,
He meant to clear the upper pasture, too.
That sounds like something you have heard before?
Warren, I wish you could have heard the way
He jumbled everything. I stopped to look
Two or three times—he made me feel so queer—
To see if he was talking in his sleep.
He ran on Harold Wilson—you remember—
The boy you had in haying four years since.
He's finished school, and teaching in his college.
Silas declares you'll have to get him back.
He says they two will make a team for work:
Between them they will lay this farm as smooth!
The way he mixed that in with other things.
He thinks young Wilson a likely lad, though daft
On education—you know how they fought
All through July under the blazing sun,
Silas up on the cart to build the load,
Harold along beside to pitch it on."

"Yes, I took care to keep well out of earshot."

"Well, those days trouble Silas like a dream.
You wouldn't think they would. How some things linger!
Harold's young college boy's assurance piqued him.
After so many years he still keeps finding

Good arguments he sees he might have used.
I sympathise. I know just how it feels
To think of the right thing to say too late.
Harold's associated in his mind with Latin.
He asked me what I thought of Harold's saying
He studied Latin like the violin
Because he liked it—that an argument!
He said he couldn't make the boy believe
He could find water with a hazel prong—
Which showed how much good school had ever done him.
He wanted to go over that. But most of all
He thinks if he could have another chance
To teach him how to build a load of hay—"

"I know, that's Silas' one accomplishment.
He bundles every forkful in its place,
And tags and numbers it for future reference,
So he can find and easily dislodge it
In the unloading. Silas does that well.
He takes it out in bunches like big birds' nests.
You never see him standing on the hay
He's trying to lift, straining to lift himself."

"He thinks if he could teach him that, he'd be
Some good perhaps to someone in the world.
He hates to see a boy the fool of books.
Poor Silas, so concerned for other folk,
And nothing to look backward to with pride,
And nothing to look forward to with hope,
So now and never any different."

Part of a moon was falling down the west,
Dragging the whole sky with it to the hills.
Its light poured softly in her lap. She saw
And spread her apron to it. She put out her hand
Among the harp-like morning-glory strings,
Taut with the dew from garden bed to eaves,

As if she played unheard the tenderness
That wrought on him beside her in the night.
"Warren," she said, "he has come home to die:
You needn't be afraid he'll leave you this time."
"Home," he mocked gently.

               "Yes, what else but home?
It all depends on what you mean by home.
Of course he's nothing to us, any more
Than was the hound that came a stranger to us
Out of the woods, worn out upon the trail."

"Home is the place where, when you have to go there,
They have to take you in."

                  "I should have called it
Something you somehow haven't to deserve."

Warren leaned out and took a step or two,
Picked up a little stick, and brought it back
And broke it in his hand and tossed it by.
"Silas has better claim on us you think
Than on his brother? Thirteen little miles
As the road winds would bring him to his door.
Silas has walked that far no doubt to-day.
Why didn't he go there? His brother's rich,
A somebody—director in the bank."

"He never told us that."

                    "We know it though."

"I think his brother ought to help, of course.
I'll see to that if there is need. He ought of right
To take him in, and might be willing to—
He may be better than appearances.
But have some pity on Silas. Do you think

If he'd had any pride in claiming kin
Or anything he looked for from his brother,
He'd keep so still about him all this time?"

"I wonder what's between them."

                    "I can tell you.
Silas is what he is—we wouldn't mind him—
But just the kind that kinsfolk can't abide.
He never did a thing so very bad.
He don't know why he isn't quite as good
As anyone. He won't be made ashamed
To please his brother, worthless though he is."

"*I* can't think Si ever hurt anyone."

"No, but he hurt my heart the way he lay
And rolled his old head on that sharp-edged chair-back.
He wouldn't let me put him on the lounge.
You must go in and see what you can do.
I made the bed up for him there to-night.
You'll be surprised at him—how much he's broken.
His working days are done; I'm sure of it."

"I'd not be in a hurry to say that."

"I haven't been. Go, look, see for yourself.
But, Warren, please remember how it is:
He's come to help you ditch the meadow.
He has a plan. You mustn't laugh at him.
He may not speak of it, and then he may.
I'll sit and see if that small sailing cloud
Will hit or miss the moon."

                    It hit the moon.
Then there were three there, making a dim row,
The moon, the little silver cloud, and she.

Warren returned—too soon, it seemed to her,
Slipped to her side, caught up her hand and waited.

"Warren," she questioned.

"Dead," was all he answered.

## After Apple-Picking

My long two-pointed ladder's sticking through a tree
Toward heaven still,
And there's a barrel that I didn't fill
Beside it, and there may be two or three
Apples I didn't pick upon some bough.
But I am done with apple-picking now.
Essence of winter sleep is on the night,
The scent of apples: I am drowsing off.
I cannot rub the strangeness from my sight
I got from looking through a pane of glass
I skimmed this morning from the drinking trough
And held against the world of hoary grass.
It melted, and I let it fall and break.
But I was well
Upon my way to sleep before it fell,
And I could tell
What form my dreaming was about to take.
Magnified apples appear and disappear,
Stem end and blossom end,
And every fleck of russet showing clear.
My instep arch not only keeps the ache,
It keeps the pressure of a ladder-round.
I feel the ladder sway as the boughs bend.
And I keep hearing from the cellar bin
The rumbling sound
Of load on load of apples coming in.
For I have had too much
Of apple-picking: I am overtired

Of the great harvest I myself desired.
There were ten thousand thousand fruit to touch,
Cherish in hand, lift down, and not let fall.
For all
That struck the earth,
No matter if not bruised or spiked with stubble,
Went surely to the cider-apple heap
As of no worth.
One can see what will trouble
This sleep of mine, whatever sleep it is.
Were he not gone,
The woodchuck could say whether it's like his
Long sleep, as I describe its coming on,
Or just some human sleep.

## The Wood-Pile

Out walking in the frozen swamp one grey day
I paused and said, "I will turn back from here.
No, I will go on farther—and we shall see."
The hard snow held me, save where now and then
One foot went down. The view was all in lines
Straight up and down of tall slim trees
Too much alike to mark or name a place by
So as to say for certain I was here
Or somewhere else: I was just far from home.
A small bird flew before me. He was careful
To put a tree between us when he lighted,
And say no word to tell me who he was
Who was so foolish as to think what *he* thought.
He thought that I was after him for a feather—
The white one in his tail; like one who takes
Everything said as personal to himself.
One flight out sideways would have undeceived him.
And then there was a pile of wood for which
I forgot him and let his little fear

Carry him off the way I might have gone,
Without so much as wishing him good-night.
He went behind it to make his last stand.
It was a cord of maple, cut and split
And piled—and measured, four by four by eight.
And not another like it could I see.
No runner tracks in this year's snow looped near it.
And it was older sure than this year's cutting,
Or even last year's or the year's before.
The wood was grey and the bark warping off it
And the pile somewhat sunken. Clematis
Had wound strings round and round it like a bundle.
What held it though on one side was a tree
Still growing, and on one a stake and prop,
These latter about to fall. I thought that only
Someone who lived in turning to fresh tasks
Could so forget his handiwork on which
He spent himself, the labour of his axe,
And leave it there far from a useful fireplace
To warm the frozen swamp as best it could
With the slow smokeless burning of decay.

## The Road Not Taken

Two roads diverged in a yellow wood,
And sorry I could not travel both
And be one traveler, long I stood
And looked down one as far as I could
To where it bent in the undergrowth;

Then took the other, as just as fair,
And having perhaps the better claim,
Because it was grassy and wanted wear;
Though as for that the passing there
Had worn them really about the same,

And both that morning equally lay
In leaves no step had trodden black.
Oh, I kept the first for another day!
Yet knowing how way leads on to way,
I doubted if I should ever come back.

I shall be telling this with a sigh
Somewhere ages and ages hence:
Two roads diverged in a wood, and I—
I took the one less traveled by,
And that has made all the difference.

## Birches

When I see birches bend to left and right
Across the lines of straighter darker trees,
I like to think some boy's been swinging them.
But swinging doesn't bend them down to stay.
Ice-storms do that. Often you must have seen them
Loaded with ice a sunny winter morning
After a rain. They click upon themselves
As the breeze rises, and turn many-colored
As the stir cracks and crazes their enamel.
Soon the sun's warmth makes them shed crystal shells
Shattering and avalanching on the snowcrust—
Such heaps of broken glass to sweep away
You'd think the inner dome of heaven had fallen.
They are dragged to the withered bracken by the load,
And they seem not to break; though once they are bowed
So low for long, they never right themselves:
You may see their trunks arching in the woods
Years afterwards, trailing their leaves on the ground
Like girls on hands and knees that throw their hair
Before them over their heads to dry in the sun.
But I was going to say when Truth broke in

With all her matter-of-fact about the ice-storm
(Now am I free to be poetical?)
I should prefer to have some boy bend them
As he went out and in to fetch the cows—
Some boy too far from town to learn baseball,
Whose only play was what he found himself,
Summer or winter, and could play alone.
One by one he subdued his father's trees
By riding them down over and over again
Until he took the stiffness out of them,
And not one but hung limp, not one was left
For him to conquer. He learned all there was
To learn about not launching out too soon
And so not carrying the tree away
Clear to the ground. He always kept his poise
To the top branches, climbing carefully
With the same pains you use to fill a cup
Up to the brim, and even above the brim.
Then he flung outward, feet first, with a swish,
Kicking his way down through the air to the ground.
So was I once myself a swinger of birches.
And so I dream of going back to be.
It's when I'm weary of considerations,
And life is too much like a pathless wood
Where your face burns and tickles with the cobwebs
Broken across it, and one eye is weeping
From a twig's having lashed across it open.
I'd like to get away from earth awhile
And then come back to it and begin over.
May no fate willfully misunderstand me
And half grant what I wish and snatch me away
Not to return. Earth's the right place for love:
I don't know where it's likely to go better.
I'd like to go by climbing a birch tree,
And climb black branches up a snow-white trunk
*Toward* heaven, till the tree could bear no more,

But dipped its top and set me down again.
That would be good both going and coming back.
One could do worse than be a swinger of birches.

———

# Design

I found a dimpled spider, fat and white,
On a white heal-all, holding up a moth
Like a white piece of rigid satin cloth—
Assorted characters of death and blight
Mixed ready to begin the morning right,
Like the ingredients of a witches' broth—
A snow-drop spider, a flower like froth,
And dead wings carried like a paper kite.

What had that flower to do with being white,
The wayside blue and innocent heal-all?
What brought the kindred spider to that height,
Then steered the white moth thither in the night?
What but designs of darkness to appal?—
If design govern in a thing so small.

———

# EDNA ST. VINCENT MILLAY
## (1892–1950)

## Renascence

All I could see from where I stood
Was three long mountains and a wood;
I turned and looked another way,
And saw three islands in a bay.
So with my eyes I traced the line
Of the horizon, thin and fine,
Straight around till I was come
Back to where I'd started from;
And all I saw from where I stood
Was three long mountains and a wood.
Over these things I could not see;
These were the things that bounded me;
And I could touch them with my hand,
Almost, I thought, from where I stand.
And all at once things seemed so small
My breath came short, and scarce at all.
But, sure, the sky is big, I said;
Miles and miles above my head;
So here upon my back I'll lie
And look my fill into the sky.
And so I looked, and, after all,
The sky was not so very tall.
The sky, I said, must somewhere stop,
And—sure enough!—I see the top!
The sky, I thought, is not so grand;
I 'most could touch it with my hand!

And, reaching up my hand to try,
I screamed to feel it touch the sky.

I screamed, and—lo!—Infinity
Came down and settled over me;
Forced back my scream into my chest,
Bent back my arm upon my breast,
And, pressing of the Undefined
The definition on my mind,
Held up before my eyes a glass
Through which my shrinking sight did pass
Until it seemed I must behold
Immensity made manifold;
Whispered to me a word whose sound
Deafened the air for worlds around,
And brought unmuffled to my ears
The gossiping of friendly spheres,
The creaking of the tented sky,
The ticking of Eternity.
I saw and heard, and knew at last
The How and Why of all things, past,
And present, and forevermore.
The universe, cleft to the core,
Lay open to my probing sense
That, sick'ning, I would fain pluck thence
But could not,—nay! But needs must suck
At the great wound, and could not pluck
My lips away till I had drawn
All venom out.—Ah, fearful pawn!
For my omniscience paid I toll
In infinite remorse of soul.
All sin was of my sinning, all
Atoning mine, and mine the gall
Of all regret. Mine was the weight
Of every brooded wrong, the hate
That stood behind each envious thrust,
Mine every greed, mine every lust.

And all the while for every grief,
Each suffering, I craved relief
With individual desire,—
Craved all in vain! And felt fierce fire
About a thousand people crawl;
Perished with each,—then mourned for all!
A man was starving in Capri;
He moved his eyes and looked at me;
I felt his gaze, I heard his moan,
And knew his hunger as my own.
I saw at sea a great fog-bank
Between two ships that struck and sank;
A thousand screams the heavens smote;
And every scream tore through my throat.
No hurt I did not feel, no death
That was not mine; mine each last breath
That, crying, met an answering cry
From the compassion that was I.
All suffering mine, and mine its rod;
Mine, pity like the pity of God.
Ah, awful weight! Infinity
Pressed down upon the finite Me!
My anguished spirit, like a bird,
Beating against my lips I heard;
Yet lay the weight so close about
There was no room for it without.
And so beneath the Weight lay I
And suffered death, but could not die.

Long had I lain thus, craving death,
When quietly the earth beneath
Gave way, and inch by inch, so great
At last had grown the crushing weight,
Into the earth I sank till I
Full six feet under ground did lie,
And sank no more,—there is no weight
Can follow here, however great.

From off my breast I felt it roll,
And as it went my tortured soul
Burst forth and fled in such a gust
That all about me swirled the dust.

Deep in the earth I rested now;
Cool is its hand upon the brow
And soft its breast beneath the head
Of one who is so gladly dead.
And all at once, and over all
The pitying rain began to fall;
I lay and heard each pattering hoof
Upon my lowly, thatchèd roof,
And seemed to love the sound far more
Than ever I had done before.
For rain it hath a friendly sound
To one who's six feet underground;
And scarce the friendly voice or face:
A grave is such a quiet place.

The rain, I said, is kind to come
And speak to me in my new home.
I would I were alive again
To kiss the fingers of the rain,
To drink into my eyes the shine
Of every slanting silver line,
To catch the freshened, fragrant breeze
From drenched and dripping apple-trees.
For soon the shower will be done,
And then the broad face of the sun
Will laugh above the rain-soaked earth
Until the world with answering mirth
Shakes joyously, and each round drop
Rolls, twinkling, from its grass-blade top.
How can I bear it; buried here,
While overhead the sky grows clear
And blue again after the storm?

O, multi-colored, multiform,
Beloved beauty over me,
That I shall never, never see
Again! Spring-silver, autumn-gold,
That I shall never more behold!
Sleeping your myriad magics through,
Close-sepulchred away from you!
O God, I cried, give me new birth,
And put me back upon the earth!
Upset each cloud's gigantic gourd
And let the heavy rain, down-poured
In one big torrent, set me free,
Washing my grave away from me!

I ceased; and, through the breathless hush
That answered me, the far-off rush
Of herald wings came whispering
Like music down the vibrant string
Of my ascending prayer, and—crash!
Before the wild wind's whistling lash
The startled storm-clouds reared on high
And plunged in terror down the sky,
And the big rain in one black wave
Fell from the sky and struck my grave.

I know not how such things can be
I only know there came to me
A fragrance such as never clings
To aught save happy living things;
A sound as of some joyous elf
Singing sweet songs to please himself,
And, through and over everything,
A sense of glad awakening.
The grass, a-tiptoe at my ear,
Whispering to me I could hear;
I felt the rain's cool finger-tips
Brushed tenderly across my lips,

Laid gently on my sealèd sight,
And all at once the heavy night
Fell from my eyes and I could see,—
A drenched and dripping apple-tree,
A last long line of silver rain,
A sky grown clear and blue again.
And as I looked a quickening gust
Of wind blew up to me and thrust
Into my face a miracle
Of orchard-breath, and with the smell,—
I know not how such things can be!—
I breathed my soul back into me.
Ah! Up then from the ground sprang I
And hailed the earth with such a cry
As is not heard save from a man
Who has been dead, and lives again.
About the trees my arms I wound;
Like one gone mad I hugged the ground;
I raised my quivering arms on high;
I laughed and laughed into the sky,
Till at my throat a strangling sob
Caught fiercely, and a great heart-throb
Sent instant tears into my eyes;
O God, I cried, no dark disguise
Can e'er hereafter hide from me
Thy radiant identity!
Thou canst not move across the grass
But my quick eyes will see Thee pass,
Nor speak, however silently,
But my hushed voice will answer Thee.
I know the path that tells Thy way
Through the cool eve of every day;
God, I can push the grass apart
And lay my finger on Thy heart!

The world stands out on either side
No wider than the heart is wide;

Above the world is stretched the sky,—
No higher than the soul is high.
The heart can push the sea and land
Farther away on either hand;
The soul can split the sky in two,
And let the face of God shine through.
But East and West will pinch the heart
That cannot keep them pushed apart;
And he whose soul is flat—the sky
Will cave in on him by and by.

## The Ballad of the Harp-Weaver

"Son," said my mother,
  When I was knee-high,
"You've need of clothes to cover you,
  And not a rag have I.

"There's nothing in the house
  To make a boy breeches,
Nor shears to cut a cloth with
  Nor thread to take stitches.

"There's nothing in the house
  But a loaf-end of rye,
And a harp with a woman's head
  Nobody will buy,"
  And she began to cry.

That was in the early fall.
  When came the late fall,
"Son," she said, "the sight of you
  Makes your mother's blood crawl,–

"Little skinny shoulder-blades
  Sticking through your clothes!

And where you'll get a jacket from
    God above knows.

"It's lucky for me, lad,
    Your daddy's in the ground,
And can't see the way I let
    His son go around!"
    And she made a queer sound.

That was in the late fall.
    When the winter came,
I'd not a pair of breeches
    Nor a shirt to my name.

I couldn't go to school,
    Or out of doors to play.
And all the other little boys
    Passed our way.

"Son," said my mother,
    "Come, climb into my lap,
And I'll chafe your little bones
    While you take a nap."

And, oh, but we were silly
    For half an hour or more,
Me with my long legs
    Dragging on the floor,

A-rock-rock-rocking
    To a mother-goose rhyme!
Oh, but we were happy
    For half an hour's time!

But there was I, a great boy,
    And what would folks say
To hear my mother singing me
    To sleep all day,
    In such a daft way?

Men say the winter
 Was bad that year;
Fuel was scarce,
 And food was dear.

A wind with a wolf's head
 Howled about our door,
And we burned up the chairs
 And sat upon the floor.

All that was left us
 Was a chair we couldn't break,
And the harp with a woman's head
 Nobody would take,
 For song or pity's sake.

The night before Christmas
 I cried with the cold,
I cried myself to sleep
 Like a two-year-old.

And in the deep night
 I felt my mother rise,
And stare down upon me
 With love in her eyes.

I saw my mother sitting
 On the one good chair,
A light falling on her
 From I couldn't tell where,

Looking nineteen,
 And not a day older,
And the harp with a woman's head
 Leaned against her shoulder.

Her thin fingers, moving
   In the thin, tall strings,
Were weav-weav-weaving
   Wonderful things.

Many bright threads,
   From where I couldn't see,
Were running through the harp-strings
   Rapidly,

And gold threads whistling
   Through my mother's hand.
I saw the web grow,
   And the pattern expand.

She wove a child's jacket,
   And when it was done
She laid it on the floor
   And wove another one.

She wove a red cloak
   So regal to see,
"She's made it for a king's son,"
   I said, "and not for me."
   But I knew it was for me.

She wove a pair of breeches
   Quicker than that!
She wove a pair of boots
   And a little cocked hat.

She wove a pair of mittens,
   She wove a little blouse,
She wove all night
   In the still, cold house.

She sang as she worked,
    And the harp-strings spoke;
Her voice never faltered,
    And the thread never broke.
    And when I awoke,—

There sat my mother
    With the harp against her shoulder
Looking nineteen
    And not a day older,

A smile about her lips,
    And a light about her head,
And her hands in the harp-strings
    Frozen dead.

And piled up beside her
    And toppling to the skies,
Were the clothes of a king's son,
    Just my size.

# WALLACE STEVENS
## (1879–1955)

## The Emperor of Ice-Cream

Call the roller of big cigars,
The muscular one, and bid him whip
In kitchen cups concupiscent curds.
Let the wenches dawdle in such dress
As they are used to wear, and let the boys
Bring flowers in last month's newspapers.
Let be be finale of seem.
The only emperor is the emperor of ice-cream.

Take from the dresser of deal,
Lacking the three glass knobs, that sheet
On which she embroidered fantails once
And spread it so as to cover her face.
If her horny feet protrude, they come
To show how cold she is, and dumb.
Let the lamp affix its beam.
The only emperor is the emperor of ice-cream.

## Disillusionment of Ten O'clock

The houses are haunted
By white night-gowns.
None are green,
Or purple with green rings,
Or green with yellow rings.

Or yellow with blue rings,
None of them are strange.
With socks of lace
And beaded ceintures.
People are not going
To dream of baboons and periwinkles.
Only, here and there, an old sailor.
Drunk and asleep in his boots.
Catches tigers
In red weather.

———

## Thirteen Ways of Looking at a Blackbird

### I

Among twenty snowy mountains,
The only moving thing
Was the eye of the blackbird.

### II

I was of three minds,
Like a tree
In which there are three blackbirds.

### III

The blackbirds whirled in the autumn winds.
It was a small part of the pantomime.

### IV

A man and a woman
Are one.
A man and a woman and a blackbird
Are one.

### V

I do not know which to prefer—
The beauty of inflections

Or the beauty of innuendoes,
The blackbird whistling
Or just after.

## VI

Icicles filled the long window
With barbaric glass.
The shadow of the blackbird
Crossed it, to and fro.
The mood
Traced in the shadow
An indecipherable course.

## VII

O thin men of Haddam,
Why do you imagine golden birds?
Do you not see how the blackbird
Walks around the feet
Of the women about you?

## VIII

I know noble accents
And lucid, inescapable rhythms;
But I know, too,
That the blackbird is involved
In what I know.

## IX

When the blackbird flew out of sight,
It marked the edge
Of one of many circles.

## X

At the sight of blackbirds
Flying in a green light,
Even the bawds of euphony
Would cry out sharply.

### XI

He rode over Connecticut
In a glass coach.
Once, a fear pierced him,
In that he mistook
The shadow of his equipage
For blackbirds.

### XII

The river is moving.
The blackbird must be flying.

### XIII

It was evening all afternoon.
It was snowing
And it was going to snow.
The blackbird sat
In the cedar-limbs.

## Of the Manner of Addressing Clouds

Gloomy grammarians in golden gowns,
Meekly you keep the mortal rendezvous,
Eliciting the still sustaining pomps
Of speech which are like music so profound
They seem an exaltation without sound.
Funest philosophers and ponderers,
Their evocations are the speech of clouds.
So speech of your processionals returns
In the casual evocations of your tread
Across the stale, mysterious seasons. These
Are the music of meet resignation; these
The responsive, still sustaining pomps for you
To magnify, if in that drifting waste
You are to be accompanied by more
Than mute bare splendors of the sun and moon.

# A High-Toned Old Christian Woman

Poetry is the supreme fiction, madame.
Take the moral law and make a nave of it
And from the nave build haunted heaven. Thus,
The conscience is converted into palms,
Like windy citherns hankering for hymns.
We agree in principle. That's clear. But take
The opposing law and make a peristyle,
And from the peristyle project a masque
Beyond the planets. Thus, our bawdiness,
Unpurged by epitaph, indulged at last,
Is equally converted into palms,
Squiggling like saxophones. And palm for palm,
Madame, we are where we began. Allow,
Therefore, that in the planetary scene
Your disaffected flagellants, well-stuffed,
Smacking their muzzy bellies in parade.
Proud of such novelties of the sublime,
Such tink and tank and tunk-a-tunk-tunk,
May, merely may, madame, whip from themselves
A jovial hullabaloo among the spheres.
This will make widows wince. But fictive things
Wink as they will. Wink most when widows wince.

# The Snow Man

One must have a mind of winter
To regard the frost and the boughs
Of the pine-trees crusted with snow;

And have been cold a long time
To behold the junipers shagged with ice,
The spruces rough in the distant glitter

Of the January sun; and not to think
Of any misery in the sound of the wind,
In the sound of a few leaves,

Which is the sound of the land
Full of the same wind
That is blowing in the same bare place

For the listener, who listens in the snow,
And, nothing himself, beholds
Nothing that is not there and the nothing that is.

## Sunday Morning

### I

Complacencies of the peignoir, and late
Coffee and oranges in a sunny chair,
And the green freedom of a cockatoo
Upon a rug mingle to dissipate
The holy hush of ancient sacrifice.
She dreams a little, and she feels the dark
Encroachment of that old catastrophe,
As a calm darkness among water-lights.
The pungent oranges and bright, green wings
Seem things in some procession of the dead,
Winding across wide water, without sound.
The day is like wide water, without sound,
Stilled for the passing of her dreaming feet
Over the seas, to silent Palestine,
Dominion of the blood and sepulchre.

### II

Why should she give her bounty to the dead?
What is divinity if it can come
Only in silent shadows and in dreams?
Shall she not find in comforts of the sun,
In pungent fruit and bright, green wings, or else
In any balm or beauty of the earth,
Things to be cherished like the thought of heaven?
Divinity must live within herself:

Passions of rain, or moods in falling snow;
Grievings in loneliness, or unsubdued
Elations when the forest blooms; gusty
Emotions on wet roads on autumn nights;
All pleasures and all pains, remembering
The bough of summer and the winter branch.
These are the measures destined for her soul.

### III

Jove in the clouds had his inhuman birth.
No mother suckled him, no sweet land gave
Large-mannered motions to his mythy mind.
He moved among us, as a muttering king,
Magnificent, would move among his hinds,
Until our blood, commingling, virginal,
With heaven, brought such requital to desire
The very hinds discerned it, in a star.
Shall our blood fail? Or shall it come to be
The blood of paradise? And shall the earth
Seem all of paradise that we shall know?
The sky will be much friendlier then than now,
A part of labor and a part of pain,
And next in glory to enduring love,
Not this dividing and indifferent blue.

### IV

She says, "I am content when wakened birds,
Before they fly, test the reality
Of misty fields, by their sweet questionings;
But when the birds are gone, and their warm fields
Return no more, where, then, is paradise?"
There is not any haunt of prophesy,
Nor any old chimera of the grave,
Neither the golden underground, nor isle
Melodious, where spirits gat them home,
Nor visionary south, nor cloudy palm
Remote on heaven's hill, that has endured

As April's green endures; or will endure
Like her remembrance of awakened birds,
Or her desire for June and evenings, tipped
By the consummation of the swallow's wings.

V

She says, "But in contentment I still feel
The need of some imperishable bliss."
Death is the mother of beauty; hence from her,
Alone, shall come fulfilment to our dreams
And our desires. Although she strews the leaves
Of sure obliteration on our paths,
The path sick sorrow took, the many paths
Where triumph rang its brassy phrase, or love
Whispered a little out of tenderness,
She makes the willow shiver in the sun
For maidens who were wont to sit and gaze
Upon the grass, relinquished to their feet.
She causes boys to pile new plums and pears
On disregarded plate. The maidens taste
And stray impassioned in the littering leaves.

VI

Is there no change of death in paradise?
Does ripe fruit never fall? Or do the boughs
Hang always heavy in that perfect sky,
Unchanging, yet so like our perishing earth,
With rivers like our own that seek for seas
They never find, the same receding shores
That never touch with inarticulate pang?
Why set the pear upon those river-banks
Or spice the shores with odors of the plum?
Alas, that they should wear our colors there,
The silken weavings of our afternoons,
And pick the strings of our insipid lutes!
Death is the mother of beauty, mystical,

Within whose burning bosom we devise
Our earthly mothers waiting, sleeplessly.

## VII

Supple and turbulent, a ring of men
Shall chant in orgy on a summer morn
Their boisterous devotion to the sun,
Not as a god, but as a god might be,
Naked among them, like a savage source.
Their chant shall be a chant of paradise,
Out of their blood, returning to the sky;
And in their chant shall enter, voice by voice,
The windy lake wherein their lord delights,
The trees, like serafin, and echoing hills,
That choir among themselves long afterward.
They shall know well the heavenly fellowship
Of men that perish and of summer morn.
And whence they came and whither they shall go
The dew upon their feet shall manifest.

## VIII

She hears, upon that water without sound,
A voice that cries, "The tomb in Palestine
Is not the porch of spirits lingering.
It is the grave of Jesus, where he lay."
We live in an old chaos of the sun,
Or an old dependency of day and night,
Or island solitude, unsponsored, free,
Of that wide water, inescapable.
Deer walk upon our mountains, and quail
Whistle about us their spontaneous cries;
Sweet berries ripen in the wilderness;
And, in the isolation of the sky,
At evening, casual flocks of pigeons make
Ambiguous undulations as they sink,
Downward to darkness, on extended wings.

# WILLIAM CARLOS WILLIAMS
## (1883–1963)

### Complaint

They call me and I go
It is a frozen road
past midnight, a dust
of snow caught
in the rigid wheeltracks.
The door opens.
I smile, enter and
shake off the cold.
Here is a great woman
on her side in the bed.
She is sick,
perhaps vomiting,
perhaps laboring
to give birth to
a tenth child. Joy! Joy!
Night is a room
darkened for lovers,
through the jalousies the sun
has sent one gold needle!
I pick the hair from her eyes
and watch her misery
with compassion.

## Queen-Ann's-Lace

Her body is not so white as
anemony petals nor so smooth—nor
so remote a thing. It is a field
of the wild carrot taking
the field by force; the grass
does not raise above it.
Here is no question of whiteness,
white as can be, with a purple mole
at the center of each flower.
Each flower is a hand's span
of her whiteness. Wherever
his hand has lain there is
a tiny purple blemish. Each part
is a blossom under his touch
to which the fibres of her being
stem one by one, each to its end,
until the whole field is a
white desire, empty, a single stem,
a cluster, flower by flower,
a pious wish to whiteness gone over—
or nothing.

## The Widow's Lament in Springtime

Sorrow is my own yard
where the new grass
flames as it has flamed
often before but not
with the cold fire
that closes round me this year.
Thirtyfive years
I lived with my husband.
The plumtree is white today
with masses of flowers.

Masses of flowers
load the cherry branches
and color some bushes
yellow and some red
but the grief in my heart
is stronger than they
for though they were my joy
formerly, today I notice them
and turn away forgetting.
Today my son told me
that in the meadows,
at the edge of the heavy woods
in the distance, he saw
trees of white flowers.
I feel that I would like
to go there
and fall into those flowers
and sink into the marsh near them.

## The Great Figure

Among the rain
and lights
I saw the figure 5
in gold
on a red
firetruck
moving
with weight and urgency
tense
unheeded
to gong clangs
siren howls
and wheels rumbling
through the dark city.

# T. S. ELIOT
## (1888–1965)

## The Love Song of J. Alfred Prufrock

*S' io credessi che mia risposta fosse*
*A persona che mai tornasse al mondo,*
*Questa fiamma staria senza piú scosse.*
*Ma perciocchè giammai di questo fondo*
*Non tornò vivo alcun, s' i' odo il vero,*
*Senza tema d' infamia ti rispondo.*

Let us go then, you and I,
When the evening is spread out against the sky
Like a patient etherized upon a table;
Let us go, through certain half-deserted streets,
The muttering retreats
Of restless nights in one-night cheap hotels
And sawdust restaurants with oyster-shells:
Streets that follow like a tedious argument
Of insidious intent
To lead you to an overwhelming question . . .

Oh, do not ask, "What is it?"
Let us go and make our visit.

In the room the women come and go
Talking of Michelangelo.

The yellow fog that rubs its back upon the window-panes,
The yellow smoke that rubs its muzzle on the window-panes,
Licked its tongue into the corners of the evening,

Lingered upon the pools that stand in drains,
Let fall upon its back the soot that falls from chimneys,
Slipped by the terrace, made a sudden leap,
And seeing that it was a soft October night,
Curled once about the house, and fell asleep.

And indeed there will be time
For the yellow smoke that slides along the street,
Rubbing its back upon the window-panes;
There will be time, there will be time
To prepare a face to meet the faces that you meet;
There will be time to murder and create,
And time for all the works and days of hands
That lift and drop a question on your plate;
Time for you and time for me,
And time yet for a hundred indecisions,
And for a hundred visions and revisions,
Before the taking of a toast and tea.

In the room the women come and go
Talking of Michelangelo.

And indeed there will be time
To wonder, "Do I dare?" and, "Do I dare?"
Time to turn back and descend the stair,
With a bald spot in the middle of my hair—
(They will say: "How his hair is growing thin!")
My morning coat, my collar mounting firmly to the chin,
My necktie rich and modest, but asserted by a simple pin—
(They will say: "But how his arms and legs are thin!")
Do I dare
Disturb the universe?
In a minute there is time
For decisions and revisions which a minute will reverse.

For I have known them all already, known them all:
Have known the evenings, mornings, afternoons,

I have measured out my life with coffee spoons;
I know the voices dying with a dying fall
Beneath the music from a farther room.
    So how should I presume?


    And I have known the eyes already, known them all—
The eyes that fix you in a formulated phrase,
And when I am formulated, sprawling on a pin,
When I am pinned and wriggling on the wall,
Then how should I begin
To spit out all the butt-ends of my days and ways?
    And how should I presume?


    And I have known the arms already, known them all—
Arms that are braceleted and white and bare
(But in the lamplight, downed with light brown hair!)
    Is it perfume from a dress
    That makes me so digress?
Arms that lie along a table, or wrap about a shawl.
    And should I then presume?
    And how should I begin?


                    *    *    *    *


    Shall I say, I have gone at dusk through narrow streets
And watched the smoke that rises from the pipes
Of lonely men in shirtsleeves, leaning out of windows? . . .


I should have been a pair of ragged claws
Scuttling across the floors of silent seas.


                    *    *    *    *


    And the afternoon, the evening, sleeps so peacefully!
Smoothed by long fingers,
Asleep . . . tired . . . or it malingers,
Stretched on the floor, here beside you and me.
Should I, after tea and cakes and ices,
Have the strength to force the moment to its crisis?

But though I have wept and fasted, wept and prayed,
Though I have seen my head (grown slightly bald) brought in upon a platter,
I am no prophet—and here's no great matter;
I have seen the moment of my greatness flicker,
And I have seen the eternal Footman hold my coat, and snicker,
    And in short, I was afraid.

    And would it have been worth it, after all,
After the cups, the marmalade, the tea,
Among the porcelain, among some talk of you and me,
Would it have been worth while,
To have bitten off the matter with a smile,
To have squeezed the universe into a ball
To roll it toward some overwhelming question,
To say: "I am Lazarus, come from the dead,
Come back to tell you all, I shall tell you all"—
If one, settling a pillow by her head,
    Should say: "That is not what I meant at all;
      That is not it, at all."

    And would it have been worth it, after all,
Would it have been worth while,
After the sunsets and the dooryards and the sprinkled streets,
After the novels, after the teacups, after the skirts that trail along the floor—
And this, and so much more?—
It is impossible to say just what I mean!
But as if a magic lantern threw the nerves in patterns on a screen:
Would it have been worth while
If one, settling a pillow or throwing off a shawl,
And turning toward the window, should say: "That is not it at all,
    That is not what I meant, at all."

        *   *   *   *

    No! I am not Prince Hamlet, nor was meant to be;
Am an attendant lord, one that will do
To swell a progress, start a scene or two,
Advise the prince; no doubt, an easy tool,

Deferential, glad to be of use,
Politic, cautious, and meticulous;
Full of high sentence, but a bit obtuse;
At times, indeed, almost ridiculous—
Almost, at times, the Fool.

I grow old . . . I grow old . . .
I shall wear the bottoms of my trowsers rolled.

   Shall I part my hair behind? Do I dare to eat a peach?
I shall wear white flannel trowsers, and walk upon the beach.
I have heard the mermaids singing, each to each.
I do not think that they will sing to me.

I have seen them riding seaward on the waves
Combing the white hair of the waves blown back
When the wind blows the water white and black.

We have lingered in the chambers of the sea
By seagirls wreathed with seaweed red and brown
Till human voices wake us, and we drown.

---

# The Waste Land

*Nam Sibyllam quidem Cumis ego ipse oculis meis
vidi in ampulla pendere, et cum illi pueri dicerent:*
Σίβυλλα τί θέλεις; *respondebut illa:* ἀποθανεῖν θ ἐλω.

### I. THE BURIAL OF THE DEAD

April is the cruellest month, breeding
Lilacs out of the dead land, mixing
Memory and desire, stirring
Dull roots with spring rain.
Winter kept us warm, covering
Earth in forgetful snow, feeding
A little life with dried tubers.

Summer surprised us, coming over the Starnbergersee
With a shower of rain; we stopped in the colonnade,
And went on in sunlight, into the Hofgarten,
And drank coffee, and talked for an hour.
Bin gar keine Russin, stamm' aus Litauen, echt deutsch.
And when we were children, staying at the archduke's,
My cousin's, he took me out on a sled,
And I was frightened. He said, Marie,
Marie, hold on tight. And down we went.
In the mountains, there you feel free.
I read, much of the night, and go south in the winter.

What are the roots that clutch, what branches grow
Out of this stony rubbish? Son of man,
You cannot say, or guess, for you know only
A heap of broken images, where the sun beats,
And the dead tree gives no shelter, the cricket no relief,
And the dry stone no sound of water. Only
There is shadow under this red rock,
(Come in under the shadow of this red rock),
And I will show you something different from either
Your shadow at morning striding behind you
Or your shadow at evening rising to meet you;
I will show you fear in a handful of dust.

> *Frisch weht der Wind*
> *Der Heimat zu*
> *Mein Irisch Kind,*
> *Wo weilest du?*

"You gave me hyacinths first a year ago;
They called me the hyacinth girl."
—Yet when we came back, late, from the Hyacinth garden,
Your arms full, and your hair wet, I could not
Speak, and my eyes failed, I was neither
Living nor dead, and I knew nothing,
Looking into the heart of light, the silence.
Od' und leer das Meer.

Madame Sosostris, famous clairvoyante,
Had a bad cold, nevertheless
Is known to be the wisest woman in Europe,
With a wicked pack of cards. Here, said she,
Is your card, the drowned Phoenician Sailor,
(Those are pearls that were his eyes. Look!)
Here is Belladonna, the Lady of the Rocks,
The lady of situations.
Here is the man with three staves, and here the Wheel,
And here is the one-eyed merchant, and this card,
Which is blank, is something he carries on his back,
Which I am forbidden to see. I do not find
The Hanged Man. Fear death by water.
I see crowds of people, walking round in a ring.
Thank you. If you see dear Mrs. Equitone,
Tell her I bring the horoscope myself:
One must be so careful these days.

Unreal City,
Under the brown fog of a winter dawn,
A crowd flowed over London Bridge, so many,
I had not thought death had undone so many.
Sighs, short and infrequent, were exhaled,
And each man fixed his eyes before his feet.
Flowed up the hill and down King William Street,
To where Saint Mary Woolnoth kept the hours
With a dead sound on the final stroke of nine.
There I saw one I knew, and stopped him, crying: "Stetson!
You who were with me in the ships at Mylae!
That corpse you planted last year in your garden,
Has it begun to sprout? Will it bloom this year?
Or has the sudden frost disturbed its bed?
Oh keep the Dog far hence, that's friend to men,
Or with his nails he'll dig it up again!
You! hypocrite lecteur!—mon semblable,—mon frère!"

## II. A GAME OF CHESS

The Chair she sat in, like a burnished throne,
Glowed on the marble, where the glass
Held up by standards wrought with fruited vines
From which a golden Cupidon peeped out
(Another hid his eyes behind his wing)
Doubled the flames of sevenbranched candelabra
Reflecting light upon the table as
The glitter of her jewels rose to meet it,
From satin cases poured in rich profusion;
In vials of ivory and coloured glass
Unstoppered, lurked her strange synthetic perfumes,
Unguent, powdered, or liquid—troubled, confused
And drowned the sense in odours; stirred by the air
That freshened from the window, these ascended
In fattening the prolonged candle-flames,
Flung their smoke into the laquearia,
Stirring the pattern on the coffered ceiling.
Huge sea-wood fed with copper
Burned green and orange, framed by the coloured stone,
In which sad light a carvèd dolphin swam.
Above the antique mantel was displayed
As though a window gave upon the sylvan scene
The change of Philomel, by the barbarous king
So rudely forced; yet there the nightingale
Filled all the desert with inviolable voice
And still she cried, and still the world pursues,
"Jug Jug" to dirty ears.
And other withered stumps of time
Were told upon the walls; staring forms
Leaned out, leaning, hushing the room enclosed.
Footsteps shuffled on the stair.
Under the firelight, under the brush, her hair
Spread out in fiery points
Glowed into words, then would be savagely still.

"My nerves are bad tonight. Yes, bad. Stay with me.
Speak to me. Why do you never speak? Speak.
What are you thinking of? What thinking? What?
I never know what you are thinking. Think."

I think we are in rats' alley
Where the dead men lost their bones.
"What is that noise?"
                                    The wind under the door.
"What is that noise now? What is the wind doing?"
                        Nothing again nothing.
                                          "Do
You know nothing? Do you see nothing? Do you remember
        Do you remember
Nothing?"
        I remember
Those are pearls that were his eyes.
"Are you alive, or not? Is there nothing in your head?"
                                          But
O O O O that Shakespeherian Rag—
It's so elegant
So intelligent
"What shall I do now? What shall I do?"
"I shall rush out as I am, and walk the street
With my hair down, so. What shall we do tomorrow?
What shall we ever do?"
                          The hot water at ten.
And if it rains, a closed car at four.
And we shall play a game of chess,
Pressing lidless eyes and waiting for a knock upon the door.


When Lil's husband got demobbed, I said—
I didn't mince my words, I said to her myself,
HURRY UP PLEASE IT'S TIME
Now Albert's coming back, make yourself a bit smart.
He'll want to know what you done with that money he gave you

To get yourself some teeth. He did, I was there.
You have them all out, Lil, and get a nice set,
He said, I swear, I can't bear to look at you.
And no more can't I, I said, and think of poor Albert,
He's been in the army four years, he wants a good time,
And if you dont give it him, there's others will, I said.
Oh is there, she said. Something o' that, I said.
Then I'll know who to thank, she said, and give me a straight look.
HURRY UP PLEASE IT'S TIME
If you dont like it you can get on with it, I said,
Others can pick and choose if you can't.
But if Albert makes off, it won't be for lack of telling.
You ought to be ashamed, I said, to look so antique.
(And her only thirty-one.)
I can't help it, she said, pulling a long face,
It's them pills I took, to bring it off, she said.
(She's had five already, and nearly died of young George.)
The chemist said it would be alright, but I've never been the same.
You *are* a proper fool, I said.
Well, if Albert wont leave you alone, there it is, I said,
What you get married for if you dont want children?
HURRY UP PLEASE IT'S TIME
Well, that Sunday Albert was home, they had a hot gammon,
And they asked me in to dinner, to get the beauty of it hot—
HURRY UP PLEASE IT'S TIME
HURRY UP PLEASE IT'S TIME
Goonight Bill. Goonight Lou. Goonight May. Goonight.
Ta ta. Goonight. Goonight.
Good night, ladies, good night, sweet ladies, good night, good night.

### III. THE FIRE SERMON

The river's tent is broken: the last fingers of leaf
Clutch and sink into the wet bank. The wind
Crosses the brown land, unheard. The nymphs are departed.
Sweet Thames, run softly, till I end my song.
The river bears no empty bottles, sandwich papers,
Silk handkerchiefs, cardboard boxes, cigarette ends

Or other testimony of summer nights. The nymphs are departed.
And their friends, the loitering heirs of city directors;
Departed, have left no addresses.
By the waters of Leman I sat down and wept . . .
Sweet Thames, run softly till I end my song,
Sweet Thames, run softly, for I speak not loud or long.
But at my back in a cold blast I hear
The rattle of the bones, and chuckle spread from ear to ear.

A rat crept softly through the vegetation
Dragging its slimy belly on the bank
While I was fishing in the dull canal
On a winter evening round behind the gashouse
Musing upon the king my brother's wreck
And on the king my father's death before him.
White bodies naked on the low damp ground
And bones cast in a little low dry garret,
Rattled by the rat's foot only, year to year.
But at my back from time to time I hear
The sound of horns and motors, which shall bring
Sweeney to Mrs. Porter in the spring.
O the moon shone bright on Mrs. Porter
And on her daughter
They wash their feet in soda water
*Et O ces voix d'enfants, chantant dans la coupole!*

Twit twit twit
Jug jug jug jug jug jug
So rudely forc'd.
Tereu

Unreal City
Under the brown fog of a winter noon
Mr. Eugenides, the Smyrna merchant
Unshaven, with a pocket full of currants
C.i.f. London: documents at sight,
Asked me in demotic French

To luncheon at the Cannon Street Hotel
Followed by a weekend at the Metropole.

At the violet hour, when the eyes and back
Turn upward from the desk, when the human engine waits
Like a taxi throbbing waiting,
I Tiresias, though blind, throbbing between two lives,
Old man with wrinkled female breasts, can see
At the violet hour, the evening hour that strives
Homeward, and brings the sailor home from sea,
The typist home at teatime, clears her breakfast, lights
Her stove, and lays out food in tins.
Out of the window perilously spread
Her drying combinations touched by the sun's last rays,
On the divan are piled (at night her bed)
Stockings, slippers, camisoles, and stays.
I Tiresias, old man with wrinkled dugs
Perceived the scene, and foretold the rest—
I too awaited the expected guest.
He, the young man carbuncular, arrives,
A small house agent's clerk, with one bold stare,
One of the low on whom assurance sits
As a silk hat on a Bradford millionaire.
The time is now propitious, as he guesses,
The meal is ended, she is bored and tired,
Endeavours to engage her in caresses
Which still are unreproved, if undesired.
Flushed and decided, he assaults at once;
Exploring hands encounter no defence;
His vanity requires no response,
And makes a welcome of indifference.
(And I Tiresias have foresuffered all
Enacted on this same divan or bed;
I who have sat by Thebes below the wall
And walked among the lowest of the dead.)
Bestows one final patronising kiss,
And gropes his way, finding the stairs unlit . . .

She turns and looks a moment in the glass,
Hardly aware of her departed lover;
Her brain allows one half-formed thought to pass:
"Well now that's done: and I'm glad it's over."
When lovely woman stoops to folly and
Paces about her room again, alone,
She smoothes her hair with automatic hand,
And puts a record on the gramophone.

"This music crept by me upon the waters"
And along the Strand, up Queen Victoria Street.
O City city, I can sometimes hear
Beside a public bar in Lower Thames Street,
The pleasant whining of a mandoline
And a clatter and a chatter from within
Where fishmen lounge at noon: where the walls
Of Magnus Martyr hold
Inexplicable splendour of Ionian white and gold.

The river sweats
Oil and tar
The barges drift
With the turning tide
Red sails
Wide
To leeward, swing on the heavy spar.
The barges wash
Drifting logs
Down Greenwich reach
Past the Isle of Dogs.
   Weialala leia
   Wallala leialala
Elizabeth and Leicester
Beating oars
The stern was formed
A gilded shell
Red and gold

The brisk swell
Rippled both shores
Southwest wind
Carried down stream
The peal of bells
White towers
                    Weialala leia
                    Wallala leialala

"Trams and dusty trees.
Highbury bore me. Richmond and Kew
Undid me. By Richmond I raised my knees
Supine on the floor of a narrow canoe."

"My feet are at Moorgate, and my heart
Under my feet. After the event
He wept. He promised 'a new start.'
I made no comment. What should I resent?"
"On Margate Sands.
I can connect
Nothing with nothing.
The broken fingernails of dirty hands.
My people humble people who expect
Nothing."
                    la la

To Carthage then I came

Burning burning burning burning
O Lord Thou pluckest me out
O Lord Thou pluckest

burning

#### IV. DEATH BY WATER

Phlebas the Phoenician, a fortnight dead,
Forgot the cry of gulls, and the deep sea swell
And the profit and loss.

                    A current under sea

Picked his bones in whispers. As he rose and fell
He passed the stages of his age and youth
Entering the whirlpool.

                      Gentile or Jew
O you who turn the wheel and look to windward,
Consider Phlebas, who was once handsome and tall as you.

## V. WHAT THE THUNDER SAID

After the torchlight red on sweaty faces
After the frosty silence in the gardens
After the agony in stony places
The shouting and the crying
Prison and palace and reverberation
Of thunder of spring over distant mountains
He who was living is now dead
We who were living are now dying
With a little patience

Here is no water but only rock
Rock and no water and the sandy road
The road winding above among the mountains
Which are mountains of rock without water
If there were water we should stop and drink
Amongst the rock one cannot stop or think
Sweat is dry and feet are in the sand
If there were only water amongst the rock
Dead mountain mouth of carious teeth that cannot spit
Here one can neither stand nor lie nor sit
There is not even silence in the mountains
But dry sterile thunder without rain
There is not even solitude in the mountains
But red sullen faces sneer and snarl
From doors of mudcracked houses
                      If there were water

  And no rock
  If there were rock
  And also water

And water
A spring
A pool among the rock
If there were the sound of water only
Not the cicada
And dry grass singing
But sound of water over a rock
Where the hermit-thrush sings in the pine trees
Drip drop drip drop drop drop drop
But there is no water

Who is the third who walks always beside you?
When I count, there are only you and I together
But when I look ahead up the white road
There is always another one walking beside you
Gliding wrapt in a brown mantle, hooded
I do not know whether a man or a woman
—But who is that on the other side of you?
What is that sound high in the air
Murmur of maternal lamentation
Who are those hooded hordes swarming
Over endless plains, stumbling in cracked earth
Ringed by the flat horizon only
What is the city over the mountains
Cracks and reforms and bursts in the violet air
Falling towers
Jerusalem Athens Alexandria
Vienna London
Unreal

A woman drew her long black hair out tight
And fiddled whisper music on those strings
And bats with baby faces in the violet light
Whistled, and beat their wings
And crawled head downward down a blackened wall
And upside down in air were towers

Tolling reminiscent bells, that kept the hours
And voices singing out of empty cisterns and exhausted wells.

In this decayed hole among the mountains
In the faint moonlight, the grass is singing
Over the tumbled graves, about the chapel
There is the empty chapel, only the wind's home.
It has no windows, and the door swings,
Dry bones can harm no one.
Only a cock stood on the rooftree
Co co rico co co rico
In a flash of lightning. Then a damp gust
Bringing rain
Ganga was sunken, and the limp leaves
Waited for rain, while the black clouds
Gathered far distant, over Himavant.
The jungle crouched, humped in silence.
Then spoke the thunder
DA
*Datta:* what have we given?
My friend, blood shaking my heart
The awful daring of a moment's surrender
Which an age of prudence can never retract
By this, and this only, we have existed
Which is not to be found in our obituaries
Or in memories draped by the beneficent spider
Or under seals broken by the lean solicitor
In our empty rooms
DA
*Dayadhvam*: I have heard the key
Turn in the door once and turn once only
We think of the key, each in his prison
Thinking of the key, each confirms a prison
Only at nightfall, aetherial rumours
Revive for a moment a broken Coriolanus

Da

*Damyata:* The boat responded
Gaily, to the hand expert with sail and oar
The sea was calm, your heart would have responded
Gaily, when invited, beating obedient
To controlling hands

       I sat upon the shore
Fishing, with the arid plain behind me
Shall I at least set my lands in order?

London Bridge is falling down falling down falling down
*Poi s'ascose nel foco che gli affina*
*Quando fiam ceu chelidon*—O swallow swallow
*Le Prince d'Aquitaine à la tour abolie*
These fragments I have shored against my ruins
Why then Ile fit you. Hieronymo's mad againe.
Datta. Dayadhvam. Damyata.

  Shantih  shantih  shantih

# About the Authors

**Matthew Arnold** (1822–1888) was an English poet, critic, and essayist. His first two collections of poetry, *The Strayed Reveller and Other Poems* (1849) and *Empedocles on Etna and Other Poems* (1852), were published pseudonymously. *Poems: A New Edition* (1853) was the first collection of his verse to appear under his own name. In a letter that dates to March 1, 1849, Arnold outlined what he believed to be the function of poetry when he wrote, "there are two offices of Poetry—one to add to one's store of thoughts and feelings—another to compose and elevate the mind by a sustained tone, numerous allusions, and a grand style."

**William Blake** (1757–1827) was an English Romantic poet and artist who worked occasionally as an engraver and printseller. Blake illuminated *Songs of Innocence and Experience* (1794), expanded from *Songs of Innocence* (1789), with color plates of his own drawings, a pattern he would follow for most publications of his verse that followed. The poems were Blake's attempt to elaborate "the two Contrary States of the Human Soul" (as he wrote in his subtitle for the book), and they express themes that Blake would return to in his later work, among them the clash of reason and imagination. Blake's greatest works include the epic cycle that comprises *The First Book of Urizen* (1794), *The Book of Los* (1795), *The Song of Los* (1795), and *The Book of Ahania* (1795), for which he conceived a universal mythology drawn from his mystic imagination.

**Rupert Brooke** (1887–1915) was an English poet who began writing verse in his teens and who became especially skilled at the sonnet form. Regarded as one of the most talented poets of his generation, he saw only one collection published in his lifetime: *Poems* (1911). At the outbreak of World War I, he joined the Royal Navy Volunteer Reserve, and was sailing to the Gallipoli Campaign in the Dardanelles when he developed a fatal case of blood poisoning. *1914 and Other Poems*, which includes the five patriotic war sonnets that were part of "1914," was published in 1915.

**Elizabeth Barrett Browning** (1806–1861) was an English poet who, in 1846, famously eloped with the poet Robert Browning, with whom she had struck up a correspondence. Browning had written her a letter of appreciation following the publication of her collection *Poems* (1844), which established her as one of the most popular poets of her age. Browning's best-known works in her lifetime were *Sonnets from the Portuguese*, a cycle of love sonnets written for her husband and published in the 1850 edition of *Poems*, and her epic poem in blank verse, *Aurora Leigh* (1857).

**Robert Browning** (1812–1889) was an English poet and the husband of Elizabeth Barrett Browning, whose popularly acclaimed work overshadowed his for much of his lifetime. With "My Last Duchess" (1842) and "The Bishop Orders His Tomb at St. Praxed's Church" (1845), Browning perfected the dramatic monologue, which was to become one of his signature contributions to poetry. Other dramatic monologues and the heroic lyric "Childe Roland to the Dark Tower Came" were collected in Browning's *Men and Women* (1855). His most highly regarded poem in his lifetime, *The Ring and the Book*, was published in four volumes between 1868 and 1869.

**William Cullen Bryant** (1794–1878) was an American poet who worked as a lawyer, newspaper editor, and politician. "Thanatopsis" and "To a Waterfowl," both of which draw philosophical insights from reflection on the natural world, were published in Bryant's *Poems* (1821).

**Robert Burns** (1759–1796) was a Scottish poet whose frequent poetic reflections on rustic life were drawn from his experiences as a farmer. Subjects from Scottish history and folklore (seen notably in "Tam O'Shanter") also dominate his verse, some of which was written as lyrics to be set to music. Burns frequently wove Scottish dialect into his poems, hence the title of the one collection of poetry he saw in his lifetime *Poems, Chiefly in the Scottish Dialect* (1786). Today, Burns is regarded as the national poet of Scotland.

**Lord Byron** (1788–1824) was an English Romantic poet who was born George Gordon Noel Byron and who in 1798 attained the title of the sixth Baron Byron of Rochedale. He achieved renown while young with the publication of the first two cantos of *Childe Harold's Pilgrimage* (1812), a meditative poem about a young man's grand tour of Europe that introduced the Byronic hero, a moody and melancholic figure who is defiant in his attitudes and behavior yet capable of strong emotions. Byron added two more cantos with strongly autobiographical content in 1817 and 1818. Many of Byron's best-known works are verse dramas, among them *Manfred* (1817), *Mazeppa* (1819), *Marino Faliero* (1821), and *Sardanapalus* (1822). At the time of his death, while participating in the Greek War for Independence, Byron was working on the seventeenth canto of *Don Juan*, a satiric epic that he had begun in 1818.

**Lewis Carroll** (1832–1898) was the pseudonym of Charles Lutwidge Dodgson, a lecturer in mathematics at Christ Church, Oxford, best known for his logically illogical children's tales *Alice's Adventures in Wonderland* (1865) and *Through the Looking-Glass* (1871). Many of Carroll's poems, including "The Walrus and the Carpenter" (from the second Alice book) and *The Hunting of the Snark* (1876), were nonsense verse. His poetry was collected in *Phantasmagoria and Other Poems* (1869) and *Rhyme and Reason?* (1883).

**Samuel Taylor Coleridge** (1772–1834) was an English Romantic poet, critic, and philosopher. In 1798, he collaborated with William Wordsworth on *Lyrical Ballads*, the collection of verse that heralded the dawn of the English Romantic movement in literature. Coleridge's meditative conversation poems "Frost at Midnight" and "Dejection: An Ode" and his more fanciful "Kubla Khan" and "The Rime of the Ancient Mariner" illustrate what he considered to be the two cardinal points of poetry: "the power of exciting the sympathy of the reader by a faithful adherence to the truth of nature, and the power of giving the interest of novelty by the modifying colors of imagination."

**Richard Crashaw** (1612–1649) was an English poet and cleric who converted from the Church of England to Roman Catholicism while living in exile in Paris during the years of the English Civil War. His verse, written mostly mostly on devotional themes, was collected in *Steps to the Temple* (1646). With Robert Herrick, Andrew Marvell, John Donne, Henry Vaughan, and others, Crashaw is considered one of the metaphysical poets.

**Walter de la Mare** (1873–1956) was an English poet and fiction writer who wrote for both adults and children. He is considered one of the last Victorian Romantic poets and much of his work is steeped in fairy tale, legend, and the atmosphere of dreams. His verse was collected in *Poems* (1906), *The Listeners and Other Poems* (1912), *The Veil and Other Poems* (1921), *The Fleeting and Other Poems* (1933), and other volumes.

**Emily Dickinson** (1830–1886) was an American poet who lived a largely reclusive life in Amherst, Massachusetts. Considered one of the greatest American poets of the nineteenth century, her poems are notable for the hymn-like rhythms of their compressed lines, their slant rhyming, and their grounding of abstract concepts such as death, immortality, love, and suffering, in metaphors that are both apt and often provocatively contrary. Dickinson published few of her nearly 1,800 poems in her lifetime; her first collection, *Poems*, was published in 1890.

**John Donne** (1572–1631) was an English poet, lawyer, and cleric. He is considered one of the leading metaphysical poets, and his verse is memorable for its witty conceits and metaphors that address themes such as romantic and erotic love, death, and religious faith. Donne was also respected as a prose writer for his meditations, devotions, and sermons.

**John Dryden** (1631–1700) was an English poet, essayist, and dramatist whose plays include *All for Love* (1677), *Don Sebastian* (1689) and *Amphitryon* (1690). He also was a translator, and his version of Vergil's *Aeneid* was considered one of the best in the English language. His clear, plainspoken style leant itself well to a variety of verse forms, including odes, elegies, and prologues, and satires such as *Absalom and Achitophel* (1681) and *Mac-Flecknoe* (1682), the latter his mock panegyric on Thomas Shadwell, a rival poet and playwright.

**T(homas) S(tearns) Eliot** (1888–1965) was a poet, playwright, literary critic, and publisher who was born in the United States but became a naturalized British citizen in 1927. His poems "The Love Song of J. Alfred Prufrock"—which became the title poem of his first collection, *Prufrock and Other Observations* (1917)—and the richly allusive *The Waste Land* (1922), are considered modernist landmarks that broke sharply with their late nineteenth-century predecessors. Eliot's other works include the play *Murder in the Cathedral* (1935) and the poems he gathered as *Four Quartets* (1943). He was awarded the Nobel Prize for Literature in 1948.

**Ralph Waldo Emerson** (1803–1882) was an American poet, minister, and philosopher and a leader of the American Transcendentalist movement, known for his championing of individualism and self-reliance. He was best known for his essays and sermons, including *Nature* (1836), "The American Scholar" (1837), and "Self Reliance" (1841). He was one of the most popular lecturers in America in the nineteenth century and a mentor to fellow transcendentalist Henry David Thoreau.

**Edward FitzGerald** (1809–1883) was an English poet and Orientalist, who translated Aeschylus and Calderon, among others, but who is remembered today almost exclusively for *The Rubáiyát of Omar Khayyám* (1859), his colorful translation of quatrains written by a twelfth-century Persian poet. The book was promoted by Dante Gabriel Rossetti and his circle and was revised and expanded several times by FitzGerald up through 1879.

**Robert Frost** (1874–1963) was one of the most popular American poets of the twentieth century, known for the rural themes of his poems and the conversational style of his verse. His many collections include *A Boy's Will* (1915), *North of Boston* (1914), *Mountain Interval* (1916), *New Hampshire* (1923), and *West Running Brook* (1928). He was a four-time winner of the Pulitzer Prize for Poetry.

**Thomas Gray** (1716–1771) was an English poet and the best known of the "grave-yard poets," whose poems were meditations on death and mortality that often featured graveyard imagery. "Elegy Written in a Country Church-Yard" was one of only thir-teen poems Gray published in his lifetime, but it was one of the most popular poems of the eighteenth century.

**Thomas Hardy** (1840–1928) was a English writer best known for *Far from the Madding Crowd* (1874), *The Return of the Native* (1878), *The Mayor of Casterbridge* (1886), *Tess of the d'Urbervilles* (1891), and other novels. Following the publication of *Jude the Obscure* (1895), Hardy gave up writing novels to concentrate on poetry, which he collected in *Poems of the Past and Present* (1901), *Time's Laughingstocks and Other Verses* (1909), *Satires of Circumstance* (1914), and other volumes.

**George Herbert** (1593–1633) was an English poet and Anglican priest, known for the devotional verse that he wrote on the Church, the majesty of God, and his personal religious duty. Herbert avoided publication of his verse in his lifetime but arranged for the publication of his collection *The Temple* shortly after his death.

**Robert Herrick** (1591–1674) was an English poet and clergyman who, as one of the "sons of Ben," was mentored by Ben Jonson. Although he took holy orders and wrote the devotional poems on religious themes collected as *Noble Numbers* (1647), much of his verse is distinguished by its sensuality and descriptions of life's pleasures. Many of his poems were collected in the volume *Hesperides* (1648).

**Gerard Manley Hopkins** (1844–1889) was an English poet who converted from Anglicanism to Roman Catholicism and was ordained a Jesuit priest. His verse is memorable for its alliteration, compound adjectives, and for what Hopkins referred to as "sprung rhythm," an irregular, more effusive rhythmic structure akin to free verse. Hopkins frequently wrote on religious themes. Most of his poetry was pub-lished posthumously.

**Samuel Johnson** (1709–1784) was a versatile English writer and leading man of letters in his day. He was best known for his *Dictionary of the English Language* (1755), the essays he published regularly in the *Rambler*, and the critical studies that make up *The Lives of the Eminent English Poets, with Critical Observations on Their Works* (1779–1781). Johnson began writing poetry while in his teens. "The Vanity of Human Wishes" was his first work to be published under his name.

**Ben Jonson** (1572–1637) was an English poet and dramatist, best known for his plays *Every Man in His Humour* (1598), *Volpone* (1606), and *The Alchemist* (1610). His classically informed verse, written in a plain and simple style and mixing wit and serious subject matter, influenced a generation of poets that included Robert Herrick, Thomas Carew, Richard Lovelace, and Thomas Randolph. Jonson and William Shakespeare were genial rivals, and Jonson's poem "To the Memory of My Beloved Master, William Shakespeare" was published as the preface to the First Folio of Shakespeare's plays in 1623.

**John Keats** (1795–1821) was an English Romantic poet who was strongly influenced by the poetry of John Milton and Edmund Spenser. He began writing poetry in his late teens and published his first collection, *Poems*, in 1817. The four odes that Keats wrote in 1819 on the theme of the power of the poetic imagination to transcend the dreariness and disappointments of existence—"Ode to Psyche," "Ode to a Nightingale," "Ode on a Grecian Urn," and "Ode on Melancholy"—and the unfinished fragment "Hyperion," are considered some of the greatest poems in the English language.

**Rudyard Kipling** (1865–1936) was an English writer best known for his books for young readers, among them *The Jungle Book* (1894), *The Second Jungle Book* (1895), *Kim* (1901), and *Just So Stories* (1902). Born in Bombay during British colonial rule, he worked in India as a journalist before moving to London in 1889. His fiction, some of which was collected in *The Phantom 'Rickshaw and Other Tales* (1888) and *Life's Handicap* (1891), and his poetry, collected in *Departmental Ditties and Other Verses* (1886) and *Barrack-Room Ballads and Other Verses* (1892), is often concerned with the differences between Eastern and Western culture. Kipling was awarded the Nobel Prize for Literature in 1907.

**Edward Lear** (1812–1888) was an English artist and poet, best known for his books of nonsense verse and limericks for children, all of which he illustrated: *A Book of Nonsense* (1846), *Nonsense Songs, Stories, Botany and Alphabets* (1870), *More Nonsense, Rhymes, Pictures, Botany, Etc.* (1872), and *Laughable Lyrics: A Fourth Book of Nonsense Poems, Songs, Botany, Music, Etc.* (1877).

**Henry Wadsworth Longfellow** (1807–1882) was an American poet who often wrote on themes from American history. His book-length narrative poems include *Evangeline, A Tale of Acadie* (1847) and *The Song of Hiawatha* (1855). His shorter verse was collected in *The Courtship of Miles Standish and Other Poems* (1858) and *Tales of a Wayside*

*Inn* (1863). Longfellow's translation of Dante's *Divine Comedy*, published in 1867, was long considered the definitive translation.

**Christopher Marlowe** (1564–1593) was an English poet and dramatist, best known for his plays *Tamburlaine the Great, Parts 1 and 2* (1587–1588) and *Dr. Faustus* (1594). He was a contemporary of William Shakespeare, whose work he influenced, and a leading literary figure of the Elizabethan era.

**Andrew Marvell** (1621–1678) was an English poet and statesman. Best known in his day as a political writer who sat in the House of Commons and served Oliver Cromwell, he is considered one of the metaphysical poets and his verse is notable for its wit and complexity. Marvell's poetry was not published in his lifetime; his *Miscellaneous Poems* appeared three years after his death, in 1681.

**Edgar Lee Masters** (1868–1950) was an American poet and novelist and a leading figure in the Chicago Renaissance, which was heralded in part with the publication of his *Spoon River Anthology* (1915), a collection of dramatic monologues presented as the "epitaphs" of the dead in a small Midwestern cemetery, speaking with bitterness and disillusionment with their lives from beyond the grave. Masters followed this volume up with *The New Spoon River* (1924), another collection of poems written in his controversial prose-in-poetry style.

**Edna St. Vincent Millay** (1892–1950) was an American poet and dramatist who was famous in her lifetime for the bohemian lifestyle she indulged in New York's Greenwich Village. She wrote frequently on the themes of love, death, and nature. Her poems were collected in *Renascence, and Other Poems* (1917), *A Few Figs from Thistles* (1921), and *The Harp-Weaver and Other Poems* (1923). She was awarded the Pulitzer Prize for Poetry in 1923.

**John Milton** (1608–1674) was an English poet and essayist, regarded as one of the most influential poets in western literature. He wrote frequently on religious and political themes, and was a staunch defender of the Commonwealth under Oliver Cromwell and the Protectorate that followed. His best-known work, the epic *Paradise Lost*, was published in 1667 and revised in 1674. Milton followed it with *Paradise Regained* (1671). His other well-known works include *Samson Agonistes* (1671); his essay in defense of freedom of the press, *Areopagitica* (1644); and the companion poems *L'Allegro* and *Il Penseroso*, both composed in 1631.

**Wilfred Owen** (1893–1918) was an English poet renowned for verse that described the horrors of war in grim, realistic detail. He died in combat, one week before the armistice that ended World War I. His poems, most unpublished in his lifetime, were collected posthumously as *Poems* (1920).

**Edgar Allan Poe** (1809–1849) was an American poet and writer of fiction, regarded as the father of the modern detective story and the author who brought psychological depth to the tale of the macabre. In his poetry, Poe frequently wrote on themes of beauty and death. In his lifetime, Poe's poetry was collected in *The Raven and Other Poems* (1845) and his fiction in *Tales* (1845).

**Alexander Pope** (1688–1744) was an English poet and essayist and is regarded as the greatest of the neoclassical poets for the wit and elegance of his verse, most of which he wrote in heroic couplet form. His best known works include *An Essay on Criticism* (1711), the four *Moral Essays* (1731–1735), "Epistle to Dr. Arbuthnot" (1735), and his famous attempt "to vindicate the ways of God to man," "An Essay on Man" (1734), as well as the mock epics *The Rape of the Lock* (1712) and *The Dunciad*, published in four versions between 1728 and 1743.

**Edward Arlington Robinson** (1869–1935) was an American poet who wrote in traditional verse forms, often on somber themes, in the late-nineteenth and early-twentieth centuries. His poems were collected in more than twenty volumes in his lifetime, including *The Torrent and the Night Before* (1896), *The Children of the Night* (1897), and *The Town Down the River* (1910). He was a three-time recipient of the Pulitzer Prize for Poetry.

**Christina Rossetti** (1830–1894) was an English poet and the younger sister of Dante Gabriel Rossetti. She wrote romantic lyrics, and occasionally on fantastic themes as in "Goblin Market," the title of her second collection, published in 1862. Her other collections include *The Prince's Progress and Other Poems* (1866) and *Poems* (1866).

**Dante Gabriel Rossetti** (1828–1882) was an English poet and painter and a leading figure in the Pre-Raphaelite Brotherhood, which he formed with John Everett Millais, William Holman Hunt, and other artists in opposition to artistic conventions of the day. In his poetry, as in his painting, Rossetti often showed an interest in idealized women, and his poetry is memorable for its colorful pictorial detail. His poems were collected as *Ballads and Sonnets* (1881), *Ballads and Narrative Poems* (1893), *Sonnets and Lyrical Poems* (1894), and other volumes.

**William Shakespeare** (1564–1616) was an English playwright and poet who is regarded as the world's greatest dramatist. In addition to acting in his plays, he was a partner in the Globe Theater, where some of his plays were performed. His extant works include thirty-eight plays, 154 sonnets, and the narrative poems "Venus and Adonis" (1593) and "The Rape of Lucrece" (1594). The First Folio, featuring thirty-six of his plays, was published in 1623.

**Percy Bysshe Shelley** (1792–1822) was an English Romantic poet whose career was intertwined with that of Lord Byron. An idealist in life, Shelley often wrote on revolutionary themes and considered poetry itself to be a form of revolution, writing in his essay *A Defence of Poetry* that "poets are the unacknowledged legislators of the world." His verse is notable for its rich symbolism, drawn from the natural world and the classics. Shelley's complete poetical works, edited by his wife, Mary Wollstonecraft Shelley, were published in 1839.

**Sir Philip Sidney** (1554–1586) was an English poet and a member of Parliament during the reign of Elizabeth I. His works include the pastoral romance *The Countess of Pembroke's Arcadia* (1590; augmented editions published 1593 and 1598), the sonnet cycle *Astrophel and Stella* (1590), and the essay *The Defence of Poetry* (1595). A militant Protestant, he died of injuries sustained in combat while fighting against the Roman Catholic Church in Spain.

**Sir Edmund Spenser** (1552–1599) was an English poet, best known for *The Faerie Queene*, his epic allegorical poem on Elizabeth I and the Tudor court that exists as six of its intended twelve books, and that was written in a stanza form (8 lines of iambic pentameter followed by a final line of hexameter) that today bears Spenser's name (i.e., the Spenserian stanza). "Epithalamion," a celebration of his marriage to his second wife, Elizabeth Boyle, was published as part of *Amoretti and Epithalamion* (1595), the *Amoretti* being a cycle of love sonnets written for her.

**Wallace Stevens** (1879–1955) was a modernist American poet who wrote in an antirationalist and antirhetorical style. He worked professionally as an insurance company executive. Collections of his verse include *Harmonium* (1923), *Ideas of Order* (1935), *The Man with the Blue Guitar and Other Poems* (1937), *Transport to Summer* (1947), and *The Auroras of Autumn* (1950). He was awarded the Pulitzer Prize for Poetry for his *Collected Poems* in 1955.

**Algernon Charles Swinburne** (1837–1909) was an English poet, playwright, novelist, and critic. The lyrical poems he collected in *Atalanta in Calydon* (1865) and *Poems and Ballads* (1866) shocked Victorian sensibilities with their atheism and erotic intensity. He invented the verse form known as the roundel, patterned on the French *rondeau*, and employed it in the poems he collected as *A Century of Roundels* (1883). His books of literary criticism include *Essays and Studies* (1875), *Studies in Prose and Poetry* (1894), and studies of William Blake, William Shakespeare, Charlotte Brontë, and Percy Bysshe Shelley.

**Alfred, Lord Tennyson** (1809–1892) is regarded as the pre-eminent poet of Victorian England. His best-known works include *Idylls of the King* (1859), a cycle of twelve narrative poems based on Arthurian romance, and *In Memoriam* (1850), an elegy on the death of his friend Arthur Henry Hallam. Tennyson's poems were collected in *Poems, Chiefly Lyrical* (1830), *Poems* (1842), *Maud, and Other Poems* (1855), and other volumes. He was appointed the poet laureate of England in 1850.

**Francis Thompson** (1859–1907) is regarded as one of the greatest English Roman Catholic poets. His poems, many of which were written on religious themes, were collected in *Poems* (1893), *New Poems* (1897), and *Poems* (1911). His works in prose include *Health and Holiness* (1905) and *A Renegade Poet, and Other Essays* (1910).

**Henry Vaughan** (1621–1695) was an English poet who wrote frequently on devotional themes. One of the metaphysical poets, his verse was collected in *Silex Scintillans* (1650). After 1655, Vaughan devoted himself mostly to the practice of medicine.

**Walt Whitman** (1819–1892) was one of the greatest American poets who wrote deeply personal confessional poems such as "Song of Myself," as well as poems on American themes such as "O Captain! My Captain!" his eulogy to the late Abraham Lincoln. Whitman's poems were collected in *Leaves of Grass*, a book criticized for its overt sexuality when it was published in 1855, and whose contents Whitman revised several times up through the "deathbed edition" of 1892.

**Oscar Wilde** (1854–1900) was an Irish poet and playwright, best known for his novel *The Picture of Dorian Gray* (1891) and such plays as *Lady Windermere's Fan* (1893) and *The Importance of Being Earnest* (1899). Wilde wrote the poem "The Ballad of Reading Gaol" following two years of imprisonment on charges of gross indecency.

**William Carlos Williams** (1883–1963) was an American poet who worked professionally as a physician. Most of his poems, long and short, have a haiku-like precision and compression of detail. They were collected in *Poems* (1909), *Spring and All* (1923), *The Desert Music and Other Poems* (1954), *Pictures from Brueghel and Other Poems* (1962), and other volumes. Williams was the recipient of the first National Book Award for Poetry in 1950.

**William Wordsworth** (1770–1850) was an English Romantic poet, who collaborated with Samuel Taylor Coleridge on the volume *Lyrical Ballads* (1798), one of the most influential volumes of poetry in English literature. Wordsworth's intention for the poems, as he wrote in his preface to the 1800 edition, was "to choose incidents and situations from common life, and to relate or describe them, throughout, as far as was possible in a selection of language really used by men, and, at the same time, to throw over them a certain colouring of imagination, whereby ordinary things should be presented to the mind in an unusual aspect." Wordsworth was living in France at the time of the outbreak of the French Revolution, an experience that shaped his reflections in his spiritual autobiography, *The Prelude*, a poem that Wordsworth wrote between 1798 and 1799 and revised over the next fifty years until his death. He was appointed the poet laureate of England in 1843.

**Sir Thomas Wyatt** (1503–1542) was an English poet and ambassador in the court of Henry VIII, credited with writing the first sonnets in English. He wrote verse on both courtly love and political themes, none of it published in his lifetime.

**William Butler Yeats** (1865–1939) was an Irish poet and playwright whose career coincides with the Celtic revival in literature of the late-nineteenth and early-twentieth centuries. He wrote frequently on themes from Irish history and folklore and collected the folktales and poems that make up the contents of *The Celtic Twilight* (1893). His poems were collected in *The Wanderings of Oisin and Other Poems* (1889), *Poems* (1895), *Michael Robartes and the Dancer* (1921), and numerous other volumes. He was awarded the Nobel Prize for Literature in 1923.